DEPARTMENT OF THE TREASURY
WASHINGTON, D.C.

A Message from the Secretary

The Financial Report of the U.S. Government for Fiscal Year 2013 provides a comprehensive overview of the government's current financial position, as well as critical insight into our long-term fiscal outlook.

Five years ago, the Administration inherited the largest deficits since the end of World War II and an economy in the grips of the worst recession since the Great Depression. Since then, the President and Congress have taken significant steps to strengthen our fiscal footing by enacting the Affordable Care Act in 2010, the Budget Control Act in 2011, and the American Taxpayer Relief Act in 2013. Together, these three laws have substantially reduced the estimated long-term fiscal gap—and thanks to the tenacity of the American people and the determination of the private sector we are moving in the right direction. In FY 2013 alone, the budget deficit declined by $409 billion since the previous year, dropping from $1.1 trillion to $680 billion. The United States has recovered faster than any other advanced economy, and our deficit today is less than half of what it was when President Obama first took office.

While this report is a testament to the strength and resilience of the U.S. economy, it also reminds us that in order to stay on the path toward fiscal sustainability, we must remain focused on enacting pro-growth, pro-jobs policies that will fuel our economy while maintaining fiscal discipline. Such policies include closing wasteful tax loopholes, reducing costs where it makes sense, and using a portion of those savings for smart investments in key areas like manufacturing, infrastructure, and education.

Through these efforts, I am confident that we can secure a strong economic future for the long term.

Jacob J. Lew

This page is intentionally blank.

Contents

Required Supplementary Information (Unaudited)

Other Information (Unaudited)

Required Supplementary Stewardship Information (Unaudited)

Appendices

List of Social Insurance Charts

This page is intentionally blank.

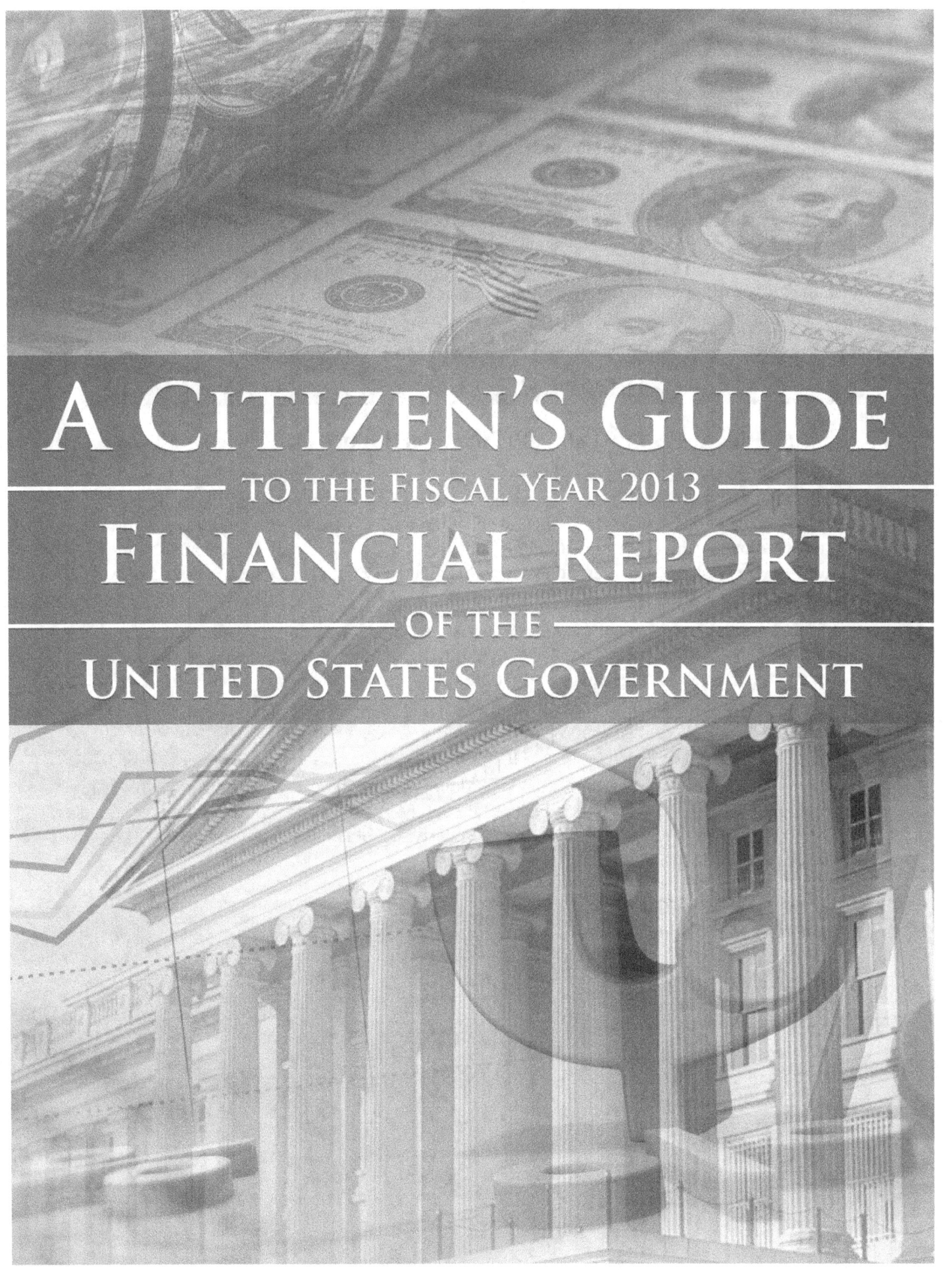

A CITIZEN'S GUIDE
TO THE FISCAL YEAR 2013
FINANCIAL REPORT
OF THE
UNITED STATES GOVERNMENT

A Citizen's Guide to the Fiscal Year 2013 Financial Report of the United States Government

The Citizen's Guide (Guide) to the Fiscal Year (FY) 2013 Financial Report of the U.S. Government (*Financial Report*) summarizes the U.S. Government's (Government) current financial position and condition and discusses key financial topics, including fiscal sustainability. This Guide and the *Financial Report* are produced by the U.S. Department of the Treasury in cooperation with the Office of Management and Budget (OMB). The Secretary of the Treasury, Director of OMB, and Comptroller General of the United States at the Government Accountability Office (GAO) believe that the information discussed in this Guide is important to all Americans.

Where We Are Now

Comparing the Budget and the Financial Report

The **Budget of the United States Government** (*Budget*) is the Government's primary financial planning and control tool. It accounts for past Government receipts and spending, and presents the President's proposed receipt and spending plan. The *Budget* compares *receipts*, or cash received by the Government, with *outlays*, or payments made by the Government to the public. An excess of receipts over outlays is called a budget *surplus*; an excess of outlays over receipts is called a budget *deficit*.

The **Financial Report of the United States Government** focuses on the Government's revenues and costs (what came in and what went out), assets and liabilities (what it owns and owes), and other important financial information. The *Financial Report* compares the Government's *revenues* (what the Government has collected and expects to collect, but has not necessarily received), with its *costs* (what the Government has incurred, but has not necessarily paid) to derive net operating cost.

Chart 1 compares the Government's budget deficit and net operating cost for FY 2009-2013. During FY 2013, increased receipts and decreased outlays combined to reduce the budget deficit by $409 billion (37.6 percent) to $680 billion. Similarly, net operating cost decreased $511 billion (38.8 percent) to $805 billion, due primarily to a $324 billion tax and other revenue increase and a $158 billion net cost decrease over the past fiscal year. The $125 billion difference between the budget deficit and the net operating cost in FY 2013 is primarily due to non-cash costs associated with an increase in estimated liabilities related to federal employee and veteran benefits that are included in net operating cost, but not the budget deficit. In addition, the difference

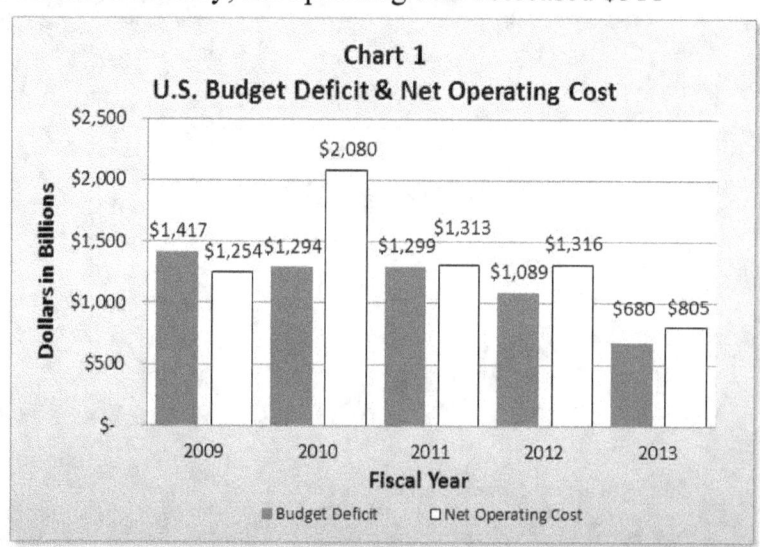

is affected by changes in various asset and liability balances, including, but not limited to: (a) net property, plant, and equipment, the costs of which are recorded in the budget as outlays when purchased but are capitalized as assets and included in net operating cost as depreciation expense over the useful life of the asset, (b) the valuation of certain assets, such as investments, and (c) insurance and guarantee loan program liabilities. Together, the *Budget* and the *Financial Report* present complementary perspectives on the Government's financial position and condition.

What Came In and What Went Out

What came in? Chart 2 shows that increases in each of the three revenue categories presented (individual income tax and withholdings, corporation income taxes, and other revenue) combined to increase total Government revenues by $324 billion (12.9 percent) to more than $2.8 trillion for FY 2013. This was primarily due to an increase in ordinary, capital gains, and dividend income tax rates for individuals, coupled with an increase in corporation income tax collections and a reduction

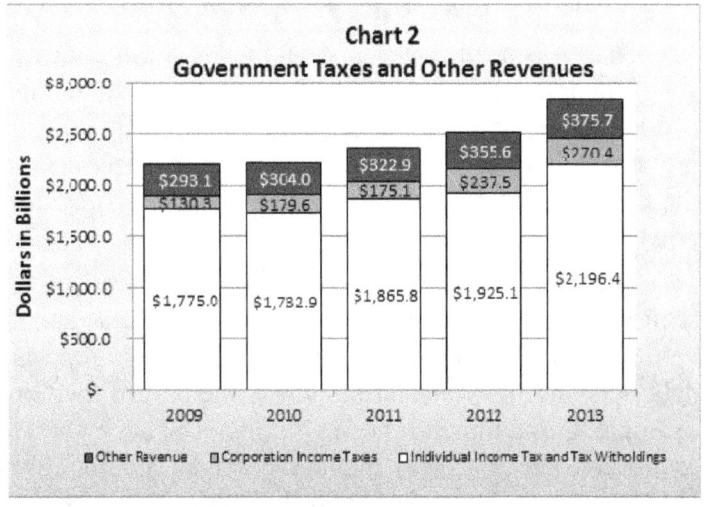

in tax refunds. These increases largely stem from the implementation of the American Taxpayer Relief Act (ATRA) of 2012, the expiration of payroll tax relief provisions, and the ongoing economic recovery. Together, individual income tax and tax withholdings, and corporation taxes accounted for about 87 percent of total revenues in FY 2013. Other revenues include excise and unemployment taxes, and customs duties.

What went out? The Government derives its net cost ($3.7 trillion in FY 2013) by subtracting revenues earned from Government programs (e.g., Medicare premiums, national park entry fees, and postal fees) from its gross costs ($3.9 trillion in FY 2013) and adjusts the amount for gains or losses from changes in actuarial assumptions used to estimate future liabilities for federal employee and veteran benefits. The Government deducts taxes and other revenues shown in Chart 2 from its net cost to arrive at its "bottom line" net operating cost, which decreased by $511 billion (38.8 percent) to $805 billion in FY 2013.[1] Much of this decrease was

attributable to the revenue increases mentioned above, as well as a $158 billion decrease in total net cost. A significant driver of this net decrease was a $189 billion decrease in certain actuarial cost estimates for federal employee and veteran benefits, especially at the Department of Defense (DOD).

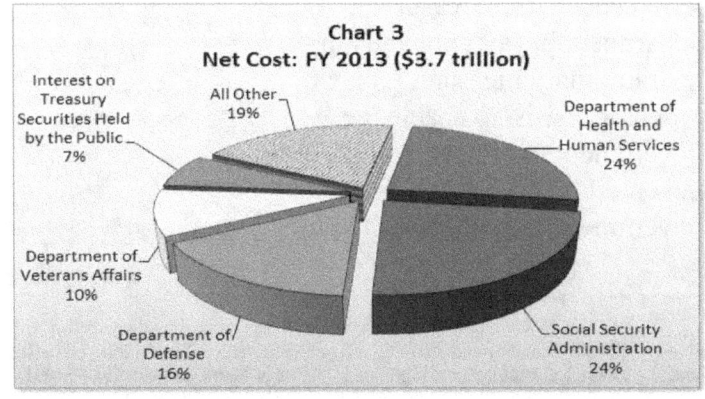

---

[1] The Government also makes adjustments for "unmatched transactions and balances" to bring certain accounts into balance for such items as restatements and errors in federal agency reporting and unreconciled intragovernmental transactions and balances between agencies.

Chart 3 shows that the largest contributors to the Government's net cost in FY 2013 include the Department of Health and Human Services (HHS) the Social Security Administration (SSA), and DOD. The bulk of HHS and SSA costs come from major social insurance programs administered by those agencies (e.g., Medicare for HHS, and Social Security for SSA). While much of DOD's total costs relate to military operations and personnel, the majority of DOD's more than $200 billion cost decrease in FY 2013 was attributed to changes in cost estimates related to its Military Retirement Fund and post-retirement health benefits programs.

What We Own and What We Owe

Chart 4 is a summary of what the Government owns in assets and what it owes in liabilities. As of September 30, 2013, the Government held about $3.0 trillion in assets, comprised mostly of $1.0 trillion in net loans receivable (primarily student loans) and $896.7 billion in net property, plant, and equipment. Beyond these assets, other significant resources are available to the Government, including stewardship assets, such as natural resources, and the Government's power to tax and set monetary policy.

The $19.9 trillion in total liabilities is comprised mostly of: (1) $12.0 trillion in federal debt securities held by the public and accrued interest[2] and (2) $6.5 trillion in federal employee and veteran benefits payable. The Government also reports about $4.8 trillion of intragovernmental debt outstanding, which arises when one part of the Government borrows from another. For example, Government funds (e.g., Social Security and Medicare trust funds) are typically required to invest excess annual receipts in federal debt securities issued by the Treasury Department, thus creating liabilities of the Treasury and assets of the trust funds. These respective amounts are included in Department of the Treasury and investing agency financial statements, but offset each other in the preparation of the Governmentwide consolidated financial statements, and thus, are not reflected in Chart 4.

The sum of debt held by the public and intragovernmental debt equals gross federal debt, which, with some adjustments, is subject to a statutory debt ceiling (i.e., the "debt limit"). The debt limit was raised by a combined $2.1 trillion to $16.394 trillion between August 2011 and January 2012 pursuant to the Budget Control Act (BCA) of 2011. In February 2013, Congress suspended the debt limit through May 18, 2013.[3] Because the debt limit had not yet been raised before the suspension period ended, the Treasury Department began implementing "extraordinary measures", on a temporary basis, to enable the Government to protect the full faith and credit of the United States Government by continuing to pay

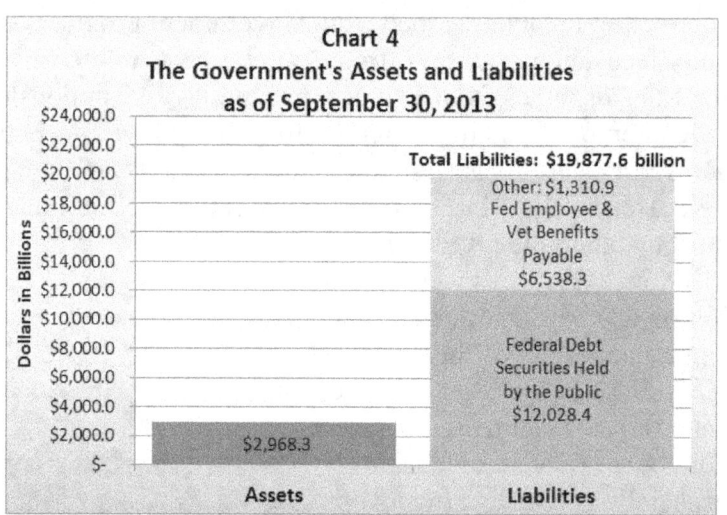

---

[2] Debt held by the public and accrued interest, as reported on the Government's balance sheet, primarily consists of Treasury securities, net of unamortized discounts and premiums, and accrued interest. The "public" consists of individuals, corporations, state and local governments, Federal Reserve Banks, foreign governments, and other entities outside the Federal Government.

[3] A delay in raising the statutory debt limit existed as of September 30, 2013. When delays in raising the statutory debt limit occur, Treasury often must deviate from its normal debt management operations and take a number of extraordinary actions to meet the Government's obligations as they come due without exceeding the debt limit. Increasing or suspending the debt limit does not increase spending or authorize new spending; rather, it permits the Government to continue to honor pre-existing commitments.

the nation's bills. At the end of the suspension period, the debt limit was raised to $16.699 trillion. As of September 30, 2013, the Government's total debt outstanding subject to the debt limit was $25 million below the $16.699 trillion statutory debt limit. In October 2013, Congress again suspended the debt limit, this time through February 7, 2014. In February 2014, Congress again suspended the debt limit, this time through March 15, 2015. As budget deficits continue to occur, the Government will have to continue to borrow from the public. Instances where the debt held by the public increases faster than the economy for extended periods can pose additional challenges to the sustainability of current fiscal policy.

Considering key macroeconomic indicators can help place the discussion of the Government's financial results in a broader context. During FY 2013, the economy continued to grow, job creation accelerated, and the unemployment rate declined. These and other economic and financial developments are discussed in greater detail in the *Financial Report*.

Where We Are Headed

An important purpose of this Guide and the *Financial Report* is to help citizens understand current fiscal policy and the importance and magnitude of policy reforms necessary to make it sustainable. A sustainable policy is one where the ratio of debt held by the public to Gross Domestic Product (GDP)[4] (the debt-to-GDP ratio) is stable or declining over the long term. To determine if current fiscal policy is sustainable, the projections discussed in this Guide assume current policy will be sustained indefinitely and draw out the implications for the growth of the debt-to-GDP ratio.[5] The projections are therefore neither forecasts nor predictions. As policy changes are enacted, actual financial outcomes will of course be different than those projected.

Receipts, Spending, and the Debt

Chart 5 shows historical and current policy projections for receipts, non-interest spending by major category, and total spending expressed as a percent of GDP. The difference between the receipts and non-interest spending shares of GDP (the primary deficit-to-GDP ratio) grew rapidly in 2009 due to the financial crisis, the recession, and the policies pursued to combat both. The ratio stayed large from 2010 to 2012, despite shrinking in each successive year, and fell significantly in 2013. The

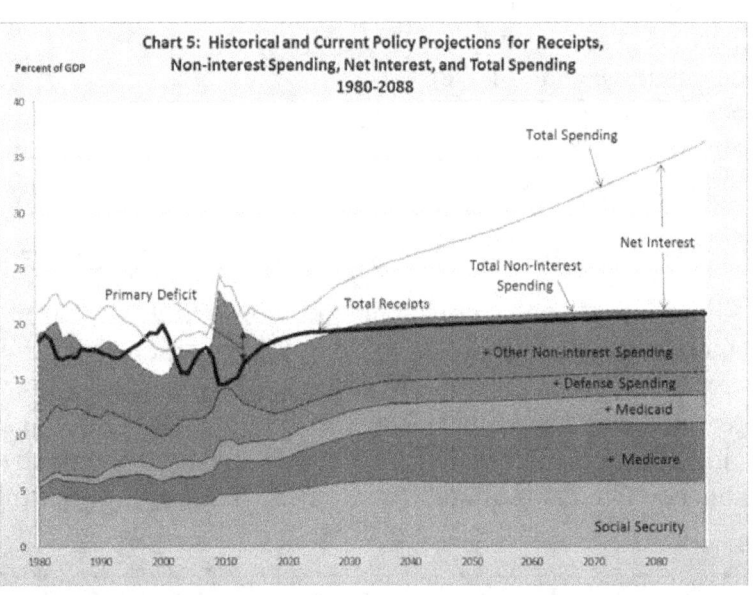

Chart 5: Historical and Current Policy Projections for Receipts, Non-interest Spending, Net Interest, and Total Spending 1980-2088

---

[4] GDP measures the size of the Nation's economy in terms of the total value of all final goods and services that are produced in a year. Considering financial results relative to GDP is a useful indicator of the economy's capacity to sustain the Government's many programs. In July 2013, the Bureau of Economic Analysis revised upward the historical values for GDP beginning with estimates for 1929. As a result, percentages or shares of GDP throughout the *Financial Report* are slightly lower than those reported in previous years.

[5] Current policy in the projections is based on current law, but includes extension of certain policies that expire under current law but are routinely extended or otherwise expected to continue.

primary deficit is projected to shrink in the next few years as spending limits called for in the BCA take effect and the economy recovers, becoming a surplus starting in 2017 that peaks at 1.1 percent of GDP in 2021. Between 2022 and 2037, however, increased spending for Social Security and health programs[6] due to continued aging of the population is expected to cause primary surpluses to steadily decline and become a deficit starting in 2029 that grows to 0.8 percent of GDP by 2036. After 2037, the projected primary deficit-to-GDP ratio slowly declines to 0.4 percent of GDP in 2088 as the impact of the baby boom generation retiring dissipates.

In these projections, the Affordable Care Act (ACA)[7] provision of health insurance subsidies and expanded Medicaid coverage boost federal spending, and other ACA provisions significantly reduce per-beneficiary Medicare and Medicaid cost growth. Overall, the ACA is projected to substantially reduce the cost growth rate of federal expenditures for Medicare over the next 75 years. However, as noted in the *Financial Report*, there is uncertainty about the extent to which

the ACA's provisions will result in reduced health care cost growth. Even if those provisions work as intended and as assumed in these projections, Chart 5 still shows a persistent gap between projected receipts and total non-interest spending.

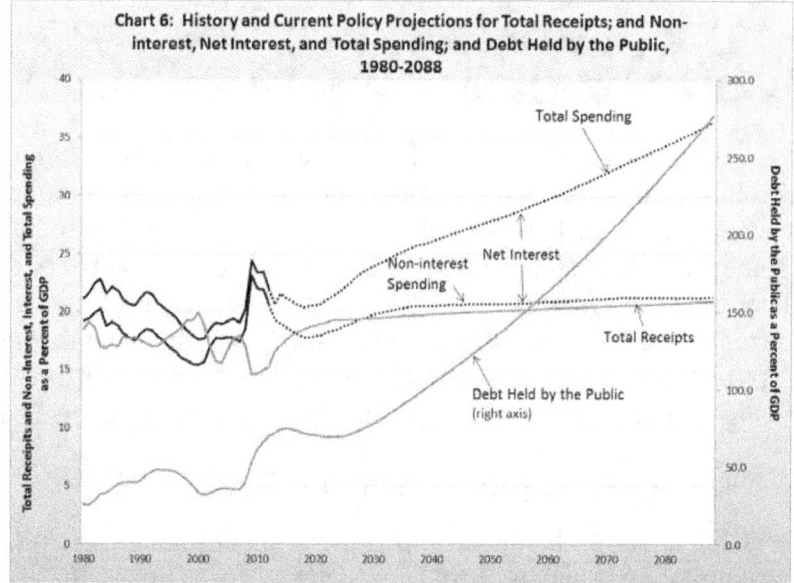

Chart 6: History and Current Policy Projections for Total Receipts; and Non-interest, Net Interest, and Total Spending; and Debt Held by the Public, 1980-2088

The primary deficit projections in Chart 5, along with those for interest rates and GDP, determine the debt-to-GDP ratio projections shown in Chart 6. That ratio was 72 percent at the end of FY 2013, and under current policy is projected to be 69 percent in 2023, 112 percent in 2043, and 277 percent in 2088. The continuous rise of the debt-to-GDP ratio after 2023 indicates that current policy is unsustainable.

The Fiscal Gap and the Cost of Delaying Policy Reform

It is estimated that preventing the debt-to-GDP ratio from rising over the next 75 years would require some combination of expenditure reductions and revenue increases that amount to 1.7 percent of GDP on average over the next 75 years. The timing of changes to non-interest spending and receipts that close this "75-year fiscal gap" has important implications for the well-being of future generations. For example, relative to a policy that begins immediately, it is estimated that the magnitude of reforms necessary to close the 75-year fiscal gap increases by

---

[6] The 2013 Medicare Trustees Report projects that, assuming full implementation of the Affordable Care Act (ACA) provisions, the Hospital Insurance (HI) Trust Fund will remain solvent under current law until 2026 (two years later than reported last year), at which point the share of estimated HI costs that could be paid from trust fund income is 87 percent, declining to 73 percent by 2087. As for Social Security, under current law, the Old-Age, Survivors, and Disability Insurance (OASDI) Trust Funds are projected to be exhausted in 2033 (unchanged from last year), at which time the projected share of scheduled benefits payable from trust fund income is 77 percent, declining to 72 percent in 2087. The projections assume full Social Security and Medicare benefits are paid after the corresponding trust funds are exhausted. See http://www.ssa.gov/oact/trsum/index.html.

[7] The ACA refers to P.L. 111-148, as amended by P.L. 111-152. The ACA expands health insurance coverage, provides health insurance subsidies for low-income individuals and families, includes many measures designed to reduce health care cost growth, and significantly reduces Medicare payment rates.

more than 20 percent if action is delayed by 10 years and by more than 50 percent if action is delayed 20 years.

This year's estimates of the magnitude of changes needed to close the 75-year fiscal gap, 1.7 percent of GDP, is down more than a third from the 2012 projection of 2.7 percent of GDP. The two largest factors behind the improvement are lower projected spending in Medicare and Medicaid and higher projected revenues (the latter reflecting the increases in high-income marginal tax rates enacted as part of the ATRA in January 2013).

Conclusion

The Government took significant steps towards fiscal sustainability by enacting the ACA in 2010, the BCA in 2011, and the ATRA in 2013. The ACA holds the prospect of lowering the long-term per beneficiary spending growth for Medicare and Medicaid, the BCA significantly curtails discretionary spending, and ATRA increased revenues. Together, these three laws substantially reduce the estimated long-term fiscal gap. But even with these new laws, the Government's debt-to-GDP ratio is projected to remain flat over the next ten years, and then commence a continuous rise over the remaining projection period and beyond if current policy is kept in place. This trend implies that current policy is not sustainable. Subject to the important caveat that changes in policy are not so abrupt that they slow the economy's recovery, the sooner policies are put in place to avert these trends, the smaller the revenue increases and/or spending decreases will need to be to return the Government to a sustainable fiscal path.[8]

The Nation By The Numbers

The *Financial Report* provides the President, Congress, and the American people a comprehensive view of how the Government is managing taxpayer dollars. It discusses the Government's financial position and condition, its revenues and costs, assets and liabilities, and other responsibilities and commitments, as well as important financial issues that affect the nation and its citizens both now and in the future. The table on the following page presents several key indicators of the Government's financial position and condition, which are summarized in this Guide and discussed in greater detail in the *Financial Report*.

> The Government Accountability Office's (GAO) audit report on the U.S. Government's consolidated financial statements can be found beginning on page 220 of the full *Financial Report*. For the reasons discussed below, GAO was prevented from expressing (disclaimed) an opinion on these consolidated financial statements, except for the 2009 Statement of Social Insurance (SOSI). GAO disclaimed an opinion on the 2013, 2012, 2011, and 2010 SOSI and the 2013 and 2012 Statements of Changes in Social Insurance Amounts because of significant uncertainties (discussed in Note 24 in the *Financial Report*) primarily related to the achievement of projected reductions in Medicare cost growth reflected in the 2013, 2012, 2011, and 2010 SOSI. However, GAO issued an unqualified or "clean" opinion on the 2009 SOSI.[9] In addition, GAO disclaimed an opinion on the remaining FY 2013 and 2012 financial statements in the *Financial Report* due to certain material financial reporting control weaknesses and other limitations on the scope of its work.

---

[8] Further information about these fiscal projections and the underlying assumptions can be found in the Required Supplementary Information section of the *Financial Report* at http://www.fiscal.treasury.gov/fsreports/fs_reports_publications.htm.

[9] In conformity with federal accounting standards, Statements of Social Insurance are presented for the current year and each of the four preceding years.

NATION BY THE NUMBERS

A Snapshot of
The Government's Financial Position & Condition

Dollars in Billions	2013	2012
Gross Costs	$ (3,940.9)	$ (3,844.9)
Less: Earned Revenues	$ 415.5	$ 350.8
Gain/(Loss) from Changes in Assumptions	$ (131.2)	$ (320.2)
Net Cost	$ (3,656.6)	$ (3,814.3)
Less: Total Taxes and Other Revenues	$ 2,842.5	$ 2,518.2
Unmatched Transactions and Balances	$ 9.0	$ (20.2)
Net Operating Cost	$ (805.1)	$ (1,316.3)
Assets:	$ 2,968.3	$ 2,748.3
Less: Liabilities, comprised of:		
Debt Held By the Public & Accrued Interest	$ (12,028.4)	$ (11,332.3)
Federal Employee & Veteran Benefits	$ (6,538.3)	$ (6,274.0)
Other	$ (1,310.9)	$ (1,243.0)
Total Liabilities	$ (19,877.6)	$ (18,849.3)
Net Position (Assets Minus Liabilities)	$ (16,909.3)	$ (16,101.0)

Sustainability Measures:

	2013	2012
Social Insurance Net Expenditures[1]	$ (39,698)	$ (38,554)
Total Non-Interest Net Expenditures[2]	$ (4,000)	$ (16,500)

Sustainability Measures as Percent of Gross Domestic Product (GDP):

	2013	2012
Social Insurance Net Expenditures[3]	(4.0%)	(4.2%)
Total Federal Government Non-Interest Net Expenditures	(0.4%)	(1.7%)

Budget Results

	2013	2012
Unified Budget Deficit	$ (680.3)	$ (1,089.4)

1 Source: Statement of Social Insurance. Amounts equal present value of projected revenues and expenditures for scheduled benefits over the next 75 years of certain benefit programs that are referred to as Social Insurance (e.g., Social Security, Medicare). Amounts represent 'open group' population (all current and future beneficiaries). These amounts are not considered liabilities on the balance sheet.

2 Represents the 75-year projection of the Federal Government's receipts less non-interest spending as reported in the 'Statement of Long Term Fiscal Projections' in the Required Supplementary Information section of the Financial Report of the U.S. Government.

3 GDP values used represent the average of 75-year present value of nominal GDP for 2013 and 2012 from the Social Security and Medicare Trustees Reports.

Find Out More

The *2013 Financial Report of the United States Government* and other information about the nation's finances are available at:

- U.S. Department of the Treasury,
  http://www.fiscal.treasury.gov/fsreports/fs_reports_publications.htm;
- OMB's Office of Federal Financial Management,
  http://www.whitehouse.gov/omb/financial/index.html; and
- GAO, http://www.gao.gov/financial.html.

MANAGEMENT'S DISCUSSION AND ANALYSIS

Introduction

The Fiscal Year (FY) *2013 Financial Report of the United States Government (Financial Report)* provides the President, Congress, and the American people with a comprehensive view of the Federal Government's finances, i.e., its financial position and condition, its revenues and costs, assets and liabilities, and other obligations and commitments. The *Financial Report* also discusses important financial issues and significant conditions that may affect future operations, including the need to achieve fiscal sustainability over the medium and long term.

Pursuant to 31 U.S.C. § 331(e)(1), the Department of the Treasury (Treasury), in cooperation with the Office of Management and Budget (OMB), must submit an audited (by the Government Accountability Office or GAO) financial statement for the preceding fiscal year, covering all accounts and associated activities of the executive branch of the United States Government[1] – the central component of the *Financial Report* – to the President and Congress no later than six months after the September 30 fiscal year end. To encourage timely and relevant reporting, OMB accelerated both individual agency and government-wide reporting deadlines.

The *Financial Report* is prepared from the audited financial statements of specifically designated federal agencies, including the Cabinet departments and many smaller, independent agencies (see organizational chart on the next page). As it has for the past sixteen years, GAO issued a "disclaimer" of opinion on the accrual-based, consolidated financial statements for the fiscal years ended September 30, 2013 and 2012. GAO also issued disclaimers of opinion on the 2013, 2012, 2011, and 2010 Statements of Social Insurance (SOSI), following an unqualified opinion on the 2009 SOSI, and a disclaimer of opinion on the 2013 and 2012 Statement of Changes in Social Insurance Amounts (SCSIA). A disclaimer of opinion indicates that sufficient information was not available for the auditors to determine whether the reported financial statements were fairly presented in accordance with Generally Accepted Accounting Principles (GAAP). In FY 2013, 32[2] of the 35 most significant agencies earned unqualified opinions on their financial statement audits.[3]

The FY 2013 *Financial Report* consists of:
- Management's Discussion and Analysis (MD&A), which provides management's perspectives on and analysis of information presented in the *Financial Report*, such as financial and performance trends;
- Principal financial statements and the related notes to the financial statements;
- Required Supplementary Information, Required Supplementary Stewardship Information, and Other Information; and
- GAO's audit report.

In addition, a Citizen's Guide is included to provide the American taxpayer with a quick reference to the key issues in the *Financial Report* and an overview of the Government's financial position and condition.

Mission & Organization

The Government's fundamental mission is derived from the Constitution: *"...to form a more perfect union, establish justice, insure domestic tranquility, provide for the common defense, promote the general welfare and secure the blessings of liberty to ourselves and our posterity."* The Congress authorizes and agencies implement programs as missions and initiatives evolve over time in pursuit of key public services and objectives, such as providing for national defense, promoting affordable health care, fostering income security, boosting agricultural productivity, providing veteran benefits and services, facilitating commerce, supporting housing and the

---

[1] The Government Management Reform Act of 1994 has required such reporting, covering the executive branch of the Government, beginning with financial statements prepared for FY 1997. Treasury and OMB have elected to include certain financial information on the legislative and judicial branches in consolidated financial statements as well.

[2] The 32 agencies include the Department of Health and Human Services, which received disclaimers of opinion on its 2013, 2012, 2011, and 2010 SOSI and on its 2013 and 2012 SCSIA.

[3] The Federal Deposit Insurance Corporation (FDIC), the National Credit Union Administration (NCUA), and the Farm Credit System Insurance Corporation (FCSIC) are among the 35 significant entities. However, because these entities operate on a calendar year basis (December 31 year-end), their 2013 audits are not yet complete. Statistic reflects 2012 audit results for these organizations.

transportation systems, protecting the environment, contributing to the security of energy resources, and helping States provide education. Exhibit 1 provides an overview of how the U.S. Government (Government) is organized.

Exhibit 1

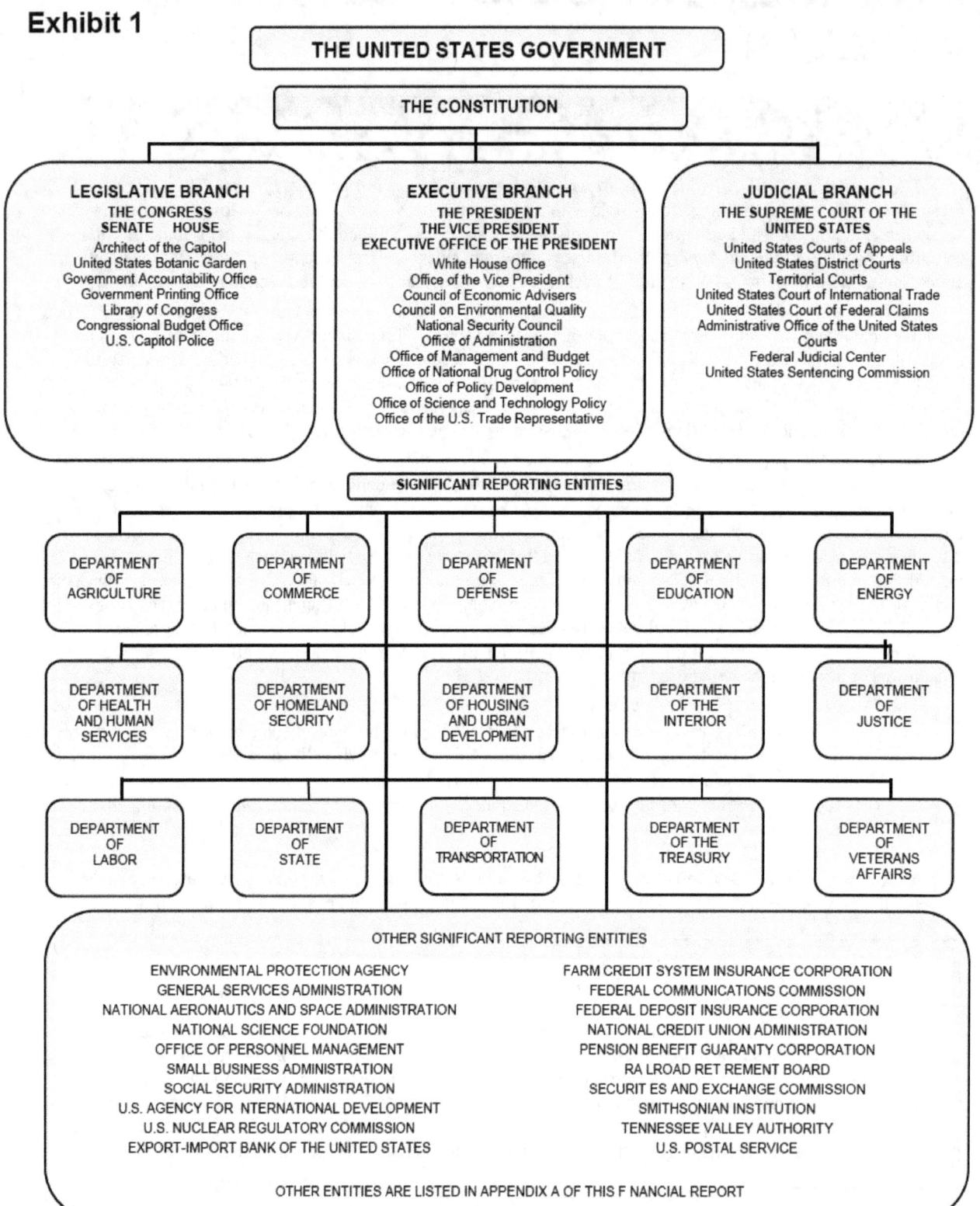

THE UNITED STATES GOVERNMENT

THE CONSTITUTION

LEGISLATIVE BRANCH
THE CONGRESS
SENATE   HOUSE
Architect of the Capitol
United States Botanic Garden
Government Accountability Office
Government Printing Office
Library of Congress
Congressional Budget Office
U.S. Capitol Police

EXECUTIVE BRANCH
THE PRESIDENT
THE VICE PRESIDENT
EXECUTIVE OFFICE OF THE PRESIDENT
White House Office
Office of the Vice President
Council of Economic Advisers
Council on Environmental Quality
National Security Council
Office of Administration
Office of Management and Budget
Office of National Drug Control Policy
Office of Policy Development
Office of Science and Technology Policy
Office of the U.S. Trade Representative

JUDICIAL BRANCH
THE SUPREME COURT OF THE
UNITED STATES
United States Courts of Appeals
United States District Courts
Territorial Courts
United States Court of International Trade
United States Court of Federal Claims
Administrative Office of the United States
Courts
Federal Judicial Center
United States Sentencing Commission

SIGNIFICANT REPORTING ENTITIES

DEPARTMENT OF AGRICULTURE

DEPARTMENT OF COMMERCE

DEPARTMENT OF DEFENSE

DEPARTMENT OF EDUCATION

DEPARTMENT OF ENERGY

DEPARTMENT OF HEALTH AND HUMAN SERVICES

DEPARTMENT OF HOMELAND SECURITY

DEPARTMENT OF HOUSING AND URBAN DEVELOPMENT

DEPARTMENT OF THE INTERIOR

DEPARTMENT OF JUSTICE

DEPARTMENT OF LABOR

DEPARTMENT OF STATE

DEPARTMENT OF TRANSPORTATION

DEPARTMENT OF THE TREASURY

DEPARTMENT OF VETERANS AFFAIRS

OTHER SIGNIFICANT REPORTING ENTITIES

ENVIRONMENTAL PROTECTION AGENCY
GENERAL SERVICES ADMINISTRATION
NATIONAL AERONAUTICS AND SPACE ADMINISTRATION
NATIONAL SCIENCE FOUNDATION
OFFICE OF PERSONNEL MANAGEMENT
SMALL BUSINESS ADMINISTRATION
SOCIAL SECURITY ADMINISTRATION
U.S. AGENCY FOR NTERNATIONAL DEVELOPMENT
U.S. NUCLEAR REGULATORY COMMISSION
EXPORT-IMPORT BANK OF THE UNITED STATES

FARM CREDIT SYSTEM INSURANCE CORPORATION
FEDERAL COMMUNICATIONS COMMISSION
FEDERAL DEPOSIT INSURANCE CORPORATION
NATIONAL CREDIT UNION ADMINISTRATION
PENSION BENEFIT GUARANTY CORPORATION
RA LROAD RET REMENT BOARD
SECURIT ES AND EXCHANGE COMMISSION
SMITHSONIAN INSTITUTION
TENNESSEE VALLEY AUTHORITY
U.S. POSTAL SERVICE

OTHER ENTITIES ARE LISTED IN APPENDIX A OF THIS F NANCIAL REPORT

The Government's Financial Position and Condition

A complete assessment of the Government's financial or fiscal condition requires analysis of historical results, projections of future revenues and expenditures, and an assessment of the Government's long-term fiscal sustainability. This *Financial Report* discusses the Government's financial position at the end of the fiscal year, explains how and why the financial position changed during the year, and provides insight into how the Government's financial condition may change in the future.

Table 1 The Federal Government's Financial Position and Condition					
Dollars in Billions	2013	2012	Increase / (Decrease)	
			$	%
FINANCIAL MEASURES					
Gross Cost	$ (3,940.9)	$ (3,844.9)	$ 96.0	2.5%
Less: Earned Revenue	$ 415.5	$ 350.8	$ 64.7	18.4%
Gain/(Loss) from Changes in Assumptions	$ (131.2)	$ (320.2)	$ (189.0)	(59%)
Net Cost[1]	**$ (3,656.6)**	**$ (3,814.3)**	**$ (157.7)**	**(4.1%)**
Less: Taxes and Other Revenue:	$ 2,842.5	$ 2,518.2	$ 324.3	12.9%
Unmatched Transactions & Balances	$ 9.0	$ (20.2)	$ (29.2)	(144.6%)
Net Operating Cost[2]	**$ (805.1)**	**$ (1,316.3)**	**$ (511.2)**	**(38.8%)**
Assets[3] :					
Cash & Other Monetary Assets	$ 206.3	$ 206.2	$ 0.1	0.0%
Loans Receivable, Net	$ 1,022.3	$ 859.6	$ 162.7	18.9%
Inventories & Related Property, Net	$ 311.1	$ 299.0	$ 12.1	4.0%
Property, Plant & Equipment, Net	$ 896.7	$ 855.0	$ 41.7	4.9%
Other	$ 531.9	$ 528.5	$ 3.4	0.6%
Total Assets	**$ 2,968.3**	**$ 2,748.3**	**$ 220.0**	**8.0%**
Liabilities[3] :					
Federal Debt Held by the Public & Accrued Interest	$ (12,028.4)	$ (11,332.3)	$ 696.1	6.1%
Federal Employee & Veterans Benefits	$ (6,538.3)	$ (6,274.0)	$ 264.3	4.2%
Other	$ (1,310.9)	$ (1,243.0)	$ 67.9	5.5%
Total Liabilities	**$ (19,877.6)**	**$ (18,849.3)**	**$ 1,028.3**	**5.5%**
Net Position (Assets minus Liabilities)	**$ (16,909.3)**	**$ (16,101.0)**	**$ (808.3)**	**(5.0%)**
SUSTAINABILITY MEASURES					
Social Insurance Net Expenditures[4] :					
Social Security (OASDI)	$ (12,294)	$ (11,278)	$ 1,016	9.0%
Medicare (Parts A, B, & D)	$ (27,302)	$ (27,174)	$ 128	0.5%
Other	$ (102)	$ (102)	$ 0	0.0%
Total Social Insurance Net Expenditures	**$ (39,698)**	**$ (38,554)**	**$ 1,144**	**3.0%**
Total Federal Government Noninterest Net Expenditures[5]	**$ (4,000)**	**$ (16,500)**	**$ (12,500)**	**(75.8%)**
BUDGET DEFICIT					
Unified Budget Deficit[6]	**$ (680.3)**	**$ (1,089.4)**	**$ (409.1)**	**(37.6%)**

1 Source: Statement of Net Cost.

2 Source: Statements of Operations and Changes in Net Position.

3 Source: Balance Sheet.

4 Source: Statements of Social Insurance (SOSI). Amounts equal estimated present value of projected revenues and expenditures for scheduled benefits over the next 75 years of certain 'Social Insurance' programs (Social Security, Medicare Parts A, B, & D, Railroad Retirement - Black Lung is projected through 2040). Amounts reflect 'Open Group' totals (all current and projected program participants during the 75-year projection period).

5 Represents the 75-year projection of the Federal Government's receipts less non-interest spending as reported in the Statement of Long-Term Fiscal Projections in the Required Supplementary Information section of the *Financial Report*.

6 Source: Final Monthly Treasury Statement (as of 9/30/2013 and 9/30/2012).

Note: totals may not equal sum of components due to rounding.

Table 1 on the previous page and the following summarize the Federal Government's financial position:

- The Government's gross costs increased by 2.5 percent to $3.9 trillion. Deducting $415.5 billion in revenues earned for goods and services provided to the public (e.g., Medicare premiums, national park entry fees, and postal service fees) and adding $131.2 billion in losses from changes in assumptions (e.g., interest rates, inflation, disability claims rates) shows that the Government's net cost decreased by $157.7 billion (4.1 percent) to $3.7 trillion during FY 2013.

- Taxes and other revenues increased $324.3 billion (12.9 percent) to $2.8 trillion, which, when offset against the Government's net cost, results in a "bottom line" net operating cost of $805.1 billion.

- Comparing total 2013 Government assets of $3.0 trillion to total liabilities of $19.9 trillion yields a negative net position of $16.9 trillion. Government liabilities are comprised mostly of $12.0 trillion in federal debt held by the public and accrued interest payable[4] and $6.5 trillion in federal employee and veteran benefits payable.

- The sum of debt held by the public ($12.0 trillion) and intragovernmental debt ($4.8 trillion) equals gross federal debt, which, with some adjustments is subject to the statutory debt limit. As of September 30, 2013, the Government's total debt subject to the debt limit was $16.699 trillion, $25 million under the limit. During 2013, Treasury began implementing "extraordinary measures" on a temporary basis, which were still in effect as of September 30, 2013, to enable the Government to protect the full faith and credit of the United States Government by continuing to pay the nation's bills.[5]

This *Financial Report* also contains information about potential impacts on the Government's future financial condition. Under federal accounting rules, social insurance expenditures, as reported in the Statement of Social Insurance (SOSI) and the Statement of Long-Term Fiscal Projections (included in the Required Supplementary Information section of the *Financial Report*) are not considered liabilities of the Government. They can, however, provide a valuable perspective on the sustainability of the Government's fiscal path:

- The SOSI compares the actuarial present value of the Government's projected expenditures for scheduled benefits for Social Security, Medicare Parts A, B and D, and other social insurance programs over 75 years[6] to a subset of the revenues[7] supporting these programs. For 2013, projected social insurance expenditures exceeded projected revenues by about $39.7 trillion, a $1.1 trillion increase over 2012 projections.

- From a government-wide perspective, projected expenditures for other major programs (including defense, Medicaid, and education) and future tax revenues will also affect the Government's future fiscal condition. Over the next 75 years, under current policy, the present value of the Government's total projected, non-interest expenditures (including its social insurance programs) are projected to exceed total projected receipts by $4.0 trillion.

The Government's current financial position and long-term financial condition can be evaluated both in dollar terms and in relation to the economy as a whole. Gross Domestic Product (GDP) measures the size of the nation's economy in terms of the total value of all final goods and services that are produced in a year. Considering financial results relative to GDP is a useful indicator of the economy's capacity to sustain the Government's many programs.[8] For example:

- The unified budget deficit decreased from 6.8 percent of GDP ($1.1 trillion) in FY 2012 to 4.1 percent of GDP ($680.3 billion in FY 2013 as a result of outlays that were 20.8 percent of GDP ($3.5 trillion)) net of receipts that were 16.7 percent of GDP ($2.8 trillion)[9]

- The budget deficit is primarily financed through borrowing from the public. As of September 30, 2013, debt held by the public, excluding interest payable, was $12.0 trillion (72 percent of GDP).

---

[4] On the Government's balance sheet, debt held by the public and accrued interest payable consists of Treasury securities, net of unamortized discounts and premiums, and accrued interest payable. The "public" consists of individuals, corporations, state and local governments, Federal Reserve Banks, foreign governments, and other entities outside the Federal Government.

[5] As of October 17, 2013, the debt limit was suspended by action of P.L. 113-46 through February 7, 2014. As of February 15, 2014, P.L. 113-83 again suspended the debt limit, this time through March 15, 2015. (see Note 26 – Subsequent Events)

[6] The Black Lung Program is projected through September 30, 2040.

[7] Social Security and Medicare Part A are funded by the payroll taxes, revenue from taxation of benefits, and premiums that support those programs. Medicare Parts B and D are primarily financed by general revenues and premiums. By accounting convention, general revenues transferred to Medicare Parts B and D are eliminated in consolidation at the government-wide level and, as such, are not included in SOSI projections.

[8] Unless otherwise noted, percentages or shares of GDP referenced in this *Financial Report* reflect revised GDP figures per the Bureau of Economic Analysis (BEA). In July 2013, the BEA revised upward the historical values for GDP beginning with estimates for 1929. As a result, shares of GDP throughout the *Financial Report* are slightly lower than those reported in previous years.

[9] Final Monthly Treasury Statement (as of September 30, 2013 and 2012), 10/30/13 press release.

- The projected $39.7 trillion net present value excess of expenditures over receipts over 75 years for the programs reported in the 2013 SOSI represents about 4.0 percent of the present value of GDP over 75 years. The excess of total projected non-interest spending over receipts of $4.0 trillion discussed in the 'Statement of Long Term Fiscal Projections' in the Required Supplementary Information (RSI) section of the *Financial Report* represents 0.4 percent of GDP. As discussed in this *Financial Report*, these projections can, in turn, have a significant impact on projected debt as a percent of GDP.

Fiscal Year 2013 Financial Statement Audit Results

For FY 2013, GAO issued a seventeenth consecutive disclaimer of audit opinion on the accrual-based, government-wide financial statements. In addition, GAO issued disclaimers of opinion on the 2013, 2012, 2011, and 2010 Statements of Social Insurance (SOSI), following an unqualified opinion on the 2009 SOSI, and disclaimers of opinion on the 2013 and 2012 Statement of Changes in Social Insurance Amounts (SCSIA). The SOSI and SCSIA disclaimers stem from significant uncertainties (discussed in note 24), primarily related to the achievement of projected reductions in Medicare cost growth as reflected in the 2013, 2012, 2011, and 2010 SOSI.

Twenty-two of the 24 agencies required to issue audited financial statements under the Chief Financial Officers (CFO) Act received unqualified audit opinions, as did 10 of 11 additional significant reporting agencies (see Table 2 and Appendix A).[10]

The Government-wide Reporting Entity

These financial statements cover the three branches of the Government (legislative, executive, and judicial). Legislative and judicial branch reporting focuses primarily on budgetary activity. Most executive branch entities, as well as certain legislative branch agencies are required, by law, to prepare audited financial statements. Some other legislative branch entities voluntarily produce audited financial reports.

A number of entities and organizations are excluded due to the nature of their operations, including the Federal Reserve System (considered to be an independent central bank under the general oversight of Congress), all fiduciary funds, and Government-Sponsored Enterprises (GSEs), including the Federal Home Loan Banks, the Federal National Mortgage Association (Fannie Mae), and the Federal Home Loan Mortgage Corporation (Freddie Mac). The Emergency Economic Stabilization Act (EESA) of 2008 gave the Secretary of the Treasury temporary authority to purchase and guarantee assets from a wide range of financial institutions through the Troubled Asset Relief Program (TARP). Following U.S. GAAP for federal entities, the Government has not consolidated into its financial statements the assets, liabilities, or results of operations of any financial organization or commercial entity in which Treasury holds either a direct, indirect, or

Table 2: FY 2013 Agency Financial Statement Audit Results	
Chief Financial Officers (CFO) Act Agency	**Audit Opinion**
Department of Agriculture (USDA)	Unqualified
Department of Commerce (DOC)	Unqualified
Department of Defense (DOD)	Disclaimer
Department of Education (Education)	Unqualified
Department of Energy (DOE)	Unqualified
Department of Health and Human Services (HHS)[1]	Unqualified
Department of Homeland Security (DHS)	Unqualified
Department of Housing and Urban Development (HUD)	Qualified
Department of the Interior (DOI)	Unqualified
Department of Labor (DOL)	Unqualified
Department of Justice (DOJ)	Unqualified
Department of State (State)	Unqualified
Department of Transportation (DOT)	Unqualified
Department of the Treasury (Treasury)	Unqualified
Department of Veterans Affairs (VA)	Unqualified
Agency for International Development (USAID)	Unqualified
Environmental Protection Agency (EPA)	Unqualified
General Services Administration (GSA)	Unqualified
National Aeronautics and Space Administration (NASA)	Unqualified
National Science Foundation (NSF)	Unqualified
Nuclear Regulatory Commission (NRC)	Unqualified
Office of Personnel Management (OPM)	Unqualified
Small Business Administration (SBA)	Unqualified
Social Security Administration (SSA)	Unqualified
Other Significant Reporting Entities	
Export-Import Bank of the United States	Unqualified
Farm Credit System Insurance Corportation (FCSIC)[2]	Unqualified
Federal Communications Commission (FCC)	Unqualified
Federal Deposit Insurance Corporation (FDIC)[2]	Unqualified
National Credit Union Administration (NCUA)[2]	Unqualified
Pension Benefit Guaranty Corporation (PBGC)	Unqualified
Railroad Retirement Board (RRB)	Disclaimer
Securities and Exchange Commission (SEC)	Unqualified
Smithsonian Institution[3]	Unqualified
Tennessee Valley Authority (TVA)	Unqualified
U.S. Postal Service (USPS)	Unqualified

[1] Recieved disclaimer of opinion on Statement of Social Insurance and Statement of Changes in Social Insurance Amounts

[2] Entities operate under calendar year (CY)-end Opinions reflect CY 2012 audit results

[3] Opinion on the most recent annual report, covering FY 2012

---

[10] The 22 agencies include the Department of Health and Human Services, which received disclaimers of opinions on its 2013, 2012, 2011, and 2010 SOSI and its 2013 and 2012 SCSIA.

beneficial majority equity investment. Even though some of the equity investments are significant, under Statement of Federal Financial Accounting Concepts (SFFAC) No. 2, these entities meet the criteria of paragraph 50 and do not appear in the Federal Budget section "Federal Programs by Agency and Account." As such, these entities are not consolidated into the financial reports of the Government. However, the values of the investments in and any related liabilities to such entities are presented on the balance sheet. Appendix A includes a list of the agencies and entities contributing to this *Financial Report*.[11]

Limitations of the Financial Statements

The principal financial statements have been prepared to report the financial position and results of operations of the Federal Government, and the financial condition and changes in financial condition of its social insurance programs, pursuant to the requirements of 31 U.S.C. § 331(e)(1). These statements are in addition to the financial reports used to monitor and control budgetary resources that are prepared from the same books and records.

The following pages contain a more detailed discussion of the Government's financial results for FY 2013, the budget, the economy, the debt, and a long-term perspective about fiscal sustainability, including the Government's ability to meet its social insurance benefits obligations. The information in this *Financial Report*, when combined with the President's Budget, collectively presents information on the Government's financial position and condition.

The President's Budget and The Financial Report

Each year, the Administration issues two reports that detail the Government's financial results: the *President's Budget*, which provides a plan for future initiatives and the resources needed to support them, as well as prior year fiscal and performance results; and this *Financial Report*, which provides the President, Congress, and the American people a broad, comprehensive overview of the cost on an accrual basis of the Government's operations, the sources used to finance them, its balance sheet, and the overall financial outlook.

Treasury generally prepares the financial statements in this *Financial Report* on an "accrual basis" of accounting as prescribed by U.S. GAAP for federal entities.[12] These principles are tailored to the Government's unique characteristics and circumstances. For example, agencies prepare a uniquely structured "Statement of Net Cost," which is intended to present net Government resources used in its operations. Also, unique to Government is the preparation of separate statements to reconcile differences and articulate the relationship between the budget and financial accounting results.

President's Budget*	Financial Report of the U.S. Government*
Prepared primarily on a *"cash basis"*	Prepared on an *"accrual and modified cash basis"*
• Initiative-based and prospective: focus on current and future initiatives planned and how resources will be used to fund them.	• Agency-based and retrospective – prior and present resources used to implement initiatives.
• Receipts ("cash in"), taxes and other collections recorded when received.	• Revenue: Tax revenue (more than 90 percent of total revenue) recognized on modified cash basis (see Financial Statement Note 1.B). Remainder recognized when earned, but not necessarily received.
• Outlays ("cash out"), largely recorded when payment is made.	• Costs: recognized when owed, but not necessarily paid.

*See Statements of Changes in Cash Balance from Unified Budget and Other Activities and Reconciliations of Net Operating Cost and Unified Budget Deficits.

---

[11] Since programs are not administered at the government-wide level, performance goals and measures for the Federal Government, as a whole, are not reported here. The outcomes and results of those programs are addressed at the individual agency level and can be found in each agency's financial report.

[12] Under U.S. GAAP, most U.S. Government revenues are recognized on a 'modified cash' basis, or when they become measurable. The Statement of Social Insurance presents the present value of the estimated future revenues and expenditures for scheduled benefits over the next 75 years for the Social Security, Medicare, Railroad Retirement programs; and through September 30, 2040 for the Black Lung program.

Budget Deficit vs. Net Operating Cost

The Government's primarily cash-based[13] budget deficit decreased nearly 38 percent from approximately $1.1 trillion in FY 2012 to about $680.3 billion in FY 2013 due to receipt increases stemming from the implementation of new tax laws under the American Taxpayer Relief Act of 2012 (ATRA), expiration of payroll tax relief provisions, and the ongoing economic recovery; as well as spending decreases associated with the defense drawdown, lower spending for unemployment claims, and budget sequester measures ushered in under the Budget Control Act (BCA) of 2011.[14] These actions had similar, corresponding effects on the Government's largely accrual-based net operating cost, which decreased nearly 39 percent from $1.3 trillion in FY 2012 to $805.1 billion in FY 2013.

The budget deficit is measured as the excess of outlays, or payments made by the Government, over receipts, or cash received by the Government. Net operating cost, on an accrual basis, is the excess of costs (what the Government has incurred, but has not necessarily paid) over revenues (what the Government has collected and expects to collect, but has not necessarily received). Net operating cost typically exceeds the budget deficit due largely to the inclusion of cost accruals associated with increases in estimated liabilities for the Government's postemployment benefit programs for its military and civilian employees and veterans. Similarly, the difference between the budget deficit and net operating cost can also be affected by changes in certain asset valuations, such as investments, and in other liabilities, such as estimated insurance and guarantee program liabilities. The longer-term estimated costs of these programs are included in the Government's net operating cost, calculated on an accrual basis as described above, but are not included in the largely cash-based budget deficit. In addition, the costs of certain assets, such as property plant and equipment, are recorded in the budget as outlays when purchased but are capitalized as assets and included in net operating cost as depreciation expense (an accrual cost) as they are used over the useful life of the asset. Significant changes in the Government's net operating cost, including those related to the aforementioned longer-term estimated costs, are discussed in the next section.

Table 3: Budget Deficit vs. Net Operating Cost				
Dollars in Billions		2013		2012
Net Operating Cost	$	**(805.1)**	$	**(1,316.3)**
Change in:				
Federal Employee and Veteran Benefits Payable	$	264.3	$	481.8
Property, Plant, and Equipment, Net[1]	$	(41.7)	$	(2.2)
Investments in Government-Sponsored Enterprises (GSEs)	$	(30.9)	$	42.3
Insurance and Guarantee Program Liabilities	$	(26.4)	$	(5.3)
Liabilities to GSEs	$	(9.0)	$	(307.2)
Other, Net	$	(31.5)	$	17.5
Subtotal - Net Difference:	$	124.8	$	226.9
Budget Deficit	$	**(680.3)**	$	**(1,089.4)**

1 Includes the net effect of: capitalized fixed assets, depreciation expense, and asset disposals and revaluations

The *Reconciliation of Net Operating Cost and Unified Budget Deficit Statement*, as summarized in Table 3, shows how the Government's net operating cost from the primarily accrual-based financial statements relates to the more widely-known and primarily cash-based budget deficit. Table 3 shows how many of the elements described above contribute to the $124.8 billion net difference between the Government's budget deficit and net operating cost for FY 2013, predominantly due to the $264.3 billion increase in liabilities for Federal employee and veteran benefits payable, the effects of which impact net operating cost, but not the budget deficit.

---

[13] Interest outlays on Treasury debt held by the public are recorded in the budget when interest accrues, not when the interest payment is made. For federal credit programs, outlays are recorded when loans are disbursed, in an amount representing the present value cost to the Government (excluding administrative costs), or the credit subsidy cost. Credit programs record cash payments to and from the public in nonbudgetary financing accounts.

[14] Joint Statement of Secretary Lew and OMB Director Burwell on Budget Results for Fiscal Year 2013.

The Government's Net Position: "Where We Are"

The Government's financial position and condition have traditionally been expressed through the *Budget*, focusing on surpluses, deficits, and debt. However, this primarily cash-based discussion of the Government's net outlays (deficit) or net receipts (surplus) tells only part of the story. The Government's accrual-based net position, (the difference between its assets and liabilities), and its "bottom line" net operating cost (the difference between its revenues and costs) are also key financial indicators.

Revenues and Costs: "What Came In & What Went Out"

The Government's *Statement of Operations and Changes in Net Position*, much like a corporation's income statement, shows the Government's "bottom line" and its impact on net position (i.e., assets net of liabilities). The Government nets its costs against both: (1) earned revenues from Government programs (e.g., Medicare premiums, national park entry fees, and postal service fees) to derive net cost; and (2) taxes and other revenue to arrive at the Government's "bottom line" net operating cost.

Table 4: Gross Cost, Revenues, Net Cost, and Net Operating Cost				
Dollars in Billions	2013	2012	Increase / (Decrease) $	%
Gross Cost	$ (3,940.9)	$ (3,844.9)	$ 96.0	2.5%
Less: Earned Revenue[1]	$ 415.5	$ 350.8	$ 64.7	18.4%
Gain/(Loss) from Changes in Assumptions[2]	$ (131.2)	$ (320.2)	$ (189.0)	(59%)
Net Cost	$ (3,656.6)	$ (3,814.3)	$ (157.7)	(4.1%)
Less: Taxes and Other Revenue	$ 2,842.5	$ 2,518.2	$ 324.3	12.9%
Unmatched Transactions and Balances[3]	$ 9.0	$ (20.2)	$ (29.2)	(144.6%)
Net Operating Cost	$ (805.1)	$ (1,316.3)	$ (511.2)	(38.8%)

1: Revenues earned for goods and services provided (e.g., Medicare premiums, national park entry fees, and postal fees)
2: Changes in assumptions used to estimate liabilities for federal employee pensions and other retirement and postemployment benefits.
3: Primarily represents net unreconciled differences in intragovernmental activity and balances between federal agencies.

Table 4 shows that the Government's "bottom line" net operating cost decreased significantly from $1,316.3 billion in FY 2012 to $805.1 billion in FY 2013. As referenced earlier and discussed further below, this nearly 39 percent decrease is attributable to both revenue increases and cost decreases over the past fiscal year.

Revenue: "What Came In"

The *Statement of Net Cost* reports "earned" revenue generated by federal programs (e.g., Medicare premiums paid by program participants, national park entry fees, and postal service fees). The *Statement of Operations and Changes in Net Position* shows the Government's taxes and other revenues (i.e., revenues other than "earned"). Chart A shows that increases in each of the three taxes and other revenue categories shown - individual income tax and withholdings, corporation income taxes, and other revenues - combined to increase total Government taxes and other revenues by $324.3 billion (12.9 percent) to more than $2.8 trillion for FY 2013. This change is

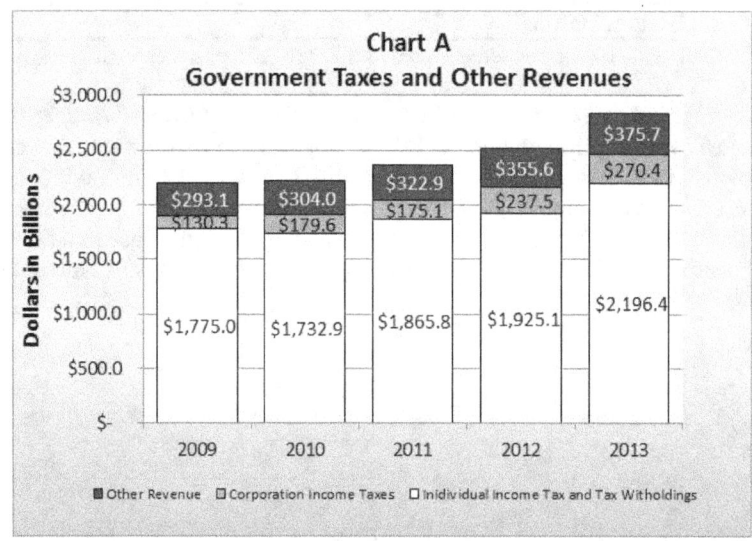

primarily attributed to an increase in ordinary, capital gains, and dividend income tax rates for individuals, coupled with an increase in corporation income tax collections and a reduction in tax refunds.[15] As noted in the earlier discussion of budget receipts, these increases largely stem from the implementation of ATRA, the expiration of payroll tax relief provisions, and the ongoing economic recovery. Earned revenues are not shown in Chart A (see Table 4 for earned revenues). Together, individual income tax and tax withholdings and corporation income taxes accounted for about 87 percent of total revenues in FY 2013. The remaining 13 percent consists of various other taxes and receipts, including excise taxes, unemployment taxes, and customs duties.

Cost: "What Went Out"

The *Statement of Net Cost* also shows how much it costs to operate the Federal Government, recognizing expenses when they happen, regardless of when payment is made (accrual basis). It shows the derivation of the Government's *net cost* or the net of: (1) the costs of goods produced and services rendered by the Government, (2) the earned revenues generated by those goods and services during the fiscal year, and (3) gains or losses from changes in assumptions impacting longer-term estimated costs. This amount, in turn, is offset against the Government's taxes and other revenue in the *Statement of Operations and Changes in Net Position* to calculate the "bottom line" or *net operating cost*.

The Government's net cost (gross cost less earned revenue and gain/loss from changes in assumptions) decreased $157.7 billion to $3,656.6 billion during FY 2013. Net cost is typically impacted by a variety of offsetting increases and decreases. For FY 2013, the single most significant driver of the decrease was a $189 billion decrease in losses from changes in assumptions associated with the Government's civilian and military benefits programs. The Department of Defense (DOD), the Department of Veterans Affairs (VA), and the Office of Personnel Management (OPM) each attributed changes in their respective agency total net costs largely to decreases in losses from changes in

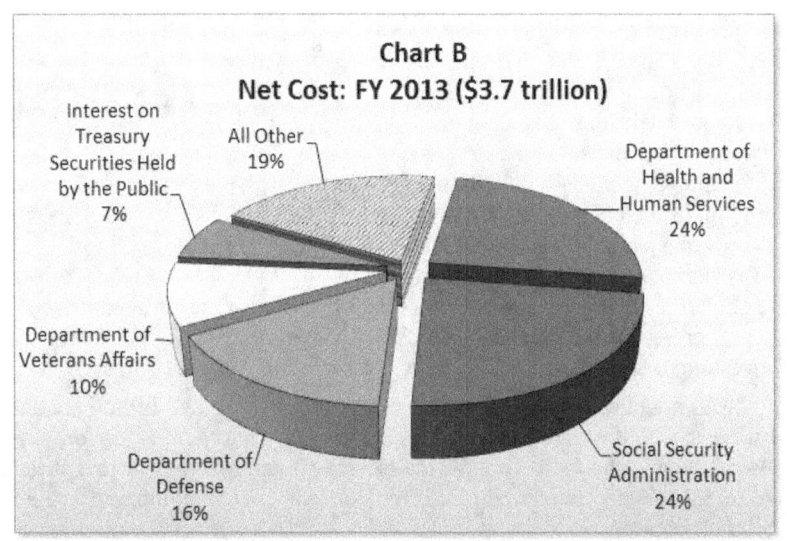

Chart B
Net Cost: FY 2013 ($3.7 trillion)

assumptions related to these programs. DOD, VA, and OPM, and other agencies administering similar programs employ a complex series of assumptions, including but not limited to interest rates, beneficiary eligibility, life expectancy, medical cost levels, compensation levels, disability claims rates, and cost of living to make annual actuarial projections of their long-term benefits liabilities and their related costs. In fact, for DOD a $133.3 billion decrease in losses from changes in actuarial assumptions accounted for the majority of the more than $200 billion decrease in DOD's total net cost during FY 2013.

Chart B shows the composition of the Government's net cost. In FY 2013, almost two-thirds of total net cost came from DOD, the Social Security Administration (SSA), and the Department of Health and Human Services (HHS), which have consistently incurred the largest agency shares of the Government's total net cost in recent years, as shown in Charts B and C. The bulk of HHS and SSA net costs (which totaled $895.7 billion and $867.0 billion in FY 2013, respectively) are attributable to major social insurance programs administered by these agencies, e.g., Medicare by HHS and Social Security by SSA. The *Statement of Social Insurance* (SOSI) and the related information in this *Financial Report*, including the broader discussion of the Government's long-term fiscal projections, discuss the projected future revenues, expenditures, and sustainability of these programs in greater detail. DOD's net costs of $577.4 billion relate primarily to operations, readiness, and support; personnel; research; procurement; and retirement and health benefits (noted earlier). Charts B and C show that the Department of Veterans Affairs (VA) as well as interest on debt held by the public were also significant contributors to the Government's net cost for FY 2013. The combined other agencies included in the Government's FY 2013 Statement of Net Cost accounted for 19 percent of the Government's total net cost for FY 2013.

Among these other agencies, according to the Statement of Net Cost in this *Financial Report*, additional significant changes in the Government's total net cost included, but were not limited to: (1) a $32.9 billion cost decrease at the Department of Education, including a $24 billion decrease associated with reductions in the projected long-term costs of its direct student loan programs; (2) a $31.4 billion decrease at the Department of Housing and Urban Development related largely to its Federal Housing Administration (FHA) programs; and (3) a $22.5 billion decrease at the Department of Labor, primarily due to decreases in unemployment benefits provided under existing statute which reduced the length of coverage, and lower levels of unemployment as compared to FY 2012.[16] These cost decreases were partially offset by cost increases in the SSA's Old Age Survivors and Disability Income (OASDI) and HHS' Medicare and Medicaid programs.

In addition, the FY 2013 Statement of Net Cost includes net revenues for Treasury for a second consecutive year. Treasury's net revenue in FY 2012 was largely attributable to a $288.7 billion reduction in the contingent liability to the GSEs associated with GSE Senior Preferred Stock Purchase Agreements (SPSPAs). In FY 2013, the remaining $9.0 billion contingent liability was eliminated.[17] Treasury investments made through the SPSPAs help maintain the solvency of GSEs, specifically Fannie Mae and Freddie Mac. During FY 2012, Treasury amended the SPSPA dividend provision, which commenced with the quarter ending March 31, 2013. Under this revision the GSEs no longer make draws to fund dividend payments to Treasury, since dividend payments are limited to the amount of the positive net worth in excess of a capital reserve amount. This change, as well as federal income tax benefits and other improvements in GSE financial performance, also contributed to a $77.3 billion increase in senior preferred stock dividends to $95.7 billion to Treasury in FY 2013. In addition, a $30.9 billion gain on GSE investments was also recognized by Treasury in FY 2013, compared to a $42.3 billion loss in 2012.[18]

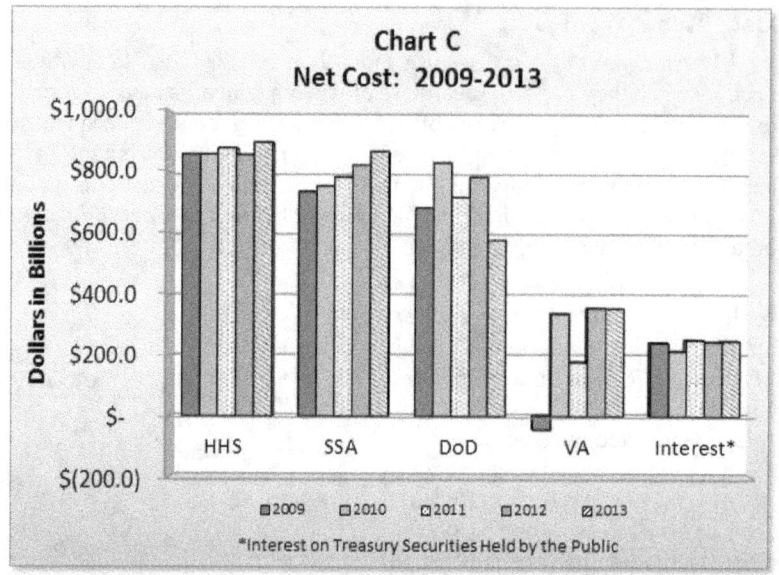

As noted earlier, taxes and other revenues of $2,842.5 billion are deducted from the total net cost of $3,656.6 billion (including actuarial costs) to derive the Government's "bottom line" net operating cost of $805.1 billion.[19] As previously shown in Table 4, the increase in taxes and other revenues, combined with the decrease in net costs, result in a net decrease of $511.2 billion or 38.8 percent compared to the FY 2012 net operating cost of $1,316.3 billion.

---

[16] Department of Labor FY 2013 Agency Financial Report, p. 25

[17] Department of the Treasury FY 2013 Agency Financial Report, p. 29. Treasury's payments to the GSEs during FY 2012 reduced its contingent liability by an additional $18.5 billion for a total contingent liability reduction of $307.2 billion. See also Note 9 – Investments in and Liabilities to GSEs – of this *Financial Report*.

[18] Department of the Treasury FY 2013 Agency Financial Report, p. 29. See also Note 9 – Investments in and Liabilities to GSEs – of this *Financial Report*.

[19] As shown in Table 4, net operating cost includes an adjustment for unmatched transactions and balances. These amounts are described in greater detail in the Other Information section of this *Financial Report*.

Assets and Liabilities: "What We Own and What We Owe"

The Government's net position at the end of the year is derived by netting the Government's assets against its liabilities, as presented in the **Balance Sheet** (summarized in Table 5). It is important to note that the balance sheet does not include the financial value of the Government's sovereign powers to tax, regulate commerce, and set monetary policy. It also excludes its control over nonoperational resources, including national and natural resources, for which the Government is a steward. In addition, as is the case with the **Statement of Operations and Changes in Net Position**, the **Balance Sheet** includes a separate presentation of the portion of

Table 5: Assets and Liabilities							
Net Position **Dollars in Billions**	**2013**		**2012**		Increase (Decrease)		
					$		**%**
Assets							
Cash & Other Monetary Assets	$	206.3	$	206.2	$	0.1	0.0%
Loans Receivable and Mortgage-Backed Securities, Net	$	1,022.3	$	859.6	$	162.7	18.9%
Inventories & Related Property, Net	$	311.1	$	299.0	$	12.1	4.0%
Property, Plant & Equipment, Net	$	896.7	$	855.0	$	41.7	4.9%
Other	$	531.9	$	528.5	$	3.4	0.6%
Total Assets	**$**	**2,968.3**	**$**	**2,748.3**	**$**	**220.0**	**8.0%**
Less: Liabilities, comprised of:							
Federal Debt Held by the Public & Accrued Interest	$	(12,028.4)	$	(11,332.3)	$	696.1	6.1%
Federal Employee & Veteran Benefits	$	(6,538.3)	$	(6,274.0)	$	264.3	4.2%
Other	$	(1,310.9)	$	(1,243.0)	$	67.9	5.5%
Total Liabilities	**$(19,877.6)**		**$(18,849.3)**		**$ 1,028.3**		**5.5%**
Net Position (Assets Minus Liabilities)	**$(16,909.3)**		**$(16,101.0)**		**$ (808.3)**		**(5.0%)**

net position related to funds from dedicated collections. Moreover, the Government's exposures are broader than the liabilities presented on the balance sheet, when such items as the Government's future social insurance exposures (namely, Medicare and Social Security), as well as other fiscal projections, commitments and contingencies, are taken into account. These exposures are discussed later in this Management Discussion and Analysis (MD&A) section as well as in the required supplementary disclosures of this *Financial Report*.

Assets – "What We Own"

As of September 30, 2013, the Government held about $3.0 trillion in assets, an increase of $220.0 billion (8.0 percent). The Government's assets are comprised mostly of net loans receivable ($1,022.3 billion) and net property, plant, and equipment ($896.7 billion).[20] The Department of Education's (Education's) direct loan programs accounted for $824.9 billion (80.7 percent) of total net loans receivable. Education's credit program receivables balances increased by 27 percent ($143.7 billion) during FY 2012 and 23 percent ($153.2 billion) during FY 2013 largely due to increased direct loan disbursements, attributable to the continued effect of 2011 legislation requiring a transition for new loans from guaranteed student loans to full direct lending by Education.[21]

Following the financial crisis in 2008, the Government's assets grew with the implementation of market stabilization and economic recovery initiatives. However, in recent years, with the ongoing wind-down of these recovery programs, the balances of many of these investments have declined principally through repayments and sales.[22] For example:

- Through the Troubled Asset Relief Program (TARP), Treasury made direct loans and equity investments, and entered into other credit programs. As of September 30, 2013, Treasury has collected a total of $273.4 billion for all TARP bank support programs through dividends, interest, repayments, sales, and other income - $27.9 billion more than the $245.5 billion originally invested. No more taxpayer money is being invested in banks under TARP. The final investment under the Capital Purchase Program (CPP) – the largest bank program under TARP – was made in December 2009. Treasury is focused on recovering

---

[20] For financial reporting purposes, other than multi-use heritage assets, stewardship assets are not recorded as part of Property, Plant, and Equipment. Stewardship assets are comprised of stewardship land and heritage assets. Stewardship land consists of public domain land (e.g., national parks, wildlife refuges). Heritage assets include national monuments and historical sites that among other characteristics are of historical, natural, cultural, educational, or artistic significance. See Note 25 – Stewardship Land and Heritage Assets.

[21] With the enactment of the SAFRA Act, formerly known as the Student Aid and Fiscal Responsibility Act, which was included as part of the Health Care and Education Reconciliation Act of 2010 (HCERA) (Pub. L. 111-152), beginning in July 2010, no new loans were originated under the Federal Family Education Loan (FFEL) Program (http://studentaid.ed.gov/sites/default/files/fsawg/datacenter/library/FY2013FederalStudentAidAnnualReport.pdf). See also: U.S. Department of Education FY 2013 Agency Financial Report p. 23.

[22] As of September 30, 2013, TARP Direct Loans and Equity Investments and Investments in GSEs represented 0.6 percent and 4.7 percent of total assets, respectively.

TARP funds in a manner that continues to promote the nation's financial stability while maximizing returns on behalf of the taxpayers.[23]

- Treasury continues to wind down the Automotive Industry Financing Program with the sale of 399 million shares of General Motors (GM) common stock during FY 2013. The remaining shares were sold in December 2013. These sales were conducted according to the plan announced in December 2012 to sell Treasury's remaining shares in GM within the next 12-15 months, subject to market conditions.[24]

- Treasury exited its remaining holdings in the American International Group, Inc. (AIG) Investment Program in December 2012 and sold remaining warrants in March 2013. As of September 30, 2013, Treasury does not hold any residual interest in AIG.[25]

- As noted earlier, amounts invested in the GSEs through the SPSPAs help maintain the solvency of Fannie Mae and Freddie Mac, since Treasury will disburse funds to the GSEs if, at the end of any quarter, the liabilities of either GSE exceeds its assets. As of September 30, 2013, the fair value of Treasury's portfolio of SPSPA investments totaled $140.2 billion compared to $109.3 billion as of September 30, 2012. Additionally, as noted earlier, as a result of the amended SPSPAs, coupled with the GSE's long-term financial forecasts within a specific time horizon, Treasury's contingent liability associated with the GSE program decreased by $9.0 billion and $288.7 billion at the end of FYs 2013 and 2012, respectively.[26]

Beyond these assets, other significant resources are available to the Government, including stewardship assets, such as natural resources, and the Government's power to tax and set monetary policy.

Liabilities – "What We Owe"

As indicated in Table 5 and Chart D, of the Government's $19.9 trillion in total liabilities, the largest liability is federal debt held by the public and accrued interest, the balance of which increased $696.1 billion (6.1 percent) to $12.0 trillion as of September 30, 2013.

The other major component of the Government's liabilities is federal employee postemployment and veteran benefits payable (i.e., the Government's pension and other benefit plans for its military and civilian employees), which increased $264.3 billion (4.2 percent) during FY 2013, from $6,274.0 billion to $6,538.3 billion. OPM administers the largest civilian pension plan, covering nearly 2.7 million current employees and

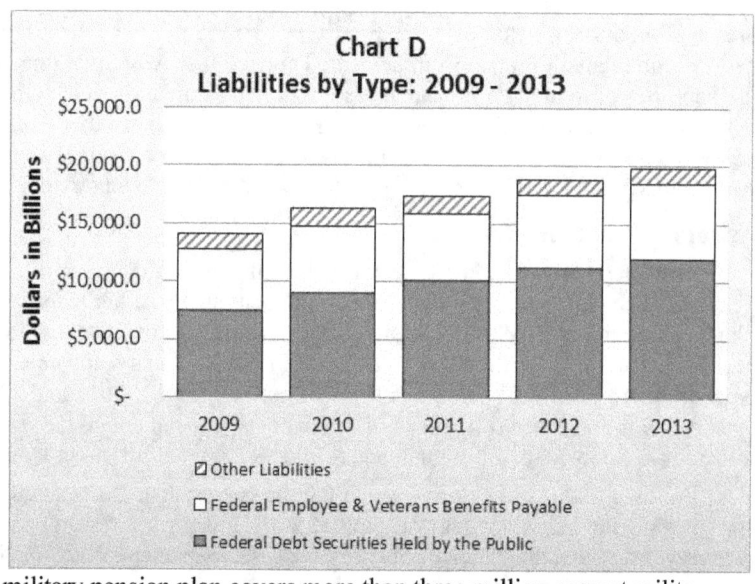

Chart D
Liabilities by Type: 2009 - 2013

☑ Other Liabilities
☐ Federal Employee & Veterans Benefits Payable
☒ Federal Debt Securities Held by the Public

2.5 million annuitants and survivors.[27] The military pension plan covers more than three million current military personnel (including active service, reserve, and National Guard) and approximately 2.2 million retirees and annuitants.[28]

Federal Debt

The unified budget surplus or deficit is the difference between total federal spending and receipts (e.g., taxes) in a given year. The Government borrows from the public (increases federal debt levels) to finance deficits. During a budget surplus (i.e., when receipts exceed spending), the Government typically uses those excess funds to reduce the debt held by the public. *The Statements of Changes in Cash Balance from Unified Budget and Other Activities* reports how the annual unified budget surplus or deficit relates to the Federal Government's borrowing

---

[23] Department of the Treasury, Office of Financial Stability FY 2013 Agency Financial Report, p. 10.

[24] Department of the Treasury, Office of Financial Stability FY 2013 Agency Financial Report, p. ix; Department of the Treasury FY 2013 Agency Financial Report, p. 27.

[25] Department of the Treasury, Office of Financial Stability FY 2013 Agency Financial Report, p. ix.

[26] U.S. Department of the Treasury FY 2013 Agency Financial Report, p. 26. Treasury's payments to the GSEs during FY 2012 reduced its contingent liability by an additional $18.5 billion for a total contingent liability reduction of $307.2 billion. See also Note 9 – Investments in and Liabilities to GSEs – of this *Financial Report.*

[27] OPM FY 2013 Agency Financial Report, p. 1.

[28] DOD FY 2013 Agency Financial Report, p.7; DOD Military Retirement Fund (MRF) financial statements, p. 13.

and changes in cash and other monetary assets. It also explains how a budget surplus or deficit normally affects changes in debt balances.

The Government's publicly-held debt, or federal debt held by the public, and accrued interest, which is reported on the Government's balance sheet as a liability, is comprised of Treasury securities, such as bills, notes, and bonds, net of unamortized discounts and premiums; and accrued interest payable. The "public" consists of individuals, corporations, state and local governments, Federal Reserve Banks, foreign governments, and other entities outside the Federal Government. Federal debt held by the public and accrued interest totaled $12.0 trillion as of September 30, 2013. As indicated above, budget surpluses have typically resulted in borrowing reductions, and budget deficits have conversely yielded borrowing increases. However, the Government's debt operations are generally much more complex than this would imply. Each year, trillions of dollars of debt matures and new debt is issued to take its place. In FY 2013, new borrowings were $8.1 trillion and repayments of maturing debt held by the public were $7.4 trillion. Both represented increases over new borrowings and debt repayments as compared to FY 2012.

In addition to debt held by the public, the Government has about $4.8 trillion in intragovernmental debt outstanding, which arises when one part of the Government borrows from another. It represents debt issued by the Treasury and held by Government accounts, including the Social Security ($2.8 trillion) and Medicare ($273.4 billion) trust funds. Intragovernmental debt is primarily held in Government trust funds in the form of special nonmarketable securities by various parts of the Government. Laws establishing Government trust funds generally require excess trust fund receipts (including interest earnings) over disbursements to be invested in these special securities. Because these amounts are both liabilities of the Treasury and assets of the Government trust funds, they are eliminated as part of the consolidation process for the government-wide financial statements (see Note 12). When those securities are redeemed, e.g., to pay future Social Security benefits, the Government will need to obtain

the resources necessary to reimburse the trust funds. The sum of debt held by the public and intragovernmental debt equals gross federal debt, which (with some adjustments), is subject to a statutory ceiling (i.e., the debt limit). At the end of FY 2013, debt subject to the statutory limit was $16.699 trillion, $25 million under the debt limit.

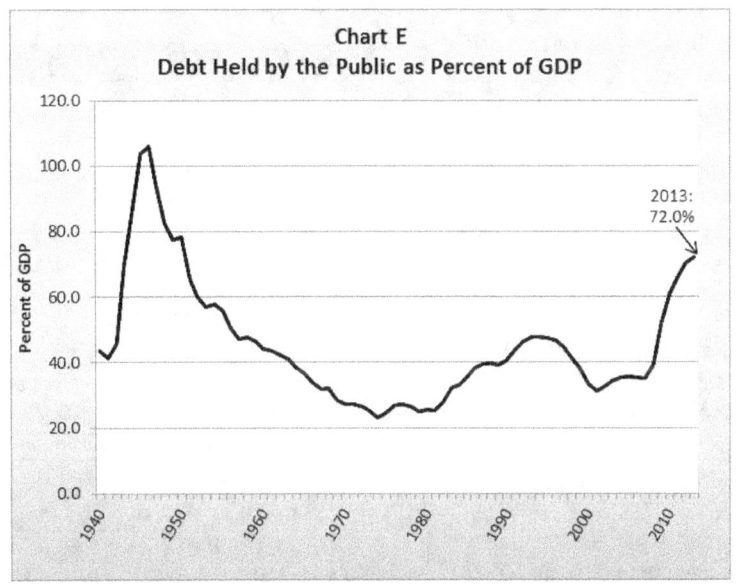

Chart E
Debt Held by the Public as Percent of GDP

Prior to 1917, the Congress approved each debt issuance. In 1917, to facilitate planning in World War I, Congress established a dollar ceiling for federal borrowing. With the Public Debt Act of 1941 (Public Law 77-7), Congress and the President set an overall limit of $65 billion on Treasury debt obligations that could be outstanding at any one time. Since then, Congress and the President have enacted a number of debt limit increases. Recently, pursuant to the BCA, the debt limit was raised by a combined $2.1 trillion to $16.394 trillion between August 2011 and January 2012. In February 2013, pursuant to the No Budget, No Pay Act of 2013 (Public Law 113-3), Congress suspended the debt limit, enabling the debt to increase as needed through May 18, 2013 in accordance with payment requirements, ultimately to an adjusted debt limit of $16.699 trillion, where it remained through the end of the fiscal year. Because the debt limit had not yet been raised before the suspension period ended, Treasury began implementing "extraordinary measures", on a temporary basis, which were still in effect on September 30, 2013, to enable the Government to protect the full faith and credit of the U.S. Government by continuing to pay the nation's bills. As of October 17, 2013, P.L. 113-46 again suspended the debt limit, this time through February 7, 2014. As of February 15, 2014, P.L. 113-83 again suspended the debt limit, this time through March 15, 2015.[29] It is important to note that increasing or suspending the debt limit does not increase

---

[29] A delay in raising the statutory debt limit existed as of September 30, 2013. When delays in raising the statutory debt limit occur, Treasury often must deviate from its normal debt management operations and take a number of extraordinary actions to meet the Government's obligations as they come due without exceeding the debt limit. Many extraordinary actions taken by Treasury during the period of May 20, 2013, through September 30, 2013 resulted in federal debt securities not being issued to certain federal government accounts. As a result of Treasury securities not being issued to the Federal Retirement Thrift Investment Board (FRTIB) Thrift Savings Plan (TSP), Treasury reported miscellaneous liabilities in the amount of $120.4 billion that represent uninvested principal of and related interest for the TSP that would have been reported as Federal Debt Securities Held by the Public and Accrued Interest had there not been a delay in raising the statutory debt limit as of September 30, 2013, and had the securities been issued. See Note 17, Other Liabilities, and Note 26, Subsequent Events, for more information.

spending or authorize new spending; rather, it permits the United States to continue to honor pre-existing commitments to its citizens, businesses, and investors domestically and around the world.

The federal debt held by the public measured as a percent of GDP (debt-to-GDP ratio) (Chart E) compares the country's debt to the size of its economy, making this measure sensitive to changes in both. Over time, the debt-to-GDP ratio has varied widely. For most of the nation's history, the debt-to-GDP ratio has tended to increase during wartime and decline during peacetime. That pattern continued to hold following World War II until the 1970s. As shown in Chart E, wartime spending and borrowing had pushed the debt-to-GDP ratio to an all-time high of 106 percent in 1946, but it decreased rapidly in the post-war years, falling to 79 percent by 1950, 44 percent in 1960, and the postwar low point of 23 percent in 1974. Since then, the ratio has increased, growing rapidly from the mid-1970s until the early 1990s. In the 1990s, strong economic growth and fundamental fiscal decisions, including measures to reduce the federal deficit and implementation of binding "Pay As You Go" ("PAYGO") rules, generated a significant decline in the debt-to-GDP ratio over the course of the 1990s, from a peak of 48 percent in 1993-1995, to 31 percent in 2001. During the last decade, much of this progress was undone as PAYGO rules were allowed to lapse, significant tax cuts were implemented, entitlements were expanded, and spending related to defense and homeland security increased. By September 2008, the debt-to-GDP ratio was 39 percent of GDP. The extraordinary demands of the recent economic and fiscal crisis and the consequent actions taken by the Federal Government, combined with slower economic growth in the wake of the crisis, pushed the debt-to-GDP ratio up to about 72 percent as of September 30, 2013.[30]

The Economy in Fiscal Year 2013

A review of the nation's key macroeconomic indicators can help place the discussion of the Government's financial results in a broader context. As summarized in Table 6, the economy continued to expand, but at a slower rate, during FY 2013. Job growth picked up. The unemployment rate declined during FY 2013 but remained above the 5.5 percent average that prevailed in the 1990s and 2000s.

Table 6: National Economic Indicators*		
	FY 2013	FY 2012
Real GDP Growth	2.0%	3.1%
Residential Investment Growth	14.2%	13.6%
Average monthly payroll job change (thousands)	198	178
Unemployment rate (percent, end of period)	7.2%	7.8%
Consumer Price Index (CPI)	1.2%	2.0%
CPI, excluding food and energy	1.7%	2.0%
Treasury constant maturity 10-year rate (end of period)	2.64%	1.65%
Moody's Baa bond rate (end of period)	4.7%	5.4%

* Some FY2012 data may differ from the FY2012 *Financial Report* due to updates and revisions

After rising 3.1 percent during FY 2012, real GDP growth slowed to 2.0 percent over the four quarters of FY 2013. Consumer spending rose 1.9 percent during FY 2013, down from a gain of 2.2 percent during FY 2012. Residential fixed investment strengthened during FY 2013, rising by 14.2 percent over the four quarters of FY 2013, compared with an increase of 13.6 percent during FY 2012. Nonresidential fixed investment grew 3.5 percent, slowing from a 5.0 percent increase during the previous fiscal year.

Labor market conditions improved further during FY 2013, despite a moderation in the pace of job growth towards the end of the fiscal year. The economy added 2.4 million total nonfarm payroll jobs during FY 2013, slightly more than the 2.1 million nonfarm payroll jobs added during FY 2012. On a monthly basis, total nonfarm payroll employment advanced at an average rate of 198,000 jobs, slightly faster than the average monthly increase of 178,000 in FY 2012. The number of unemployed persons fell from 12.1 million in September 2012 to 11.2 million in September 2013. The unemployment rate declined 0.6 percentage point, from 7.8 percent in September 2012 to 7.2 percent in September 2013. At the end of FY 2013, the unemployment rate was 2.8 percentage points lower than the recent peak of 10.0 percent, reached in October 2009.

Inflation continued to decelerate, mainly reflecting lower energy and food price inflation. The overall price level, as measured by the consumer price index (CPI), rose 1.2 percent during FY 2013. In FY 2012, the CPI had increased by 2.0 percent. Underlying core inflation (the CPI excluding food and energy) also decelerated, increasing 1.7 percent during FY 2013, down from 2.0 percent the previous fiscal year. The level of core inflation in FY 2013 was low by historical standards.

---

[30] The debt/GDP ratios were calculated using National Income and Product Accounts (NIPA)-revised GDP figures, resulting in a slight decline in the debt/GDP ratio when compared to the unrevised historical series (see MD&A footnote 8).

Real wages for private production and nonsupervisory workers rose during FY 2013, following a decline in the previous fiscal year, as nominal wage growth accelerated and inflation moderated. The level of corporate profits increased in FY 2013, but at a somewhat slower pace than in the previous fiscal year. Federal spending declined, and federal tax receipts grew in FY 2013. As a result, the federal unified budget deficit fell to $680.3 billion in FY 2013, and also narrowed as a share of the economy to 4.1 percent of GDP from 6.8 percent in FY 2012.

This economic performance occurred against a backdrop of generally stable conditions in financial markets in FY 2013. Yields on corporate bonds of moderate risk were about 307 basis points above the rate on 10-year Treasury securities at the end of FY 2012. This spread decreased and remained below that level throughout the following fiscal year, ending FY 2013 at 275 basis points. The difference between the 3-month London Interbank Offered Rate (LIBOR) and the 3-month Treasury rate stood at 30 basis points at the end of FY 2012. This spread generally narrowed over the course of the latest fiscal year, ending FY 2013 at 26 basis points.

The Long-Term Fiscal Outlook: "Where We Are Headed"

While the Government's immediate priority is to continue to foster economic recovery, there are longer-term fiscal challenges that must ultimately be addressed. Persistent growth of health care costs and the aging of the population due to the retirement of the "baby boom" generation and increasing longevity will make it increasingly difficult to fund critical social programs, including Medicare, Medicaid, and Social Security.

Fiscal Sustainability

An important purpose of the *Financial Report* is to help citizens understand current fiscal policy and the importance and magnitude of policy reforms necessary to make it sustainable. A sustainable policy is one where the debt-to-GDP ratio is stable or declining over the long term.

To determine if current fiscal policies are sustainable, the projections discussed here assume current policy will be sustained indefinitely and draw out the implications for the growth of debt held by the public as a share of GDP.[31] The projections are therefore neither forecasts nor predictions. As policy changes are enacted, actual financial outcomes will of course be different than those projected.

The projections in this *Financial Report* indicate that current policy is not sustainable. The debt-to-GDP ratio is projected to reach 277 percent in 2088 and to rise continuously thereafter. Preventing the debt-to-GDP ratio from rising over the next 75 years is estimated to require some combination of spending reductions and revenue increases that amount to 1.7 percent of GDP over the period. While this estimate of the "75-year fiscal gap" is highly uncertain, it is nevertheless nearly certain that current fiscal policies cannot be sustained indefinitely.

It is important to address the Government's fiscal imbalances soon. Delaying action increases the magnitude of spending reductions and/or revenue increases necessary to stabilize the debt-to-GDP ratio. Relative to a reform that begins immediately, for example, it is estimated that the magnitude of reforms necessary to close the 75-year fiscal gap is more than 20 percent larger if reforms are delayed by just ten years, and more than 50 percent larger if reform is delayed 20 years.

The estimates of the cost of policy delay in this *Financial Report* assume policy does not affect GDP or other economic variables. Reducing deficits too abruptly would be counterproductive if it slows the economy's recovery. Conversely, delaying fiscal adjustments for too long raises the risk that growing federal debt would increase interest rates and slow economic growth. In the near term, it is crucial to strike the proper balance between deficit reduction and economic growth.

---

[31] Current policy in the projections is based on current law, but includes extension of certain policies that expire under current law but are routinely extended or otherwise expected to continue, such as reauthorization of the Supplemental Nutrition Assistance Program.

The Primary Deficit, Interest, and Debt

The primary deficit – the difference between non-interest spending and receipts – is the only determinant of the debt-to-GDP ratio that the Government controls directly. (The other determinants are interest rates and growth in GDP). Chart F shows receipts, non-interest spending, and the difference – the primary deficit – expressed as a share of GDP (primary deficit-to-GDP ratio). The primary deficit-to-GDP ratio grew rapidly in 2009 due to the financial crisis and the recession and the policies pursued to combat both. The ratio stayed large from 2010 to 2012 despite shrinking in each successive year, and fell significantly in 2013. The primary deficit is projected to shrink in the next few years as spending reductions called for in the BCA take effect and the economy recovers, becoming a primary surplus in 2017 that peaks at 1.1 percent of GDP in 2021. Between 2022 and 2037, however, increased spending for Social Security and health programs due to continued aging

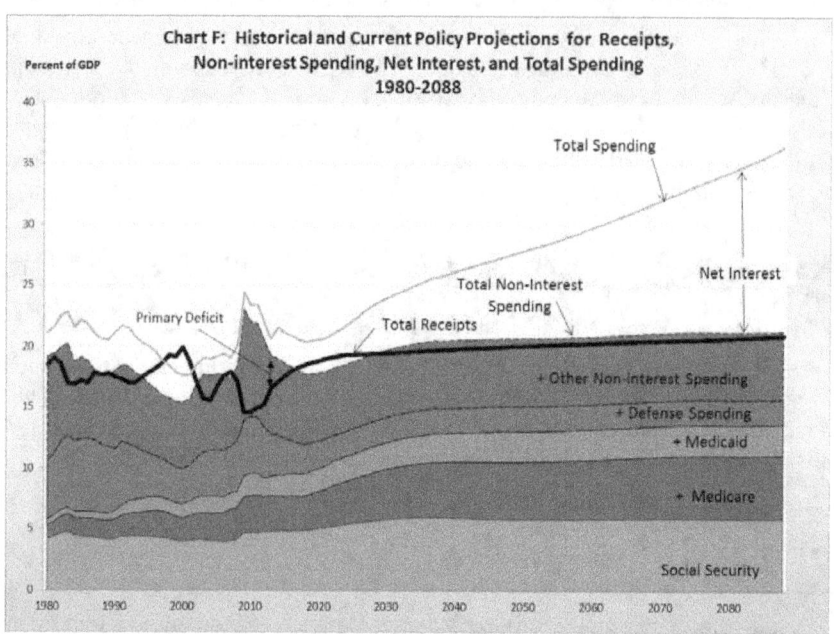

Chart F: Historical and Current Policy Projections for Receipts, Non-interest Spending, Net Interest, and Total Spending 1980-2088

of the population is expected to cause the primary balance to steadily decline and become a primary deficit starting in 2029 that grows to 0.8 percent of GDP by 2036. After 2037, the projected primary deficit-to-GDP ratio slowly declines to 0.4 percent in 2088 as the impact of the baby boom generation retiring dissipates.

The revenue share of GDP fell substantially in 2009 and 2010 and remained low in 2011 and 2012 because of the recession and tax reductions enacted as part of the American Recovery and Reinvestment Act of 2009 (ARRA) and the Tax Relief, Unemployment Insurance Reauthorization, and Job Creation Act of 2010. The share rose to 17 percent in 2013 and is projected to return to near its long-run average as the economy recovers and higher tax rates called for by ATRA take effect. After the economy has fully recovered around 2020, receipts are projected to grow slightly more rapidly than GDP as increases in real incomes cause more taxpayers and a larger share of income to fall into the higher individual income tax brackets.

The non-interest spending share of GDP is projected to stay at or below its current level of about 19 percent until 2026, and to then rise gradually to 20.6 percent of GDP in 2042 and 21.3 percent of GDP in 2088. The reductions in the non-interest spending share of GDP over the next two years are mostly due to the expected reductions in spending for overseas contingency operations, caps on discretionary spending, and the automatic spending limits mandated by the BCA, and the subsequent increases are principally due to growth in Medicare, Medicaid, and Social Security spending (see Chart F). The retirement of the baby boom generation over the next 25 years is projected to increase the Social Security, Medicare, and Medicaid spending shares of GDP by about 1.2 percentage points, 1.6 percentage points and 0.8 percentage points, respectively. After 2038, the Social Security spending share of GDP gradually declines and then returns to 2038 levels, while the Medicare and Medicaid spending share of GDP continues to increase, albeit at a slower rate, due to projected increases in health care costs. The Affordable Care Act (ACA)[32] provision of health insurance subsidies and expanded Medicaid coverage boost federal spending and other ACA provisions significantly reduce per-beneficiary Medicare and Medicaid cost growth. On net, the ACA is projected to substantially reduce the cost growth rate of federal expenditures for Medicare over the next 75 years. However, there is uncertainty about whether the projected cost savings, productivity improvements, and reductions in physician payment rates will be sustained in a manner consistent with the projected cost growth over time.

---

[32] P.L. 111-148, as amended by P.L. 111-152. The ACA expands health insurance coverage, provides health insurance subsidies for low-income individuals and families, includes many measures designed to reduce health care cost growth, and reduces the annual increases in Medicare payment rates.

The primary deficit-to-GDP projections and Chart F, along with projections for interest rates, determine the debt-to-GDP ratio projections shown in Chart G. That ratio was 72 percent at the end of FY 2013 and under current policy is projected to be 69 percent in 2023, 112 percent in 2043, and 277 percent in 2088. The continuous rise of the debt-to-GDP ratio after 2023 indicates that current policy is unsustainable.

The debt projections in Chart G are substantially lower than those projected in last year's *Financial Report*. The projected debt-to-GDP ratio in 2087 shown in Chart G is 272 percent, which compares with 395 percent projected in last year's *Financial Report*. Many factors contributed to the improvement. Most notable were: (i) improvements in the outlook for Medicare finances and for Medicaid spending as reflected in the 2013 Medicare Trustees report and the 2012 Medicaid Actuarial Report, respectively, and (ii) the enactment of the ATRA, which allowed the 2001/2003 tax cuts to expire for taxpayers with incomes above \$400,000 for individuals and above \$450,000 for couples. The long-term projections of current policy in the FY 2012 *Financial Report* assumed that all of the 2001/2003 tax cuts would be extended.

Chart G: History and Current Policy Projections for Total Receipts; and Non-interest, Net Interest, and Total Spending; and Debt Held by the Public, 1980-2088

The Fiscal Gap and the Cost of Delaying Policy Reform

The 75-year fiscal gap is one measure of the degree to which current fiscal policy is unsustainable. It is the amount by which primary surpluses over the next 75 years must rise above current-policy levels in order to prevent the debt-to-GDP ratio from rising. It is estimated that running primary surpluses that average 1.3 percent of GDP over the next 75 years would result in the 2088 debt-to-GDP ratio equaling its level in fiscal year 2013, which compares with primary deficits that average 0.4 percent of GDP under current policies. The 75-year fiscal gap is therefore 1.7 percent of GDP, which is 8.6 percent of the 75-year present value of projected receipts and 8.4 percent of the 75-year present value of non-interest spending.

It is noteworthy that preventing the debt-to-GDP ratio from rising over the next 75 years requires that primary surpluses be substantially positive on average. This is true because projected GDP growth rates are, on average, smaller than the projected government borrowing rate over the next 75 years. The implication is that debt would grow faster than GDP if primary surpluses were zero on average. For example, if the primary surplus was precisely zero in every year, then debt would grow at the rate of interest in every year, which would be faster than GDP growth.

Table 7 illustrates the cost of delaying policy to close the fiscal gap by comparing three policies that begin on different dates. The first policy begins immediately and calls for increasing primary surpluses by 1.7 percent of GDP in every year between 2014 and 2088. This is accomplished by invoking some combination of spending reductions and revenue increases that amount to 1.7 percent of GDP in every year over the 75-year projection period. The second policy in Table 7 begins in 2024. Because debt grows unabated between 2014 and 2024 and the

Table 7	
Costs of Delaying Fiscal Reform	
Period of Delay	**Change in Average Primary Surplus**
No Delay: Reform in 2014.........	1.7 percent of GDP between 2014 and 2088
Ten Years: Reform in 2024.......	2.1 percent of GDP between 2024 and 2088
Twenty Years: Reform in 2034..	2.6 percent of GDP between 2034 and 2088

Note: Reforms taking place in 2013, 2023, and 2033 from the 2012 Finanical Report were 2.7, 3 2, and 4 1 percent of GDP.

same fiscal consolidation must be compressed into ten fewer years, this policy change is more abrupt, calling for primary surplus increases amounting to 2.1 percent of GDP in every year between 2024 and 2088. Similarly, if debt is allowed to accumulate unabated for 20 years, then closing the 75-year fiscal gap would require even more abrupt primary surplus increases amounting to 2.6 percent of GDP in every year between 2034 and 2088. The differences between the primary surplus boost starting in 2024 and 2034 (2.1 and 2.6 percent of GDP, respectively) and the primary surplus boost starting in 2014 (1.7 percent of GDP) is a measure of the additional burden policy delay would impose on future generations. Future generations are harmed by a policy delay of this sort because the higher the primary surplus is during their lifetimes the greater the difference is between the taxes they pay and the programmatic spending from which they benefit.

Conclusion

The Government took significant steps towards a sustainable fiscal policy by enacting the ACA in 2010, the BCA in 2011, and ATRA in 2013. The ACA holds the prospect of lowering long-term per-beneficiary spending growth for Medicare and Medicaid, the BCA significantly curtails discretionary spending, and ATRA increases revenues. Together, these three laws substantially reduce the estimated long-term fiscal gap. But even with the new laws, the debt-to-GDP ratio is projected to remain about flat over the next ten years and then commence a continuous rise over the remaining projection period and beyond if current policies are kept in place. This trend implies that current policies are not sustainable. Subject to the important caveat that changes in policy are not so abrupt that they slow the economy's recovery, the sooner policies are put in place to avert these trends, the smaller the revenue increases and/or spending decreases will need to be to return the Government to a sustainable fiscal path over the long term.

While this *Financial Report's* projections of expenditures and receipts under current policy are highly uncertain, it is nevertheless nearly certain that current policy cannot be sustained indefinitely.

These and other issues concerning fiscal sustainability are discussed in further detail in the Required Supplementary Information section of this *Financial Report*.

Statement of Social Insurance – Challenges Continue

The preceding analysis of the Government's long-term fiscal projections considered Government receipts and spending as a whole. The Statement of Social Insurance (SOSI) provides a more focused perspective of the Government's "social insurance" programs: Social Security, Medicare, Railroad Retirement, and Black Lung.[33] For these programs, the SOSI reports: (1) the actuarial present value of all future program revenue (mainly taxes and premiums) - excluding interest - to be received from or on behalf of current and future participants; (2) the estimated future scheduled expenditures to be paid to or on behalf of current and future participants; and (3) the difference between (1) and (2). Amounts reported in the SOSI and in the Required Supplementary Information section in this *Financial Report* are based on each program's official actuarial calculations. By accounting convention, the transfers of general revenues are eliminated in the consolidation of the SOSI at the government-wide level and as such, the general revenues that are used to finance Medicare Parts B and D are not included in these calculations even though the expenditures on these programs are included. For the FY 2013 and 2012 SOSI, the amounts eliminated totaled $22.5 trillion and $21.6 trillion, respectively. SOSI programs and amounts are included in the broader fiscal sustainability analysis in the previous section, although on a slightly different basis (as described in the Required Supplementary Information section of this *Financial Report*).

The SOSI provides perspective on the Government's long-term estimated exposures and costs for social insurance programs. While these expenditures are not considered Government liabilities, they do have the potential to become expenses and liabilities in the future, based on the continuation of the social insurance programs' provisions contained in current law. The social insurance trust funds account for all related program income and expenses. Medicare and Social Security taxes, premiums, and other income are credited to the funds; fund disbursements may only be made for benefit payments and program administrative costs. Any excess revenues are invested in special non-marketable U.S. Government securities at a market rate of interest. The trust funds represent the accumulated value, including interest, of all prior program surpluses, and provide automatic funding authority to pay for future benefits.

---

[33] The Black Lung Benefits Act (BLBA) provides for monthly payments and medical benefits to coal miners totally disabled from pneumoconiosis (black lung disease) arising from their employment in or around the nation's coal mines. See http://www.dol.gov/compliance/topics/benefits-comp-blacklung.htm

Table 8 summarizes amounts reported in the SOSI, showing that net social insurance expenditures are projected to be $39.7 trillion as of January 1, 2013 for the "Open Group", an increase of $1.1 trillion over net expenditures of $38.6 trillion projected in the 2012 *Financial Report*.[34] Table 9 summarizes the principal reasons for the changes in projected social insurance amounts during 2013 and 2012. For the current valuation (as of January 1, 2013), most of the combined change from the past year is attributable to a $1.8 trillion increase in the present value of negative net cash outflow attributable to a change in the valuation period (e.g., replacing a small negative net cash flow for 2012 with a much larger negative net cash flow for 2087). This was largely offset by a $1.0 trillion decrease in the present value of negative net cash outflow from changes in methodology and

Table 8: Social Insurance Future Expenditures in Excess of Future Revenues				
Dollars in Billions	2013	2012	Increase / (Decrease) $	%
Open Group (Net):				
Social Security (OASDI)	$ (12,294)	$ (11,278)	$ 1,016	9.0%
Medicare (Parts A, B, & D)	$ (27,302)	$ (27,174)	$ 128	0.5%
Other	$ (102)	$ (102)	$ 0	0.0%
Total Social Insurance Expenditures, Net (Open Group)	**$ (39,698)**	**$ (38,554)**	**$ 1,144**	**3.0%**
Total Social Insurance Expenditures, Net (Closed Group)	**$ (53,974)**	**$ (51,604)**	**$ 2,370**	**4.6%**
Social Insurance Net Expenditures as a % of Gross Domestic Product (GDP)*				
Open Group				
Social Security (OASDI)	(1.2%)	(1.2%)		
Medicare (Parts A, B, & D)	(2.9%)	(3.0%)		
Other	0.0%	0.0%		
Total (Open Group)	**(4.0%)**	**(4.2%)**		
Total (Closed Group)	**(5.5%)**	**(5.6%)**		

Source: Statement of Social Insurance (SOSI). Amounts equal estimated present value of projected revenues and expenditures for scheduled benefits over the next 75 years of certain 'Social Insurance' programs (e.g., Social Security, Medicare). 'Open Group' totals reflect all current and projected program participants during the 75-year projection period. 'Closed Group' totals reflect only current participants.

* GDP values used are from the 2013 & 2012 Social Security and Medicare Trustees Reports and represent the present value of GDP over the 75-year projection period. As the GDP used for Social Security and Medicare differ slightly in the Trust Fund Reports, the two values are averaged to estimate the 'Other' and Total Net Social Insurance Expenditures as % of GDP.

Note - some totals may not equal sum of components due to rounding.

programmatic data for the OASDI program, including, but not limited to: (1) modifying the alignment of projected labor force participation with future trends in disability, longevity, and population levels, (2) updating ultimate age-sex specific unemployment rates based on the relative levels of long-term historical patterns, and (3) modeling the insured status of citizens and legal permanent residents separately from other immigrants. Projections for both the OASDI and Medicare Part A (Hospital Insurance) programs (were also affected by changes in: (1) law – particularly various provisions of the ATRA; and (2) demographic assumptions (e.g., increased assumed immigration of individuals attaining legal permanent resident (LPR) status, decreased assumed immigration of those without LPR status, and lower assumed mortality and fertility rates). Economic and health care (for Medicare) assumptions (e.g., health care costs, taxable earnings, price inflation, and real interest rates) also impact the projections. For both OASDI and Medicare Part A: (1) the real interest rate is projected to be lower over the first 10 years of the current valuation; and (2) the starting economic values and near-term economic growth rates were updated. The effects of these changes on HHS are reported separately in Table 9 as HHS also includes the effect of specific healthcare assumptions in this category, including but not limited to utilization rate and case mix increase assumptions for skilled nursing facilities and lower projected Medicare Advantage program costs.[35]

As shown in the five-year SOSI, projected net expenditures for Medicare Parts A and B declined significantly between FY 2009 and FY 2010 reflecting provisions of the ACA. As reported in Note 24, there continues to be uncertainty about whether the projected cost savings, productivity improvements, and reductions in physician payment rates will be sustained in a manner consistent with the projected cost growth over time. Note 24 includes an alternative projection to illustrate the uncertainty of projected Medicare costs. As indicated earlier, GAO disclaimed opinions on the 2013, 2012, 2011 and 2010 SOSI because of these significant uncertainties.

---

[34] 'Closed' Group and 'Open' Group differ by the population included in each calculation. From the SOSI, the 'Closed' Group includes: (1) participants who have attained eligibility and (2) participants who have not attained eligibility. The 'Open' Group adds future participants to the 'Closed' Group. See 'Social Insurance' in the Required Supplementary Information section in this *Financial Report* for more information.

[35] FY 2013 HHS Agency Financial Report, pp 118-123, FY 2013 SSA Agency Financial Report, pp 70-73

Costs as a percent of GDP of both Medicare and Social Security, which are analyzed annually in the Medicare and Social Security Trustees' Reports, are projected to increase substantially through 2035, because: (1) the number of beneficiaries rises rapidly as the "baby-boom" generation retires; and (2) the lower birth rates that have persisted since the baby boom cause slower growth in the labor force and GDP.[36] According to the Medicare Trustees' Report, under current law, including the assumption of the full implementation of ACA program changes, spending on Medicare is projected to rise from 3.6 percent of GDP in 2011 to 6.5 percent in 2086 (based on the Trustees intermediate set of assumptions). The Hospital Insurance (HI) Trust Fund is now expected to remain solvent until 2026, (two years later than reported last year), at which point tax income is estimated to be sufficient to pay 87 percent of estimated HI costs, declining to 73 percent by 2087.

As for Social Security, combined spending is projected to increase gradually from its current level of 5.0 percent of GDP to about 6.2 percent by 2035, declining to 6.0 percent by 2050 and remaining between 6.0 and 6.2 percent through 2087. The Social Security Trustees' Report indicates that annual OASDI income, including interest on trust fund assets, will exceed annual cost and trust fund assets will increase every year until 2021, at which time it will be necessary to begin drawing down on trust fund assets to cover part of expenditures until assets are exhausted in 2033 (no change from last year's Report), at which point continuing tax income would be sufficient to pay 77 percent of scheduled benefits in 2033 and 72 percent in 2087.[37]

Table 9: Changes in Social Insurance Projections		
Dollars in Billions	2013	2012
Net Present Value (NPV) - Open Group (Beginning of the Year)	**$ (38,554)**	**(33,830)**
Changes In:		
Valuation Period	$ (1,813)	$ (1,613)
Demographic data and assumptions	$ (285)	$ 518
Economic data and assumptions[1]	$ (273)	$ (1,039)
Law or policy	$ (520)	$ 193
Methodology and programmatic data[1]	$ 1,034	$ (471)
Economic and other healthcare assumptions[2]	$ (94)	$ (2,601)
Change in projection base[2]	$ 807	$ 289
Net Change in Open Group measure	$ (1,144)	$ (4,724)
NPV - Open Group (End of the Year)	**$ (39,698)**	**$ (38,554)**

1 Relates to SSA.

2 Relates to HHS.

Note - totals may not equal sum of components due to rounding.

As noted earlier, it is apparent that these programs are on a fiscally unsustainable path (as was previously discussed and as noted in the Trustees' Reports). Additional information from the Trustees Reports may be found in the Required Supplementary Information section of this *Financial Report*.

Systems, Controls, and Legal Compliance

Systems

As federal agencies demonstrate success in obtaining opinions on their audited financial statements, the Federal Government continues to face challenges in implementing financial systems that meet federal requirements. The number of CFO Act agencies reporting non-compliance with one or more of the three Section 803(a) requirements of the Federal Financial Management Improvement Act (FFMIA) in FY 2013 was 9 in both FY 2013 and FY 2012, and the number of auditors reporting non-compliance with one or more of the three Section 803(a) FFMIA requirements was 11 in both FY 2013 and FY 2012. These results underscore the importance of current initiatives to standardize the financial management practices across the Federal Government.

Building on recent policies—including OMB Memoranda M-10-26, *Immediate Review of Financial Systems IT Projects*, and M-13-08, *Improving Financial Systems through Shared Services*— OMB issued Appendix D to Circular No. A-123 which defines new requirements for determining compliance with the FFMIA. The goal of this Appendix is to transform the Federal Government's compliance framework so that it will contribute to efforts to reduce the cost, risk, and complexity of financial system modernizations. The objective of this approach will be to provide additional flexibility for federal agencies to initiate smaller-scale financial modernizations as long as relevant financial management outcomes (e.g., clean audits, proper controls, timely reporting) are maintained. The Appendix:

- Replaces "check the box" compliance approaches with an outcome-based approach to assess FFMIA compliance and establishes a series of financial management goals that are common to all federal agencies;

---

[36] 2013 Annual Trustees Reports on Social Security and Medicare (Summary), p. 2.

[37] 2013 Annual Trustees Reports on Social Security and Medicare (Summary), pp. 3, 10.

- Removes unnecessary financial management system requirements that drive complexity and cost and focuses on requirements that emphasize the Federal Government's business and information needs;

- Eliminates the lengthy and resource-intensive financial system software test and certification program and the requirement that financial management system requirements be met through a single technology product and emphasizes the deployment of newer, cost-effective technology through shared service approaches; and

- Solidifies Treasury's role in achieving Government-wide financial systems policy goals by adding responsibilities to develop and maintain, in coordination with OMB and Federal agencies, Federal Financial Management System Requirements and to publish the requirements in the *Treasury Financial Manual.*

Appendix D will be effective for FY 2014 and OMB plans to continue to work closely with Treasury, the Chief Financial Officers Council and the President's Council of Inspectors General on Integrity and Efficiency to implement the guidance.

Controls

Federal managers have a fundamental responsibility to develop and maintain effective internal controls. Effective internal controls help to ensure that programs are managed with integrity and resources are used efficiently and effectively through three objectives: effective and efficient operations, reliable financial reporting, and compliance with applicable laws and regulations. The safeguarding of assets is a subcomponent of each objective.

OMB Circular No. A-123, *Management's Responsibility for Internal Control,* is the policy document that implements the requirements of 31 U.S.C. 3512 (c), (d) (commonly known as the Federal Managers' Financial Integrity Act or FMFIA). Circular No. A-123 primarily focuses on providing agencies with a framework for assessing and managing risks more strategically and effectively. The Circular contains multiple appendices that address, at a more detailed level, one or more of the objectives of effective internal control. Appendix A provides a methodology for agency management to assess, document, test, and report on internal controls over financial reporting. Appendix B requires agencies to maintain internal controls that reduce the risk of fraud, waste, and error in Government charge card programs. Appendix C implements the requirements for Effective Measurement and Remediation of Improper Payments.

In FY 2013, the total number of material weaknesses for Chief Financial Officers (CFO) Act agencies decreased to 29, compared to 32 in FY 2012. Effective internal controls are a challenge not only at the agency level, but also at the government-wide level. GAO reported that at the government-wide level, material weaknesses resulted in ineffective internal control over financial reporting. While progress is being made at many agencies and across the Government in identifying and resolving internal control deficiencies, continued diligence and commitment are needed.

Legal Compliance

Federal agencies are required to comply with a wide range of laws and regulations, including appropriations, employment, health and safety, and others. Responsibility for compliance primarily rests with agency management. Compliance is addressed as part of agency financial statement audits. Agency auditors test for compliance with selected laws and regulations related to financial reporting. Certain individual agency audit reports contain instances of noncompliance. None of these instances were material to the government-wide financial statements. However, GAO reported that its work on compliance with laws and regulations was limited by the material weaknesses and scope limitations discussed in its report.

Financial Management Progress and Priorities

Since the passage of the CFO Act of 1990, the federal financial community has made important strides in instilling strong accounting and financial reporting practices. This year, 23 of the 24 CFO Act agencies obtained an opinion from the independent auditors on their financial statements. Out of the 24 major "CFO Act" agencies, there were 22 clean opinions, [38] 1 qualified opinion, and only one remaining disclaimer in FY 2013. In addition, 29 auditor-identified material weaknesses were reported in FY 2013, an approximate 52 percent decline from the 61 material weaknesses that were identified at the start of this past decade. An increasing number of federal agencies have initiated and sustained disciplined and consistent financial reporting operations, implemented effective internal

---

[38] The 22 agencies include HHS, which received a clean opinion on all statements except the Statement of Social Insurance and the Statement of Changes in Social Insurance, both of which received a disclaimer of opinion.

controls around financial reporting, and have successfully integrated transaction processing and accounting records. These efforts have resulted in improved results on financial statement audits. However, weaknesses in basic financial management practices and other limitations continue to prevent one major agency, and the Government as a whole, from achieving an audit opinion.

Today, accountability means providing transparent information to the public about where and how federal dollars are being spent. It means protecting against fraud. It means avoiding wasteful or excessive use of taxpayer funds. It means ensuring that we are not only responsible stewards of taxpayer dollars, but frugal stewards as well, looking for every opportunity to save money and create greater efficiencies.

We have come a long way since the passage of the CFO Act in 1990. Today, the federal financial management community is focused on three important improvement initiatives:

- Improving the quality, utility, and transparency of financial information;
- Protecting against waste, fraud, and abuse; and
- Helping agencies maximize the impact of their limited financial resources.

Improve the Quality, Utility, and Transparency of Federal Financial Information

USAspending.gov was established to provide clear information on federal award spending. Continuing to improve the quality, utility and transparency of this federal spending information is a foundational Administration commitment to open government, as identified in the U.S. Government's National Action Plan for Open Government. To continue our efforts to improve the quality of spending data, OMB issued guidance in June 2013, directing agencies to validate the award-level data submitted to USAspending.gov. To align our federal spending and financial management transparency efforts, the Administration has transferred responsibility for USAspending.gov from GSA to Treasury. Treasury's leadership in executing a government-wide federal spending transparency vision will leverage existing financial reporting and offer opportunities to link data across multiple data sources for a more comprehensive public view. Treasury's work will enable the Federal Government to move forward in achieving the objective of making spending data more useful, accurate, and timely – consistent with the agency's other work through financial reporting, work on improper payment, among other priority areas. Over the next year, USAspending.gov will reflect improvements in both website usability and functionality, leveraging the lessons and successes learned from Recovery Act reporting and data display.

Moving forward, in concert with the Government Accountability & Transparency Board, OMB will continue to collaborate with both federal and non-federal stakeholders to evolve our government wide spending transparency framework to effectively provide the public with transparent information about how federal dollars are being spent. In addition, we will strengthen linkages between agency financial and performance data to provide better information on federal spending and impact.

Protect Against Waste, Fraud, and Abuse
Improper Payments

Addressing improper payments is a central component of the Administration's overall efforts to eliminate waste, fraud, and abuse. In FY 2009, the improper payment rate was 5.42 percent. Since then, the Administration, working together with Congress, has substantially reduced improper payments by strengthening accountability and transparency through annual reviews by agency inspectors general, and expanded requirements for high-priority programs. As a result of this concerted effort, the improper payment rate declined from 3.74 percent in FY 2012 to 3.53 percent in FY 2013, when Department of Defense (DOD) commercial payments are considered. When DOD commercial payments are excluded from the government-wide figures, the rate declined from 4.35 percent in FY 2012 to 4.00 percent in FY 2013[39]. Over the past year, we reduced improper payment rates in major programs across the government, including Medicaid, Medicare Advantage (Part C), Unemployment Insurance, and others. Furthermore, agencies recovered more than $22 billion in overpayments through payment recapture audits and other methods in FY 2013.

Moving forward, we are focusing our actions toward a specific goal: to reach a government-wide improper payment rate of 3 percent or less by the end of FY 2016. In doing so, we are revising OMB Circular A-123, Appendix C, in order to reduce reporting burden and create a more granular taxonomy of improper payments. We are also conducting a comprehensive analysis of agency-specific corrective actions to identify programs with the highest potential for substantially reducing improper payments. In addition, we are working to improve the completeness of government-wide improper payment testing of all high risk programs. Finally, we are advancing

---

[39] More information about DOD improper payments can be found in DOD's Agency Financial Report (see http://comptroller.defense.gov/FinancialManagement/Reports/afr2013.aspx).

data analytics and improved technologies to prevent improper payments before they happen. In doing so, we established a Do Not Pay System of Record and strategy to screen federal payments. This includes obtaining necessary authorities and agreements to utilize the Full Death Master File, verifying that privacy protections are in place, and enforcing the disposition process on payments to deceased individuals, among other things.

Improving Grants Management

On December 26, 2013, OMB published final guidance to better target risk and reduce waste, fraud, and abuse (2 CFR Part 200—Uniform Administrative Requirements, Cost Principles, And Audit Requirements for Federal Awards). This final guidance was developed by the interagency Council on Financial Assistance Reform (COFAR) to improve effectiveness for the approximately $600 billion awarded annually in federal financial assistance. Representing a two-year collaborative effort across the Federal Government and its partners -- State and local governments, Indian tribes, research and higher education institutions, nonprofit organizations, and the audit community, the guidance rethinks and reforms the rules that govern our stewardship of federal dollars. It streamlines eight existing OMB Circulars on financial management into one consolidated set of guidance in the CFR. Specifically, the revised policies emphasize risk-based decision making to reduce administrative burden and waste, fraud, and abuse by:

- Eliminating duplicative and conflicting guidance;
- Focusing on performance over compliance for accountability;
- Encouraging efficient use of information technology and shared services;
- Providing for consistent and transparent treatment of costs;
- Limiting allowable costs to make the best use of federal resources;
- Setting standard business processes using data definitions;
- Encouraging non-federal entities to have family-friendly policies;
- Strengthening oversight; and
- Targeting audit requirements on risk of waste, fraud, and abuse.

Moving forward, the COFAR will work closely with federal agencies to develop, issue, and implement regulations for the new guidance by the effective date of December 26, 2014. The COFAR will also work with federal and non-federal stakeholders to develop additional training and outreach resources, and establish metrics that will measure the effectiveness of the new policies. In addition, OMB and its partners are continuing complementary work to strengthen program outcomes through innovative and effective use of grant-making models, performance metrics, and evaluation, as described in OMB Memorandum M-13-17 on *Next Steps in the Evidence and Innovation Agenda*.

Help Agencies Maximize the Impact of their Limited Financial Resources

Improving Effectiveness and Efficiency in Financial Operations and Systems

The Administration is making significant progress in the effort to minimize the costs and risks associated with agency financial systems modernization. In 2013, OMB issued M-13-08: *Improving Financial Systems Through Shared Services*. This new guidance directs all executive agencies to use, with limited exceptions, a shared service solution for future modernizations of core accounting or mixed systems and names the Office of Financial Innovation and Transformation (FIT) at the Department of the Treasury as OMB's partner in evaluating shared service providers and agency modernization plans. In 2013, two cabinet level Departments began working with Federal Shared Service Providers (FSSPs) to plan migration to shared services.

In 2014, OMB and FIT will build on these efforts and focus on improving cost, quality, and performance in agency and shared service financial management. Major emphasis areas will be:

- Identifying and naming any new entrants to the FSSP community;
- Developing and publishing performance and cost information for all FSSPs in a product services catalog;
- Developing meaningful benchmarks and metrics to measure the cost, quality, and performance of financial operations throughout the government; and
- Developing a sound governance model to support greater use of shared services by agencies while ensuring adequate input on major decisions by customer agencies.

Driving Real Property Efficiencies through Better Data and Data Analytics

The federal real estate inventory contains over 360,000 building assets, 485,000 separate structures, and 43 million acres of federal land. Within the inventory, there are opportunities for savings by reducing federally-occupied space and using space more efficiently. The Government is pursuing a long-term strategy to maximize the efficiency of the real estate portfolio by implementing a policy to freeze growth in the portfolio, improving the quality of real property data, and using quality data to identify opportunities to consolidate and reduce the size of the real estate inventory. Over the next year, the Government intends to continue its efforts to freeze real property growth under the existing "Freeze the Footprint" Policy (OMB Memorandum 12-12), develop and collect performance metrics/benchmarks to measure efficiency/effectiveness of real property use, improve the consistency and quality of inventory real property data, and identify government-wide standards to continue to improve the efficiency of our real property use.

Conclusion

The Federal Government has seen significant progress in financial management since the passage of the CFO Act more than 20 years ago. Yet significant challenges remain. The issues we face in the Government today require our financial managers to move beyond the status quo and to generate a higher return on investment for our financial management activities. The steps outlined above leverage the tools and capacities in place today, and refocus energies on critical and emerging priorities – cutting wasteful spending, improving the efficiency of our operations and information technology, and laying a foundation for data quality and collaboration as we enter a new era of transparency and open Government.

Additional Information

This *Financial Report's* Appendix contains the names and websites of the significant Government entities included in the *Financial Report's* financial statements. Details about the information in this *Financial Report* can be found in these entities' financial statements included in their Performance and Accountability and Agency Financial Reports. This *Financial Report*, as well as those from previous years, is also available at the Treasury, OMB, and GAO websites at: http://www.fiscal.treasury.gov/fsreports/fs_reports_publications.htm; http://www.whitehouse.gov/omb/financial/index_html; and http://www.gao.gov/financial.html, respectively. Other related Government publications include, but are not limited to the:

- *Budget of the United States Government,*
- *Treasury Bulletin,*
- *Monthly Treasury Statement of Receipts and Outlays of the United States Government,*
- *Monthly Statement of the Public Debt of the United States,*
- *Economic Report of the President,* and
- *Trustees' Reports* for the Social Security and Medicare Programs.

This page is intentionally blank.

U.S. GOVERNMENT ACCOUNTABILITY OFFICE

441 G St. N.W.
Washington, DC 20548

Comptroller General
of the United States

February 27, 2014

The President
The President of the Senate
The Speaker of the House of Representatives

During fiscal year 2013, the federal government's reported unified budget deficit decreased by about $409 billion to approximately $680 billion. However, the federal government continues to face an unsustainable long-term fiscal path. To operate as effectively and efficiently as possible and to make difficult decisions to address the federal government's fiscal challenges, Congress, the administration, and federal managers must have ready access to reliable and complete financial and performance information—both for individual federal entities and for the federal government as a whole. Overall, significant progress has been made since the enactment of key federal financial management reforms in the 1990s; however, our report on the U.S. government's consolidated financial statements underscores that much work remains to improve federal financial management, and these improvements are urgently needed.

Our audit report on the U.S. government's consolidated financial statements is enclosed. In summary, we found the following:

- Certain material weaknesses[1] in internal control over financial reporting and other limitations on the scope of our work resulted in conditions that prevented us from expressing an opinion on the accrual-based consolidated financial statements as of and for the fiscal years ended September 30, 2013, and 2012.[2] About 33 percent of the federal government's reported total assets as of September 30, 2013, and approximately 16 percent of the federal government's reported net cost for fiscal year 2013 relate to the Department of Defense (DOD), which received a disclaimer of opinion on its consolidated financial statements.

- Significant uncertainties, primarily related to the achievement of projected reductions in Medicare cost growth reflected in the 2013, 2012, 2011, and 2010 Statements of

---

[1]A material weakness is a deficiency, or a combination of deficiencies, in internal control over financial reporting such that there is a reasonable possibility that a material misstatement of the entity's financial statements will not be prevented, or detected and corrected, on a timely basis. A deficiency in internal control exists when the design or operation of a control does not allow management or employees, in the normal course of performing their assigned functions, to prevent, or detect and correct, misstatements on a timely basis.

[2]The accrual-based consolidated financial statements as of and for the fiscal years ended September 30, 2013, and 2012 consist of the (1) Statements of Net Cost, (2) Statements of Operations and Changes in Net Position, (3) Reconciliations of Net Operating Cost and Unified Budget Deficit, (4) Statements of Changes in Cash Balance from Unified Budget and Other Activities, and (5) Balance Sheets, including the related notes to these financial statements. Most revenues are recorded on a modified cash basis. The 2013, 2012, 2011, 2010, and 2009 Statements of Social Insurance and the 2013 and 2012 Statements of Changes in Social Insurance Amounts, including the related notes, are also included in the consolidated financial statements.

Social Insurance, prevented us from expressing an opinion on those statements as well as on the 2013 and 2012 Statements of Changes in Social Insurance Amounts. About $27.3 trillion, or 68.8 percent, of the reported total present value of future expenditures in excess of future revenue presented in the 2013 Statement of Social Insurance relates to Medicare programs reported in the Department of Health and Human Services' 2013 Statement of Social Insurance, which received a disclaimer of opinion.[3]

- Material weaknesses resulted in ineffective internal control over financial reporting for fiscal year 2013.

- Our tests of compliance with selected provisions of applicable laws, regulations, contracts, and grant agreements for fiscal year 2013 were limited by the material weaknesses and other scope limitations discussed in our audit report.

While significant progress has been made in improving federal financial management since the federal government began preparing consolidated financial statements 17 years ago, three major impediments continued to prevent us from rendering an opinion on the federal government's accrual-based consolidated financial statements over this period: (1) serious financial management problems at DOD that have prevented its financial statements from being auditable, (2) the federal government's inability to adequately account for and reconcile intragovernmental activity and balances between federal entities, and (3) the federal government's ineffective process for preparing the consolidated financial statements.

Importantly, almost all of the 24 Chief Financial Officers (CFO) Act agencies received unmodified ("clean") opinions on their respective entities' fiscal year 2013 financial statements, including the Department of Homeland Security (DHS). This was the first time that DHS has received an unmodified opinion on all of its financial statements—a significant achievement.

DOD, however, has consistently been unable to receive such an audit opinion on its financial statements. Following years of unsuccessful financial improvement efforts, the DOD Comptroller established the Financial Improvement and Audit Readiness (FIAR) Directorate to develop, manage, and implement a strategic approach for addressing internal control weaknesses and for achieving auditability, and to integrate those efforts with other improvement activities, such as the department's business systems modernization efforts. DOD's current FIAR strategy and methodology focus on two priorities—budgetary information and asset accountability—with an overall goal of

---

[3]We issued an unmodified opinion on the Statement of Social Insurance for 2009. Statements of Social Insurance are presented for the current year and each of the 4 preceding years in accordance with U.S. generally accepted accounting principles. Also, both the Statements of Social Insurance and the Statements of Changes in Social Insurance Amounts do not interrelate with the accrual-based consolidated financial statements.

preparing auditable department-wide financial statements by September 30, 2017.[4] Because budgetary information is widely and regularly used for management, one of DOD's highest interim priorities is the improvement of its budgetary information and processes underlying its Statement of Budgetary Resources (SBR).

Based on difficulties encountered in auditing the SBR of the U.S. Marine Corps, DOD made a significant change to its FIAR Guidance that will limit the scope of the first-year SBR audits for all DOD components.[5] As outlined in the March 2013 revised FIAR Guidance, the scope of the SBR audits beginning in fiscal year 2015 will be on budget activity only in the current year appropriations as an interim step toward achieving an audit of the SBR. In subsequent years, the components will commence audits of schedules of both current year and prior year audited appropriations and all related activity against those appropriated funds. DOD also reported this scope change in its May 2013 FIAR Plan Status Report and reiterated the department's commitment to achieving its audit readiness goals, but noted that absent a stable budget environment, DOD efforts were subject to increased risk.[6] Moreover, the results of our prior work have raised concerns about the ability of DOD components to implement the FIAR Plan effectively.[7]

Various efforts are also under way to address the other two major impediments. During fiscal year 2013, the Department of the Treasury (Treasury) continued to actively work with federal entities to resolve intragovernmental differences. These efforts included expanding the implementation of a quarterly scorecard process[8] to the 35 significant federal entities[9] and encouraging the use of the dispute resolution process.[10] In addition, Treasury further developed and began implementing a methodology to reconcile certain

---

[4]Section 1003 of the National Defense Authorization Act for Fiscal Year 2010, Pub. L. No. 111-84, 123 Stat. 2190, 2439-41 (Oct. 28, 2009), made the development and maintenance of the FIAR Plan a statutory requirement. Under the act, the FIAR Plan must describe specific actions to be taken and the costs associated with ensuring that DOD's financial statements are validated as ready for audit by September 30, 2017. More recently, section 1005 of the National Defense Authorization Act for Fiscal Year 2013, Pub. L. No. 112-239, 126 Stat. 1632 (Jan. 2, 2013), added a new requirement for DOD's FIAR Plan to describe specific actions to be taken and the costs associated with ensuring that one of DOD's financial statements, the Statement of Budgetary Resources, is validated as ready for audit by September 30, 2014.

[5]The FIAR Guidance was first issued by the DOD Comptroller in May 2010 and provides a standardized methodology for DOD components to follow for achieving financial management improvements and auditability. The DOD Comptroller periodically updates this guidance.

[6]In accordance with the National Defense Authorization Act for fiscal year 2010, the DOD Comptroller provides reports to relevant congressional committees on the status of DOD's implementation of the FIAR Plan twice a year—no later than May 15 and November 15.

[7]GAO, *DOD Financial Management: Marine Corps Statement of Budgetary Resources Audit Results and Lessons Learned*, GAO-11-830 (Washington, D.C.: Sept. 15, 2011, reissued Oct. 17, 2011); *DOD Financial Management: Improvement Needed in DOD Components' Implementation of Audit Readiness Effort*, GAO-11-851 (Washington, D.C.: Sept. 13, 2011); and *DOD Financial Management: Ongoing Challenges with Reconciling Navy and Marine Corps Fund Balance with Treasury*, GAO-12-132 (Washington, D.C.: Dec. 20, 2011).

[8]For each quarter, Treasury produces a scorecard for each significant entity that reports various aspects of the entity's intragovernmental differences with its trading partners, including the composition of the differences by trading partner and category. Entities are expected to resolve, with the respective trading partners, the differences identified in their scorecards.

[9]The Office of Management and Budget and Treasury have identified 35 federal entities that are significant to the U.S. government's consolidated financial statements, consisting of the 24 CFO Act agencies, several other federal executive branch agencies, and some government corporations.

[10]When an entity and respective trading partner cannot resolve an intragovernmental difference, the entities must request Treasury to resolve the dispute. Treasury will review the dispute and issue a decision on how to resolve the difference, which the entities must follow.

outlays and receipts between Treasury's records used to compute the budget deficit reported in the consolidated financial statements and underlying federal entity financial information and records. To help address the numerous issues in these areas, it will be important that Treasury has adequate systems and personnel to address the magnitude of the issues, and that Treasury and the Office of Management and Budget (OMB) develop and implement adequate corrective action plans for addressing the internal control deficiencies involving the process for preparing the consolidated financial statements. In addition to continued leadership by Treasury and OMB, strong and sustained commitment by federal entities is critical to fully address the numerous issues in these areas.

The material weaknesses underlying these three major impediments continued to (1) hamper the federal government's ability to reliably report a significant portion of its assets, liabilities, costs, and other related information; (2) affect the federal government's ability to reliably measure the full cost as well as the financial and nonfinancial performance of certain programs and activities; (3) impair the federal government's ability to adequately safeguard significant assets and properly record various transactions; and (4) hinder the federal government from having reliable financial information to operate in an efficient and effective manner.

In addition to the material weaknesses referred to above, we identified three other material weaknesses. These are the federal government's inability to (1) determine the full extent to which improper payments occur and reasonably assure that appropriate actions are taken to reduce them, (2) identify and resolve information security control deficiencies and manage information security risks on an ongoing basis, and (3) effectively manage its tax collection activities. Additional details concerning these material weaknesses and their effect on the accrual-based consolidated financial statements and on the management of federal government operations are presented in our audit report. Until the problems outlined in our audit report are adequately addressed, they will continue to have adverse implications for the federal government and American taxpayers.

The federal government reported a net operating cost of about $805 billion for fiscal year 2013 compared to the approximate $1.3 trillion reported for fiscal year 2012. Significant increases in taxes and other revenues and reductions in net costs were responsible for the decrease. The reported unified budget deficit of approximately $680 billion for fiscal year 2013 was down from the approximate $1.1 trillion reported for fiscal year 2012. The federal government's reported assets increased from about $2.7 trillion as of September 30, 2012, to about $3 trillion as of September 30, 2013, and its reported liabilities increased from about $18.8 trillion to about $19.9 trillion. Most of the increase in the federal government's assets and liabilities was due to student loans made by the Department of Education and a net increase in federal debt held by the public, respectively. As of September 30, 2013, federal debt held by the public totaled about 72 percent of gross domestic product (GDP).

While the federal government has significantly reduced the assets and liabilities related to actions it had taken to stabilize the financial markets and promote economic recovery during and after the last recession, the accrual-based consolidated financial statements, as of September 30, 2013, and 2012, continue to include significant equity investments in certain entities. For example, as of September 30, 2013, the reported investments in the Federal National Mortgage Association (Fannie Mae) and the Federal Home Loan

Mortgage Corporation (Freddie Mac) totaled about $140 billion (reported net of about $54 billion in valuation reserves). In valuing these equity investments, management considered and selected assumptions and data that it believed provided a reasonable basis for the estimated values reported in the accrual-based consolidated financial statements; however, there are many factors affecting these assumptions and estimates that are inherently subject to substantial uncertainty arising from the uniqueness of the transactions and the likelihood of future changes in general economic, regulatory, and market conditions. As such, there will be differences between the estimated values as of September 30, 2013, and the actual results, and such differences may be material.

In addition, there are risks that other factors could affect the federal government's financial condition in the future, including the following:

- The U.S. Postal Service (USPS) is facing a deteriorating financial situation with a lack of liquidity as it has reached its borrowing limit of $15 billion and finished fiscal year 2013 with a reported net loss of $5 billion.

- The Federal Housing Administration's (FHA) mortgage insurance portfolio continues to grow, and its insurance fund has experienced major financial difficulties. FHA's capital ratio for its Mutual Mortgage Insurance Fund remained below the required 2 percent level as of the end of fiscal year 2013. The ultimate roles of Fannie Mae and Freddie Mac in the mortgage market may further affect FHA's financial condition.

- The Pension Benefit Guaranty Corporation's (PBGC) financial future is uncertain because of long-term challenges related to PBGC's governance and funding structure. PBGC's liabilities exceeded its assets by about $36 billion as of September 30, 2013. PBGC reported that it is subject to further losses if plan terminations that are reasonably possible occur.

- Several initiatives undertaken during the last 5 years by the Board of Governors of the Federal Reserve System to stabilize the financial markets have led to a significant change in the composition and size of reported securities on the Federal Reserve's balance sheet. The value of these securities, which include Treasury securities and mortgage-backed securities guaranteed by Fannie Mae, Freddie Mac, and the Government National Mortgage Association (Ginnie Mae), is subject to interest rate risk and may decline or increase depending on interest rate changes. If the Federal Reserve sells these securities at a loss, future payments of Federal Reserve earnings to the federal government may be reduced.[11]

GAO's High-Risk list includes several of these issues, such as information security, USPS's business model, DOD financial management, and the PBGC and FHA insurance programs.[12] Every 2 years, GAO provides Congress with an update on its High-Risk Series, which highlights federal entities and program areas that are high risk due to their vulnerabilities to fraud, waste, abuse, and mismanagement or are most in need of broad reform. We updated our High-Risk Series in early 2013.

---

[11]Under Federal Reserve System policy, excess Federal Reserve Bank earnings are paid to the federal government. The federal government reported such net earnings of about $76 billion for fiscal year 2013, still well above its historical levels.
[12]GAO, *High-Risk Series: An Update*, GAO-13-283 (Washington, D.C.: February 2013).

Increased attention to risks that could affect the federal government's financial condition is made more important because of the nation's longer-term fiscal challenges. The comprehensive long-term fiscal projections presented in the unaudited Required Supplementary Information section of the *Fiscal Year 2013 Financial Report of the United States Government* (*2013 Financial Report*) show that—absent policy changes—the federal government continues to face an unsustainable long-term fiscal path. The oldest members of the baby-boom generation are already eligible for Social Security retirement benefits and for Medicare benefits. Under these projections, spending for the major health and retirement programs will increase in coming decades as more members of the baby-boom generation become eligible for benefits and the health care cost for each enrollee increases. Over the long term, the imbalance between spending and revenue that is built into current law and policy will lead to continued growth of debt held by the public as a share of GDP. This situation—in which debt grows faster than GDP—means the current federal fiscal path is unsustainable. Further, without legislative action, the Social Security Disability Insurance Trust Fund's assets are projected to be exhausted in 2016, at which time the Social Security Administration would need to reduce benefits consistent with available funds.

These projections, with regard to Social Security and Medicare, are based on the same assumptions underlying the information presented in the Statement of Social Insurance and assume that the provisions in law designed to slow the growth of Medicare costs are sustained and remain effective throughout the projection period. If, however, the cost containment measures are not sustained over the long term—a concern expressed by the Trustees of the Medicare trust funds, the Centers for Medicare & Medicaid Services' (CMS) Chief Actuary, the Congressional Budget Office, and others—spending on federal health care programs will grow much more rapidly.

GAO also prepares long-term federal fiscal simulations, which continue to show debt rising as a share of GDP.[13] Under GAO's Alternative simulation,[14] which uses the CMS Office of the Actuary's alternative health care cost projections, future spending in excess of receipts would be greater and debt held by the public as a share of GDP would grow more quickly than the projections in the *2013 Financial Report*.

---

[13]GAO, *The Federal Government's Long-Term Fiscal Outlook: Spring 2013 Update*, GAO-13-481SP (Washington, D.C.: Apr. 11, 2013).
[14]GAO's Spring 2013 Alternative simulation incorporates the CMS Office of the Actuary's alternative projections for health care cost growth, which assume physician payments are not reduced as specified under current law and certain cost controls are not maintained over the long term. Also in this simulation, expiring tax provisions, such as the research and experimentation tax credit, are extended to 2023. In the Alternative simulation, discretionary spending follows the original discretionary spending caps set by the Budget Control Act of 2011 but not the lower caps triggered by the automatic enforcement procedures. Over the long term, discretionary spending and revenue are held at their historical average share of GDP.

The Bipartisan Budget Act of 2013 (budget agreement),[15] which amended the Balanced Budget and Emergency Deficit Control Act (BBEDCA),[16] established new (higher) limits on defense and nondefense discretionary appropriations for fiscal years 2014 and 2015, extended sequestration for direct spending programs by 2 years through fiscal year 2023, and made other changes to direct spending and revenue. As a result, the budget agreement is projected to reduce the deficit over the next 10 years, but would not make a significant change in the long-term outlook for the federal budget.

Reliable financial and performance information is even more critical as (1) federal managers likely face increasingly tight budget constraints and need to operate their respective entities as efficiently and effectively as possible and (2) decision makers carry out the important task of deciding how to use multiple tools (tax provisions, discretionary spending, mandatory spending, and credit programs) to address the federal government's fiscal challenges.

As we reported in December 2013, Treasury twice deviated from its normal debt management operations during fiscal year 2013, for almost half the fiscal year, due to delays in raising the debt limit.[17] During those delays, Treasury took a number of extraordinary actions—consistent with relevant laws and regulations—to avoid exceeding the debt limit. The first delay occurred from December 31, 2012, through February 3, 2013. On February 4, 2013, the debt limit was suspended through May 18, 2013, by the No Budget, No Pay Act of 2013.[18] The second delay occurred from May 20, 2013, through October 16, 2013. On October 17, 2013, the debt limit was suspended through February 7, 2014, by the Continuing Appropriations Act, 2014.[19] On February 15, 2014, the debt limit was suspended through March 15, 2015, by the Temporary Debt Limit Extension Act.[20]

As we have previously reported, the debt limit does not restrict Congress's ability to enact spending and revenue legislation that affects the level of federal debt or otherwise constrains fiscal policy; it restricts Treasury's authority to borrow to finance the decisions already enacted by Congress and the President.[21] The United States benefits from the confidence investors have that debt backed by the full faith and credit of the United

---

[15]Pub. L. No. 113-67, div. A, tit. I, § 101, 127 Stat. 1165, 1166-69 (Dec. 26, 2013). The Continuing Appropriations Act, 2014, Pub. L. No. 113-76, 128 Stat. 5 (Jan. 17, 2014), enacted discretionary appropriations for fiscal year 2014 consistent with the limits established in the budget agreement and the Balanced Budget and Emergency Deficit Control Act (BBEDCA), as amended.

[16]The Budget Control Act of 2011, Pub. L. No. 112-25, 125 Stat. 240 (Aug. 2, 2011), which amended BBEDCA, imposed discretionary spending limits for fiscal years 2012 through 2021 to reduce projected spending by about $1 trillion. The Budget Control Act also established the Joint Select Committee on Deficit Reduction, which was tasked with proposing legislation to reduce the deficit by an additional $1.2 trillion through fiscal year 2021. The Joint Committee did not report a proposal, and Congress and the President did not enact legislation. This triggered the sequestration process in section 251A of BBEDCA, which is classified, as amended, at 2 U.S.C. § 901a. Section 251A also provides for an annual reduction of the discretionary spending limits and a sequestration of direct spending from fiscal years 2014 through 2021. The budget agreement enacted further changes amending section 251A of BBEDCA.

[17]GAO, *Financial Audit: Bureau of the Fiscal Service's Fiscal Years 2013 and 2012 Schedules of Federal Debt*, GAO-14-173 (Washington, D.C.: Dec. 12, 2013).

[18]Pub. L. No. 113-3, § 2, 127 Stat. 51 (Feb. 4, 2013).

[19]Pub. L. No. 113-46, § 1002, 127 Stat. 558, 566-67 (Oct. 17, 2013).

[20]Pub. L. No. 113-83, § 2, 128 Stat. 1011 (Feb. 15, 2014).

[21]GAO, *Debt Limit: Analysis of 2011-2012 Actions Taken and Effect of Delayed Increase on Borrowing Costs*, GAO-12-701 (Washington, D.C.: July 23, 2012), and *Debt Limit: Delays Create Debt Management Challenges and Increase Uncertainty in the Treasury Market*, GAO-11-203 (Washington, D.C.: Feb. 22, 2011).

States will be honored. As we have also previously reported, delays in raising the debt limit can create uncertainty in the Treasury market and lead to higher Treasury borrowing costs. To avoid such uncertainty and related borrowing costs, we noted, in our February 2011 and July 2012 reports related to the debt limit, that Congress should consider ways to better link decisions about the debt limit with decisions about spending and revenue at the time those decisions are made to avoid potential disruptions to the Treasury market and to help inform the fiscal policy debate in a timely way.

Our audit report on the U.S. government's consolidated financial statements would not be possible without the commitment and professionalism of inspectors general throughout the federal government who are responsible for annually auditing the financial statements of individual federal entities. We also appreciate the cooperation and assistance of Treasury and OMB officials as well as the federal entities' chief financial officers. We look forward to continuing to work with these individuals, the administration, and Congress to achieve the goals and objectives of federal financial management reform.

Our audit report begins on page 220. Our guide to the *Financial Report of the United States Government (Financial Report)* is intended to help those who seek to obtain a better understanding of the *Financial Report* and is available on GAO's website at www.gao.gov.[22] In addition, the website includes a guide to understanding the differences between accrual and cash measures of the deficit and provides a useful perspective on the different purposes cash and accrual measures serve in providing a comprehensive picture of the federal government's fiscal condition today and over time.[23]

---

[22]GAO, *Understanding the Primary Components of the Annual Financial Report of the United States Government*, GAO-09-946SP (Washington, D.C.: September 2009).

[23]See http://www.gao.gov/special.pubs/longterm/deficit/, which is based on information in GAO, *Understanding Similarities and Differences between Accrual and Cash Deficits*, GAO-07-117SP (Washington, D.C.: December 2006). In January 2007 and 2008, we issued updates to this guide for fiscal years 2006 and 2007; see GAO-07-341SP (Washington, D.C.: January 2007) and GAO-08-410SP (Washington, D.C.: January 2008).

Our audit report was prepared under the direction of Robert F. Dacey, Chief Accountant, and Gary T. Engel, Director, Financial Management and Assurance. If you have any questions, please contact me on (202) 512-5500 or them on (202) 512-3406.

Gene L. Dodaro
Comptroller General
of the United States

cc: The Majority Leader of the Senate
      The Minority Leader of the Senate
      The Majority Leader of the House of Representatives
      The Minority Leader of the House of Representatives

Financial Statements of the United States Government for the Years Ended September 30, 2013, and 2012

Statements of Net Cost

These statements present the net cost of the United States Government (Government)[1] operations for fiscal years 2013 and 2012, including the operations related to funds from dedicated collections (funds financed by specifically identified revenues, often supplemented by other financing sources, which remain available over time). The Government's fiscal year begins October 1 and ends September 30. Costs and earned revenues are categorized on the Statement of Net Cost by significant entity, providing greater accountability by showing the relationship of the agencies' net cost to the Governmentwide net cost. Costs and earned revenues are presented in this *Financial Report* by significant entity on an accrual basis, while the budget presents costs and revenues by obligations and receipts, generally on a cash basis. The focus of the budget of the United States is by agency. Budgets are prepared, defended, and monitored by agency. In reporting by agency, we are assisting the external users in assessing the budget integrity, operating performance, stewardship, and systems and controls of the Government.

These statements contain the following four components:

- Gross cost—is the full cost of all the departments and entities excluding (gain)/loss from changes in assumptions. These costs are assigned on a cause-and-effect basis, or reasonably allocated to the corresponding departments and entities.
- Earned revenue—is exchange revenue resulting from the Government providing goods and services to the public at a price.
- (Gain)/loss from changes in assumptions—is the gain or loss from changes in long-term assumptions used to measure the liabilities reported for federal civilian and military employee pensions, other post-employment benefits, and other retirement benefits, including veterans' compensation.
- Net cost—is computed by subtracting earned revenue from gross cost, adjusted by the (gain)/loss from changes in assumptions.

Individual agency net cost amounts will differ from the agency's financial statements primarily because of allocations of Office of Personnel Management (OPM) benefit program costs and intragovernmental eliminations, as adjusted for buy/sell cost, buy/sell revenues and imputed costs. Because of its specific function, most of the costs originally associated with OPM have been allocated to their user agencies for Governmentwide reporting purposes. The remaining costs for OPM on the Statements of Net Cost are the administrative operating costs, the expenses from prior and past costs from health and pension plan amendments, and the actuarial gains and losses, if applicable. With regard to intragovernmental buy/sell costs and related revenues, the amounts recognized by each agency are added to, and subtracted from, respectively, the individual agency non-federal net cost amounts. Because of the specific functions of the General Services Administration (GSA), as the primary provider of goods and services to federal agencies, once GSA's net cost is adjusted for its intragovernmental buy/sell costs and related revenues, the remaining costs for GSA on the Statements of Net Cost are its administrative operating costs. In addition, the intragovernmental imputed costs recognized for the receipt of goods and services, financed in whole or part by the providing agencies, are added to the individual agency non-federal net cost amounts. The interest on securities issued by the Department of the Treasury (Treasury) and held by the public is reported on Treasury's financial statements, but, because of its importance and the dollar amounts involved, it is reported separately in these statements.

---

[1] For purposes of this document, "Government" refers to the U.S. Government.

Statements of Operations and Changes in Net Position

These statements report the results of Government operations, which include the results of operations for funds from dedicated collections. They include nonexchange revenues which are generated from transactions where the government gives (or receives) value without giving (or receiving) equal value in return. These are generated principally by the Government's sovereign power to tax, levy duties, and assess fines and penalties. These statements also present the cost of Government operations, net of revenue earned from the sale of goods and services to the public (exchange revenue). They further include certain adjustments and unreconciled transactions that affect the net position.

Revenue

Individual income tax and tax withholdings include Federal Insurance Contributions Act (FICA)/Self-Employment Contributions Act (SECA) taxes and other taxes. These taxes are characterized as nonexchange revenue.

Excise taxes consist of taxes collected for various items, such as airline tickets, gasoline products, distilled spirits and imported liquor, tobacco, firearms, and other items. These also are characterized as nonexchange revenue.

Other taxes and receipts include Federal Reserve Banks (FRBs) earnings, tax related fines, penalties and interest, and railroad retirement taxes.

Miscellaneous earned revenues consist of earned revenues received from the public with virtually no associated cost. These revenues include rents and royalties on the Outer Continental Shelf Lands resulting from the leasing and development of mineral resources on public lands.

Generally, funds from dedicated collections are financed by specifically identified revenues, provided to the government by non-federal sources, often supplemented by other financing sources, which remain available over time. These specifically identified revenues and other financing sources are required by statute to be used for designated activities, benefits or purposes, and must be accounted for separately from the Government's general revenue. See Note 22—Funds from Dedicated Collections for detailed information.

Intragovernmental interest represents interest earned from the investment of surplus dedicated collections, which finance the deficit spending of all other fund's non-dedicated operations. These investments are recorded as intragovernmental debt holdings and are included in Note 12—Federal Debt Securities Held by the Public and Accrued Interest, in the table titled Intragovernmental Debt Holdings: Federal Debt Securities Held as Investments by Government Accounts. These interest payments and the associated investments are eliminated in the consolidation process.

Net Cost of Government Operations

The net cost of Government operations (gross cost [including (gains)/losses from changes in assumptions] less earned revenue) flows through from the Statements of Net Cost. The net cost associated with funds from dedicated collections activities is separately reported.

Intragovernmental Transfers

Intragovernmental transfers reflect budgetary and other financing sources for funds from dedicated collections, excluding financing sources related to nonexchange, intragovernmental interest and miscellaneous revenues. These intragovernmental transfers include appropriations, transfers and other financing sources. These amounts are labeled as "other changes in fund balance" in Note 22—Funds from Dedicated Collections. Some transfers reflect amounts required by statute to be transferred from the General Fund of the Treasury to funds from dedicated collections. An example is the annual transfer to the Department of Health and Human Services' (HHS) Supplementary Medical Insurance Trust Fund Medicare Parts B and D which received approximately 75 percent and 74 percent, respectively, of 2013 program costs, from the General Fund.

Unmatched Transactions and Balances

Unmatched transactions and balances are adjustments needed to bring the change in net position into balance due to unreconciled intragovernmental differences and unreconciled General Fund differences, agency reporting errors and restatements in the consolidated financial statements. See Note 1.T—Unmatched Transactions and Balances for detailed information.

The unmatched transactions and balances are included in net operating cost to make the sum of net operating costs and prior period adjustments for the year equal to the change in the net position balance.

Net Position, Beginning of Period

The net position, beginning of period, reflects the net position reported on the prior year's balance sheet as of the end of that fiscal year. The net position for funds from dedicated collections is shown separately.

Prior-period adjustments are revisions to adjust the beginning net position and balances presented on the prior year financial statements due to corrections of errors or changes in accounting principles. See Note 19—Prior Period Adjustments for detailed information.

Net Position, End of Period

The net position, end of period, amount reflects the net position as of the end of the fiscal year. The net position for funds from dedicated collections is separately shown.

Reconciliations of Net Operating Cost and Unified Budget Deficit

These statements reconcile the results of operations (net operating cost) on the Statements of Operations and Changes in Net Position to the unified budget deficit. The premise of the reconciliation is that the accrual and budgetary accounting bases share transaction data.

Receipts and outlays in the budget are measured primarily on a cash basis and differ from the accrual basis of accounting used in the *Financial Report*. Refer to Note 1.B—Basis of Accounting and Revenue Recognition for details. These statements begin with the net results of operations (net operating cost), where operating revenues are reported on a modified cash basis of accounting and the net cost of Government operations on an accrual basis of accounting and report activities where the bases of accounting for the components of net operating cost and the unified budget deficit differ.

Components of Net Operating Cost Not Part of the Budget Deficit

This information includes the operating components, such as the changes in benefits payable for veterans, military and civilian employees, the environmental and disposal liabilities, and depreciation expense, not included in the budget results.

Components of the Budget Deficit Not Part of Net Operating Cost

This information includes the budget components, such as capitalized fixed assets (that are recorded as outlays in the budget when purchased and reflected in net operating cost through depreciation expense over the useful life of the asset), and increases in other assets that are not included in the operating results.

Statements of Changes in Cash Balance from Unified Budget and Other Activities

The primary purpose of these statements is to report how the annual unified budget deficit relates to the change in the Government's cash and other monetary assets and debt held by the public. It explains why the unified budget deficit normally would not result in an equivalent change in the Government's cash and other monetary assets.

These statements reconcile the unified budget deficit to the change in cash and other monetary assets during the fiscal year and explain how the budget deficits were financed. A budget deficit is the result of outlays (expenditures) exceeding receipts (revenue) during a particular fiscal year.

The budget deficit is primarily financed through borrowings from the public. Other transactions such as the payment of interest on debt held by the public also require cash disbursements and are not part of the deficit. The budget deficit also includes certain amounts that are recognized in the budget and will be disbursed in a future period or are adjustments that did not affect the cash balance. These amounts include interest accrued on debt issued by Treasury and held by the public and subsidy expense related to direct and guaranteed loans.

These statements show the adjustments for noncash outlays included in the budget and items affecting the cash balance not included in the budget to explain the change in cash and other monetary assets.

Balance Sheets

The balance sheets show the Government's assets, liabilities, and net position. When combined with stewardship information, this information presents a more comprehensive understanding of the Government's financial position. The net position for funds from dedicated collections is shown separately.

Assets

Assets included on the balance sheets are resources of the Government that remain available to meet future needs. The most significant assets that are reported on the balance sheets are loans receivable, net; property, plant, and equipment (PP&E), net; inventories and related property, net; and cash and other monetary assets. There are, however, other significant resources available to the Government that extend beyond the assets presented in these balance sheets. Those resources include the Government's sovereign powers to tax, and set monetary policy.

Liabilities and Net Position

Liabilities are obligations of the Government resulting from prior actions that will require financial resources. The most significant liabilities reported on the balance sheets are Federal debt securities held by the public and accrued interest and Federal employee and veteran benefits payable. Liabilities also include environmental and disposal liabilities, benefits due and payable, and insurance and guarantee program liabilities.

As with reported assets, the Government's responsibilities, policy commitments, and contingencies are much broader than these reported balance sheet liabilities. They include the social insurance programs reported in the Statements of Social Insurance and disclosed in the Required Supplementary Information—Social Insurance section, the fiscal long-term projections of non-interest spending disclosed in the Required Supplementary Information (RSI)—Statement of Fiscal Projections for the United States Government (Government) section, and a wide range of other programs under which the Government provides benefits and services to the people of this Nation, as well as certain future loss contingencies.

The Government has entered into contractual commitments requiring the future use of financial resources and has unresolved contingencies where existing conditions, situations, or circumstances create uncertainty about future losses. Commitments, as well as contingencies that do not meet the criteria for recognition as liabilities on the balance sheets, but for which there is at least a reasonable possibility that losses have been incurred, are disclosed in Note 20—Contingencies and Note 21—Commitments.

The collection of taxes and other revenue is credited to the corresponding funds from dedicated collections that will use these funds to meet a particular Government purpose. If the collections from taxes and other sources exceed the payments to the beneficiaries, the excess revenue is invested in Treasury securities or "loaned" to Treasury's General Fund; therefore, the trust fund balances do not represent cash. An explanation of the trust funds for social insurance is included in Note 22—Funds from Dedicated Collections. That note also contains information about trust fund receipts, disbursements, and assets.

Because of its sovereign power to tax and borrow, and the country's wide economic base, the Government has unique access to financial resources through generating tax revenues and issuing Federal debt securities. This provides the Government with the ability to meet present obligations and those that are anticipated from future operations, and are not reflected in net position.

The net position is the residual difference between assets and liabilities and is the cumulative results of operations since inception. For detailed components that comprise the net position, refer to the section "Statement of Operations and Changes in Net Position."

Statements of Social Insurance and Changes in Social Insurance Amounts

The Statements of Social Insurance provide estimates of the status of the most significant social insurance programs: Social Security, Medicare, Railroad Retirement, and Black Lung social insurance programs. They are administered by the Social Security Administration (SSA), HHS, the Railroad Retirement Board (RRB), and the Department of Labor (DOL), respectively. The estimates are actuarial present values[2] of the projections and are based on the economic and demographic assumptions representing the trustees' reasonable estimates as set forth in the relevant Social Security and Medicare trustees' reports and in the agency financial reports of HHS, SSA, and DOL (Black Lung) and in the relevant agency performance and accountability report for the RRB. The projections are based on the continuation of program provisions contained in current law.

The magnitude and complexity of social insurance programs, coupled with the extreme sensitivity of projections relating to the many assumptions of the programs, produce a wide range of possible results. In preparing the Statements of Social Insurance, Government management considers and selects assumptions and data that it believes provide a reasonable basis for the assertions in the statements. However, because of the large number of factors that affect the Statements of Social Insurance and the fact that such assumptions are inherently subject to substantial uncertainty (arising from the likelihood of future events, significant uncertainties, and contingencies), there will be differences between the estimates in the Statements of Social Insurance and the actual results, and those differences may be material. Note 24—Social Insurance describes the social insurance programs, reports long-range estimates that can be used to assess the financial condition of the programs, and explains some of the factors that impact the various programs. The Statements of Changes in Social Insurance Amounts reconcile the change between the current valuation period and the prior valuation period.

---

[2] Present values recognize that a dollar paid or collected in the future is worth less than a dollar today, because a dollar today could be invested and earn interest. To calculate a present value, future amounts are thus reduced using an assumed interest rate, and those reduced amounts are summed.

United States Government
Statement of Net Cost
for the Year Ended September 30, 2013

(In billions of dollars)	Gross Cost	Earned Revenue	Subtotal	(Gain)/Loss from Changes in Assumptions	Net Cost
Department of Health and Human Services	968.4	72.9	895.5	0.2	895.7
Social Security Administration	867.4	0.4	867.0	-	867.0
Department of Defense	685.1	44.9	640.2	(62.8)	577.4
Department of Veterans Affairs	243.3	4.5	238.8	114.1	352.9
Interest on Treasury Securities Held by the Public	247.6	-	247.6	-	247.6
Department of Agriculture	147.6	7.5	140.1	-	140.1
Office of Personnel Management	67.3	19.2	48.1	81.9	130.0
Department of Labor	80.1	-	80.1	-	80.1
Department of Transportation	77.3	0.9	76.4	-	76.4
Department of Homeland Security	70.7	9.7	61.0	(2.4)	58.6
Department of Housing and Urban Development	42.6	1.5	41.1	-	41.1
Department of Energy	38.5	4.3	34.2	-	34.2
Department of Justice	31.8	1.3	30.5	-	30.5
Department of State	29.4	4.2	25.2	0.4	25.6
National Aeronautics and Space Administration	18.1	0.2	17.9	-	17.9
Department of the Interior	16.9	2.7	14.2	-	14.2
Agency for International Development	10.6	0.2	10.4	-	10.4
Department of Education	32.9	23.2	9.7	-	9.7
Federal Communications Commission	9.9	0.4	9.5	-	9.5
Railroad Retirement Board	13.5	4.2	9.3	-	9.3
Environmental Protection Agency	9.8	0.5	9.3	-	9.3
Department of Commerce	11.1	2.9	8.2	-	8.2
National Science Foundation	7.1	-	7.1	-	7.1
U.S. Postal Service	72.4	66.3	6.1	-	6.1
Smithsonian Institution	0.8	-	0.8	-	0.8
Small Business Administration	0.7	0.4	0.3	-	0.3
U.S. Nuclear Regulatory Commission	1.0	0.8	0.2	-	0.2
Export-Import Bank of the United States	1.1	1.0	0.1	-	0.1
Farm Credit System Insurance Corporation	-	0.1	(0.1)	-	(0.1)
Pension Benefit Guaranty Corporation	9.1	9.4	(0.3)	-	(0.3)
Securities and Exchange Commission	1.3	1.8	(0.5)	-	(0.5)
Tennessee Valley Authority	10.7	11.0	(0.3)	(0.2)	(0.5)
General Services Administration	0.1	0.7	(0.6)	-	(0.6)
National Credit Union Administration	(1.8)	0.9	(2.7)	-	(2.7)
Federal Deposit Insurance Corporation	(2.9)	12.7	(15.6)	-	(15.6)
Department of the Treasury	75.3	103.5	(28.2)	-	(28.2)
All other entities	46.1	1.3	44.8	-	44.8
Total	3,940.9	415.5	3,525.4	131.2	3,656.6

The accompanying notes are an integral part of these financial statements.

United States Government
Statement of Net Cost
for the Year Ended September 30, 2012 (See Note 1.U.)

(In billions of dollars)	Gross Cost	Earned Revenue	Subtotal	Loss from Changes in Assumptions	Net Cost
Department of Health and Human Services	922.4	67.8	854.6	0.3	854.9
Social Security Administration	822.9	0.3	822.6	-	822.6
Department of Defense...	769.6	56.0	713.6	70.4	784.0
Department of Veterans Affairs..................................	209.9	4.1	205.8	149.3	355.1
Interest on Treasury Securities Held by the Public	245.4	-	245.4	-	245.4
Department of Agriculture...	158.8	12.0	146.8	-	146.8
Office of Personnel Management	82.0	19.1	62.9	98.9	161.8
Department of Labor..	102.6	-	102.6	-	102.6
Department of Transportation....................................	77.3	0.8	76.5	-	76.5
Department of Homeland Security..............................	58.9	9.9	49.0	0.4	49.4
Department of Housing and Urban Development	74.0	1.5	72.5	-	72.5
Department of Energy..	60.2	4.3	55.9	-	55.9
Department of Justice..	38.8	1.3	37.5	-	37.5
Department of State..	29.5	3.5	26.0	0.8	26.8
National Aeronautics and Space Administration	18.1	0.2	17.9	-	17.9
Department of the Interior..	21.7	2.7	19.0	-	19.0
Agency for International Development.........................	11.4	0.2	11.2	-	11.2
Department of Education	62.6	20.0	42.6	-	42.6
Federal Communications Commission	10.0	0.4	9.6	-	9.6
Railroad Retirement Board	15.2	5.1	10.1	-	10.1
Environmental Protection Agency..............................	10.7	0.3	10.4	-	10.4
Department of Commerce..	12.0	2.6	9.4	-	9.4
National Science Foundation	7.3	-	7.3	-	7.3
U.S. Postal Service..	81.5	64.2	17.3	-	17.3
Smithsonian Institution..	0.7	-	0.7	-	0.7
Small Business Administration...................................	1.5	0.4	1.1	-	1.1
U.S. Nuclear Regulatory Commission	1.0	0.8	0.2	-	0.2
Export-Import Bank of the United States	1.2	0.8	0.4	-	0.4
Farm Credit System Insurance Corporation...............	-	0.1	(0.1)	-	(0.1)
Pension Benefit Guaranty Corporation	20.2	10.4	9.8	-	9.8
Securities and Exchange Commission	1.2	1.6	(0.4)	-	(0.4)
Tennessee Valley Authority	11.0	11.3	(0.3)	0.1	(0.2)
General Services Administration................................	0.1	0.5	(0.4)	-	(0.4)
National Credit Union Administration	1.3	1.0	0.3	-	0.3
Federal Deposit Insurance Corporation	2.4	19.3	(16.9)	-	(16.9)
Department of the Treasury.......................................	(152.9)	27.5	(180.4)	-	(180.4)
All other entities	54.4	0.8	53.6	-	53.6
Total..	3,844.9	350.8	3,494.1	320.2	3,814.3

The accompanying notes are an integral part of these financial statements.

United States Government
Statement of Operations and Changes in Net Position
for the Year Ended September 30, 2013

(In billions of dollars)	Funds other than those from Dedicated Collections (Combined)	Funds from Dedicated Collections (Note 22) (Combined)	Eliminations	Consolidated
		2013		
Revenue (Note 18):				
Individual income tax and tax withholdings	1,294.0	902.4	-	2,196.4
Corporation income taxes	270.4	-	-	270.4
Excise taxes	32.8	52.8	-	85.6
Unemployment taxes	-	54.0	-	54.0
Customs duties	30.6	-	-	30.6
Estate and gift taxes	18.8	-	-	18.8
Other taxes and receipts	139.7	36.4	(0.6)	175.5
Miscellaneous earned revenues	7.0	4.2	-	11.2
Intragovernmental interest	-	119.6	(119.6)	-
Total Revenue	1,793.3	1,169.4	(120.2)	2,842.5
Net Cost of Government Operations:				
Net cost	2,175.2	1,482.0	(0.6)	3,656.6
Intragovernmental interest	119.6	-	(119.6)	-
Total net cost	2,294.8	1,482.0	(120.2)	3,656.6
Intragovernmental transfers	(307.6)	307.6	-	-
Unmatched transactions and balances (Note 1.T)	9.0	-	-	9.0
Net operating (cost)/revenue	(800.1)	(5.0)	-	(805.1)
Net position, beginning of period	(19,248.8)	3,147.8	-	(16,101.0)
Prior period adjustments—changes in accounting principles (Note 19)	(4.1)	0.9	-	(3.2)
Net operating (cost)/revenue	(800.1)	(5.0)	-	(805.1)
Net position, end of period	(20,053.0)	3,143.7	-	(16,909.3)

The accompanying notes are an integral part of these financial statements.

United States Government
Statement of Operations and Changes in Net Position
for the Year Ended September 30, 2012 (Restated - See Note 22)

(In billions of dollars)	Funds other than those from Dedicated Collections (Combined)	Funds from Dedicated Collections (Note 22) (Combined)	Eliminations	Consolidated
		2012		
Revenue (Note 18):				
Individual income tax and tax withholdings	1,135.2	789.9	-	1,925.1
Corporation income taxes	237.5	-	-	237.5
Excise taxes	24.6	56.5	-	81.1
Unemployment taxes	-	66.5	-	66.5
Customs duties	28.6	-	-	28.6
Estate and gift taxes	13.9	-	-	13.9
Other taxes and receipts	115.3	31.3	(0.8)	145.8
Miscellaneous earned revenues	13.5	6.2	-	19.7
Intragovernmental interest	-	128.4	(128.4)	-
Total Revenue	1,568.6	1,078.8	(129.2)	2,518.2
Net Cost of Government Operations:				
Net cost	2,381.8	1,433.3	(0.8)	3,814.3
Intragovernmental interest	128.4	-	(128.4)	-
Total net cost	2,510.2	1,433.3	(129.2)	3,814.3
Intragovernmental transfers	(419.7)	419.7	-	-
Unmatched transactions and balances (Note 1.T)	(20.2)	-	-	(20.2)
Net operating (cost)/revenue	(1,381.5)	65.2	-	(1,316.3)
Net position, beginning of period	(15,533.6)	748.2	-	(14,785.4)
Prior period adjustments–changes in accounting principles (Note 19)	(2,333.7)	2,334.4	-	0.7
Net operating (cost)/revenue	(1,381.5)	65.2	-	(1,316.3)
Net position, end of period	(19,248.8)	3,147.8	-	(16,101.0)

The accompanying notes are an integral part of these financial statements.

United States Government
Reconciliations of Net Operating Cost and Unified Budget Deficit
for the Year Ended September 30, 2013, and 2012

(In billions of dollars)	2013	2012
Net operating cost	(805.1)	(1,316.3)
Components of net operating cost not part of the budget deficit:		
(Decrease)/increase in liability for military employee benefits (Note 13):		
Increase in military pension liabilities...	42.2	120.7
(Decrease) in military health liabilities..	(85.7)	(9.0)
(Decrease) in other military benefits	(0.4)	(0.6)
(Decrease)/increase in liability for military employee benefits	(43.9)	111.1
Increase in liability for veteran's compensation (Note 13)..	213.2	227.9
Increase in liabilities for civilian employee benefits (Note 13):		
Increase in civilian pension liabilities..	95.6	152.6
(Decrease) in civilian health liabilities	(1.4)	(14.4)
Increase in other civilian benefits..	0.8	4.6
Increase in liabilities for civilian employee benefits....................................	95.0	142.8
Increase in environmental and disposal liabilities (Note 14):		
Increase in Energy's environmental and disposal liabilities....................................	11.8	17.8
(Decrease) in all others' environmental and disposal liabilities....................................	(1.7)	(2.9)
Increase in environmental and disposal liabilities..	10.1	14.9
Property, plant, and equipment depreciation expense....................................	62.1	59.1
Property, plant, and equipment disposals and revaluations	(36.2)	9.4
Increase/(decrease) in benefits due and payable	8.1	(4.8)
(Decrease) in insurance and guarantee program liabilities	(26.4)	(5.3)
(Decrease)/increase in other liabilities..	(20.9)	5.6
Increase in accounts payable	1.0	1.8
Decrease/(increase) in net accounts and taxes receivable....................................	8.0	(4.9)
TARP yearend (downward) re-estimate	(8.1)	(9.0)
(Decrease) in liabilities to Government-Sponsored enterprises (GSEs)...........................	(9.0)	(307.2)
(Decrease)/increase in valuation loss on investments in GSEs....................................	(30.9)	42.3
Components of the budget surplus (or deficit) that are not part of		
net operating revenue/(or cost):		
Capitalized property, plant, and equipment:		
Department of Defense..	(37.0)	(33.6)
All other agencies	(30.6)	(37.1)
Total capitalized property, plant, and equipment	(67.6)	(70.7)
Effect of prior year TARP downward/(upward) re-estimate....................................	9.0	(23.3)
(Increase) in inventory	(12.1)	(2.9)
(Increase) in investments in GSEs	-	(18.6)
Decrease in debt and equity securities..	2.4	0.4
(Increase)/decrease in other assets	(5.2)	21.7
Credit reform and other loan activities..	(25.4)	38.6
All other reconciling items...	1.6	(2.0)
Unified budget deficit	(680.3)	(1,089.4)

The accompanying notes are an integral part of these financial statements.

United States Government
Statements of Changes in Cash Balance from Unified Budget and Other Activities
for the Years Ended September 30, 2013, and 2012

(In billions of dollars)	2013		2012	
Unified budget deficit	(680.3)		(1,089.4)	
Adjustments for Noncash Outlays Included in the budget:				
Interest accrued by Treasury on debt held by the public	242.7		240.1	
TARP yearend re-estimates...	(0.9)		32.3	
TARP Subsidy (income) (Note 5)	(11.9)		(10.8)	
Other Federal entity subsidy (income) (Note 4)....................	(63.4)		(29.4)	
Subtotal		166.5		232.2
Items Affecting the Cash Balance Not Included in the budget:				
Net Transactions from financing activity:				
Borrowings from the public	8,145.4		7,766.9	
Repayment of debt held by the public	(7,444.0)		(6,614.0)	
Agency securities..	0.7		(0.4)	
Subtotal		702.1		1,152.5
Transactions from monetary and other activity:				
Interest paid by Treasury on debt held by the public	(248.7)		(234.3)	
Net TARP direct loans and equity investments activity	31.7		52.3	
Net GSEs-mortgage-backed securities activity	-		70.6	
Net loan receivable activity	(125.6)		(153.7)	
Allocations of special drawing rights....................................	(0.2)		(0.7)	
Uninvested principal from the Thrift Savings Plan (TSP) G Fund	119.9		-	
Other	34.7		(0.3)	
Subtotal		(188.2)		(266.1)
Cash and other monetary assets: (Note 2)				
Increase in Cash and other monetary assets		0.1		29.2
Balance, beginning of period		206.2		177.0
Balance, end of period...		206.3		206.2

The accompanying notes are an integral part of these financial statements.

For budgetary purposes, the effect of the yearend downward re-estimates (reduction of net outlays) and upward re-estimates (increase of net outlays) is not recognized until the subsequent fiscal year.

United States Government
Balance Sheets
as of September 30

(In billions of dollars)	2013	2012 (Restated - See Note 22)
Assets:		
Cash and other monetary assets (Note 2)	206.3	206.2
Accounts and taxes receivable, net (Note 3)	103.2	111.2
Loans receivable, net (Note 4)	1,022.3	859.6
TARP direct loans and equity investments, net (Note 5)	17.9	40.2
Inventories and related property, net (Note 6)	311.1	299.0
Property, plant and equipment, net (Note 7)	896.7	855.0
Debt and equity securities (Note 8)	107.8	110.2
Investments in GSEs (Note 9)	140.2	109.3
Other assets (Note 10)	162.8	157.6
Total assets	2,968.3	2,748.3
Stewardship land and heritage assets (Note 25)		
Liabilities:		
Accounts payable (Note 11)	66.2	65.2
Federal debt securities held by the public and accrued interest (Note 12)	12,028.4	11,332.3
Federal employee and veteran benefits payable (Note 13)	6,538.3	6,274.0
Environmental and disposal liabilities (Note 14)	349.1	339.0
Benefits due and payable (Note 15)	174.3	166.2
Insurance and guarantee program liabilities (Note 16)	130.0	156.4
Loan guarantee liabilities (Note 4)	59.2	74.6
Liabilities to GSEs (Note 9)	-	9.0
Other liabilities (Note 17)	532.1	432.6
Total liabilities	19,877.6	18,849.3
Contingencies (Note 20) and Commitments (Note 21)		
Net Position:		
Funds from Dedicated Collections (Note 22)	3,143.7	3,147.8
Funds other than those from Dedicated Collections	(20,053.0)	(19,248.8)
Total net position	(16,909.3)	(16,101.0)
Total liabilities and net position	2,968.3	2,748.3

The accompanying notes are an integral part of these financial statements.

United States Government
Statements of Social Insurance (Note 24)
Present Value of Long-Range (75 Years, except Black Lung) Actuarial Projections

(In billions of dollars)	2013	2012	2011	2010	2009
Federal Old-age, Survivors and Disability Insurance (Social Security): [14]					
Revenue (Contributions and Dedicated Taxes) from:					
Participants who have attained eligibility age (age 62 and over)	908	847	726	672	575
Participants who have not attained eligibility age	24,591	22,703	20,734	19,914	18,559
Future participants	23,419	21,649	20,144	19,532	18,082
All current and future participants	48,918	45,198	41,603	40,118	37,217
Expenditures for Scheduled Future Benefits for:					
Participants who have attained eligibility age (age 62 and over)	(11,021)	(9,834)	(8,618)	(8,096)	(7,465)
Participants who have not attained eligibility age	(40,591)	(37,753)	(34,042)	(32,225)	(30,207)
Future participants	(9,600)	(8,890)	(8,100)	(7,744)	(7,223)
All current and future participants	(61,212)	(56,477)	(50,760)	(48,065)	(44,894)
Present value of future expenditures in excess of future revenue	(12,294)[1]	(11,278)[2]	(9,157)[3]	(7,947)[4]	(7,677)[5]
Federal Hospital Insurance (Medicare Part A): [14]					
Revenue (Contributions and Dedicated Taxes) from:					
Participants who have attained eligibility age (age 65 and over)	301	302	262	248	209
Participants who have not attained eligibility age	8,147	7,929	7,581	7,216	6,348
Future participants	7,744	7,367	7,260	6,944	5,451
All current and future participants	16,192	15,598	15,104	14,408	12,008
Expenditures for Scheduled Future Benefits for:					
Participants who have attained eligibility age (age 65 and over)	(3,422)	(3,369)	(2,923)	(2,648)	(2,958)
Participants who have not attained eligibility age	(14,629)	(14,919)	(12,887)	(12,032)	(18,147)
Future participants	(2,913)	(2,891)	(2,546)	(2,411)	(4,673)
All current and future participants	(20,964)	(21,179)	(18,356)	(17,091)	(25,778)
Present value of future expenditures in excess of future revenue	(4,772)[1]	(5,581)[2]	(3,252)[3]	(2,683)[4]	(13,770)[5]
Federal Supplementary Medical Insurance (Medicare Part B): [14]					
Revenue (Premiums) from:					
Participants who have attained eligibility age (age 65 and over)	701	635	570	538	498
Participants who have not attained eligibility age	4,073	3,826	3,651	3,460	4,224
Future participants	944	884	865	839	1,270
All current and future participants	5,718	5,344	5,086	4,836	5,992
Expenditures for Scheduled Future Benefits for:					
Participants who have attained eligibility age (age 65 and over)	(2,887)	(2,646)	(2,343)	(2,166)	(2,142)
Participants who have not attained eligibility age	(15,075)	(14,303)	(13,489)	(12,587)	(16,342)
Future participants	(3,415)	(3,211)	(3,108)	(2,984)	(4,672)
All current and future participants	(21,377)	(20,159)	(18,940)	(17,737)	(23,156)
Present value of future expenditures in excess of future revenue [6]	(15,659)[1]	(14,815)[2]	(13,854)[3]	(12,901)[4]	(17,165)[5]

Totals may not equal the sum of components due to rounding.

The accompanying notes are an integral part of these financial statements.

United States Government
Statements of Social Insurance (Note 24), continued
Present Value of Long-Range (75 Years, except Black Lung) Actuarial Projections

(In billions of dollars)	2013	2012	2011	2010	2009
Federal Supplementary Medical Insurance (Medicare Part D): [14]					
Revenue (Premiums and State Transfers) from:					
Participants who have attained eligibility age (age 65 and over).....	184	179	173	165	140
Participants who have not attained eligibility age	1,491	1,510	1,608	1,626	1,442
Future participants...	665	661	703	694	618
All current and future participants..	2,340	2,349	2,484	2,486	2,199
Expenditures for Scheduled Future Benefits for:					
Participants who have attained eligibility age (age 65 and over).....	(722)	(694)	(695)	(646)	(595)
Participants who have not attained eligibility age	(5,871)	(5,866)	(6,438)	(6,355)	(6,144)
Future participants...	(2,617)	(2,568)	(2,817)	(2,714)	(2,632)
All current and future participants..	(9,211)	(9,128)	(9,950)	(9,715)	(9,371)
Present value of future expenditures in excess of future revenue [6]	(6,871)[1]	(6,778)[2]	(7,466)[3]	(7,229)[4]	(7,172)[5]
Railroad Retirement:					
Revenue (Contributions and Dedicated Taxes) from :					
Participants who have attained eligibility	7	7	6	5	5
Participants who have not attained eligibility	60	56	46	47	48
Future participants...	79	78	65	66	70
All current and future participants..	146	141	117	118	123
Expenditures for Scheduled Future Benefits for:					
Participants who have attained eligibility	(123)	(119)	(109)	(105)	(102)
Participants who have not attained eligibility	(96)	(95)	(86)	(88)	(91)
Future participants...	(34)	(34)	(28)	(27)	(30)
All current and future participants..	(253)	(248)	(223)	(220)	(223)
Present value of future expenditures in excess of future revenue [7]	(107)[1]	(107)[2]	(106)[3]	(103)[4]	(100)[5]
Black Lung (Part C):					
Present value of future revenue in excess of future expenditures [8]	5[9]	5[10]	5[11]	6[12]	6[13]
Total present value of future expenditures in excess of future revenue	(39,698)	(38,554)	(33,830)	(30,857)	(45,878)

Totals may not equal the sum of components due to rounding.

The accompanying notes are an integral part of these financial statements.

United States Government
Statements of Social Insurance (Note 24), continued
Present Value of Long-Range (75 Years, except Black Lung) Actuarial Projections

(In billions of dollars)	2013	2012	2011	2010	2009
Social Insurance Summary [14]					
Participants who have attained eligibility age:					
Revenue (e.g., Contributions and dedicated taxes).........................	2,101	1,970	1,737	1,628	1,427
Expenditures for scheduled future benefits	(18,175)	(16,662)	(14,688)	(13,661)	(13,262)
Present value of future expenditures in excess of future revenue	(16,074)	(14,692)	(12,951)	(12,033)	(11,835)
Participants who have not attained eligibility age:					
Revenue (e.g., Contributions and dedicated taxes)........................	38,362	36,024	33,620	32,263	30,621
Expenditures for scheduled future benefits	(76,262)	(72,936)	(66,942)	(63,287)	(70,931)
Present value of future expenditures in excess of future revenue	(37,900)	(36,912)	(33,322)	(31,024)	(40,310)
Closed-group – Total present value of future expenditures in excess of future revenue...	(53,974)	(51,604)	(46,272)	(43,057)	(52,145)
Future participants:					
Revenue (e.g., Contributions and dedicated taxes)........................	32,851	30,639	29,037	28,075	25,491
Expenditures for scheduled future benefits	(18,575)	(17,589)	(16,594)	(15,875)	(19,224)
Present value of future revenue in excess of future expenditure..	14,276	13,050	12,443	12,200	6,267
Open-group – Total present value of future expenditures in excess of future revenue	(39,698)	(38,554)	(33,830)	(30,857)	(45,878)

[1] The projection period is 1/1/2013-12/31/2087 and the valuation date is 1/1/2013.
[2] The projection period is 1/1/2012-12/31/2086 and the valuation date is 1/1/2012.
[3] The projection period is 1/1/2011-12/31/2085 and the valuation date is 1/1/2011.
[4] The projection period is 1/1/2010-12/31/2084 and the valuation date is 1/1/2010.
[5] The projection period is 1/1/2009-12/31/2083 and the valuation date is 1/1/2009.
[6] These amounts represent the present value of the future transfers from the General Fund of the Treasury to the Supplementary Medical Insurance Trust Fund. These future intragovernmental transfers are included as income in both HHS' and the Centers for Medicare & Medicaid Services' Financial Reports but are not income from the Governmentwide perspective of this report.
[7] These amounts approximate the present value of the future financial interchange and the future advances from the General Fund of the Treasury to the Social Security Equivalent Benefit Account and future repayments from the Social Security Equivalent Benefit Account to the General Fund (see discussion of Railroad Retirement Program in the unaudited required supplementary information section of this report). They are included as income in the Railroad Retirement Financial Report but are not income from the Governmentwide perspective of this report.
[8] Does not include interest expense accruing on the outstanding debt.
[9] The projection period is 9/30/2013-9/30/2040 and the valuation date is 9/30/2013.
[10] The projection period is 9/30/2012-9/30/2040 and the valuation date is 9/30/2012.
[11] The projection period is 9/30/2011-9/30/2040 and the valuation date is 9/30/2011.
[12] The projection period is 9/30/2010-9/30/2040 and the valuation date is 9/30/2010.
[13] The projection period is 9/30/2009-9/30/2040 and the valuation date is 9/30/2009.
[14] Current participants for the Social Security and Medicare programs are assumed to be the "closed-group" of individuals who are at least 15 years of age at the start of the projection period, and are participating as either taxpayers, beneficiaries, or both.

Totals may not equal the sum of components due to rounding.

The accompanying notes are an integral part of these financial statements.

United States Government
Statement of Changes in Social Insurance Amounts
for the Year Ended September 30, 2013 (Note 24)

(In billions of dollars)	Social Security[1]	Medicare HI[1]	Medicare SMI[1]	Other[2]	Total
Net present value (NPV) of future revenue less future expenditures for current and future participants (the "open group") over the next 75 years, beginning of the year	(11,278)	(5,581)	(21,593)	(102)	(38,554)
Reasons for changes in the NPV during the year:					
Changes in valuation period	(543)	(285)	(983)	(2)	(1,813)
Changes in demographic data and assumptions	(681)	724	(330)	2	(285)
Changes in economic data and assumptions	(273)	-	-	-	(273)
Changes in law or policy	(553)	31	2	-	(520)
Changes in methodology and programmatic data	1,034	-	-	-	1,034
Changes in economic and other health care assumptions	-	31	(125)	-	(94)
Change in projection base	-	308	499	-	807
Net change in open group measure	(1,016)	809	(937)	-	(1,144)
Open group measure, end of year	(12,294)	(4,772)	(22,530)	(102)	(39,698)

Totals may not equal the sum of components due to rounding.

The accompanying notes are an integral part of these financial statements.

1 Amounts represent changes between valuation dates 1/1/2012 and 1/1/2013.
2 Includes Railroad Retirement changes between valuation dates 1/1/2012 and 1/1/2013 and Black Lung changes between 9/30/2012 and 9/30/2013.

United States Government
Statement of Changes in Social Insurance Amounts
for the Year Ended September 30, 2012 (Note 24)

(In billions of dollars)	Social Security[1]	Medicare HI[1]	Medicare SMI[1]	Other[2]	Total
Net present value (NPV) of future revenue less future expenditures for current and future participants (the "open group") over the next 75 years, beginning of the year	(9,157)	(3,252)	(21,320)	(101)	(33,830)
Reasons for changes in the NPV during the year:					
Change in valuation period	(473)	(125)	(1,013)	(2)	(1,613)
Changes in demographic data and assumptions	(140)	(97)	752	3	518
Changes in economic data and assumptions	(1,037)	-	-	(2)	(1,039)
Changes in law or policy	-	153	40	-	193
Changes in methodology and programmatic data	(471)	-	-	-	(471)
Changes in economic and other health care assumptions	-	(2,546)	(55)	-	(2,601)
Change in projection base	-	286	3	-	289
Net change in open group measure	(2,121)	(2,329)	(273)	(1)	(4,724)
Open group measure, end of year	(11,278)	(5,581)	(21,593)	(102)	(38,554)

Totals may not equal the sum of components due to rounding.

The accompanying notes are an integral part of these financial statements.

[1] Amounts represent changes between valuation dates 1/1/2011 and 1/1/2012.
[2] Includes Railroad Retirement changes between valuation dates 1/1/2011 and 1/1/2012 and Black Lung changes between 9/30/2011 and 9/30/12.

United States Government
Notes to the Financial Statements
for the Years Ended September 30, 2013, and 2012

Note 1. Summary of Significant Accounting Policies

A. Reporting Entity

This *Financial Report* includes the financial status and activities of the executive branch, the legislative branch (the U.S. Senate and the U.S. House of Representatives are included on a cash basis), and the judicial branch (which also is included on a cash basis) of the Government. The legislative and judicial branches are included on a limited basis and are not required by law to submit financial statement information to Treasury. Appendix A of this report contains a list of organizations and agencies encompassed in the reporting entity for the *Financial Report*, as well as some organizations excluded from the reporting entity. Certain entities are excluded from the *Financial Report* because they are Government-Sponsored Enterprises (GSEs), such as the Federal National Mortgage Association (Fannie Mae) and the Federal Home Loan Mortgage Corporation (Freddie Mac). Other entities are excluded from the *Financial Report* because their activities are not included in the Federal budget, such as the Thrift Savings Fund and the Board of Governors of the Federal Reserve System.

During fiscal year 2008, the Government began a number of emergency economic measures relating to the economy that involved various financing programs. Key initiatives beginning in fiscal year 2008 involved programs concerning Fannie Mae and Freddie Mac (GSEs), provision of a credit facility for GSEs and Federal Home Loan Banks, purchase of Mortgage-Backed Securities (MBSs), and setup of a Money Market Guarantee Program (see Note 1.I—Investments in and Liabilities to Government-Sponsored Enterprises and Note 9—Investments in and Liabilities to Government-Sponsored Enterprises). The Emergency Economic Stabilization Act of 2008 (EESA) gave the Secretary of the Treasury temporary authority to purchase and guarantee assets from a wide range of financial institutions through the Troubled Asset Relief Program (TARP) (see Note 5—TARP Direct Loans and Equity Investments, Net).

Following U.S. Generally Accepted Accounting Principles (U.S. GAAP) for Federal entities, the Government has not consolidated into its financial statements the assets, liabilities, or results of operations of any financial organization or commercial entity in which Treasury holds either a direct, indirect, or beneficial equity investment. Even though some of the equity investments are significant, under Statement of Federal Financial Accounting Concepts (SFFAC) No. 2, these entities meet the criteria of paragraph 50 and do not appear in the Federal budget section "Federal Programs by Agency and Account." As such, these entities are not consolidated into the financial reports of the Government. However, the values of the investment in such entities are presented on the balance sheet.

Material intragovernmental transactions are eliminated in consolidation, except as described in the Other Information—Unmatched Transactions and Balances (see Note 1.T). The financial reporting period ends September 30 and is the same as used for the annual budget.

B. Basis of Accounting and Revenue Recognition

These financial statements were prepared using U.S. GAAP, primarily based on Statement of Federal Financial Accounting Standards (SFFAS). Under these principles:

- Expenses are generally recognized when incurred.
- Nonexchange revenues, including taxes, duties, fines, and penalties, are recognized when collected and adjusted for the change in net measurable and legally collectable amounts receivable. Related refunds and other offsets, including those that are measurable and legally payable, are netted against nonexchange revenue.
- Exchange (earned) revenues are recognized when the Government provides goods and services to the public for a price. Exchange revenues include user charges such as admission to Federal parks and premiums for certain Federal insurance.

The basis of accounting used for budgetary purposes, which is primarily on a cash and obligation basis and follows budgetary concepts and policies, differs from the basis of accounting used for the financial statements which follow U.S. GAAP. See the Reconciliations of Net Operating Cost and Unified Budget Deficit in the Financial Statements section.

The basis of accounting used and the detail of the basis for the Statement of Social Insurance (SOSI) and the Statement of Changes in Social Insurance (SCSIA) Amounts are covered in Note 24—Social Insurance.

New Standards Issued and Implemented

Beginning in fiscal year 2013, the Government implemented the requirements of new standards related to the reporting for: federal oil and gas resources, funds from dedicated collections, and asbestos-related clean-up costs. The new standards being implemented are:

- SFFAS No. 38, *Accounting for Federal Oil and Gas Resources*. SFFAS No. 38 requires the value of the Government's estimated petroleum royalties from the production of federal oil and gas proved reserves to be reported in a schedule of estimated federal oil and gas petroleum royalties. In addition, this standard requires the quantity of proved reserves, the average prices, and average royalty rates for oil and gas to be reported in a schedule. These schedules are to be presented in required supplementary information (RSI) as part of a discussion of all significant federal oil and gas resources under management by the Government. SFFAS No. 41 amended the effective date of SFFAS No. 38 to fiscal year 2013.

- SFFAS No. 43, *Funds from Dedicated Collections: Amending Statement of Federal Financial Accounting Standards 27, Identifying and Reporting Earmarked Funds*. SFFAS No. 43 changes the term "earmarked funds" to "funds from dedicated collections;" clarifies that at least one source of funds external to the Government must exist for a fund to qualify as a fund from dedicated collections; and adds an explicit exclusion for any fund established to account for pensions, other retirement benefits, other postemployment or other benefits provided for federal employees (civilian and military). In addition, the disclosure of such funds may be presented on a combined or consolidated basis and the presentation must be labeled accordingly. When implemented in fiscal year 2013, SFFAS No. 43 requires that prior period (i.e., fiscal year 2012) amounts displayed on the face of the financial statements and disclosed in notes be restated.

- Technical Bulletin (TB) 2006-1, *Recognition and Measurement of Asbestos-Related Cleanup Costs*. This technical bulletin clarifies the required reporting of liabilities and related expenses arising from asbestos-related cleanup costs. TBs 2009-1 and 2011-2 amended the effective date of TB 2006-1 to fiscal year 2013. TB 2006-1 requires that the unrecognized portion of estimated asbestos-related cleanup costs associated with general property, plant and equipment be disclosed, if material.

New Standards Issued and Not Yet Implemented

The Federal Accounting Standards Advisory Board (FASAB) issued the following new standards that are applicable to the *Financial Report*, but are not yet implemented at the Governmentwide level for fiscal year 2013:

- In July 2011, FASAB issued TB 2011-1, *Accounting for Federal Natural Resources Other than Oil and Gas*. TB 2011-1 clarifies that the Government should report the value of its estimated royalties and other revenue from federal natural resources that are (1) under lease, contract, or other long-term agreement, and (2) reasonably estimable as of the reporting date in RSI, consistent with the guidance contained in SFFAS No. 38. TB 2011-1 becomes effective in fiscal year 2014. The specific impact on implementing the new technical bulletin has not yet been determined.

- In April 2012, FASAB issued SFFAS No. 42, *Deferred Maintenance and Repairs, Amending SFFAS No. 6, 14, 29, and 32*. SFFAS No. 42 replaces the definition, measurement and reporting requirements for deferred maintenance and repairs established in SFFAS No. 6. SFFAS No. 42 paragraph 19 rescinds the current Governmentwide disclosures required for deferred maintenance established in SFFAS 32 paragraph 24. SFFAS 42 paragraph 16 requires the Governmentwide financial statements to disclose as RSI a description of what constitutes deferred maintenance and repairs (DM&R) and how it was measured; amounts of DM&R for each major category of property, plant and equipment; and a general reference to specific component entity reports for additional information. SFFAS No. 42 becomes effective in fiscal year 2015. The specific impact of implementing the new standard has not yet been determined.
- In January 2013, FASAB issued SFFAS No. 44, *Accounting for Impairment of General Property, Plant and Equipment Remaining in Use*. SFFAS No. 44 amends SFFAS No. 6, *Accounting for Property, Plant and Equipment*, by providing accounting and reporting requirements for partial impairments of general property, plant and equipment (G-PP&E) remaining in use and construction work-in-process. SFFAS No. 44 requires description of what constitutes G-PP&E impairment and the disclosure of related losses, if material. SFFAS No. 44 becomes effective in fiscal year 2015. The specific impact on implementing the new standard has not yet been determined.
- In July 2013, FASAB issued SFFAS No. 45, *Deferral of the Transition to Basic Information for Long-Term Projections; Amending SFFAS No. 36.* Issued on September 2009, SFFAS No. 36, *Comprehensive Long-Term Projections for the U.S. Government* required that certain information currently included as RSI be reclassified as basic information. This included the statement of long-term fiscal projections and related disclosures on the assumptions underlying the projections. SFFAS No. 45 amends the effective date for the reclassification to fiscal year 2014.

C. Accounts and Taxes Receivable

Accounts receivable represent claims to cash or other assets from entities outside the Government that arise from the sale of goods or services, duties, fines, certain license fees, recoveries, or other provisions of the law. Accounts receivable are reported net of an allowance for uncollectible accounts. An allowance is established when it is more likely than not the receivables will not be totally collected. The allowance method varies among the agencies in the Government and is usually based on past collection experience and is re-estimated periodically as needed. Methods include statistical sampling of receivables, specific identification and intensive analysis of each case, aging methodologies, and percentage of total receivables based on historical collection.

Taxes receivable consist primarily of uncollected tax assessments, penalties, and interest when taxpayers have agreed or a court has determined the assessments are owed. The Balance Sheet does not include unpaid assessments when taxpayers or a court have not agreed that the amounts are owed (compliance assessments) or the Government does not expect further collections due to factors such as the taxpayer's death, bankruptcy, or insolvency (write-offs). Taxes receivable are reported net of an allowance for the estimated portion deemed to be uncollectible. The allowance for doubtful accounts is based on projections of collectibles from a statistical sample of unpaid tax assessments.

D. Loans Receivable, and Loan Guarantee Liabilities, Net

Direct loans obligated and loan guarantees committed after fiscal year 1991 are reported based on the present value of the net cashflows estimated over the life of the loan or guarantee. The difference between the outstanding principal of the direct loans and the present value of their net cash inflows is recognized as a subsidy cost allowance. The present value of estimated net cashflows of the loan guarantees is recognized as a liability for loan guarantees.

The subsidy expense for direct or guaranteed loans disbursed during a fiscal year is the present value of estimated net cashflows for those loans or guarantees. A subsidy expense also is recognized for modifications made during the year to loans and guarantees outstanding and for reestimates made as of the end of the fiscal year to the subsidy allowances or loan guarantee liability for loans and guarantees outstanding.

Direct loans obligated and loan guarantees committed before fiscal year 1992 are valued under two different methodologies within the Government: the allowance-for-loss method and the present-value method. Under the allowance-for-loss method, the outstanding principal of direct loans is reduced by an allowance for uncollectible amounts; the liability for loan guarantees is the amount the agency estimates would more likely than not require future cash outflow to pay default claims. Under the present-value method, the outstanding principal of direct loans is reduced by an allowance equal to the difference between the outstanding principal and the present value of the expected net cashflows. The liability for loan guarantees is the present value of expected net cash outflows due to the loan guarantees.

E. TARP Direct Loans and Equity Investments, Net

Troubled Asset Relief Program (TARP) equity investments are accounted for at fair value, which is defined as the estimated amount of proceeds that would be received if the equity investments were sold to a market participant in an orderly transaction. Consistent with the present value accounting concepts embedded in SFFAS No. 2, *Accounting for Direct Loans and Loan Guarantees*, TARP direct loans and equity investments, net, disbursed and outstanding are recognized as assets at the net present value of their estimated future cashflows and outstanding asset guarantees are recognized as liabilities or assets at the net present value of their estimated future cashflows. Market risk is considered in the calculation and determination of the estimated net present values.

The subsidy allowance for TARP's direct loans and equity investments represents the difference between the face value of the outstanding direct loan and equity investment balance and the net present value of the expected future cashflows and is reported as an adjustment to the face value of the direct loan or equity investment.

The recorded subsidy allowance for a direct loan or equity investment is based on a set of assumptions regarding estimated future cashflows.

The Government used the following methodologies for valuation of the TARP direct loans and equity investments:

- The estimated future cashflows for TARP direct loans were derived using analytical models that estimate the cashflows to and from the Government over the life of the loan. These cashflows include the scheduled principal, interest, and other payments to the Government, including estimated proceeds from equity interest obtained or additional notes. These models also include estimates of default and recoveries, incorporating the value of any collateral provided by the contract. The probability and timing of default and losses relating to a default are estimated by using applicable historical data when available, or publicly available proxy data, including credit rating agency historical performance data. The models include an adjustment for market risk which is intended to capture the risk of unexpected losses, but are not intended to represent fair value, i.e., the proceeds that would be expected to be received if the loans were sold to a market participant.
- TARP preferred stock cashflows are projected using an analytical model developed to incorporate the risk of losses associated with adverse events, such as failure of the institution or increases in market interest rates. The model estimates how cashflows vary depending on: (1) current interest rates, which may affect the decision whether to repay the preferred stock; and (2) the strength of a financial institution's assets. Inputs to the model include institution specific accounting data obtained from regulatory filings, an institution's stock price volatility, and historical bank failure information, as well as market prices of comparable securities trading in the market. The Government estimates the values and projects the cashflows of warrants using an option-pricing approach based on the current stock price and its volatility. Investments in common stock which are exchange traded are valued at the market price. The result of using market prices, either quoted prices for the identical asset or quoted prices for comparable assets, is that the equity investments are recorded at estimated fair value.

For more details on TARP, see Note 5—TARP Direct Loans and Equity Investments, Net.

F. Inventories and Related Property

Inventory is tangible personal property that is (1) held for sale, principally to Federal agencies, (2) in the process of production for sale, or (3) to be consumed in the production of goods for sale or in the provision of services for a fee. SFFAS No. 3, *Accounting for Inventory and Related Property*, requires inventories held for sale and held in reserve for future sale within the Government to be valued using either historical cost or latest acquisition cost (LAC). Historical cost methods include first-in-first-out, weighted average, and moving average. When LAC methods are used, the inventory is revalued periodically and an allowance account should be established for unrealized holding gains and losses.

The Department of Defense (DOD) holds the majority of the inventories within the Government and uses standard price and moving average cost methods for valuing most of its inventory. To a lesser degree, DOD also uses first-in-first-out methods and LAC methods adjusted for holding gains and losses to approximate the historical cost of resale inventory items remaining in its legacy system. DOD is continuing to transition inventories currently accounted for under the LAC methods, to be accounted for under the moving average cost methods. However, DOD still has issues supporting inventory valuations.

When using historical cost valuation, estimated repair costs reduce the value of inventory held for repair. Excess, obsolete, and unserviceable inventories are valued at estimated net realizable value. When latest acquisition cost is used to value inventory held for sale, it is adjusted for holding gains and losses in order to approximate historical cost.

Related property includes commodities, seized monetary instruments, forfeited and foreclosed property, raw materials and work in process. Operating materials and supplies are valued at historical cost, latest acquisition cost, and standard price using the purchase and consumption method of accounting. Operating materials and supplies that are valued at latest acquisition cost and standard pricing are not adjusted for holding gains and losses.

G. Property, Plant, and Equipment

PP&E consists of tangible assets including buildings, equipment, construction in progress, and internal use software, assets acquired through capital leases, including leasehold improvements, and other assets used to provide goods and services.

PP&E used in Government operations are carried at acquisition cost, with the exception of DOD military equipment (e.g., ships, aircraft, combat vehicles, and weapons) and some National Aeronautics and Space Administration (NASA) equipment. DOD military equipment is valued at estimated historical costs, which are calculated using internal DOD records. DOD identified the universe of military equipment by accumulating information relating to program funding and associated military equipment, equipment useful life, and program acquisitions and disposals to create a baseline. The equipment baseline is updated using expenditure information and information related to acquisition and logistics to identify acquisitions and disposals. NASA also uses estimates of historical cost to value some of its equipment for which historical cost information is not readily available, such as components of the International Space Station.

All PP&E is capitalized if the acquisition costs (or estimated acquisition cost for DOD) are in excess of capitalization thresholds that vary considerably between the Federal entities. Depreciation and amortization expense applies to PP&E reported on the balance sheets except for land, unlimited duration land rights and construction in progress. Depreciation and amortization are recognized using the straight-line method over the estimated useful lives of the assets. All PP&E are assigned useful lives depending on their category. The cost of acquisition, betterment, or reconstruction of all multi-use heritage assets is capitalized as general PP&E and is depreciated. Construction in progress is used for the accumulation of the cost of construction or major renovation of fixed assets during the construction period. The assets are transferred out of construction in progress when the project is substantially completed. Internal use software includes purchased commercial off-the-shelf software, contractor-developed software, and software internally developed.

For financial reporting purposes, other than multi-use heritage assets, stewardship assets are not recorded as part of PP&E. Stewardship Assets consist of public domain land (Stewardship Land) and Heritage Assets. Examples of stewardship land include national parks, wildlife refuges, national forests, and other lands of national and historical significance. Heritage assets include national monuments, and historical sites that among other characteristics are of historical, natural, cultural, educational or artistic significance. Stewardship land and most heritage assets are considered priceless and irreplaceable, and as such they are measured in physical units with no financial value assigned to them. Some heritage assets have been designated as multi-use heritage assets, for example the White House, the predominant use of which is in government operations. For more details on stewardship assets, see Note 25—Stewardship Land and Heritage Assets.

H. Debt and Equity Securities

Debt and equity securities are classified as held-to-maturity, available-for-sale, and trading. Held-to-maturity debt and equity securities are reported at amortized cost, net of unamortized premiums and discounts. Available-for-sale debt and equity securities are reported at fair value. Trading debt and equity securities are reported at fair value.

I. Investments in and Liabilities to Government-Sponsored Enterprises

The senior preferred stock and associated common stock warrant (warrant(s)) in GSEs are presented at their fair value. Treasury has an annual process, as of September 30th, to provide a "sufficiently reliable" estimate of the outstanding commitments, if any, in order for Treasury to calculate the remaining liability in accordance with SFFAS No. 5, *Accounting for Liabilities of the Federal Government*. The process incorporates various forecasts, projections, and cash-flow analyses to develop an estimate of the potential liability. These valuations are performed on the senior preferred stock and warrants and any changes in valuation, including impairment, are recorded and disclosed in accordance with SFFAS No. 7, *Accounting for Revenue and Other Financing Sources*. Since the valuation is an annual process, the changes in valuation of the senior preferred stock and warrants are deemed usual and recurring. Accordingly, changes in valuation are recorded as an exchange transaction which is either an expense or revenue. Since the costs of the senior preferred stock and warrants are reflected in exchange transactions, any change in valuation is also recorded as an exchange transaction.

The *Housing and Economic Recovery Act of 2008 (HERA)* established the Federal Housing Finance Agency (FHFA), which was created to enhance authority over the GSEs, and provide the Secretary of the Treasury with certain authorities to support the financial stability of the GSEs. In September 2008, Treasury entered into a Senior Preferred Stock Purchase Agreement (SPSPA) with each GSE. Based on U.S. GAAP, these contingent commitments, predicated on the future occurrence of any stockholders' equity net deficits of the GSEs, at the end of any reporting quarter are potential liabilities of Treasury. The potential liabilities to the GSEs are assessed annually and recorded at the gross amount. For more detailed information on investments in and liabilities to GSEs, refer to Note 9—Investments in and Liabilities to Government-Sponsored Enterprises.

J. Federal Debt

Accrued interest on Treasury securities held by the public is recorded as an expense when incurred, instead of when paid. Certain Treasury securities are issued at a discount or premium. These discounts and premiums are amortized over the term of the security using an interest method for all long-term securities and the straight line method for short-term securities. Treasury also issues Treasury Inflation-Protected Securities (TIPS). The principal for TIPS is adjusted daily over the life of the security based on the Consumer Price Index (CPI) for all Urban Consumers.

K. Federal Employee and Veteran Benefits Payable

Generally, Federal employee and veteran benefits payable are recorded during the time employee services are rendered. The related liabilities for defined benefit pension plans, veterans' compensation and burial benefits, post-retirement health benefits, and post-retirement life insurance benefits, are recorded at estimated present value of future benefits, less any estimated present value of future normal cost contributions. Normal cost is the portion of the actuarial present value of projected benefits allocated as an expense for employee services rendered in the current year. Actuarial gains and losses (and prior service cost, if any) are recognized immediately in the year they occur without amortization.

The Department of Veterans Affairs (VA) also provides certain veterans and/or their dependents with pension benefits, based on annual eligibility reviews, if the veteran died or was disabled for nonservice-related causes. The actuarial present value of the future liability for these VA pension benefits is a nonexchange transaction and is not required to be recorded on the Balance Sheet. These benefits are expenses when benefits are paid rather than when employee services are rendered.

The liabilities for Federal Employees' Compensation Act (workers compensation) benefits are recorded at estimated present value of future benefits for injuries and deaths that have already been incurred.

Gains and losses from changes in long-term assumptions used to estimate Federal employee pensions, Other Retirement Benefits (ORB), and Other Postemployment Benefits (OPEB) liabilities are reflected separately on the Statement of Net Cost and the components of the expense related to Federal employee pension, ORB, and OPEB liabilities are disclosed in Note 13—Federal Employee and Veteran Benefits Payable as prescribed by SFFAS No. 33. In addition, SFFAS No. 33 also provides a standard for selecting the discount rate assumption for present value estimates of Federal employee pension, ORB, and OPEB liabilities.

L. Environmental and Disposal Liabilities

Environmental and disposal liabilities are recorded at the estimated current cost of removing, containing, treating, and/or disposing of radioactive waste, hazardous waste, chemical and nuclear weapons, and other environmental contaminations, including asbestos, assuming the use of current technology. Hazardous waste is a solid, liquid, or gaseous waste that, because of its quantity or concentration, presents a potential hazard to human health or the environment. Remediation consists of removal, decontamination, decommissioning, site restoration, site monitoring, closure and post-closure cost, treatment, and/or safe containment. Where technology does not exist to clean up radioactive or hazardous waste, only the estimable portion of the liability, typically monitoring and safe containment is recorded.

M. Insurance and Guarantee Program Liabilities

Insurance and guarantee programs provide protection to individuals or entities against specified risks except for those specifically covered by Federal employee and veteran benefits, social insurance, and loan guarantee programs. Insurance and guarantee program funds are commonly held in revolving funds in the Government and losses sustained by participants are paid from these funds. Many of these programs receive appropriations to pay excess claims and/or have authority to borrow from the Treasury. The values of insurance and guarantee program liabilities are particularly sensitive to changes in underlying estimates and assumptions. Insurance and guarantee programs with recognized liabilities in future periods (i.e., liabilities that extend beyond one year) are reported at their actuarial present value.

N. Deferred Maintenance and Repairs

Deferred maintenance and repairs are maintenance and repairs that were not performed when they should have been or scheduled maintenance and repairs that were delayed or postponed. Maintenance is the act of keeping fixed assets in acceptable condition, including preventative maintenance, normal repairs, and other activities needed to preserve the assets, so they continue to provide acceptable service and achieve their expected life. Maintenance and repairs exclude activities aimed at expanding the capacity of assets or otherwise upgrading them to serve needs different from those originally intended. Deferred maintenance and repairs expenses are not accrued in the Statements of Net Cost or recognized as liabilities on the Balance Sheet. However, deferred maintenance and repairs information is disclosed in the Unaudited Required Supplementary Information section of this report.

O. Contingent Liabilities

Liabilities for contingencies are recognized on the Balance Sheet when both:
- A past transaction or event has occurred, and
- A future outflow or other sacrifice of resources is probable and measurable.

The estimated contingent liability may be a specific amount or a range of amounts. If some amount within the range is a better estimate than any other amount within the range, then that amount is recognized. If no amount within the range is a better estimate than any other amount, then the minimum amount in the range is recognized and the range is disclosed.

Contingent liabilities that do not meet the above criteria for recognition, but for which there is at least a reasonable possibility that a loss may be incurred, are disclosed in Note 20—Contingencies.

P. Commitments

In the normal course of business, the Government has a number of unfulfilled commitments that may require the use of its financial resources. Note 21—Commitments describes the components of the Government's actual commitments that are disclosed due to their nature and/or their amount. They include long-term leases, undelivered orders, and other commitments.

Q. Social Insurance

A liability for social insurance programs (Social Security, Medicare, Railroad Retirement, Black Lung, and Unemployment) is recognized for any unpaid amounts currently due as of the reporting date. No liability is recognized for future benefit payments not yet due. For further information, see the Unaudited Required Supplementary Information—Social Insurance section, and Note 24—Social Insurance.

R. Funds from Dedicated Collections

Generally, funds from dedicated collections are financed by specifically identified revenues, provided to the Government by non-federal sources, often supplemented by other financing sources that remain available over time. These specifically identified revenues and other financing sources are required by statute to be used for designated activities, benefits, or purposes, and must be accounted for separately from the Government's general revenues. The three required criteria for a fund from dedicated collections are:

- A statute committing the Government to use specifically identified revenues and/or other financing sources that are originally provided to the Government by a non-federal source only for designated activities, benefits or purposes;
- Explicit authority for the fund to retain revenues and/or other financing sources not used in the current period for future use to finance the designated activities, benefits, or purposes; and
- A requirement to account for and report on the receipt, use, and retention of the revenues and/or other financing sources that distinguishes the fund from the Government's general revenues.

For more details on funds from dedicated collections, see Note 22—Funds from Dedicated Collections.

S. Related Party Transactions

Federal Reserve System

The Federal Reserve System (FR System) was created by Congress under the Federal Reserve Act of 1913. The FR System consists of the Federal Reserve Board of Governors (Board), the Federal Open Market Committee (FOMC), and the FRBs. Collectively, the FR System serves as the nation's central bank and is responsible for formulating and conducting monetary policy, issuing and distributing currency (Federal Reserve Notes), supervising and regulating financial institutions, providing nationwide payments systems (including large-dollar transfers of funds, Automated Clearing House (ACH) operations, and check collection), providing certain financial services to federal agencies and fiscal principals, and serving as the Government's bank. Monetary policy includes actions undertaken by the FR System that influence the availability and cost of money and credit as a means of helping to promote national economic goals. The FR System also conducts operations in foreign markets in order to counter disorderly conditions in exchange markets or to meet other needs specified by the FOMC to carry out its central bank responsibilities. The FR System is not included in the federal budget. It is considered an independent central bank, and its decisions are not ratified by the executive branch of the Federal Government.

The Government interacts with the FRBs in a variety of ways, including the following:

- The FRBs serve as the Government's fiscal agent and depositary, executing banking and other financial transactions on the Government's behalf. The Government reimburses the FRBs for these services, the cost of which is included on the Statements of Net Cost

- The FRBs hold Treasury and other federal securities in the FRBs' System Open Market Account (SOMA) for the purpose of conducting monetary policy (Note 12—Federal Debt Securities Held by the Public and Accrued Interest)
- The FRBs hold gold certificates issued by the Government in which the certificates are collateralized by gold (Note 2—Cash and Other Monetary Assets)
- The FRBs hold Special Drawing Rights (SDR) certificates issued by the Government which are collateralized by SDRs (see Note 2—Cash and Other Monetary Assets)
- The FRBs are required by Board policy to transfer their excess earnings to the Government

The Government also consults with the FR System on matters affecting the economy and certain financial stability activities (Note 4—Loans Receivable and Loan Guarantee Liabilities, Net, and Note 5—Troubled Asset Relief Program (TARP)—Direct Loans and Equity Investments, Net). The above financial activities involving the Government are accounted for and disclosed in the Government consolidated financial statements. In accordance with SFFAC No. 2, *Entity and Display*, the FR System's assets, liabilities, and operations are not consolidated into the Government's financial statements, and are, therefore, not a part of the reporting entity.

Federal Reserve System Structure

The Board is an independent organization governed by seven members who are appointed by the President and confirmed by the Senate. The full term of a Board member is 14 years, and the appointments are staggered so that one term expires on January 31 of each even-numbered year. The Board has a number of supervisory and regulatory responsibilities for institutions including, among others, state-chartered banks that are members of the FR System, bank holding companies, and savings and loan holding companies. In addition, the Board has general supervisory responsibilities for the 12 FRBs, and issues currency (Federal Reserve Notes) to the FRBs for distribution. The FOMC is comprised of the seven Board members and five of the 12 FRB presidents, and is charged with formulating and conducting monetary policy primarily through open market operations (the purchase and sale of certain securities in the open market), the principal tool of national monetary policy. These operations affect the amount of reserve balances available to depository institutions, thereby influencing overall monetary and credit conditions. The 12 FRBs are chartered under the Federal Reserve Act, which requires each member bank to own the capital stock of its FRB. Supervision and control of each FRB is exercised by a board of directors, of which three are appointed by the Board of Governors of the FR System, and six are elected by their member banks.

The FRBs participate in formulating and conducting monetary policy, distribute currency and coin, and serve as fiscal agents for the Government, other federal agencies and fiscal principals. Additionally, the FRBs provide short-term loans to depository institutions and loans to participants in programs or facilities with broad-based eligibility in unusual and exigent circumstances when approved by the Board.

Federal Reserve System Assets and Liabilities

The FRBs hold Treasury and other securities in the SOMA for the purpose of conducting monetary policy. Treasury securities held by the FRBs totaled $1,930.2 billion and $1,646.8 billion at September 30, 2013, and 2012, respectively (Note 12—Federal Debt Securities Held by the Public and Accrued Interest). These assets are generally subject to the same market (principally interest-rate) and credit risks as other financial instruments. In the open market, the FR System purchases and sells Treasury securities as a mechanism for controlling the money supply.

The FRBs have deposit liabilities with Treasury and depository institutions. The FRBs issue Federal Reserve Notes, the circulating currency of the United States, which are collateralized by the Treasury securities and other assets held by the FRBs. Financial and other information concerning the FR System, including financial statements for the Board and the FRBs, may be obtained at http://www.federalreserve.gov.

FRB Residual Earnings Transferred to the Government

FRBs generate income from interest earned on securities, reimbursable services provided to federal agencies, and the provision of priced services to depository institutions, as specified by the Monetary Control Act of 1980. Although the FRBs generate earnings from carrying out open market operations (via the earnings on securities held in the SOMA account), their execution of these operations is for the purpose of accomplishing monetary policy rather than generating earnings. Each FRB is required by Board policy to transfer to the Government its residual (or excess) earnings, after providing for the cost of operations, payment of dividends, and reservation of an amount necessary to equate surplus with paid-in capital. These residual earnings may vary due to, among other things, changes in the SOMA balance levels that may occur in conducting monetary policy. The FRB residual earnings of $75.8 billion and $82.0 billion for fiscal years ended September 30, 2013, and 2012, respectively, are reported as other taxes and receipts on the Statements of Operations and Changes in Net Position. Accounts and taxes receivables, net, includes a receivable for FRB's residual earnings which represents the earnings due to the Treasury General Fund as of September 30, but not collected by the Treasury General Fund until after the end of the month. As of September 30, 2013, and 2012, interest receivable on FRB's residual earnings are $3.1 billion and $2.3 billion, respectively (Note 3—Accounts and Taxes Receivables, Net).

Other Related Parties

The Government generally does not guarantee payment for the liabilities of GSEs such as Fannie Mae, Freddie Mac, or the Federal Home Loan Banks, which are privately owned. For further details regarding investments in or liabilities to Fannie Mae and Freddie Mac, see Note 9—Investments in and Liabilities to Government-Sponsored Enterprises.

The Secretary of Transportation has possession of two long term notes with the National Railroad Passenger Service Corporation (more commonly referred to as Amtrak). The first note is for $4 billion and matures in 2975 and the second note is for $1.1 billion and matures in 2082 with renewable 99 year terms. Interest is not accruing on these notes as long as the current financial structure of Amtrak remains unchanged. If the financial structure of Amtrak changes, both principal and accrued interest are due and payable. The Department of Transportation (DOT) does not record the notes in its financial statements because the present value of the notes was immaterial at September 30, 2013. These notes were discounted according to rates published in OMB M-13-4, Appendix C, *Discount Rates for Cost Effectiveness Lease Purchase and Related Analyses* with maturity dates of 2975 and 2082.

In addition, DOT has possession of all the preferred stock shares (109.4 million) of Amtrak. Congress, through DOT, has continued to fund Amtrak since approximately 1972; originally through grants, then, beginning in 1981, through the purchase of preferred stock, and then through grants again after 1997. The *Amtrak Reform and Accountability Act of 1997* changed the structure of the preferred stock by rescinding the voting rights with respect to the election of the Board of Directors and by eliminating the preferred stock's liquidation preference over the common stock. The Act also eliminated further issuance of preferred stock to DOT. DOT does not record the Amtrak preferred stock in its financial statements because, under the Corporation's current financial structure, the preferred shares do not have a liquidation preference over the common shares, the preferred shares do not have any voting rights, and dividends are neither declared nor in arrears.

Amtrak is not a department, agency or instrumentality of the Government or DOT. The nine members of Amtrak's Board of Directors are appointed by the President of the United States and are subject to confirmation by the U.S. Senate. Once appointed, Board members, as a whole, act independently without the consent of the Government or any of its officers to set Amtrak policy, determine its budget and decide operational issues. The Secretary of Transportation is statutorily appointed to the nine-member Board. Traditionally, the Secretary of Transportation has designated the Administrator of the Federal Railroad Administration to represent the Secretary at Board meetings.

The Export-Import Bank of the United States (Ex-Im Bank) has contractual agreements with the Private Export Funding Corporation (PEFCO). PEFCO, which is owned by a consortium of private-sector banks, industrial companies and financial services institutions, makes medium-term and long-term fixed-rate and variable-rate loans to foreign borrowers to purchase U.S.-made equipment when such loans are not available from traditional private sector lenders on competitive terms. Ex-Im Bank's credit and guarantee agreement with PEFCO extends through December 31, 2020. Through its contractual agreements with PEFCO, Ex-Im Bank exercises a broad measure of supervision over PEFCO's major financial management decisions, including approval of both the terms of individual loan commitments and the terms of PEFCO's long-term debt issues, and is entitled to representation at all meetings of PEFCO's board of directors, advisory board and its exporters' council.

The contractual agreements provide that Ex-Im Bank will (1) guarantee the due and punctual payment of principal and interest on export loans made by PEFCO and (2) guarantee the due and punctual payment of interest on PEFCO's long-term secured debt obligations when requested by PEFCO. Related to the amounts for Ex-Im Bank as shown in Note 4—Loans Receivable and Loan Guarantee Liabilities, Net, these guarantees to PEFCO, aggregating $7.5 billion and $6.1 billion at September 30, 2013 and 2012, respectively, are included within the principal amounts guaranteed by the United States. The allowance related to these transactions is included within the guaranteed loan liability. Ex-Im Bank received fees totaling $0.04 billion and $0.03 billion for fiscal years 2013 and 2012 respectively, for the agreements, which are included as earned revenue on the Statements of Net Cost.

T. Unmatched Transactions and Balances

The reconciliation of the change in net position requires that the difference between ending and beginning net position equals the difference between revenue and cost, plus or minus prior-period adjustments.

The unmatched transactions and balances are needed to bring the change in net position into balance. The primary factors affecting this out of balance situation are:

- Unmatched intragovernmental transactions and balances between federal agencies,
- Unmatched intragovernmental transactions and balances between federal agencies and General Fund
- Errors and restatements in federal agencies' reporting.

Refer to the Other Information (unaudited) —Unmatched Transactions and Balances for detailed information.

U. Reclassifications

Certain amounts were reclassified in the fiscal year 2012 consolidated statement of net cost due to a change in the methodology for cost allocation. The allocation of federal employee benefit expenses from OPM to all other agencies formerly included an allocation of non-normal costs (e.g., interest cost, actuarial gains/losses, etc.) included within OPM's pre-allocation gross cost related to its pension, other retirement benefit, and other post-employment benefit programs. In addition, the allocation was formerly based on OPM provided data on average wages and headcount for each agency. Beginning in fiscal year 2013, and retroactive to fiscal year 2012, only normal costs (i.e., the full benefit program expense recognized by each agency) will be included in this allocation and will be based on agencies' financial reporting instead of the OPM provided wage and headcount data. This is considered a change in accounting method with regard to allocation of federal employee benefit cost. This change in methodology did not affect fiscal year 2012 total gross and net cost reflected on the consolidated statements of net cost as published in the fiscal year 2012 *Financial Report*.

As a result of this cost allocation methodology change, with the exception of OPM, USPS and DHS, the gross and net cost for the agencies decreased collectively by $43.2 billion, with the largest decrease being DOD's gross and net cost decrease of $15.1 billion. USPS's and DHS's gross and net cost increased by $8.7 billion and $0.7 billion, respectively. The majority of the increase was due to these agencies recognizing federal benefit expense greater than what was allocated using the prior allocation methodology. Additionally, the $8.7 billion increase for USPS also includes $3.1 billion of imputed costs that were not reflected in the former cost allocation methodology for USPS. The OPM increase of $33.8 billion is primarily due to the $76.9 billion of OPM's fiscal year 2012 non-normal costs (primarily interest and actuarial gains due to experience) that are now completely within OPM's gross and net cost. These non-normal costs are offset by current health and life insurance benefit expense of $30.9 billion and imputed costs of $3.7 billion (including the $3.1 billion imputed cost for USPS mentioned above) that were not reflected in the former cost allocation methodology.

Certain loan balances separately reported in the prior year have been reclassified into the "All Other Programs" line. Additionally, Education's Perkins and Facilities Loans, which were previously reported as part of Federal Direct Student Loans, were reclassified into the "All Other Programs" line. As a result, the Federal Direct Student Loan Receivable, Net, was reduced by $1.2 billion and the All Other Programs, Net, for prior year, was increased by $38.0 billion. In addition, "All Other Guaranteed Loan Programs" under Loan Guarantee Liabilities for the prior year also increased by $2.8 billion as a result of reclassification of loans which were previously reported separately. The prior year's subsidy expense related to "All Other Programs Loans" and "All Other Loan Programs" decreased by $0.2 billion and increased by $0.1 billion, respectively.

V. Restatements

In accordance with the implementation of SFFAS No. 43, retroactive to fiscal year 2012, certain funds previously classified in fiscal year 2012 as earmarked funds were excluded from the reporting requirements of SFFAS No. 43. Therefore, the fiscal year 2012 amounts for funds from dedicated collections were restated in the consolidated statements of operations and changes in net position and in Note 22—Funds from Dedicated Collections, and the net position attributable to funds from dedicated collections and funds other than those from dedicated collections were restated on the consolidated balance sheet.

W. Fiduciary Activities

Fiduciary activities are the collection or receipt, and the management, protection, accounting, investment and disposition by the Government of cash or other assets in which non-Federal individuals or entities have an ownership interest that the Government must uphold. Fiduciary cash and other fiduciary assets are not assets of the Government and are not recognized on the Balance Sheet. See Note 23—Fiduciary Activities, for further information.

X. Use of Estimates

The Government has made certain estimates and assumptions relating to the reporting of assets, liabilities, revenues, expenses, and the disclosure of contingent liabilities to prepare these financial statements. There are a large number of factors that affect these assumptions and estimates, which are inherently subject to substantial uncertainty arising from the likelihood of future changes in general economic, regulatory and market conditions. As such, actual results will differ from these estimates and such differences may be material.

Significant transactions subject to estimates include loans receivable, TARP direct loans and equity investments; investments in other non-Federal securities (including GSEs and foreign and domestic public entities) and related impairment, if any; tax receivables; loan guarantees; depreciation; actuarial liabilities; contingent legal liabilities; environmental and disposal liabilities; credit reform subsidy costs; and insurance and guarantee program liabilities.

The Government recognizes the sensitivity of credit reform modeling to slight changes in some model assumptions and uses regular review of model factors, statistical modeling, and annual reestimates to reflect the most accurate cost of the credit programs to the U.S. Government. *Federal Credit Reform Act of 1990* (FCRA) loan receivables and loan guarantees are disclosed in Note 4—Loans Receivable and Loan Guarantee Liabilities, Net. Additionally, all TARP credit activity, including investments in common and preferred stock and loans and asset guarantees, are also subject to credit reform accounting (see Note 5—TARP Direct Loans and Equity Investments, Net).

The forecasted future cashflows used to determine credit reform amounts as of September 30, 2013, and 2012, are sensitive to slight changes in model assumptions, such as general economic conditions, specific stock price volatility of the entities in which the Government has an equity interest, estimates of expected default, and prepayment rates. Forecasts of future financial results have inherent uncertainty and the TARP Direct Loans and Equity Investments, Net line item as of September 30, 2013, and 2012, is reflective of relatively illiquid, troubled assets whose values are particularly sensitive to future economic conditions and other assumptions.

The GSE senior preferred stock purchase agreements (SPSPAs) provide that the Government will fund the GSEs, if needed at the end of any quarter. The FHFA, acting as the conservator, determines whether the liabilities of either GSE, individually, exceed its respective assets. Valuation analyses are performed to attempt to provide a "sufficiently reliable" estimate of the outstanding commitment which is recorded as a liability in accordance with SFFAS No. 5. As part of the valuation process, Treasury prepared a series of long-range financial forecasts through 2038 to determine the implied amount of total liability. In fiscal year 2012, the SPSPAs were amended. For more detailed information on investments in and liabilities to GSEs and the amended SPSPAs, see Note 9—Investments in and Liabilities to Government-Sponsored Enterprises.

Y. Credit Risk

Credit risk is the potential, no matter how remote, for financial loss from a failure of a borrower or a counterparty to perform in accordance with underlying contractual obligations. The Government takes on credit risk when it makes direct loans or credits to foreign entities or becomes exposed to institutions which engage in financial transactions with foreign countries.

The Government also takes on credit risk related to committed, but undisbursed direct loans, investment commitment to GSEs, investments, loans, and asset guarantees of the TARP, guarantee of money market funds, and the Terrorism Risk Insurance Program. Except for the Terrorism Risk Insurance Program, these activities focus on the underlying problems in the credit markets, and the ongoing instability in those markets exposes the Government to potential unknown costs and losses. The extent of the risk assumed is described in more detail in the notes to the financial statements, and where applicable, is factored into credit reform models and reflected in fair value measurements.

Note 2. Cash and Other Monetary Assets

Cash and Other Monetary Assets as of September 30, 2013, and 2012

(In billions of dollars)	2013	2012
Unrestricted cash:		
Cash held by Treasury for Governmentwide operations	82.8	79.2
Other	6.3	5.9
Restricted cash	21.5	20.9
Total Cash	110.6	106.0
International Monetary assets	72.9	76.8
Gold and silver	11.1	11.1
Foreign Currency	11.7	12.3
Total cash and other monetary assets	206.3	206.2

Unrestricted cash includes cash held by Treasury for Governmentwide operations (Operating Cash) and all other unrestricted cash held by the Federal agencies. Operating Cash represents balances from tax collections, other revenue, Federal debt receipts, and other various receipts net of cash outflows for budget outlays and other payments. Treasury checks outstanding are netted against Operating Cash until they are cleared by the Federal Reserve System. Other unrestricted cash not included in Treasury's Operating Cash balance includes balances representing cash, cash equivalents, and other funds held by agencies, such as undeposited collections, deposits in transit, demand deposits, amounts held in trust, imprest funds, and amounts representing the balances of petty cash. Operating Cash held by the Treasury increased by $3.6 billion (an increase of approximately 5 percent) in fiscal year 2013 due to Treasury's investment and borrowing decisions to manage the balance and timing of the Government's cash position.

Restricted cash is restricted due to the imposition on cash deposits by law, regulation, or agreement. Restricted cash is primarily composed of cash held by the Executive Office of the President (EOP) Foreign Military Sales program. The Foreign Military Sales program included $20.6 billion and $20.1 billion as of September 30, 2013, and 2012, respectively.

International monetary assets include the U.S. reserve position in the International Monetary Fund (IMF) and U.S. holdings of Special Drawing Rights (SDRs). The U.S. reserve position in the IMF is an interest-bearing claim on the IMF that includes the reserve asset portion of the financial subscription that the United States has paid in as part of its participation in the IMF as well as any amounts drawn by the IMF from a letter of credit made available by the United States as part of its financial subscription to the IMF. The IMF promotes international monetary cooperation and a stable payment system to facilitate growth in the world economy. Its primary activities are surveillance of member economies, financial assistance as appropriate and technical assistance.

Only a portion of the U.S. financial subscriptions to the IMF is made in the form of reserve assets; the remainder is provided in the form of a letter of credit from the United States to the IMF. The balance available under the letter of credit totaled $44.6 billion and $41.3 billion as of September 30, 2013, and 2012, respectively. The U.S. reserve position in the IMF has a U.S. dollar equivalent of $19.8 billion and $23.5 billion as of September 30, 2013, and 2012, respectively.

The SDR is an international reserves asset created by the IMF to supplement the existing reserve assets of its members. These interest-bearing assets can be obtained by IMF allocations, transactions with IMF member countries, or in the form of interest earnings on SDR holdings and reserve position in the IMF. U.S. SDR holdings are an interest-bearing asset of Treasury's Exchange Stabilization Fund (ESF). The total amount of SDR holdings of the United States was the equivalent of $55.0 billion and $55.2 billion as of September 30, 2013, and 2012, respectively.

The IMF allocates SDRs to its members in proportion to each member's quota in the IMF. The SDR Act, enacted in 1968, authorized the Secretary of the Treasury to issue SDR Certificates (SDRCs) to the Federal Reserve in exchange for dollars. The amount of SDRCs outstanding cannot exceed the dollar value of SDR holdings. The Secretary of the Treasury determines when Treasury will issue or redeem SDRCs. SDRCs outstanding totaled $5.2 billion as of September 30, 2013, and 2012, and are included in Note 17—Other Liabilities.

As of September 30, 2013, and 2012, other liabilities included $54.2 billion and $54.5 billion of interest-bearing liability to the IMF for SDR allocations. The SDR allocation item represents the cumulative total of SDRs distributed by the IMF to the United States in allocations that occurred in 1970, 1971, 1972, 1979, 1980, 1981, and 2009. The United States has received no SDR allocations since 2009.

Gold is valued at the statutory price of $42.2222 per fine troy ounce. The number of fine troy ounces of gold was 261,498,927 as of September 30, 2013 and 2012. The market value of gold on the London Fixing was $1,327 and $1,776 per fine troy ounce as of September 30, 2013, and 2012, respectively. In addition, silver is valued at the statutory price of $1.2929 per fine troy ounce. The number of fine troy ounces of silver was 16,000,000 as of September 30, 2013, and 2012. The market value of silver on the London Fixing was $21.68 and $34.65 per fine troy ounce as of September 30, 2013, and 2012, respectively. Gold totaling $11.0 billion as of September 30, 2013, and 2012, was pledged as collateral for gold certificates issued and authorized to the FRBs by the Secretary of the Treasury. Gold certificates were valued at $11.0 billion as of September 30, 2013, and 2012, which are included in Note 17—Other Liabilities. Treasury may redeem the gold certificates at any time. Foreign currency is translated into U.S. dollars at the exchange rate at fiscal year-end. The foreign currency is maintained by the ESF and various U.S. Federal agencies and foreign banks.

Note 3. Accounts and Taxes Receivable, Net

Accounts and Taxes Receivable as of September 30, 2013, and 2012

(In billions of dollars)	2013	2012
Accounts receivable:		
Gross accounts receivable	89.1	92.6
Allowance for uncollectible accounts	(23.6)	(23.1)
Accounts receivable, net	65.5	69.5
Taxes receivable:		
Gross taxes receivable	164.0	156.8
Allowance for doubtful accounts	(126.3)	(115.1)
Taxes receivable, net	37.7	41.7
Total accounts and taxes receivable, net	103.2	111.2

Accounts receivable includes related interest receivable of $8.1 billion and $7.5 billion as of September 30, 2013, and 2012, respectively.

Treasury comprises approximately 37.4 percent of the Government's reported accounts and taxes receivable, net, as of September 30, 2013. Refer to the individual financial statements of the Department of the Treasury, the Social Security Administration, the Department of Defense, the Department of Health and Human Services, the Department of Agriculture, the Federal Deposit Insurance Corporation, the Department of Veterans Affairs, the Tennessee Valley Authority, the Department of Energy, the Department of Homeland Security, the Department of the Interior, and the Department of Labor for significant detailed information on gross accounts and taxes receivable and the related allowance for doubtful accounts. These agencies comprise 91.7 percent of the Government's accounts and taxes receivable, net, of $103.2 billion as of September 30, 2013.

Note 4. Loan Receivable and Loan Guarantee Liabilities, Net

Direct Loan and Defaulted Guaranteed Loan Programs as of September 30, 2013, and 2012

(In billions of dollars)	Face Value of Loans Outstanding		Long-term Cost of (Income from) Direct Loans and Defaulted Guaranteed Loans Outstanding		Loans Receivable, Net		Subsidy Expense (Income) for the Fiscal Year	
	2013	2012	2013	2012	2013	2012	2013	2012
Federal Direct Student Loans - Education	613.9	493.8	(65.3)	(32.1)	679.2	525.9	(39.7)	(10.7)
Federal Family Education Loans - Education	143.6	147.0	(2.1)	0.9	145.7	146.1	(0.9)	(2.8)
Electric Loans - USDA	49.5	43.3	2.2	1.4	47.3	41.9	0.2	-
Rural Housing Services - USDA ..	31.8	31.5	3.4	6.8	28.4	24.7	0.4	0.3
Export-Import Bank Loans	19.7	13.9	3.0	2.8	16.7	11.1	(0.9)	(0.6)
International Monetary Fund Program- Treasury	15.8	13.9	0.2	0.3	15.6	13.6	-	-
Water and Environmental Loans - USDA	12.3	12.1	0.2	0.5	12.1	11.6	(0.1)	(0.1)
Housing and Urban Development Loans	15.7	15.5	3.9	1.9	11.8	13.6	(0.3)	(0.9)
All other programs........................	82.9	88.6	17.4	17.5	65.5	71.1	2.9	1.1
Total direct loans and defaulted guaranteed loans	985.2	859.6	(37.1)	(0.0)	1,022.3	859.6	(38.4)	(13.7)

Loan Guarantees as of September 30, 2013, and 2012

(In billions of dollars)	Principal Amount of Loans Under Guarantee		Principal Amount Guaranteed by the United States		Loan Guarantee Liabilities		Subsidy Expense (Income) for the Fiscal Year	
	2013	2012	2013	2012	2013	2012	2013	2012
Federal Housing Administration Loans - HUD	1,282.9	1,253.4	1,191.9	1,170.2	41.5	55.0	(18.4)	(6.0)
Federal Family Education Loans - Education	264.0	290.7	258.4	284.6	-	1.0	(7.8)	(11.6)
Veterans Housing Benefit Programs - VA	339.2	286.6	89.2	76.1	7.9	5.6	1.5	0.6
Rural Housing Services - USDA	90.2	77.0	82.5	69.3	3.8	3.2	0.6	0.7
Export-Import Bank Guarantees	79.5	76.4	79.5	76.4	1.6	1.8	(0.3)	(0.4)
Small Business Loans - SBA	93.1	87.4	79.1	74.4	3.0	3.7	(0.5)	0.3
All other guaranteed loan programs	58.3	58.3	53.8	53.8	1.4	4.3	(0.1)	0.7
Total loan guarantees	2,207.2	2,129.8	1,834.4	1,804.8	59.2	74.6	(25.0)	(15.7)

The Government has two different types of loans and loan guarantees. One major type of loan is direct loans such as the Department of Education's (Education) Federal Direct Student Loans. The second type is loan guarantee programs, such as the Department of Housing and Urban Development's (HUD's) Federal Housing Administration Loans program.

Direct loans and loan guarantee programs are used to promote the Nation's welfare by making financing available to segments of the population not served adequately by non-Federal institutions, or otherwise providing for certain activities or investments. For those unable to afford credit at the market rate, Federal credit programs provide subsidies in the form of direct loans offered at an interest rate lower than the market rate. For those to whom non-Federal financial institutions are reluctant to grant credit because of the high risk involved, Federal credit programs guarantee the payment of these non-Federal loans and absorb the cost of defaults.

The amount of the long-term cost of post-1991 direct loans and loan guarantees outstanding equals the subsidy cost allowance for direct loans and the liability for loan guarantees as of September 30. The amount of the long-term cost of pre-1992 direct loans and loan guarantees equals the allowance for uncollectible amounts (or present value allowance) for direct loans and the liability for loan guarantees. The long-term cost is based on all direct loans and guaranteed loans disbursed in this fiscal year and previous years that are outstanding as of September 30. It includes the subsidy cost of these loans and guarantees estimated as of the time of loan disbursement and subsequent adjustments such as modifications, reestimates, amortizations, and write-offs.

Net loans receivable includes related interest and foreclosed property. Foreclosed property is property that is transferred from borrowers to a Federal credit program, through foreclosure or other means, in partial or full settlement of post-1991 direct loans or as a compensation for losses that the Government sustained under post-1991 loan guarantees. Please refer to the individual financial statements of the VA and HUD for significant detailed information regarding foreclosed property.

The total subsidy expense/(income) is the cost of direct loans and loan guarantees recognized during the fiscal year. It consists of the subsidy expense/(income) incurred for direct and guaranteed loans disbursed during the fiscal year, for modifications made during the fiscal year of loans and guarantees outstanding, and for upward or downward re-estimates as of the end of the fiscal year of the cost of loans and guarantees outstanding. This expense/(income) is included in the Statements of Net Cost.

Loan Programs

The majority of the loan programs are provided by Education, HUD, United States Department of Agriculture (USDA), Treasury, Small Business Administration (SBA), VA, and Export-Import Bank. For significant detailed information regarding the direct and guaranteed loan programs listed in the tables above, please refer to the individual financial statements of the agencies.

Education has two major loan programs, authorized by Title IV of the *Higher Education Act of 1965 (HEA)*. The first program is the William D. Ford Federal Direct Student Loan Program, (referred to as the Direct Loan Program) that was established in fiscal year 1994. The Direct Loan Program offers four types of educational loans: Stafford, Unsubsidized Stafford, PLUS for parents and graduate or professional students, and consolidation loans. With this program, the Government makes loans directly to students and parents through participating institutions of higher education. Direct loans are originated and serviced through contracts with private vendors. Education disbursed approximately $130.0 billion in Direct Loans to eligible borrowers in fiscal year 2013 and approximately $142.0 billion in fiscal year 2012. The second program is the Federal Family Education Loan (FFEL) Program. This program was established in fiscal year 1965, and is a guaranteed loan program. Like the William D. Ford Federal Direct Student Loan Program, it offers four types of loans: Stafford, Unsubsidized Stafford, PLUS for parents and graduate or professional students, and consolidation loans. The *Student Aid and Fiscal Responsibility Act (SAFRA)*, which was enacted as part of the *Health Care Education and Reconciliation Act of 2010* (Public Law 111-152), eliminated the authority to guarantee new FFEL after June 30, 2010. During fiscal year 2013, Education net loans receivable increased by $153.2 billion, largely the result of increased Direct Loan Program disbursements for new loan originations and FFEL consolidations, net of borrower principal and interest collections.

HUD's Federal Housing Administration (FHA) provides mortgage insurance to encourage lenders to make credit available to expand home ownership. FHA serves many borrowers that the conventional market does not serve adequately. This includes first-time homebuyers, minorities, low-income, and other underserved households to realize the benefit of home ownership. Borrowers obtain an FHA insured mortgage and pay an upfront premium and an annual premium to FHA. The proceeds from those premiums are used to fund FHA program costs, including claims on defaulted mortgages and holding costs, property management fees, property sales, and other associated costs. The possibility of a sizable volume of delinquencies remains a significant risk for the housing market and for FHA in the near term. The number of FHA mortgages has risen dramatically. FHA has taken a number of steps to help improve its financial health and reduce its market share, including fee increases and underwriting changes.

In 2009, Congress passed the *Supplemental Appropriations Act of 2009* which authorized an increase in the U.S. quota in the IMF, as well as an increase in U.S. participation in the New Arrangements to Borrow, one of the IMF's supplemental borrowing arrangements. For the first time, Congress subjected both program increases to FCRA. Under FCRA, both program increases are treated as direct loans to the IMF.

USDA offers direct and guaranteed loans through credit programs in the Farm and Foreign Agricultural Services (FFAS) mission area through the Farm Service Agency (FSA), and the Commodity Credit Corporation (CCC), and in the Rural Development (RD) mission area. The FFAS delivers commodity, credit, conservation, disaster and emergency assistance programs that help strengthen and stabilize the agricultural economy. The FSA offers direct and guaranteed loans to farmers who are temporarily unable to obtain private, commercial credit. Through this supervised credit offered by FSA, the goal is to graduate its borrowers to commercial credit. The CCC offers both credit guarantee and direct credit programs for buyers of U.S. exports, suppliers, and sovereign countries in need of food assistance. The RD provides affordable housing and essential community facilities to rural communities through its rural housing loan and grant programs. The Rural Utilities Program helps to improve the quality of life in rural America through a variety of loan programs for electric energy, telecommunications, and water and environmental projects.

The Export-Import Bank aids in financing and promoting U.S. exports. The average repayment term for these loans is approximately 7 years.

The SBA's Disaster Assistance Loan Program makes direct loans to disaster victims primarily for homes and personal property.

VA operates the following direct loan and loan guaranty programs: Home Loans, Vocational Rehabilitation and Employment, and Insurance. The VA Home Loans program is the largest of the VA loan programs. The Home Loan program provides loan guarantees and direct loans to veterans, service members, qualifying dependents, and limited non-veterans to purchase homes and retain homeownership with favorable market terms. During fiscal year 2013, the VA principal amount of loans under guarantee increased by $52.6 billion. This increase was primarily due to new loans under guarantee with a principal amount totaling $128.2 billion, offset by guaranteed loan terminations with a principal amount of $74.1 billion.

Note 5. Troubled Asset Relief Program (TARP) — Direct Loans and Equity Investments, Net

The TARP was authorized by the EESA. This Act gave the Secretary of the Treasury broad flexible authority to establish the TARP to purchase and guarantee mortgages, mortgage related securities, and other troubled assets from financial institutions. This permitted the Secretary of the Treasury to inject capital into, and receive equity interests in, banks and other financial institutions. Treasury established several programs under the TARP designed to help stabilize the financial system, restore the flow of credit to consumers and businesses, and help prevent avoidable foreclosures. Under the TARP programs, Treasury made direct loans, equity investments, and entered into other credit programs. This authority to make new commitments to purchase or guarantee troubled assets expired on October 3, 2010.

The following table lists the TARP programs and types:

Program	Program Type
American International Group, Inc. Investment Program	Equity Investment
Public-Private Investment Program	Equity Investment and Direct Loan
Automotive Industry Financing Program	Equity Investment and Direct Loan
Capital Purchase Program	Equity Investments/Subordinated Debentures
Other Programs	Direct Loan, Subordinated Debentures, and Equity Investments
Housing Programs under TARP*	Expenditure and Loss Sharing

*Housing Programs under TARP are not designed to recoup money spent on loan modifications or payments on the loss sharing agreement. As such, these programs do not include direct loans, equity investments, or asset guarantees.

The table below is a summary of TARP - Direct Loans and Equity Investments, Net of Allowance

Troubled Asset Relief Program Direct Loans and Equity Investments

(In billions of dollars)	Direct Loans and Equity Investments		Subsidy Cost Allowance		Net Direct Loans and Equity Investments		Subsidy Expense (Income) for the Fiscal Year	
	2013	2012	2013	2012	2013	2012	2013	2012
Automotive Industry Financing Program	19.9	37.2	(4.3)	(19.7)	15.6	17.5	(10.2)	0.2
Capital Purchase Program	3.1	8.7	(1.3)	(2.9)	1.8	5.8	(1.1)	(1.9)
American International Group, Inc. (AIG), Investment Program	-	6.7	-	(1.7)	-	5.0	-	(9.2)
Public-Private Investment Program	-	9.8	-	1.0	-	10.8	(0.4)	0.2
All other	0.5	0.7	-	0.4	0.5	1.1	(0.2)	(0.1)
Total Troubled Asset Relief Program	23.5	63.1	(5.6)	(22.9)	17.9	40.2	(11.9)	(10.8)

Automotive Industry Financing Program

The Automotive Industry Financing Program was designed to help prevent a significant disruption of the American automotive industry, which could have had a negative effect on the economy of the United States. The various activities undertaken by Treasury in the automotive industry include:

General Motors (GM)—In fiscal year 2009, Treasury provided $51.0 billion to Old GM through various loan agreements while Old GM was in bankruptcy. During fiscal year 2009, New GM was created through various sales and restructuring of its investment, Treasury held 500 million shares of New GM common stock, or 31.9 percent of New GM's total outstanding common shares, as of September 30, 2012. During fiscal year 2013, Treasury sold 399 million shares of the New GM common stock for $12.0 billion, which resulted in net proceeds less than cost of $5.4 billion. There were no sales of common stock during fiscal year 2012. As of September 30, 2013, Treasury held 101 million shares of New GM common stock, or 7.3 percent of New GM's total outstanding common shares. The fair value of the New GM common shares held as of September 30, 2013, and 2012 was $3.6 billion and $11.4 billion, respectively.

Ally Financial Inc. (formerly known as GMAC Inc.)—Between December 2008 and December 2009, Treasury invested a total of $16.3 billion in GMAC Inc. to help support its ability to originate new loans to GM and Chrysler dealers and consumers, and to help address GMAC's capital needs. GMAC changed its corporate name to Ally Financial, Inc. (Ally) in May 2010. As of September 30, 2012, Treasury held 981,971 shares of Ally's outstanding common stock (or 73.8 percent) and 119 million shares of Series F-2 Mandatorily Convertible Preferred Securities, with a stated dividend rate of 9.0 percent. Per an August 2013 agreement, Ally repurchased all the Series F-2 from Treasury in November 2013 for $5.2 billion and Treasury received an additional $ 0.7 billion for the elimination of certain rights under the original agreement. The August 2013 agreement also included terms for Ally to issue a November 2013 private offering of new common stock at a price of $6,000 per share. Following this private offering, Treasury's ownership was reduced to 63.4 percent of Ally's outstanding common stock. As of September 30, 2013, and 2012 Treasury's investment was valued at $12.0 billion and $6.2 billion, respectively.

Public Private Investment Program (PPIP)

The PPIP is part of Treasury's efforts to help restart the markets and provide liquidity for legacy assets. Under this program, Treasury made equity investments and loans to nine investment vehicles (referred to as Public Private Investment

Funds or "PPIFs") established by private investment managers. The PPIFs were allowed to purchase commercial MBS and non-agency residential MBS. As of September 30, 2012, Treasury held investments in six PPIFs comprising $4.1 billion of equity investments outstanding and $5.7 billion of loans outstanding, for an aggregate total of $9.8 billion. These investments and loans were valued at $10.8 billion as of September 30, 2012. During fiscal year 2013, all of the PPIFs fully liquidated their portfolios and repaid investors including Treasury. Treasury made no disbursements to the PPIFs during fiscal year 2013, compared to fiscal year 2012 in which Treasury disbursed $0.2 billion as equity investment and $0.8 billion as loans to these PPIFs. At September 30, 2013, Treasury had no PPIF equity investments or loans outstanding. The legal commitments to disburse up to $1.8 billion in additional loans to remaining PPIFs as of September 30, 2012, were canceled in 2013 since all PPIFs had ceased operations. Commitments of $1.0 billion to disburse additional equity to PPIFs will remain until all distributions have been received from PPIFs and all PPIF liabilities have been settled, although a requirement for additional disbursement by Treasury is highly unlikely.

Capital Purchase Program

In October 2008, Treasury began implementation of the Capital Purchase Program (CPP), designed to help stabilize the financial system by assisting in building the capital base of certain viable U.S. financial institutions to increase the capacity of those institutions to lend to businesses and consumers and support the economy. Under this program, Treasury purchased senior perpetual preferred stock with a stated dividend rate of 5.0 percent through year five, increasing to 9.0 percent in subsequent years, from qualifying U.S. controlled banks, savings associations, and certain bank and savings and loan holding companies (Qualified Financial Institution). The dividends are cumulative for bank holding companies and subsidiaries of bank holding companies and non-cumulative for others and payable when and if declared by the institution's board of directors. In addition to the senior preferred stock, Treasury received warrants, with a ten-year term, from public QFIs to purchase shares of common stock. QFIs that are Sub-chapter S corporations issued subordinated debentures with a maturity of 30 years and interest rates of 7.7 percent to 13.8 percent. For fiscal years 2013 and 2012, repayments and sales totaled $4.8 billion and $8.2 billion, respectively. As of September 30, 2013, and 2012, Treasury's investment was valued at $1.8 billion and $5.8 billion, respectively.

American International Group, Inc. Investment Program (AIG)

Treasury provided assistance to help AIG in order to prevent its disorderly failure as well as to prevent broader disruption to the financial markets. In fiscal year 2009, Treasury made an investment in AIG under TARP of $40.0 billion in the form of AIG's cumulative 10.0 percent Series D preferred stock. Additionally, Treasury made available under TARP an equity capital facility under which AIG drew $27.8 billion, and Treasury received additional AIG preferred stock and common stock warrants. By January 2011, and as a result of various restructurings, Treasury's investments in AIG under TARP consisted of $20.3 billion of interest in AIG Special Purpose Vehicles (SPVs), and 1.1 billion shares of AIG common stock. Since the January 2011 restructuring, Treasury sold 154 million and 806 million shares of AIG's common stock under TARP in fiscal years 2013 and 2012 for $5.0 billion and $25.2 billion, respectively. As of September 30, 2012, Treasury held 154 million shares of AIG's common stock under TARP, with a fair value of approximately $5.1 billion representing 10.5 percent of the AIG shares outstanding. As of September 30, 2013, Treasury retained no ownership interest in AIG, common or preferred stock, nor any interests in SPVs.

Other Programs

Treasury implemented other programs under TARP to help unlock the flow of credit to consumers and small businesses. Several programs, including the following, were established to help accomplish this: Term Asset-Backed Securities Loan Facility (TALF), and the Community Development Capital Initiative (CDCI).

TALF was created by the Federal Reserve Board to provide low cost funding to investors in certain classes of Asset-Backed Securities (ABS). Treasury participated in the program by providing liquidity and credit protection to the Federal Reserve Board. As implementer of the TALF program, the FRBNY originated loans on a non-recourse basis to holders of certain AAA rated ABS. As part of the program, the FRBNY created the TALF, LLC, an SPV that agreed to purchase from the FRBNY any collateral it has seized because of borrower default. In the event there are insufficient funds to purchase the collateral, Treasury committed to invest up to $20.0 billion in non-recourse subordinate notes issued by the TALF, LLC. Since 2010, the commitment amount has been reduced periodically and in fiscal year 2013 was terminated. As of September 30, 2013 and 2012, approximately $0.1 billion and $1.5 billion of loans due to FRBNY remained outstanding, respectively.

The CDCI Initiative was created to provide additional low-cost capital to Community Development Financial Institutions (CDFI) to encourage more lending to small businesses. Under the terms of the initiatives, Treasury purchased senior preferred stock (or subordinated debt) from eligible CDFI financial institutions with an initial dividend rate of 2.0 percent, increasing up to a maximum rate of 9.0 percent after 8 years.

Housing Programs under TARP

Housing Programs under TARP are not designed to recoup money spent on loan modifications or payments on the loss sharing agreement. As such, these programs do not include direct loans, equity investments, or asset guarantees.

The following housing programs under TARP are designed to help prevent avoidable foreclosures. These programs provide incentives for mortgage modifications and other types of assistance in order to enable homeowners who are experiencing financial hardships to remain in their homes until their financial position improves or relocate to more sustainable living situations. These programs fall into three initiatives:

- Making Home Affordable Program;
- Housing Finance Agency Hardest-Hit Fund, and
- Federal Housing Administration Refinance Program.

As of September 30, 2013, and 2012, Treasury has committed up to $38.5 billion and $45.6 billion, respectively for these programs. Payments made under the housing programs under TARP for fiscal years 2013 and 2012, amounted to $3.9 billion and $3.1 billion, respectively. As of September 30, 2013, Treasury had $28.7 billion in total commitments outstanding for future payments under the housing programs.

For more details on the TARP, please see the Treasury's Annual Financial Report.

Note 6. Inventories and Related Property, Net

Inventories and Related Property, Net as of September 30, 2013, and 2012

(In billions of dollars)	Defense	All Others	Total	Defense	All Others	Total
		2013			2012	
Inventory purchased for resale	57.1	0.5	57.6	61.6	0.6	62.2
Inventory and operating material and supplies						
held for repair	59.6	1.5	61.1	52.8	1.4	54.2
Inventory—excess, obsolete, and unserviceable	7.0	-	7.0	6.8	0.1	6.9
Operating materials and supplies held for use	142.8	3.5	146.3	134.6	3.2	137.8
Operating materials and supplies held in						
reserve for future use	-	0.2	0.2	-	0.1	0.1
Operating materials and supplies— excess,						
obsolete, and unserviceable	2.1	-	2.1	1.9	0.1	2.0
Stockpile materials	0.1	50.9	51.0	-	49.9	49.9
Stockpile materials held for sale	0.4	0.1	0.5	0.5	0.1	0.6
Other related property	1.5	1.0	2.5	1.4	0.8	2.2
Allowance for loss	(16.6)	(0.6)	(17.2)	(16.3)	(0.6)	(16.9)
Total inventories and related property, net	254.0	57.1	311.1	243.3	55.7	299.0

Inventory purchased for resale is the cost or value of tangible personal property purchased by an agency for resale. As of September 30, 2013, DOD values approximately 84 percent of its resale inventory using the moving average cost (MAC) method. An additional 13 percent (fuel inventory) is reported using the first-in-first-out method. DOD reports the remaining 3 percent of resale inventories at an approximation of historical cost using LAC adjusted for holding gains and losses. The LAC method is used because DOD's legacy inventory systems do not maintain historical cost data.

Please refer to the individual financial statements of DOD for significant detailed information regarding its inventories.

Inventory and operating materials and supplies held for repair are damaged inventory that require repair to make them suitable for sale (inventory) or is more economical to repair than to dispose of (operating materials and supplies).

Inventory—excess, obsolete, and unserviceable consists of:

- Excess inventory that exceeds the demand expected in the normal course of operations and which does not meet management's criteria to be held in reserve for future sale.
- Obsolete inventory that is no longer needed due to changes in technology, laws, customs, or operations.
- Unserviceable inventory that is damaged beyond economic repair.

Excess, obsolete, and unserviceable inventory is reported at net realizable value.

Operating materials and supplies held for use are tangible personal property to be consumed in normal operations.

Operating materials and supplies held in reserve for future use are materials retained because they are not readily available in the market or because they will not be used in the normal course of operations, but there is more than a remote chance they will eventually be needed. DOD, which accounts for most of the reported operating materials and supplies held for use, uses LAC, MAC, and Standard Price and expenses a significant amount when purchased instead of when consumed.

Operating materials and supplies—excess, obsolete, and unserviceable consists of:

- Excess operating materials and supplies are materials that exceed the demand expected in the normal course of operations, and do not meet management's criteria to be held in reserve for future use.

- Obsolete operating materials and supplies are materials no longer needed due to changes in technology, laws, customs, or operations.

- Unserviceable operating materials and supplies are materials damaged beyond economic repair.

DOD, which accounts for most of the reported excess, obsolete, and unserviceable operating materials and supplies, revalues it to a net realizable value of zero through the allowance account.

Please refer to the individual financial statements of DOD for significant detailed information regarding operating materials and supplies.

Stockpile materials include strategic and critical materials held in reserve for use in national defense, conservation, or national emergencies due to statutory requirements; for example, nuclear materials and oil, and stockpile materials that are authorized to be sold. The majority of the amount reported by DOD is stockpile materials held for sale, and the amount reported by others is stockpile materials held in reserve, with the majority of it being reported by the Department of Energy (DOE). Please refer to their individual financial statements for more information on stockpile materials.

Other related property consists of the following:

- Commodities include items of commerce or trade that have an exchange value used to stabilize or support market prices. Please refer to the financial statements of the USDA for detailed information regarding commodities.

- Seized monetary instruments are comprised only of monetary instruments that are awaiting judgment to determine ownership. The related liability is included in other liabilities. Other property seized by the Government, such as real property and tangible personal property, is not considered a Government asset. It is accounted for in agency property-management records until the property is forfeited, returned, or otherwise liquidated. Please refer to the individual financial statements of the Department of Justice (DOJ), Treasury, and the Department of Homeland Security (DHS) for significant detailed information regarding seized property.

- Forfeited property is comprised of monetary instruments, intangible property, real property, and tangible personal property acquired through forfeiture proceedings; property acquired by the Government to satisfy a tax liability; and unclaimed and abandoned merchandise. Please refer to the individual financial statements of DOJ, Treasury, and DHS for significant detailed information regarding forfeited property.

- Foreclosed property is comprised of assets received in satisfaction of a loan receivable or as a result of payment of a claim under a guaranteed or insured loan (excluding commodities acquired under price support programs). All properties included in foreclosed property are assumed to be held for sale. Please refer to the individual financial statements of USDA and HUD for significant detailed information regarding foreclosed property.

Note 7. Property, Plant, and Equipment, Net

Property, Plant, and Equipment as of September 30, 2013

(In billions of dollars)	Cost		Accumulated Depreciation/ Amortization		Net	
	Defense	All Others	Defense	All Others	Defense	All Others
Buildings, structures, and facilities	269.8	249.7	127.9	130.0	141.9	119.7
Furniture, fixtures, and equipment	983.6	165.1	547.5	102.5	436.1	62.6
Construction in progress	46.6	41.6	N/A	N/A	46.6	41.6
Land	10.8	12.5	N/A	N/A	10.8	12.5
Internal use software	11.0	25.0	8.0	14.2	3.0	10.8
Assets under capital lease	0.6	3.3	0.4	1.7	0.2	1.6
Leasehold improvements	0.4	8.6	0.2	4.5	0.2	4.1
Other property, plant, and equipment	1.0	7.6	-	3.6	1.0	4.0
Subtotal	1,323.8	513.4	684.0	256.5	639.8	256.9
Total property, plant, and equipment, net		1,837.2		940.5		896.7

Property, Plant, and Equipment as of September 30, 2012

(In billions of dollars)	Cost		Accumulated Depreciation/ Amortization		Net	
	Defense	All Others	Defense	All Others	Defense	All Others
Buildings, structures, and facilities	248.9	234.0	120.9	123.4	128.0	110.6
Furniture, fixtures, and equipment	984.4	160.8	570.4	99.1	414.0	61.7
Construction in progress	42.8	50.8	N/A	N/A	42.8	50.8
Land	10.7	12.2	N/A	N/A	10.7	12.2
Internal use software	11.3	22.1	7.6	12.3	3.7	9.8
Assets under capital lease	0.9	3.1	0.5	1.5	0.4	1.6
Leasehold improvements	0.9	7.6	0.3	4.0	0.6	3.6
Other property, plant, and equipment	1.2	6.7	-	3.4	1.2	3.3
Subtotal	1,301.1	497.3	699.7	243.7	601.4	253.6
Total property, plant, and equipment, net		1,798.4		943.4		855.0

For further information related to multi-use heritage assets, see Note 25—Stewardship Land and Heritage Assets.

DOD comprises approximately 71.3 percent of the Government's reported property, plant, and equipment, net, as of September 30, 2013. Refer to the individual financial statements of DOD, DOE, the Tennessee Valley Authority (TVA), GSA, the Department of Interior (DOI), VA, DHS, USPS, Department of State, and DOT for significant detailed information on the useful lives and related capitalization thresholds for property, plant, and equipment. These agencies comprise 94.1 percent of the Government's total cost of property, plant, and equipment net of $896.7 billion as of September 30, 2013.

Note 8. Debt and Equity Securities

Debt and Equity Securities as of September 30, 2013

(In billions of dollars)	Held-To-Maturity			Available-for-Sale			Trading Securities			Total
	Cost Basis	Unamortized Premium/ Discount	Net Investment	Cost Basis	Unrealized Gain (Loss)	Fair Value	Cost Basis	Unrealized Gain (Loss)	Fair Value	
Debt Securities:										
Non-U.S. Government	0.2	-	0.2	14.2	(0.1)	14.1	10.1	(0.1)	10.0	24.3
Commercial	-	-	-	-	-	-	0.1	-	0.1	0.1
Mortgage/asset backed	-	-	-	-	-	-	3.0	0.1	3.1	3.1
Corporate and other bonds	-	-	-	-	-	-	10.0	0.4	10.4	10.4
All other debt securities	-	-	-	-	-	-	2.0	(0.1)	1.9	1.9
Equity Securities:										
Common stocks	-	-	-	-	-	-	2.2	0.6	2.8	2.8
Unit trust	-	-	-	-	-	-	12.0	7.1	19.1	19.1
All other equity securities	0.1	-	0.1	-	-	-	2.8	0.1	2.9	3.0
Other	3.7	-	3.7	-	-	-	15.1	-	15.1	18.8
Total debt and equity securities categorized as held-to-maturity, available-for-sale or trading	4.0	-	4.0	14.2	(0.1)	14.1	57.3	8.1	65.4	83.5
Total RRB debt and equity securities										24.3
Total debt and equity securities										107.8

Debt and Equity Securities as of September 30, 2012

(In billions of dollars)	Held-To-Maturity			Available-for-Sale			Trading Securities			
	Cost Basis	Unamortized Premium/ Discount	Net Investment	Cost Basis	Unrealized Gain (Loss)	Fair Value	Cost Basis	Unrealized Gain (Loss)	Fair Value	Total
Debt securities:										
Non-U.S. Government	0.2	-	0.2	15.1	0.3	15.4	8.5	0.7	9.2	24.8
Commercial	-	-	-	-	-	-	0.4	-	0.4	0.4
Mortgage/asset backed	-	-	-	-	-	-	3.5	0.2	3.7	3.7
Corporate and other bonds ..	-	-	-	-	-	-	9.8	1.3	11.1	11.1
All other debt securities	-	-	-	-	-	-	0.6	-	0.6	0.6
Equity securities:										
Common stocks	-	-	-	3.6	(1.0)	2.6	2.1	0.4	2.5	5.1
Unit trust	-	-	-	-	-	-	14.6	5.7	20.3	20.3
All other equity securities	3.1	-	3.1	-	-	-	2.2	-	2.2	5.3
Other	10.7	-	10.7	-	-	-	5.2	0.1	5.3	16.0
Total debt and equity securities categorized as held-to-maturity, available-for-sale or trading	14.0	-	14.0	18.7	(0.7)	18.0	46.9	8.4	55.3	87.3
Total RRB debt and equity securities										22.9
Total debt and equity securities										110.2

Debt and Equity Securities as of September 30, 2013, and 2012

(In billions of dollars)	By Agency	
	2013	2012
Debt and Equity Securities:		
Pension Benefit Guaranty Corporation	54.7	52.8
Railroad Retirement Board	24.3	22.9
Department of the Treasury	14.1	18.0
Tennessee Valley Authority	10.6	9.5
All Other	4.1	7.0
Total Securities and Investments	107.8	110.2

These debt and equity securities do not include nonmarketable Treasury securities, which have been eliminated in consolidation. Held-to-maturity debt and equity securities are reported at amortized cost, net of unamortized discounts and premiums. Available-for-sale debt and equity securities are reported at fair value. Trading debt and equity securities are reported at fair value. The Pension Benefit Guaranty Corporation (PBGC) and the TVA invest primarily in fixed maturity and equity securities, classified as trading. Treasury invests primarily in fixed maturity and equity securities, classified as available-for-sale securities. Treasury's Exchange Stabilization Fund invests primarily in foreign fixed maturity debt, with a fair value of $14.1 billion and $15.4 billion as of September 30, 2013, and 2012, respectively. The General Fund also owned shares of AIG common stock until the remaining shares were sold in mid-December 2012. These non-TARP investments had a fair value of $2.6 billion as of September 30, 2012. The National Railroad Retirement Investment Trust (NRRIT), on behalf of the RRB, manages and invests railroad retirement assets that are to be used to pay retirement benefits to the Nation's railroad workers under the Railroad Retirement Program. As an investment company, NRRIT is subject to different accounting standards that do not require the classifications presented above. NRRIT's total debt and equity securities are presented as a separate line item. Please refer to NRRIT's financial statements for more detailed information concerning this specific investment information. The TVA balance includes $7.4 billion and $7.2 billion as of September 30, 2013, and 2012, respectively, for the Tennessee Valley Authority Retirement System. Please refer to the individual financial statements of PBGC, NRRIT, Treasury, and TVA for more detailed information related to debt and equity securities. These agencies comprise 96.2 percent of the total reported debt and equity securities of $107.8 billion as of September 30, 2013.

Note 9. Investments in and Liabilities to Government-Sponsored Enterprises

Congress established Fannie Mae and Freddie Mac as GSEs to support the supply of mortgage loans. A key function of the GSEs is to package purchased mortgages into securities, which are subsequently sold to investors.

Leading up to the financial crisis, increasingly difficult conditions in the housing market challenged the soundness and profitability of the GSEs, thereby undermining the entire housing market. This led Congress to pass the HERA. This Act created the FHFA, with enhanced regulatory authority over the GSEs, and provided the Secretary of the Treasury with certain authorities intended to ensure the financial stability of the GSEs, if necessary. In September 2008, FHFA placed the GSEs under conservatorship and Treasury entered into a SPSPA with each GSE. These actions were taken to preserve the GSEs' assets, ensure a sound and solvent financial condition, and mitigate systemic risks that contributed to market instability. The SPSPAs were amended in August 2012 (the amended SPSPAs) and changed, among other things, the basis by which quarterly dividends are paid by the GSEs to the U.S. Government. The dividend change in the amended SPSPAs became effective commencing with the quarter ending March 31, 2013.

The actions taken by Treasury, as authorized by section 1117 of HERA, thus far are temporary and are intended to provide financial stability. The purpose of Treasury's actions is to maintain the solvency of the GSEs so they can continue to fulfill their vital roles in the home mortgage market while the Administration and Congress determine what structural changes should be made. Draws under the SPSPAs are designed to enable the GSEs to maintain a positive net worth. The SPSPAs were structured to ensure any draws result in an increased nominal investment as further discussed below. Per SFFAC No. 2, *Entity and Display*, these entities meet the criteria of "bailed out" entities. Accordingly, the Government has not consolidated them into the financial statements, but included disclosure of the relationship(s) with the bailed out entities and any actual or potential material costs or liabilities in the consolidated financial statements.

Senior Preferred Stock Purchase Agreements (SPSPAs)

Under the SPSPAs, Treasury initially received from each GSE: 1) 1,000,000 shares of non-voting variable liquidation preference senior preferred stock with a liquidation preference value of $1,000 per share and 2) a non-transferable warrant for the purchase, at a nominal cost, of 79.9 percent of common stock on a fully-diluted basis. The warrants expire on September 7, 2028. Through December 31, 2012, the senior preferred stock accrued dividends at 10.0 percent per year, payable quarterly. Under the amended SPSPAs, the quarterly dividend payment changed from a 10.0 percent per annum fixed rate dividend to an amount equivalent to the GSE's net worth above a capital reserve amount. The capital reserve amount was initially set at $3.0 billion for calendar year 2013, and declines by $600 million at the beginning of each calendar year thereafter until it reaches zero by calendar year 2018. The GSEs will not pay a quarterly dividend if their positive net worth is below the required capital reserve threshold.

Cash dividends of $95.7 billion and $18.4 billion were declared and received during fiscal years ended September 30, 2013, and 2012, respectively. The significant increase in dividends received in fiscal year 2013 compared to fiscal year 2012 was primarily attributable to a federal income tax benefit that was recognized in the 2013 earnings of Fannie Mae resulting in improved net worth and increased dividends remitted to Treasury.

The SPSPAs, which have no expiration date, provide that Treasury will disburse funds to the GSEs if at the end of any quarter, the FHFA determines that the liabilities of either GSE exceed its assets. The maximum amount available to each GSE under this agreement was previously based on a formula that allowed the cap to increase by the amount of actual draws made for a 3-year period that ended December 31, 2012, at which time, the maximum amount was automatically adjusted downward by each GSE's positive net worth, as of December 31, 2012, and became fixed effective as of that date. Draws against the funding commitment of the SPSPAs do not result in the issuance of additional shares of senior preferred stock; instead the liquidation preference of the initial 1,000,000 shares is increased by the amount of the draw.

There were no payments to the GSEs for the fiscal year ended September 30, 2013. Payments to the GSEs for the fiscal year ended 2012, were $18.5 billion.

OMB issued guidance to Treasury on October 7, 2009, allowing the use of fair value accounting for non-Federal securities beginning with reporting for fiscal year 2009. The GSE investments are reported at fair value as of September 30, 2013, and 2012. In accordance with SFFAS No. 7, the annual valuation is classified as usual and recurring and thus a change in value is recorded as an expense or revenue to the financial statements. Annual valuations are performed as of September 30 for the senior preferred stock and warrants.

Contingent Liability to GSEs

As part of the annual process undertaken by Treasury, a series of long-term forecasts are prepared to assess the probability and magnitude of draws under the SPSPAs as of September 30. Treasury used financial forecasts prepared through 2038 and 2025 in estimating the contingent liability as of September 30, 2013 and 2012, respectively. If future payments under the SPSPAs are deemed to be probable within the forecast horizon, Treasury will estimate and accrue a contingent liability to the GSEs to reflect the forecasted equity deficits of the GSEs.

Based on the annual assessment of Treasury's estimated future contingent liability under the SPSPAs, Treasury estimated and accrued no contingent liability as of September 30, 2013. Treasury's estimated contingent liability decreased by $9.0 billion and $307.2 billion at the end of fiscal years 2013 and 2012, respectively. The reduction in the estimated liability is primarily due to a decrease in the amount of estimated future draws forecasted to be required by the GSEs within the forecast time horizon. Such recorded accruals are adjusted as new information develops or circumstances change. The $307.2 billion decrease in fiscal year 2012 resulted in a remaining contingent liability of $9.0 billion at the end of that fiscal year to reflect the 10.0 percent per annum dividend payment requirement in accordance with the pre-amended SPSPAs. As a result of the amended SPSPAs in which the new dividend payment requirement became operationally effective commencing with the quarter ended March 31, 2013, coupled with the long-term financial forecasts of the GSEs, Treasury reduced by $9.0 billion the contingent liability as of September 30, 2013.

As of September 30, 2013, the maximum remaining contractual commitment to the GSEs for the remaining life of the SPSPAs was $258.1 billion, which was established at a fixed amount on December 31, 2012. As of September 30, 2012, the maximum remaining potential commitment to the GSEs for the remaining life of the SPSPAs was estimated at $282.3 billion, which was based upon case scenario estimates ranging from $274.0 billion to $291.5 billion.

Senior Preferred Stock and Warrants for Common Stock

In determining the fair value of the senior preferred stock and warrants for common stock, Treasury relied on the GSEs' public filings and press releases concerning their financial statements, as well as non-public, long-term financial forecasts, monthly summaries, quarterly credit supplements, independent research regarding high-yield bond and preferred stock trading, independent research regarding the GSEs' common stock trading, discussions with each of the GSEs and FHFA, and other information pertinent to the fair valuations. Because of the nature of the senior preferred stock and warrants, which are not publicly traded and for which there is no comparable trading information available, the fair valuations rely on significant unobservable inputs that reflect assumptions about the expectations that market participants would use in pricing.

The fair value of the senior preferred stock considers the amount of forecasted dividend payments. The fair valuations assume that a hypothetical buyer would acquire the discounted dividend stream as of the transaction date. The increase in the fair value of the senior preferred stock at September 30, 2013, compared to 2012, is primarily due to the GSEs' improved financial performance.

The fair value of the warrants is impacted by the nominal exercise price and the large number of potential exercise shares, the market trading of the common stock that underlies the warrants as of September 30, the principal market, and the market participants. Other factors are the holding period risk related directly to the amount of time that it will take to sell the exercised shares without depressing the market. The fair value of the warrants increased at the end of fiscal year 2013 when compared to 2012 primarily due to increases in the market price of the underlying common stock of each GSE.

Regulatory Environment

Pursuant to a provision within the Dodd Frank Act, the Secretary of the Treasury conducted a study and developed recommendations regarding the options for ending the conservatorship. In February 2011, the President delivered to Congress a report from the Secretary of the Treasury that provided recommendations regarding the options for ending the conservatorship and plans to wind down the GSEs. To date, Congress has not approved a plan to address the future of the GSEs, and thus the GSEs continue to operate under the direction of their conservator, the FHFA, whose stated strategic goals for the GSEs are to: (i) build a new infrastructure for the secondary mortgage market; (ii) reduce the GSEs' presence in the marketplace, and (iii) maintain foreclosure prevention activities and credit availability.

In December 2011, Congress passed the Temporary Payroll Tax Cut Continuation Act of 2011 (TPTCCA), which included an increase in the GSEs' guarantee fees that would expire on October 1, 2021. Under TPTCCA, the amount of the fee increase shall not be less than an average increase of 10-basis points above the average fees imposed in 2011 for such guarantees. The increased fees are to be remitted to Treasury and not retained by the GSEs.

Accordingly, the increased fees do not affect the profitability of the GSEs. Treasury received its first remittance of the increased fees from the GSEs on September 28, 2012. For fiscal years 2013 and 2012, the GSEs remitted to the Treasury the increased fees totaling $946 million and $35 million, respectively.

As of September 30, 2013, and 2012, GSE investments consisted of the following:

Investments in GSE as of September 30, 2013

(In billions of dollars)	Gross Investments as of 9/30/13	Cumulative Valuation Gain/(Loss)	9/30/13 Fair Value
Fannie Mae Senior Preferred Stock	117.0	(40.4)	76.6
Freddie Mac Senior Preferred Stock	72.1	(16.3)	55.8
Fannie Mae Warrants Common Stock	3.1	2.0	5.1
Freddie Mac Warrants Common Stock	2.3	0.4	2.7
Total GSE Investment	194.5	(54.3)	140.2

Investments in GSE as of September 30, 2012

(In billions of dollars)	Gross Investments as of 9/30/12	Cumulative Valuation (Loss)	9/30/12 Fair Value
Fannie Mae Senior Preferred Stock	117.0	(51.3)	65.7
Freddie Mac Senior Preferred Stock	72.1	(30.2)	41.9
Fannie Mae Warrants Common Stock	3.1	(2.0)	1.1
Freddie Mac Warrants Common Stock	2.3	(1.7)	0.6
Total GSE Investment	194.5	(85.2)	109.3

Note 10. Other Assets

Other Assets as of September 30, 2013, and 2012

(In billions of dollars)	2013	2012
Advances and prepayments	106.0	96.5
FDIC receivable from resolution activity	17.0	18.9
Regulatory assets	21.6	18.9
Other	18.2	23.3
Total Other Assets	162.8	157.6

Advances and prepayments are assets that represent funds disbursed in contemplation of the future performance of services, receipt of goods, the incurrence of expenditures, or the receipt of other assets. These include advances to contractors and grantees, travel advances, and prepayments for items such as rents, taxes, insurance, royalties, commissions, and supplies.

The Federal Deposit Insurance Corporation (FDIC) has the responsibility for resolving failed institutions in an orderly and efficient manner. The resolution process involves valuing a failing institution, marketing it, soliciting and accepting bid for the sale of the institution, determining which bid is least costly to the insurance fund, and working with the acquiring institution through the closing process. FDIC records receivables for resolutions that include payments by the Deposit Insurance Fund to cover obligations to insured depositors, advances to receiverships and conservatorships for working capital, and administrative expenses paid on behalf of receiverships and conservatorships.

With regard to regulatory assets, the DOE's Power Marketing Authorities (PMAs) and the TVA record certain amounts as assets in accordance with FASB ASC Topic 980, *Regulated Operations*. The provisions of FASB ASC Topic 980 require that regulated enterprises reflect rate actions of the regulator in their financial statements, when appropriate. These rate actions can provide reasonable assurance of the existence of an asset, reduce or eliminate the value of an asset, or impose a liability on a regulated enterprise. In order to defer incurred costs under FASB ASC Topic 980, a regulated entity must have the statutory authority to establish rates that recover all costs, and those rates must be charged to and collected from customers. If the PMAs' or TVA's rates should become market-based, FASB ASC Topic 980 would no longer be applicable, and all of the deferred costs under that standard would be expensed.

Other items included in "other" are purchased power generating capacity, deferred nuclear generating units, nonmarketable equity investments in international financial institutions, and the balance of assets held by the experience rated carriers participating in the Health Benefits and Life Insurance Program (pending disposition on behalf of OPM).

Note 11. Accounts Payable

Accounts Payable as of September 30, 2013, and 2012

(In billions of dollars)	2013	2012
Department of Defense	20.2	19.5
Department of Veterans Affairs	10.8	9.7
Department of Justice	4.2	4.1
Department of Education	4.1	4.1
Department of the Treasury	3.9	4.9
Department of State	2.8	2.8
Department of Agriculture	2.1	2.0
General Services Administration	2.1	2.0
Department of Homeland Security	2.1	1.9
Tennessee Valley Authority	1.9	1.9
U.S. Postal Service	1.8	1.7
Agency for International Development	1.6	1.9
Department of Energy	1.5	1.7
National Aeronautics and Space Administration	1.3	1.4
Department of the Interior	1.0	0.8
All other	4.8	4.8
Total accounts payable	66.2	65.2

Accounts payable includes amounts due for goods and property ordered and received, services rendered by other than Federal employees, accounts payable for cancelled appropriations, and non-debt related interest payable.

Note 12. Federal Debt Securities Held by the Public and Accrued Interest

Federal Debt Securities Held by the Public and Accrued Interest

(In billions of dollars)	Balance September 30, 2012	Net Change During Fiscal Year 2013	Balance September 30, 2013	Average Interest Rate 2013	Average Interest Rate 2012
Treasury securities (public):					
Marketable securities:					
Treasury bills.................................	1,613.0	(85.1)	1,527.9	0.1%	0.1%
Treasury notes	7,115.0	635.3	7,750.3	1.8%	2.0%
Treasury bonds	1,194.7	168.4	1,363.1	5.1%	5.4%
Treasury inflation-protected securities (TIPS)	807.5	128.6	936.1	1.1%	1.4%
Total marketable Treasury securities	10,730.2	847.2	11,577.4		
Nonmarketable securities	539.4	(140.5)	398.9	2.4%	2.1%
Net unamortized premiums/ (discounts)	(19.2)	(5.3)	(24.5)		
Total Treasury securities, net (public)	11,250.4	701.4	11,951.8		
Agency securities:					
Tennessee Valley Authority	24.0	0.8	24.8		
All other agencies	0.3	(0.1)	0.2		
Total agency securities, net of unamortized premiums and discounts	24.3	0.7	25.0		
Accrued interest payable..............	57.6	(6.0)	51.6		
Total Federal debt securities held by the public and accrued interest	11,332.3	696.1	12,028.4		

Types of marketable securities:
Bills–Short-term obligations issued with a term of 1 year or less.
Notes–Medium-term obligations issued with a term of 2-10 years.
Bonds–Long-term obligations of more than 10 years.
TIPS–Term of more than 5 years.

Federal debt securities held by the public outside the Government are held by individuals, corporations, state or local governments, FRBs, foreign governments, and other entities outside the Federal Government. The above table details Government borrowing primarily to finance operations and shows marketable and nonmarketable securities at face value less net unamortized premiums and discounts including accrued interest.

Securities that represent Federal debt held by the public are issued primarily by the Treasury and include:

- Interest-bearing marketable securities (bills, notes, bonds, and inflation-protected).
- Interest-bearing nonmarketable securities (government account series held by deposit and fiduciary funds, foreign series, State and local government series, domestic series, and savings bonds).
- Non-interest-bearing marketable and nonmarketable securities (matured and other).

Section 3111 of Title 31, United States Code (U.S.C.) authorizes the Secretary of the Treasury to use money received from the sale of an obligation and other money in the General Fund of the Treasury to buy, redeem, or refund, at or before maturity, outstanding bonds, notes, certificates of indebtedness, Treasury bills, or savings certificates of the Government. There were no buyback operations in fiscal years 2013 and 2012.

Gross federal debt (with some adjustments) is subject to a statutory ceiling (i.e., the debt limit). Prior to 1917, the Congress approved each debt issuance. In 1917, to facilitate planning in World War I, Congress and the President first enacted a statutory dollar ceiling for federal borrowing. With the Public Debt Act of 1941 (Public Law 77-7), Congress and the President set an overall limit of $65 billion on Treasury debt obligations that could be outstanding at any one time; since then, Congress and the President have enacted a number of debt limit increases. Most recently, Public Law 113 was enacted, which increased the statutory debt limit to the amount of qualifying federal debt securities outstanding as of May 19, 2013, or $16,699.4 billion. During fiscal year 2013, Treasury faced two periods that required it to depart from its normal debt management operations and to invoke legal authorities to avoid exceeding the statutory debt limit. As of September 30, 2013, and 2012, debt subject to the statutory debt limit was $16,699.4 billion and $16,027.0 billion, respectively. The debt subject to the limit includes Treasury securities held by the public and Government guaranteed debt of federal agencies (shown in the table above) and intragovernmental debt holdings (shown in the following table). A delay in raising the statutory debt limit existed as of September 30, 2013. Extraordinary measures taken by Treasury during the period of May 20, 2013, through September 30, 2013, resulted in federal debt securities not being issued to certain federal accounts. Please see Note 17—Other Liabilities, Note 23—Fiduciary Activities, and Note 26—Subsequent Events for additional information.

Intragovernmental Debt Holdings: Federal Debt Securities Held as Investments by Government Accounts as of September 30, 2013, and 2012

(In billions of dollars)	Balance 2012	Net Change During Fiscal Year 2013	Balance 2013
Social Security Administration, Federal Old-Age and Survivors Insurance Trust Fund	2,586.7	68.9	2,655.6
Office of Personnel Management, Civil Service Retirement and Disability Fund	826.5	(107.1)	719.4
Department of Defense, Military Retirement Fund	376.4	44.9	421.3
Department of Health and Human Services, Federal Hospital Insurance Fund	228.3	(22.3)	206.0
Department of Defense, Medicare-Eligible Retiree Health Care Fund	176.1	12.6	188.7
Social Security Administration, Federal Disability Insurance Trust Fund	132.3	(31.5)	100.8
Department of Health and Human Services, Federal Supplementary Medical Insurance Trust Fund	69.3	(1.9)	67.4
Department of Energy, Nuclear Waste Disposal Fund	49.6	1.0	50.6
Office of Personnel Management, Postal Service Retiree Health Benefits Fund	45.3	(3.0)	42.3
Office of Personnel Management, Employees Life Insurance Fund	41.3	0.7	42.0
Federal Deposit Insurance Corporation Funds	41.0	(3.3)	37.7
Department of Labor, Unemployment Trust Fund	20.7	8.8	29.5
Office of Personnel Management, Employees Health Benefits Fund	21.3	2.1	23.4
Department of the Treasury, Exchange Stabilization Fund	22.7	-	22.7
Pension Benefit Guaranty Corporation Fund	21.1	1.5	22.6
Department of State, Foreign Service Retirement and Disability Fund	16.9	0.5	17.4
Department of Transportation, Airport and Airway Trust Fund	10.4	1.4	11.8
National Credit Union Share Insurance Fund	10.3	0.3	10.6
All other programs and funds	100.4	(8.3)	92.1
Subtotal	4,796.6	(34.7)	4,761.9
Total Net Unamortized Premiums/(Discounts) for Intragovernmental	56.3	13.1	69.4
Total intragovernmental debt holdings, net	4,852.9	(21.6)	4,831.3

Intragovernmental debt holdings represent the portion of the gross Federal debt held as investments by Government entities such as trust funds, revolving funds, and special funds. As noted above, the delay in raising the debt limit still existed as of September 30, 2013. As such, suspension of certain investments to the Civil Service Retirement and Disability Fund contributed to the decrease in the intragovernmental debt holdings balance for the fund. Government entities that held investments in Treasury securities include trust funds that have funds from dedicated collections. For more information on funds from dedicated collections, see Note 22—Funds from Dedicated Collections. These intragovernmental debt holdings are eliminated in the consolidation of these financial statements.

Note 13. Federal Employee and Veteran Benefits Payable

Federal Employee and Veteran Benefits Payable as of September 30, 2013, and 2012

(In billions of dollars)	Civilian		Military		Total	
	2013	2012	2013	2012	2013	2012
Pension and accrued benefits..........	1,867.9	1,772.3	1,524.2	1,482.0	3,392.1	3,254.3
Post-retirement health and accrued benefits..	326.7	328.1	747.6	833.3	1,074.3	1,161.4
Veterans compensation and burial benefits......................................	N/A	N/A	1,974.8	1,761.6	1,974.8	1,761.6
Life insurance and accrued benefits.	47.6	47.2	9.9	10.6	57.5	57.8
FECA benefits................................	27.4	27.0	9.0	8.6	36.4	35.6
Liability for other benefits...............	0.8	0.8	2.4	2.5	3.2	3.3
Total Federal employee and veteran benefits payable.........................	2,270.4	2,175.4	4,267.9	4,098.6	6,538.3	6,274.0

Change in Pension and Accrued Benefits

(In billions of dollars)	Civilian		Military		Total	
	2013	2012	2013	2012	2013	2012
Actuarial accrued pension liability, beginning of fiscal year	1,772.3	1,619.7	1,482.0	1,361.3	3,254.3	2,981.0
Pension Expense:						
Expected normal costs	38.1	36.3	32.0	34.3	70.1	70.6
Interest on pension liability during the period	76.7	74.4	67.5	64.8	144.2	139.2
Prior (or past) service cost from plan amendments or new plans..............	-	0.1	-	-	-	0.1
Actuarial (gains)/losses (from experience)	(19.4)	9.7	(14.7)	(3.2)	(34.1)	6.5
Actuarial (gains)/losses (from assumption changes).......................	80.8	109.6	11.9	77.2	92.7	186.8
Total pension expense	176.2	230.1	96.7	173.1	272.9	403.2
Less benefits paid.............................	(80.6)	(77.5)	(54.5)	(52.4)	(135.1)	(129.9)
Actuarial accrued pension liability, end of fiscal year..........	1,867.9	1,772.3	1,524.2	1,482.0	3,392.1	3,254.3

Change in Post-Retirement Health and Accrued Benefits

(In billions of dollars)	Civilian		Military		Total	
	2013	2012	2013	2012	2013	2012
Actuarial accrued post-retirement health benefits liability, beginning of fiscal year	328.1	342.5	833.3	842.3	1,161.4	1,184.8
Post-Retirement health benefits expense:						
Prior (and past) service costs from plan amendments or new plans	-	-	(46.8)	(31.9)	(46.8)	(31.9)
Normal costs	11.8	13.8	22.1	21.4	33.9	35.2
Interest on liability	15.1	16.4	38.8	41.7	53.9	58.1
Actuarial (gains)/losses (from experience)	(14.7)	(21.2)	(3.8)	(12.3)	(18.5)	(33.5)
Actuarial (gains)/losses (from assumption changes)	-	(9.8)	(74.8)	(6.8)	(74.8)	(16.6)
Total post-retirement health benefits expense	12.2	(0.8)	(64.5)	12.1	(52.3)	11.3
Less claims paid	(13.6)	(13.6)	(21.2)	(21.1)	(34.8)	(34.7)
Actuarial accrued post-retirement health benefits liability, end of fiscal year	326.7	328.1	747.6	833.3	1,074.3	1,161.4

The Government offers its employees life and health insurance, as well as retirement and other benefits. The liabilities for these benefits, which include both actuarial amounts and amounts due and payable to beneficiaries and health care carriers, apply to current and former civilian and military employees.

OPM administers the largest civilian plan. DOD administers the largest military plan. Other significant pension plans with more than $10 billion in accrued benefits payable include those of the Coast Guard (DHS), Foreign Service (Department of State), TVA, and HHS's Public Health Service Commissioned Corps Retirement System. Please refer to the individual financial statements of the agencies listed for further details regarding their pension plans and other benefits.

Change in Civilian Life Insurance and Accrued Benefits

(In billions of dollars)	2013	2012
Actuarial accrued life insurance benefits liability, beginning of fiscal year	47.2	44.6
Life insurance benefits expense:		
New entrant expense	0.4	0.3
Interest on liability	2.1	2.1
Actuarial (gains)/losses (from experience)	(0.7)	-
Actuarial (gains)/losses (from assumption changes)	(0.9)	0.7
Total life insurance benefits expense	0.9	3.1
Less costs paid	(0.5)	(0.5)
Actuarial accrued life insurance benefits liability, end of fiscal year	47.6	47.2

Significant Long-Term Economic Assumptions Used in Determining Pension Liability and the Related Expense

| | Civilian | | | | Military | |
| | 2013 | | 2012 | | 2013 | 2012 |
	FERS	CSRS	FERS	CSRS		
Rate of interest	4.40%	4.10%	4.70%	4.30%	4.30%	4.60%
Rate of inflation	2.50%	2.50%	2.50%	2.50%	2.40%	2.60%
Projected salary increases	2.20%	2.20%	2.60%	2.60%	2.80%	3.00%
Cost of living adjustment	2.00%	2.50%	2.00%	2.50%	-	-

Significant Long-Term Economic Assumptions Used in Determining Post-Retirement Health Benefits and the Related Expense

| | Civilian | | Military | |
	2013	2012	2013	2012
Rate of interest	4.40%	4.70%	4.40%	4.60%
Single equivalent medical trend rate	-	-	4.80%	5.10%
Ultimate medical trend rate	4.20%	4.40%	5.15%	5.35%

Significant Long-Term Economic Assumptions Used in Determining Life Insurance Benefits and the Related Expense

| | Civilian | |
	2013	2012
Rate of interest	4.30%	4.50%
Rate of increase in salary	2.20%	2.60%

With the implementation of SFFAS No. 33, *Pension, Other Retirement Benefits, and Other Postemployment Benefits: Reporting the Gains and Losses from Changes in Assumptions and Selecting Discount Rates and Valuation Dates*, agencies are required to separately present gains and losses from changes in long-term assumptions used to estimate liabilities associated with pensions, ORB, and OPEB on the Statement of Net Cost. SFFAS No. 33 also provides a standard for selecting the discount rate assumption for present value estimates of Federal employee pension, ORB, and OPEB liabilities. In addition, SFFAS No. 33 provides a standard for selecting the valuation date for estimates of Federal employee pension, ORB, and OPEB liabilities that will establish a consistent method for such measurements.

DOD's long-term ultimate medical trend rate for post-retirement health benefits liability is 5.15 percent for fiscal year 2013 and 5.35 percent for fiscal year 2012. For disclosure and comparison purposes, DOD's estimate of a single equivalent medical trend rate for fiscal year 2013 is 4.8 percent and for fiscal year 2012 is 5.10 percent, which is an approximation of the single equivalent rate that would produce that same actuarial liability as the actual rates used. Please refer to the individual financial statements of DOD for further details regarding Military Retirement Health Benefits-Medical Trend.

Civilian Employees

Pensions

OPM administers the largest civilian pension plan, which covers substantially all full-time, permanent civilian Federal employees. This plan includes two components of defined benefits. These are the Civil Service Retirement System (CSRS) and the Federal Employees' Retirement System (FERS). The basic benefit components of the CSRS and the FERS are financed and operated through the Civil Service Retirement and Disability Fund (CSRDF).

CSRDF monies are generated primarily from employees' contributions, agency contributions, payments from the General Fund, and interest on investments in Treasury securities. See Note 22—Funds from Dedicated Collections.

The Federal Retirement Thrift Investment Board administers the TSP Fund. The TSP Fund investment options include two fixed income funds (the G and F Funds), three stock funds (the C, S, and I Funds) and five lifecycle funds (L 2050, L 2040, L 2030, L 2020, and L Income). The L Funds diversify participant accounts among the G, F, C, S, and I Funds, using professionally determined investment mixes (allocations) that are tailored to different time horizons. Treasury securities held in the G Fund are included in Federal debt securities held by the public and accrued interest on the Balance Sheet. The G Fund held $52.5 billion and $153.9 billion in nonmarketable Treasury securities as of September 30, 2013, and 2012, respectively. The decrease in nonmarketable Treasury securities held in the G Fund relates to the delay in raising the statutory debt limit. The Secretary of the Treasury has authority to take extraordinary measures to stay within the statutory debt limit imposed by Congress.

One such measure involves the suspension of the issuance of securities to the G Fund if the issuance cannot be made without causing the debt limit to be exceeded. Please see Note 17—Other Liabilities for additional information.

Post-Retirement Health Benefits

The post-retirement civilian health benefit liability is an estimate of the Government's future cost of providing post-retirement health benefits to current employees and retirees. Although active and retired employees pay insurance premiums under the Federal Employees Health Benefits Program (FEHB), these premiums cover only a portion of the costs. The OPM actuary applies economic assumptions to historical cost information to estimate the liability. The Postal Accountability and Enhancement Act of 2006 (Postal Act of 2006) (Public Law No. 109-435, Title VIII), made significant changes in the funding of future retiree health benefits for employees of the USPS, including the requirement for the USPS to make scheduled payments to the third Health Benefits Program (HBP) fund, the Postal Service Retiree Health Benefits (PSRHB) Fund. Public Law No.109-435 requires the USPS to make scheduled payment contributions to the PSRHB Fund ranging from $5.4 billion to $5.8 billion per year from fiscal year 2007 through fiscal year 2016. (The fiscal year 2009 payment was subsequently reduced to $1.4 billion.) Thereafter, the USPS will make annual payments in the amount of the normal cost payment plus or minus an amount to amortize the unfunded liability or surplus. The payment originally due by September 30, 2011, was deferred by Public Law No. 112-74, resulting in two payments due in fiscal year 2012, one for $5.5 billion due by August 1, 2012, and a second payment of $5.6 billion due by September 30, 2012, a total of $11.1 billion. Both were defaulted upon by USPS. At this time, Congress has not taken further action on these payments due to the PSRHB from USPS. In addition, there was a $5.6 billion payment due by September 30, 2013, which USPS also did not make. The cost for these annual payments, including any defaulted payments, along with all its other benefit program costs, are included in USPS' net cost in the consolidated Statements of Net Cost.

Life Insurance Benefits

One of the largest other employee benefits is the Federal Employee Group Life Insurance (FEGLI) Program. Employee and annuitant contributions and interest on investments fund a portion of this liability. The actuarial life insurance liability is the expected present value of future benefits to pay to, or on behalf of, existing FEGLI participants. The OPM actuary uses interest rate, inflation, and salary increase assumptions that are consistent with the pension liability.

Workers' Compensation Benefits

The DOL determines both civilian and military agencies' liabilities for future workers' compensation benefits for civilian Federal employees, as mandated by the Federal Employees' Compensation Act (FECA), for death, disability, medical, and miscellaneous costs for approved compensation cases, and a component for incurred, but not reported, claims. The FECA liability is determined annually using historical benefit payment patterns related to injury years to predict the ultimate payments. These estimated payments have been discounted to present value using OMB's interest rate assumptions for 10-year U.S. Treasury notes. For 2013, a 2.73 percent interest rate was assumed in year one and 3.13 percent was assumed for year two and thereafter.

The DOL calculates the FECA liability using wage inflation factors, cost of living adjustments (COLA), and medical inflation factors (Consumer Price Index–Medical or (CPIM)). The table below reflects the compensation COLAs and CPIMs used in the estimations for various charge-back years.

Fiscal Year	COLA	CPIM
2014	1.67%	3.46%
2015	1.80%	3.82%
2016	2.20%	3.83%
2017	2.20%	3.82%
2018+	2.20%	3.82%

Military Employees (Including Veterans)

Pensions

The DOD Military Retirement Fund finances military retirement and survivor benefit programs. The increase in the Military Retirement Pension liability is due to additional benefit accruals (normal cost), interest on the pension liability and assumption and benefit changes. Liabilities in the future will depend on expected changes due to interest and benefit accruals, future benefit changes, assumption changes, and actuarial experience.

This Fund receives income from three sources: monthly normal cost payments from the Services to pay for the current years' service cost; annual payments from Treasury to amortize the unfunded liability and pay for the increase in the normal cost attributable to Concurrent Receipt per Public Law 108-136; and investment income.

The military retirement system consists of a funded, noncontributory, defined benefit plan. It applies to military personnel (Departments of Army, Navy, Air Force, and the Marine Corps). This system includes non-disability retirement pay, disability retirement pay, and survivor annuity programs. Military personnel who remain on active duty for 20 years or longer are eligible for retirement. There are three different retirement benefit formulas that are currently being used by the military: Final Pay, High-3 Year Average, and Career Status Bonus/Military Retirement Reform Act of 1986. The date an individual enters the military determines which retirement system they would fall under and if they have the option to pick their retirement system. For more information on these benefits, see DOD's Website http://www.dfas.mil/retiredmilitary/plan/estimate/csbredux.html.

Post-Retirement Health Benefits

Military retirees and their dependents are entitled to health care in military medical facilities if a facility can provide the needed care. Prior to becoming Medicare eligible, military retirees and their dependents also are entitled to participate in TRICARE, which reimburses (net of beneficiary copay and deductible requirements) for the cost of health care from civilian providers. TRICARE options are available in indemnity, preferred provider organization, and health maintenance organization (HMO) designs.

Since fiscal year 2002, TRICARE, as second payer to Medicare, covers military retirees and their dependents after they become Medicare eligible. This TRICARE coverage for Medicare eligible beneficiaries requires that the beneficiary enroll in Medicare Part B and is referred to as TRICARE for Life (TFL). Health care under TFL can be obtained from military medical facilities on an "as available" basis or from civilian providers. Military retiree health care actuarial liability figures include costs incurred in military medical facilities, as well as claims paid to civilian providers and certain administrative costs. Costs paid to civilian providers are net of Medicare's portion of the cost.

Chapter 56 of Title 10, United States Code (U.S.C.) created the DOD Medicare-Eligible Retiree Health Care Fund, which became operative on October 1, 2002. The purpose of this fund is to account for the health benefits of Medicare-eligible military retirees, their dependents, and survivors who are Medicare eligible. The Fund receives contributions from the Uniformed Services and Treasury, as well as interest earnings on its investments and pays costs incurred in military medical facilities, as well as claims for care provided by civilian providers under TFL, administration costs associated with processing the TFL claims, and capitated payments for coverage provided by U.S. Family Health Plans.

In addition to the health care benefits for civilian and military retirees and their dependents, the VA also provides medical care to veterans on an "as available" basis, subject to the limits of the annual appropriations. In accordance with 38 CFR 17.36 (c), VA's Secretary makes an annual enrollment decision that defines the veterans, by priority, who will be treated for that fiscal year subject to change based on funds appropriated, estimated collections, usage, the severity index of enrolled veterans, and changes in cost. Accordingly, VA recognizes the medical care expenses in the period the medical care services are provided. For the fiscal years 2009 through 2013, the average medical care cost per year was $39.0 billion.

Veterans Compensation and Burial Benefits

The Government compensates disabled veterans and their survivors. Veterans compensation is payable as a disability benefit or a survivor's benefit. Entitlement to compensation depends on the veteran's disabilities having been incurred in, or aggravated during, active military service; death while on duty; or death resulting from service-connected disabilities, if not on active duty.

Burial benefits include a burial and plot or interment allowance payable for a veteran who, at the time of death, is qualified to receive compensation or a pension, or whose death occurred in a VA facility.

The liability for veterans' compensation and burial benefits payable increased by $213.2 billion in fiscal year 2013. Substantially all the $213.2 billion increase in the Federal Employee and Veterans Benefits Liabilities relates to 1) changes in experience related primarily to increased disability claims filed and processed for presumptive disability benefits associated with Vietnam Veterans, including Agent Orange and 2) changes in actuarial liability assumptions used to project future cashflows related primarily to higher disability claims rates and the decrease in the rate used to discount future cashflows.

Several significant actuarial assumptions were used in the valuation of compensation, pension, and burial benefits to calculate the present value of the liability. A liability was recognized for the projected benefit payments to: 1) those beneficiaries, including veterans and survivors, currently receiving benefit payments; 2) current Veterans who will in the future become beneficiaries of the compensation and pension programs; and 3) a proportional share of those in active military service as of the valuation date who will become veterans in the future.

The veterans compensation and burial benefits liability is a valuation of a long period of estimated cashflows. As a result, changes in long-term assumptions can have a dramatic effect on the liability and net cost.

Change in Veterans Compensation and Burial Benefits

(In billions of dollars)	Compensation		Burial		Total	
	2013	2012	2013	2012	2013	2012
Actuarial accrued liability, beginning of fiscal year	1,757.1	1,529.2	4.5	4.5	1,761.6	1,533.7
Current Year Expenses:						
Interest on the liability balance	75.7	69.3	0.2	0.2	75.9	69.5
Prior (and past) service costs from program amendments or new programs during the period	1.2	0.4	-	-	1.2	0.4
Actuarial (gain)/losses (from experience)	86.8	61.7	(0.1)	(0.1)	86.7	61.6
Actuarial (gain)/losses (from assumption changes)	113.9	149.2	0.2	0.1	114.1	149.3
Total current year expense	277.6	280.6	0.3	0.2	277.9	280.8
Less benefits paid	(64.5)	(52.7)	(0.2)	(0.2)	(64.7)	(52.9)
Actuarial accrued liability, end of fiscal year	1,970.2	1,757.1	4.6	4.5	1,974.8	1,761.6

Significant Economic Assumptions Used in Determining Veterans Compensation and Burial Benefits as of September 30, 2013, and 2012

	2013	2012
Rate of interest	4.20%	4.31%
Rate of inflation	2.57%	2.61%

Life Insurance Benefits

The largest veterans' life insurance programs consist of the following:

- National Service Life Insurance (NSLI) covers policyholders who served during World War II.
- Veterans' Special Life Insurance (VSLI) was established in 1951 to meet the insurance needs of veterans who served during the Korean Conflict and through the period ending January 1, 1957.
- Veterans' Reopened Insurance (VRI), which provided a 1-year reopening for insurance coverage in 1965 for those eligible to have obtained NSLI or VSLI and were disabled.

The components of veteran life insurance liability for future policy benefits are presented below.

Veterans Life Insurance Liability as of September 30, 2013, and 2012

(In billions of dollars)	2013	2012
Insurance death benefits:		
NSLI	5.0	5.7
VSLI	1.5	1.5
VRI	0.2	0.2
Other	0.7	0.7
Total death benefits	7.4	8.1
Death benefit annuities	0.1	0.1
Disability income & waiver	0.8	0.7
Insurance dividends payable	1.5	1.6
Unearned premiums	0.1	0.1
Total veterans life insurance liability	9.9	10.6

Insurance dividends payable consists of dividends left on a deposit with VA, related interest payable, and dividends payable to policyholders.

The VA supervises Servicemembers Group Life Insurance and Veterans Group Life Insurance programs that provide life insurance coverage to members of the uniformed armed services and veterans who served during the Vietnam era or thereafter. The VA also provides certain veterans and/or their dependents with pension benefits, based on annual eligibility reviews, if the veteran died or was disabled for nonservice-related causes. The actuarial present value of the future liability for pension benefits is a non-exchange transaction and is not required to be recorded on the Balance Sheet. The projected amounts of future payments for pension benefits (presented for informational purposes only) as of September 30, 2013, and 2012, were $97.5 billion and $92.8 billion, respectively.

Note 14. Environmental and Disposal Liabilities

Environmental and Disposal Liabilities as of September 30, 2013, and 2012

(In billions of dollars)	2013	2012
Department of Energy:		
Environmental and Disposal Liabilities	280.2	268.4
Department of Defense:		
Environmental Restoration	26.6	28.4
Disposal of Weapon Systems Program	21.8	24.5
Environmental Corrective Other	5.7	5.4
Base Realignment and Closure	4.3	4.3
Total Department of Defense	58.4	62.6
All other agencies	10.5	8.0
Total environmental and disposal liabilities	349.1	339.0

During World War II and the Cold War, DOE (or predecessor agencies) developed a massive industrial complex to research, produce, and test nuclear weapons. This included nuclear reactors, chemical-processing buildings, metal machining plants, laboratories, and maintenance facilities that manufactured tens of thousands of nuclear warheads and conducted more than one thousand nuclear tests.

At all sites where these activities took place, some environmental contamination occurred. This contamination was caused by the production, storage, and use of radioactive materials and hazardous chemicals, which resulted in contamination of soil, surface water, and groundwater. The environmental legacy of nuclear weapons production also includes thousands of contaminated buildings and large volumes of waste and special nuclear materials requiring treatment, stabilization, and disposal.

Estimated cleanup costs at sites for which there are no current feasible remediation approaches, such as the Nevada nuclear test site, are excluded from the estimates, although applicable stewardship and monitoring costs for these sites are included. DOE has not been required through regulation to establish remediation activities for these sites.

Estimating DOE's environmental cleanup liability requires making assumptions about future activities and is inherently uncertain. The future course of DOE's environmental cleanup and disposal will depend on a number of fundamental technical and policy choices, many of which have not been made. The sites and facilities could be restored to a condition suitable for any desirable use, or could be restored to a point where they pose no near-term health risks. Achieving the former conditions would have a higher cost, but may or may not, warrant the costs, or be legally required. The environmental and disposal liability estimates include contingency estimates intended to account for the uncertainties associated with the technical cleanup scope of the program.

DOE's environmental and disposal liabilities estimates are dependent on annual funding levels and achievement of work as scheduled. Congressional appropriations at lower than anticipated levels or unplanned delays in project completion would cause increases in life-cycle costs.

DOE's environmental and disposal liabilities also include the estimated cleanup and post-closure responsibilities, including surveillance and monitoring activities, soil and groundwater remediation, and disposition of excess material for sites. The Department is responsible for the post-closure activities at many of the closure sites as well as other sites. The costs for these post-closure activities are estimated for a period of 75 years after the balance sheet date, i.e., through 2088 in fiscal year 2013 and through 2087 in fiscal year 2012. While some post-cleanup monitoring and other long-term stewardship activities post-2088 are included in the liability, there are others the Department expects to continue beyond 2088 for which the costs cannot reasonably be estimated.

A portion of DOE's environmental and disposal liabilities at various field sites includes anticipated costs for facilities managed by DOE's ongoing program operations which will ultimately require stabilization, deactivation and decommissioning. The estimate is largely based upon a cost-estimating model. Site specific estimates are used in lieu of the cost-estimating model, when available. Cost estimates for ongoing program facilities are updated each year. For facilities newly contaminated since fiscal year 1997, cleanup costs allocated to future periods and not included in environmental and disposal liabilities amounted to $766.0 million and $808.0 million for fiscal years 2013 and 2012, respectively.

Please refer to the financial statements of the DOE for significant detailed information regarding DOE's environmental and disposal liabilities, including cleanup costs.

DOD follows the Comprehensive Environmental Response, Compensation, and Liability Act (CERCLA), Superfund Amendments and Reauthorization Act, Resource Conservation and Recovery Act (RCRA) and other applicable Federal or State laws to clean up contamination. The CERCLA and RCRA require the DOD to clean up contamination in coordination with regulatory agencies, current owners of property damaged by the Department, and third parties that have a partial responsibility for the environmental restoration. Failure to comply with agreements and legal mandates puts the DOD at risk of incurring fines and penalties.

DOD must restore active installations, installations affected by base realignment and closure, and other areas formerly used as Defense sites. DOD also bears responsibility for disposal of chemical weapons and environmental costs associated with the disposal of weapons systems (primarily nuclear powered aircraft carriers and submarines).

DOD uses engineering estimates and independently validated models to estimate environmental costs. The engineering estimates are used after obtaining extensive data during the remedial investigation/feasibility phase of the environmental project.

For general PP&E placed into service after September 30, 1997, DOD expenses associated environmental costs systematically over the life of the asset using two methods: physical capacity for operating landfills and life expectancy in years for all other assets. The Department expenses the full cost to clean up contamination for stewardship property, plant, and equipment at the time the asset is placed into service. DOD has expensed the costs for cleanup associated with general property, plant, and equipment placed into service before October 1, 1997, except for costs intended to be recovered through user charges; for those costs, DOD has expensed cleanup costs associated with that portion of the asset life that has passed since it was placed into service. DOD systematically recognizes the remaining cost over the remaining life of the asset. The unrecognized portion of the cleanup cost associated with general property, plant, and equipment is $3.2 billion for both fiscal years 2013 and 2012. Not all components of DOD are able to compile the necessary information for this disclosure, thus the amount reported may not accurately reflect DOD's total unrecognized costs associated with general property, plant, and equipment. DOD is implementing procedures to address these deficiencies.

DOD is unable to estimate and report a liability for environmental restoration and corrective action for buried chemical munitions and agents, because the extent of the buried chemical munitions and agents is unknown at this time. DOD is also unable to provide a complete estimate for the Formerly Utilized Sites Remedial Action Program. DOD has ongoing studies and will update its estimate as additional liabilities are identified. DOD has the potential to incur costs for restoration initiatives in conjunction with returning overseas Defense facilities to host nations. However, DOD is unable to provide a reasonable estimate at this time because the extent of required restoration is unknown.

Please refer to the financial statements of the DOD for further detailed information regarding DOD's environmental and disposal liabilities, including cleanup costs.

In addition, due to the implementation of TB 2006-1, as stated in Note 1.B, various agencies within the "all other agencies" line recorded an environmental and disposal liability for asbestos-related cleanup costs totaling $3.0 billion as of September 30, 2013. Combined with DOD's liability of $1.0 billion for asbestos-related cleanup costs, total asbestos-related environmental and disposal liability as of September 30, 2013 is $4.0 billion. Prior to the implementation of TB 2006-1, asbestos-related environmental and disposal liability was $1.1 billion, solely due to DOD.

Note 15. Benefits Due and Payable

Benefits Due and Payable as of September 30, 2013, and 2012

(In billions of dollars)	2013	2012
Federal Old-Age and Survivors Insurance	60.0	56.8
Federal Supplementary Medical Insurance (Medicare Parts B and D)	27.8	26.2
Grants to States for Medicaid	27.6	24.9
Federal Disability Insurance	24.2	24.4
Federal Hospital Insurance (Medicare Part A)	20.8	20.2
Supplemental Security Income	5.2	5.4
Unemployment Insurance	2.4	2.1
All other benefits programs	6.3	6.2
Total benefits due and payable	174.3	166.2

Benefits due and payable are amounts owed to program recipients or medical service providers as of September 30 that have not been paid. HHS and the SSA administer the majority of the medical service programs and the DOL administers the Unemployment Insurance program. For a description of the programs, see Note 24—Social Insurance and the Unaudited Required Supplementary Information—Social Insurance section.

Note 16. Insurance and Guarantee Program Liabilities

Insurance and Guarantee Program Liabilities as of September 30, 2013, and 2012

(In billions of dollars)	2013	2012
Insurance and Guarantee Program Liabilities:		
Pension Benefit Guaranty Corporation - Benefit Pension Plans	105.0	105.6
Federal Deposit Insurance Corporation Funds	16.9	26.5
Department of Agriculture - Federal Crop Insurance	6.9	20.0
All other insurance and guarantee programs	1.2	4.3
Total insurance and guarantee program liabilities	130.0	156.4

PBGC insures pension benefits for participants in covered defined benefit pension plans. As a wholly-owned corporation of the Government, PBGC's financial activity and balances are included in the consolidated financial statements of the Government. However, under current law, PBGC's liabilities may be paid only from PBGC's assets and not from the General Fund of the Treasury or assets of the Government in general. As of September 30, 2013, and 2012, PBGC had total liabilities of $120.6 billion and $119.2 billion, and its total liabilities exceeded its total assets by $35.6 billion and $34.4 billion, respectively. In addition, as discussed in Note 20—Contingencies, PBGC reported reasonably possible contingent losses of about $328.9 billion and $321.8 billion as of September 30, 2013, and 2012, respectively.

Of the total FDIC amount as of September 30, 2013, and 2012, $1.2 billion and $3.6 billion, respectively, represents the recorded contingent liability and loss provision for institutions insured by the Deposit Insurance Fund that are likely to fail. In addition, $15.8 billion and $21.2 billion pertain to liabilities due to resolutions of failed or failing institutions and to pending depositor claims as of September 30, 2013, and 2012, respectively. Liabilities due to resolutions of failed or failing institutions declined as a result of either sending cash to the receivership to fund shared-loss agreements and other expenses or by offsetting receivables from resolutions when the receivership declared a dividend. Another $1.7 billion as of September 30, 2012, pertains to the Temporary Liquidity Guarantee Program, which guaranteed, certain newly issued debt and certain noninterest-bearing transaction accounts in an effort to counter the system-wide crisis in the nation's financial sector. The guarantees expired no later than December 31, 2012. The remaining amounts represent contingent liabilities for litigation.

As of September 30, 2013, and 2012, $6.9 billion and $20.0 billion, respectively, pertain to the USDA's Federal Crop Insurance Program. The decrease in the estimated indemnities is due to the return of normal weather conditions after experiencing the most severe drought in the farm belt since 1988 during fiscal year 2012. The Federal Crop Insurance Program is administered by the Federal Crop Insurance Corporation, whose mission is to provide an actuarially sound risk management program to reduce agricultural producers' economic losses due to natural disasters. Also, $3.4 billion relates to recorded contingent liabilities for the National Credit Union Administration's Temporary Corporate Credit Union Stabilization Fund as of September 30, 2012. These programs guarantee the timely payment of interest and principal on certain unsecured debt of participating credit unions and to holders of NCUA Guaranteed Notes (NGNs) under certain conditions outlined in the respective indentures and related agreements. As of December 31, 2012, the only remaining guarantee obligation was for the NGN program. NCUA uses both internal and external models, as well as external valuations to some extent, to estimate contingent liabilities associated with the Stabilization Fund. Actual results could differ materially from current estimates and expectations.

Note 17. Other Liabilities

Other Liabilities as of September 30, 2013, and 2012
(In billions of dollars)

	2013	2012
Unearned revenue and assets held for others:		
Unearned fees for nuclear waste disposal (DOE) and other unearned revenue	48.5	56.2
Assets held on behalf of others	79.5	74.5
Subtotal	128.0	130.7
Employee-related liabilities:		
Accrued Federal employees' wages and benefits	38.2	40.0
Selected DOE contractors' and D.C. employees' pension benefits	46.5	57.0
Subtotal	84.7	97.0
International monetary liabilities and gold certificates:		
Exchange Stabilization Fund	59.4	59.7
Gold Certificates (see Note 2)	11.0	11.0
Subtotal	70.4	70.7
Subsidies and grants:		
Farm and other subsidies	10.6	11.8
Grant payments due to State and local governments and others	15.6	16.8
Subtotal	26.2	28.6
Miscellaneous liabilities:		
Legal and other contingencies	43.4	41.9
Bonneville Power Administration non-Federal power projects and capital lease liabilities, and disposal liabilities	12.8	13.2
Liability for restoration of Federal debt principal and interest	120.4	-
Other miscellaneous	46.2	50.5
Subtotal	222.8	105.6
Total other liabilities	532.1	432.6

Other liabilities represent liabilities that are not separately identified on the Balance Sheet and are presented on a comparative basis by major category.

Unearned Revenue and Assets Held for Others

The Government recognizes a liability when it receives money in advance of providing goods and services or assumes custody of money belonging to others. The Government's unearned revenue from fees DOE has collected from utility companies for the future cost of managing the disposal of nuclear waste is about $34.1 billion and $32.1 billion as of September 30, 2013, and 2012, respectively. Other unearned revenue includes USPS income for such things as prepaid postage, outstanding money orders, and prepaid P.O. Box rentals. FDIC collected prepaid assessments from the financial institutions to address the Deposit Insurance Fund (DIF) liquidity needs to pay for projected near-term failures and to ensure that the deposit insurance system remained industry-funded. The prepaid collection was based on maintaining assessment rates at their current levels through the end of 2010 and adopting a uniform three basis point increase in assessment rates effective January 1, 2011. An institution's quarterly risk-based deposit insurance assessment thereafter is offset by the amount prepaid until that amount is exhausted or until June 30, 2013, when any amount remaining would be returned to the institution. The DIF's unearned revenue liability was $9.2 billion as of September 30, 2012. The final offset of prepaid assessments occurred for the period ending March 31, 2013, and in June 2013, as required by regulation, the DIF refunded $5.8 billion of unused prepaid assessments to Insured Depository Institutions. Assets held on behalf of others include funds collected in advance and undelivered Defense articles. The Foreign Military Sales program holds $67.0 billion and $61.8 billion as of September 30, 2013, and 2012, respectively for articles and services for future delivery to foreign governments.

Employee-Related Liabilities

This category includes amounts owed to employees at year-end and actuarial liabilities for certain non-Federal employees. Actuarial liabilities for Federal employees and veteran benefits are included in Note 13 and are reported on another line on the Balance Sheet. The largest liability in the employee-related liabilities category is the amount owed at the end of the fiscal year to Federal employees for wages and benefits (including accrued annual leave). In addition, DOE is liable to certain contractors such as the University of California, which operates the Lawrence Livermore National Laboratory, for contractor employee pension and postretirement benefits, which is about $21.3 billion and $31.4 billion as of September 30, 2013, and 2012, respectively. Also, the Government owed about $9.2 billion and $10.1 billion as of September 30, 2013, and 2012, respectively, for estimated future pension benefits of the District of Columbia's judges, police, firefighters, and teachers.

International Monetary Liabilities and Gold Certificates

Consistent with U.S. obligations in the IMF on orderly exchange arrangements and a stable system of exchange rates, the Secretary of the Treasury, with the approval of the President, may use the Exchange Stabilization Fund to deal in gold, foreign exchange, and other instruments of credit and securities.

Gold certificates are issued in nondefinitive or book-entry form to the Federal Reserve Banks. The Government's liability incurred by issuing the gold certificates, as reported on the Balance Sheet, is limited to the gold being held by the Department of the Treasury at the standard value established by law. Upon issuance of gold certificates to the Federal Reserve Banks, the proceeds from the certificates are deposited into the operating cash of the U.S. Government. All of the Department of the Treasury's certificates issued are payable to the Federal Reserve Banks.

Subsidies and Grants

The Government supports the public good through a wide variety of subsidy and grant programs in such areas as agriculture, medical and scientific research, education, and transportation. USDA programs such as the Conservation Reserve, Tobacco Transition Payment, and Direct and Counter-Cyclical Payment programs account for the majority of the subsidies due, about $6.8 billion, and $8.1 billion as of September 30, 2013, and 2012, respectively.

The Government awards hundreds of billions of dollars in grants annually. These include project grants that are competitively awarded for agency-specific projects, such as HHS grants to fund projects to "enhance the independence, productivity, integration and inclusion into the community of people with developmental disabilities." Other grants are formula grants, such as matching grants. Formula grants go to State governments for such things as education and transportation programs. These grants are paid in accordance with distribution formulas that have been provided by law or administrative regulations. Of the total liability reported for grants as of September 30, 2013, and 2012, DOT, Education, and HHS collectively owed their grantees about $12.7 billion and $13.0 billion, respectively. Refer to the financial statements and footnotes of the respective agencies for additional information.

Miscellaneous Liabilities

Some of the more significant liabilities included in this category are for (1) legal and other contingencies (see Note 20—Contingencies), (2) Bonneville Power Administration liability to pay annual budgets of several power projects for its electrical generating capacity, (3) payables due to the purchases of securities, and (4) other liabilities reported by Treasury as a result of the occurrence of a delay in raising the statutory debt limit as of September 30, 2013. When delays in raising the statutory debt limit occur, Treasury often must deviate from its normal debt management operations and take a number of extraordinary measures to meet the Government's obligations as they come due without exceeding the debt limit. Many extraordinary measures taken by Treasury during the period of May 20, 2013, through September 30, 2013, resulted in federal debt securities not being issued to certain federal government accounts. As a result of Treasury securities not being issued to the Federal Retirement Thrift Investment Board (FRTIB) for the Government Securities Investment Fund (G Fund), Treasury reported miscellaneous liabilities in the amount of $120.4 billion that represent uninvested principal of and related interest for the Thrift Savings Plan's (TSP) G Fund that would have been reported in Note 12—Federal Debt Securities Held by the Public and Accrued Interest had there not been a delay in raising the statutory debt limit as of September 30, 2013, and had the securities been issued. For further information related to the impact on TSP, see Note 23—Fiduciary Activities and Note 26—Subsequent Events.

In addition, many Federal agencies reported relatively small amounts of miscellaneous liabilities that are not otherwise classified.

Note 18. Collections and Refunds of Federal Revenue

Collections of Federal Tax Revenue for the Year Ended September 30, 2013

(In billions of dollars)	Federal Tax Revenue Collections	Tax Year to Which Collections Relate			
		2013	2012	2011	Prior Years
Individual income and tax withholdings	2,448.5	1,580.4	821.5	22.3	24.3
Corporation income taxes	312.0	217.6	83.6	2.0	8.8
Unemployment taxes	54.1	28.0	15.3	10.7	0.1
Excise taxes	87.1	64.0	22.9	0.1	0.1
Estate and gift taxes	19.8	-	10.3	0.6	8.9
Railroad retirement taxes	5.5	4.2	1.3	-	-
Fines, penalties, interest, and other revenue	7.5	7.2	0.2	0.1	-
Customs duties	31.8	31.8	-	-	-
Subtotal	2,966.3	1,933.2	955.1	35.8	42.2
Less: amounts collected for non-Federal entities	(0.4)				
Total	2,965.9				

Treasury is the Government's principal revenue-collecting agency. Collections of individual income and tax withholdings include FICA/SECA and individual income taxes. These taxes are characterized as non-exchange revenue.

Excise taxes, also characterized as non-exchange revenue, consist of taxes collected for various items, such as airline tickets, gasoline products, distilled spirits and imported liquor, tobacco, firearms, and others.

Federal Tax Refunds Disbursed for the Year Ended September 30, 2013

(In billions of dollars)	Refunds Disbursed	Tax Year to Which Refunds Relate			
		2013	2012	2011	Prior Years
Individual income and tax withholdings	320.4	0.7	287.1	21.9	10.7
Corporation income taxes	41.6	5.4	12.9	6.7	16.6
Unemployment taxes	0.1	-	0.1	-	-
Excise taxes	1.6	0.6	0.8	0.1	0.1
Estate and gift taxes	1.0	-	0.2	0.3	0.5
Customs duties	1.2	1.2	-	-	-
Total	365.9	7.9	301.1	29.0	27.9

Reconciliation of Revenue to Tax Collections for the Year Ended September 30, 2013, and 2012

(In billions of dollars)	2013	2012
Consolidated revenue per the Statements of Operations and Changes in Net Position	2,842.5	2,518.2
Tax refunds	365.9	375.7
Earned income tax and child tax credit imputed revenue	(79.1)	(77.0)
Other tax credits and accrual adjustments	(9.5)	(16.1)
Federal Insurance Contributions Act - Tax	20.3	-
Federal Reserve earnings	(75.8)	(82.0)
Nontax-related fines and penalties reported by agencies	(87.2)	(52.7)
Nontax-related earned revenue	(11.2)	(19.7)
Collections of Federal tax revenue	2,965.9	2,646.4

Consolidated revenue in the Statements of Operations and Changes in Net Position is presented on a modified cash basis, is net of tax refunds, and includes other non-tax related revenue. Earned Income Tax Credit and Child Tax Credit, other tax credits amounts (unaudited) are included in gross cost in the Statements of Net Cost. The Federal Insurance Contributions Act – Tax is included in the Individual income and tax withholdings line in the Collections of Federal tax revenue; however, it is not reported on the SOCNP as these collections are intragovernmental revenue and eliminated in consolidation. The table above reconciles total revenue to Federal tax collections.

Collections of Federal Revenue for the Year Ended September 30, 2012

(In billions of dollars)	Federal Tax Revenue Collections	Tax Year to Which Collections Relate			
		2012	2011	2010	Prior Years
Individual income and tax withholdings	2,160.0	1,415.4	699.5	20.7	24.4
Corporation income taxes	281.5	197.3	73.1	0.7	10.4
Unemployment taxes	66.6	34.8	18.0	13.7	0.1
Excise taxes	82.6	62.2	20.2	-	0.2
Estate and gift taxes	14.5	0.1	6.8	0.2	7.4
Railroad retirement taxes	4.8	3.6	1.2	-	-
Fines, penalties, interest, and other revenue	6.3	6.1	0.1	0.1	-
Customs duties	30.5	30.5	-	-	-
Subtotal	2,646.8	1,750.0	818.9	35.4	42.5
Less: amounts collected for non-Federal entities	(0.4)				
Total	2,646.4				

Federal Tax Refunds Distributed for the Year Ended September 30, 2012

(In billions of dollars)	Refunds Distributed	Tax Year to Which Refunds Relate			
		2012	2011	2010	Prior Years
Individual income and tax withholdings	327.7	0.5	293.5	23.7	10.0
Corporation income taxes	44.0	5.1	10.6	7.4	20.9
Unemployment taxes	0.1	-	0.1	-	-
Excise taxes	1.5	0.5	0.8	0.1	0.1
Estate and gift taxes	0.5	-	0.2	0.1	0.2
Customs duties	1.9	1.9	-	-	-
Total	375.7	8.0	305.2	31.3	31.2

Note 19. Prior-Period Adjustments

Prior-Period Adjustments for the Year Ended September 30, 2013, and 2012

(In billions of dollars)	Changes to Net Position	
	2013	2012
Prior-period adjustments		
Department of Homeland Security	-	0.7
General Services Administration	(1.8)	-
Department of the Interior	(0.5)	-
Department of Justice	(0.3)	-
Other prior-period adjustments	(0.6)	-
Total prior-period adjustments	(3.2)	0.7

For fiscal year 2013, GSA and DOI applied a change in accounting principle for the recognition of environmental liabilities related to asbestos, as required by FASAB Technical Bulletin 2006-1. GSA recognized a total asbestos liability of $1.8 billion attributable to prior years' amortized cost. This was recognized as a prior-period adjustment in fiscal year 2013. The DOI recognized a liability and an adjustment to ending net position for the total estimated asbestos cleanup cost of $0.5 billion. Also, in fiscal year 2013, DOJ recognized adjustments relating to the change in the capitalization thresholds as changes to the General PP&E net book value primarily for real property, including leasehold improvements, personal property, and internal use software. This change was reported as a change in accounting principles. The other prior-period adjustment line includes Department of Commerce, Department of Agriculture, and Department of State and non-verifying agencies reporting. The Departments of Commerce, Agriculture, and State also implemented FASAB Technical Bulletin 2006-1.

For fiscal year 2012, DHS applied a change in accounting principle that changed activity previously classified as General PP&E to operating materials and supplies. This change by DHS ultimately resulted in an adjustment to beginning of the year cumulative results of operations totaling $711.0 million on their Statement of Changes in Net Position. Please refer to DHS audited financial statements for detailed information pertaining to their change in accounting principles.

For fiscal year 2012, as discussed in Note 1.V—Restatements and Note 22—Funds from Dedicated Collections, certain funds that were previously reported as earmarked funds were excluded from being reported as funds from dedicated collections with the implementation of SFFAS 43. This was reported as a prior-period adjustment due to a change in accounting principle. As shown in the Statement of Operations and Changes in Net Position, this restatement had no effect on the total net position, however, the fiscal year 2012 amounts for funds from dedicated collections and funds other than those from dedicated collections were restated to reflect the retroactive implementation of SFFAS No. 43.

Note 20. Contingencies

Financial Treatment of Loss Contingencies

Loss contingencies that are assessed to be at least reasonably possible are disclosed in this note. Loss contingencies involve situations where there is an uncertainty of a possible loss. The reporting of loss contingencies depends on the likelihood that a future event or events will confirm the loss or impairment of an asset or the incurrence of a liability. Terms used to assess the range for the likelihood of loss are probable, reasonably possible, and remote. Loss contingencies that are assessed as probable and measurable are accrued in the financial statements. Loss contingencies that are assessed as remote are not reported in the financial statements, nor disclosed in the notes. All other material loss contingencies are disclosed in this note. The following table provides criteria for how Federal agencies are to account for loss contingencies, based on the likelihood of the loss and measurability.[1]

Likelihood of future outflow or other sacrifice of resources	Loss amount can be reasonably measured	Loss range can be reasonably measured	Loss amount or range cannot be reasonably measured
Probable Future confirming event(s) are more likely to occur than not.[2]	Accrue the liability. Report on Balance Sheet and Statement of Net Cost.	Accrue liability of the best estimate or minimum amount in loss range if there is no best estimate, and disclose nature of contingency and range of estimated liability.	Disclose nature of contingency and include a statement that an estimate cannot be made.
Reasonably possible Possibility of future confirming event(s) occurring is more than remote and less than likely.	Disclose nature of contingency and estimated loss amount.	Disclose nature of contingency and estimated loss range.	Disclose nature of contingency and include a statement that an estimate cannot be made.
Remote Possibility of future event(s) occurring is slight	No disclosure	No disclosure	No disclosure

---

[1] In addition, a third condition must be met to be a loss contingency: a past event or an exchange transaction must occur.
[2] For loss contingencies related to litigation, probable is defined as the future confirming event or events are more likely than not to occur, with the exception of pending or threatened litigation and unasserted claims. For the pending or threatened litigation and unasserted claims, the future confirming event or events are likely to occur.

The Government is subject to loss contingencies that include insurance and litigation cases. These loss contingencies arise in the normal course of operations and their ultimate disposition is unknown. Based on information currently available, however, it is management's opinion that the expected outcome of these matters, individually or in the aggregate, will not have a material adverse effect on the financial statements, except for the insurance and litigation described in the following section, which could have a material adverse effect on the financial statements.

Insurance Contingencies

At the time an insurance policy is issued, a contingency arises. The contingency is the risk of loss assumed by the insurer, that is, the risk of loss from events that may occur during the term of the policy. The Government has insurance contingencies that are reasonably possible in the amount of $332.8 billion as of September 30, 2013, and $329.0 billion as of September 30, 2012. The major programs are identified below:

- PBGC reported $328.9 billion and $321.8 billion as of September 30, 2013, and 2012, respectively, for the estimated aggregate unfunded vested benefits exposure to the PBGC for private-sector single-employer and multiemployer defined benefit pension plans that are classified as a reasonably possible exposure to loss.
- FDIC reported $3.6 billion and $6.9 billion as of September 30, 2013, and 2012, respectively, for identified additional risk in the financial services industry that could result in additional loss to the DIF should potentially vulnerable insured institutions ultimately fail. Actual losses, if any, will largely depend on future economic and market conditions.

Deposit Insurance

Deposit insurance covers all types of deposit accounts such as checking, Negotiable Order of Withdrawal and savings accounts, money market deposit accounts, and certificates of deposit received at an insured bank, savings association, or credit union. The insurance covers the balance of each depositor's account and shares, dollar-for-dollar, up to the insurance limit, including principal and any accrued interest through the date of the insured financial institution's closing. As a result, the Government has the following exposure from Federally-insured financial institutions:

- FDIC has estimated insured deposits of $5,969.0 billion as of September 30, 2013, and $7,250.7 billion as of September 30, 2012, for the DIF.
- National Credit Union Administration (NCUA) has estimated insured shares of $869.0 billion as of September 30, 2013, and $834.3 billion as of September 30, 2012, for the National Credit Union Share Insurance Fund.

Legal Contingencies

Legal contingencies as of September 30, 2013, and 2012, are summarized in the table below:

| (In billions of dollars) | 2013 | | | 2012 | | |
| | Accrued Liabilities [1] | Estimated Range of Loss for Certain Cases [2] | | Accrued Liabilities [1] | Estimated Range of Loss for Certain Cases [2] | |
		Lower End	Upper End		Lower End	Upper End
Legal contingencies:						
Probable	7.2	7.2	9.2	9.9	9.9	11.1
Reasonably possible	-	9.2	15.1	-	12.8	15.2

[1] Accrued liabilities are recorded and presented in the related line items of the Balance Sheet.
[2] Does not reflect the total range of loss; many cases assessed as reasonably possible of an unfavorable outcome did not include estimated losses that could be determined.

The Government is party to various administrative claims and legal actions brought against it, some of which may ultimately result in settlements or decisions against the Government.

Management and legal counsel have determined that it is "probable" that some of these actions will result in a loss to the Government and the loss amounts are reasonably measurable. The estimated liabilities for these cases are $7.2 billion and $9.9 billion as of September 30, 2013, and 2012, respectively, and are included in "Other Liabilities" on the Balance Sheet. For example, HHS is subject to various claims and contingencies related to lawsuits. For cases in which payment has been deemed probable and for which the amount of potential liability has been estimated, about $2.8 billion and $2.9 billion has been accrued in the financial statements as of September 30, 2013, and 2012, respectively. The U.S. Supreme Court decision in Salazar v. Ramah Navajo Chapter, dated June 18, 2012, is likely to result in increased claims against the Indian Health Service, a component within HHS. Tribes are expected to file claims for prior years and seek to consolidate their claims in a class action lawsuit. It is not clear if these will be filed as administrative cases or filed in Federal District Court. Also, the following matters had significant impact on DOI's contingent liabilities in fiscal years 2013 and 2012. The Cobell settlement under the Claims Resolution Act of 2010, which President Obama signed into law on December 8, 2010, resolved a class action lawsuit regarding the U.S. Government's trust management and accounting of Native American trust accounts and resources. Under the settlement, $1.5 billion was distributed to class members in compensation for claims alleging historical accounting problems and to resolve potential claims that the United States mismanaged the administration of trust assets. The agreement also established a $1.9 billion fund for the voluntary buy-back and consolidation of fractionated land interests to address the continued proliferation of thousands of new trust accounts caused by the division of land interests through succeeding generations. With the establishment of the Trust Land Consolidation Fund in the amount of $1.9 billion and the distribution of $1.5 billion of compensation to class members during fiscal year 2013, the case was considered final and resulted in the decrease of $3.4 billion in DOI's contingent liabilities in fiscal year 2013.

There are also administrative claims and legal actions pending where adverse decisions are considered by management and legal counsel as "reasonably possible" with an estimate of potential loss or a range of potential loss. The estimated potential losses for such claims and actions range from $9.2 billion to $15.1 billion as of September 30, 2013, and from $12.8 billion to $15.2 billion as of September 30, 2012.

Numerous litigation cases are pending where the outcome is uncertain or it is reasonably possible that a loss has been incurred and where estimates cannot be made. There are other litigation cases where the plaintiffs have not made claims for specific dollar amounts, but the settlement may be significant. The ultimate resolution of these legal actions for which the potential loss could not be determined may materially affect the U.S. Government's financial position or operating results. An example of a specific case is summarized below:

- Various parties filed administrative claims and lawsuits against the U.S. Army Corps of Engineers as a result of Hurricane Katrina in 2005. A class action case was filed on behalf of residents of St. Bernard Parish and the Lower Ninth Ward of Orleans Parish who were flooded as a result of Hurricane Katrina. These plaintiffs' original claims amount to $5.0 billion, and the likelihood of an unfavorable outcome is reasonably possible. The plaintiffs filed a second complaint asking the case to be treated as a class action lawsuit on behalf of 65,000 residents from the Ninth Ward in New Orleans, LA. Plaintiffs' request to have the case certified as a class action lawsuit has been pending since January 2006. Since the Federal District Court has not ruled on these plaintiffs' request to be certified as a class action lawsuit, an evaluation of the likelihood of an unfavorable outcome is reasonably possible but an estimate of the amount or range of any potential loss cannot be determined at this time.

Environmental and Disposal Contingencies

Environmental and disposal contingencies as of September 30, 2013, and 2012, are summarized in the table below:

| (In billions of dollars) | 2013 | | | 2012 | | |
| | | Estimated Range of Loss for Certain Cases [2] | | | Estimated Range of Loss for Certain Cases [2] | |
	Accrued Liabilities [1]	Lower End	Upper End	Accrued Liabilities [1]	Lower End	Upper End
Environmental and disposal contingencies:						
Probable	24.0	24.0	24.1	20.7	20.7	21.0
Reasonably possible	-	0.5	0.5	-	0.6	0.6

[1] Accrued liabilities are recorded and presented in the related line items of the Balance Sheet.
[2] Does not reflect the total range of loss; many cases assessed as reasonably possible of an unfavorable outcome did not include estimated losses that could be determined.

The Government is subject to loss contingencies for a variety of environmental cleanup costs for the storage and disposal of hazardous material and the operations and closures of facilities at which environmental contamination may be present.

Management and legal counsel have determined that it is "probable" that some of these actions will result in a loss to the Government and the loss amounts are reasonably measurable. The estimated liabilities for these cases are $24.0 billion and $20.7 billion as of September 30, 2013, and 2012, respectively, and are included in "Other Liabilities" on the Balance Sheet. DOE is subject to Spent Nuclear Fuel litigation for damages suffered by all utilities as a result of the delay in beginning disposal of spent nuclear fuel and also damages for alleged exposure to radioactive and/or toxic substances. Significant claims for partial breach of contract and a large number of class action and/or multiple plaintiff tort suits have been filed with estimated liability amounts of $21.4 billion and $19.7 billion as of September 30, 2013, and 2012, respectively.

Other Contingencies

DOT and HHS reported the following other contingencies:

- The Federal Highway Administration (FHWA) reimburses states for construction costs on projects related to the Federal Highway System of roads. FHWA has pre-authorized $45.9 billion and $44.3 billion to the states to establish budgets for its construction projects for fiscal years ending September 30, 2013, and 2012, respectively. Congress has not provided appropriations for these projects and no liability is accrued in the consolidated financial statements.
- Contingent liabilities have been accrued as a result of Medicaid audit and program disallowances that are currently being appealed by the States and for reimbursement of State Plan amendments. The Medicaid amounts are $6.1 billion and $3.9 billion for fiscal years ending September 30, 2013, and 2012, respectively. In all cases, the funds have been returned to HHS. HHS will be required to pay these amounts if the appeals are decided in favor of the States. In addition, certain amounts for payment have been deferred under the Medicaid program when there is

reasonable doubt as to the legitimacy of expenditures claimed by a State. There are also outstanding reviews of the State expenditures in which a final determination has not been made.

Treaties

The U.S. Government is a party to major treaties and other international agreements. These treaties and other international agreements address various issues including, but not limited to, trade, commerce, security, and arms that may involve financial obligations or give rise to possible exposure to losses. A comprehensive analysis to determine any such financial obligations or possible exposure to loss and their related effect on the consolidated financial statements of the U.S. Government has not yet been performed.

Note 21. Commitments

Long-Term Operating Leases as of September 30, 2013, and 2012

(In billions of dollars)	2013	2012
General Services Administration	23.6	29.5
U.S. Postal Service	6.7	7.0
Department of State	1.3	1.6
Department of Defense	1.3	1.6
Department of Health and Human Services	0.9	1.2
Department of Agriculture	0.8	0.8
Department of Homeland Security	0.8	0.6
Other operating leases	4.0	4.2
Total long-term operating leases	39.4	46.5

The Government has entered into contractual commitments that require future use of financial resources. It has significant amounts of long-term lease obligations and undelivered orders. Undelivered orders represent the value of goods and services ordered that have not yet been received.

The Government has other commitments that may require future use of financial resources. For example, the Government has callable subscriptions in certain Multilateral Development Banks (MDBs), which are international financial institutions that finance economic and social development projects in developing countries. Callable capital stock shares in the MDBs serve as a supplemental pool of resources that may be redeemed, and converted into ordinary paid in shares, if the MDB cannot otherwise meet certain obligations through its other available resources. MDBs are able to use callable capital as backing to obtain very favorable financing terms when borrowing from world capital markets. To date, there has never been a call on this capital for any of the major MDBs and none are anticipated.

Undelivered Orders and Other Commitments as of September 30, 2013, and 2012

(In billions of dollars)	2013	2012
Undelivered Orders:		
Department of Education	215.6	230.8
Department of Defense	201.8	211.7
Department of the Treasury	171.3	186.9
EOP Foreign Military Sales Program	153.9	163.5
Department of Transportation	101.5	104.0
Department of Health and Human Services	88.4	91.8
Department of Agriculture	46.4	49.1
Department of Housing and Urban Development	45.7	49.7
Department of Homeland Security	31.2	33.3
Department of Energy	21.8	29.1
Department of State	20.0	20.8
Agency for International Development	17.2	16.3
Export-Import Bank of the United States	15.9	17.3
Department of Veterans Affairs	13.9	9.7
National Science Foundation	11.2	11.4
Department of Labor	9.6	9.9
All other agencies	36.8	57.3
Total undelivered orders	1,202.2	1,292.6
Other Commitments:		
GSE Senior Preferred Stock Purchase Agreement	258.1	273.2
Callable Capital Subscriptions for Multilateral Development Banks	90.8	82.3
Fuel Purchase Obligations	6.3	7.1
Agriculture Direct Loans and Guarantees	5.4	6.0
Power Purchase Obligations	4.4	4.3
Long-term Satellite and Systems	3.6	4.2
Conservation Reserve Program	2.0	1.8
All other commitments	6.3	5.7
Total other commitments	376.9	384.6

Other Commitments and Risks

Commitments to GSE

At September 30, 2013, the maximum remaining contractual commitment to the GSEs for the remaining life of the SPSPAs was $258.1 billion which, was established on December 31, 2012. At September 30, 2012, the maximum remaining potential commitment to the GSEs for the remaining life of the SPSPAs was estimated at $282.3 billion, which was based upon case scenario estimates ranging from $274.0 billion to $291.5 billion.

Refer to Note 9—Investments in and Liabilities to Government-Sponsored Enterprises for a full description of the SPSPA agreements, related contingent liability and additional information.

Terrorism Risk Insurance Program

The Government has entered into agreements that could potentially require claims on Government resources in the future. For example, the Terrorism Risk Insurance Act of 2002 (TRIA or the Act) was signed into law on November 26, 2002. This law was enacted to address market disruptions resulting from terrorist attacks on September 11, 2001. On December 26, 2007, the *Terrorism Risk Insurance Program Reauthorization Act of 2007* (Reauthorization Act) was enacted extending the Program through December 31, 2014. The Act helps to ensure available and affordable commercial property and casualty insurance for terrorism risk, and simultaneously allows private markets to stabilize. The Terrorism Risk Insurance Program is activated upon the certification of an "act of terrorism" by the Secretary of the Treasury in concurrence with the Secretary of State and the Attorney General. If a certified act of terrorism occurs, insurers may be eligible to receive reimbursement from the Government for insured losses above a designated deductible amount. Insured losses above this amount will be shared between insurance companies and the Government. The Act also gives Treasury authority to recoup Federal payments made under the Program through policyholder surcharges under certain circumstances and contains provisions designed to manage litigation arising from or relating to a certified act of terrorism. There were no claims under TRIA as of September 30, 2013, or September 30, 2012.

Note 22. Funds from Dedicated Collections

Funds from Dedicated Collections as of September 30, 2013[1]

(In billions of dollars)	Federal Old-Age and Survivors Insurance Trust Fund	Federal Hospital Insurance Trust Fund (Medicare Part A)	Federal Disability Insurance Trust Fund	Federal Supplementary Medical Insurance Trust Fund (Medicare Parts B and D)	All Other -Funds from Dedicated Collections	Total Funds From Dedicated Collections (Combined)
Assets:						
Cash and other monetary assets	-	-	-	-	65.4	65.4
Fund balance with Treasury	(0.3)	2.0	(0.4)	7.5	104.1	112.9
Investments in U.S. Treasury securities, net of unamortized premiums/discounts	2,655.6	206.0	100.8	67.4	163.8	3,193.6
Other Federal assets	24.0	30.8	1.1	45.6	17.4	118.9
Non-Federal assets	2.0	-	3.8	-	108.4	114.2
Total assets	2,681.3	238.8	105.3	120.5	459.1	3,605.0
Liabilities and net position:						
Due and payable to beneficiaries	60.1	20.8	24.4	27.8	3.7	136.8
Other Federal liabilities	4.9	27.3	1.4	38.0	89.3	160.9
Other non-Federal liabilities	-	0.7	-	2.0	160.9	163.6
Total liabilities	65.0	48.8	25.8	67.8	253.9	461.3
Total net position	2,616.3	190.0	79.5	52.7	205.2	3,143.7
Total liabilities and net position	2,681.3	238.8	105.3	120.5	459.1	3,605.0
Change in net position:						
Beginning net position	2,551.6	212.3	111.3	70.1	202.5	3,147.8
Prior-period adjustment	-	-	-	-	0.9	0.9
Beginning net position, adjusted	2,551.6	212.3	111.3	70.1	203.4	3,148.7
Investment revenue	99.1	9.5	5.1	2.4	3.5	119.6
Individual income taxes	589.4	212.9	100.1	-	-	902.4
Unemployment and excise taxes	-	-	-	-	106.8	106.8
Other taxes and receipts	-	1.3	0.1	3.4	31.6	36.4
Miscellaneous earned revenues	-	-	-	-	4.2	4.2
Other changes in fund balance (e.g., appropriations, transfers)	43.2	15.4	2.4	213.9	32.7	307.6
Program gross cost and non-program expenses	667.0	265.2	139.5	302.6	211.2	1,585.5
Less: program revenue	-	3.8	-	65.5	34.2	103.5
Net cost	667.0	261.4	139.5	237.1	177.0	1,482.0
Ending net position	2,616.3	190.0	79.5	52.7	205.2	3,143.7

[1] By law, certain expenses (costs), revenues, and other financing sources related to the administration of the above funds are not charged to the funds and are therefore financed and/or credited to other sources.

Funds from Dedicated Collections as of September 30, 2012 (Restated)[1]

(In billions of dollars)	Federal Old-Age and Survivors Insurance Trust Fund	Federal Hospital Insurance Trust Fund (Medicare Part A)	Federal Disability Insurance Trust Fund	Federal Supplementary Medical Insurance Trust Fund (Medicare Parts B and D)	All Other -Funds from Dedicated Collections	Total Funds From Dedicated Collections (Combined)
Assets:						
Cash and other monetary assets	-	-	-	-	66.1	66.1
Fund balance with Treasury	(0.5)	1.5	(0.5)	21.8	99.0	121.3
Investments in U.S. Treasury securities, net of unamortized premiums/discounts	2,586.7	228.3	132.3	69.3	155.8	3,172.4
Other Federal assets	25.0	27.6	1.6	30.8	23.0	108.0
Non-Federal assets	2.0	1.4	3.8	7.8	103.7	118.7
Total assets	2,613.2	258.8	137.2	129.7	447.6	3,586.5
Liabilities and net position:						
Due and payable to beneficiaries	56.9	20.2	24.6	26.2	3.3	131.2
Other Federal liabilities	4.7	25.7	1.3	31.4	86.3	149.4
Other non-Federal liabilities	-	0.6	-	2.0	155.5	158.1
Total liabilities	61.6	46.5	25.9	59.6	245.1	438.7
Total net position	2,551.6	212.3	111.3	70.1	202.5	3,147.8
Total liabilities and net position	2,613.2	258.8	137.2	129.7	447.6	3,586.5
Change in net position:						
Beginning net position	2,462.1	226.8	141.9	66.4	(2,149.0)	748.2
Prior-period adjustment	-	-	-	-	2,334.4	2,334.4
Beginning net position, adjusted	2,462.1	226.8	141.9	66.4	185.4	3,082.6
Investment revenue	104.0	10.9	6.8	2.9	3.8	128.4
Individual income taxes	500.1	204.8	85.0	-	-	789.9
Unemployment and excise taxes	-	-	-	-	123.0	123.0
Other taxes and receipts	0.1	0.6	-	2.8	27.8	31.3
Miscellaneous earned revenue	-	-	-	-	6.2	6.2
Other changes in fund balance (e.g. appropriations, transfers)	116.7	19.7	13.3	225.2	44.8	419.7
Program gross cost and non-program expenses	631.4	254.2	135.7	288.4	220.9	1,530.6
Less: program revenue	-	3.7	-	61.2	32.4	97.3
Net cost	631.4	250.5	135.7	227.2	188.5	1,433.3
Ending net position	2,551.6	212.3	111.3	70.1	202.5	3,147.8

[1] By law, certain expenses (costs), revenues, and other financing sources related to the administration of the above funds are not charged to the funds and are therefore financed and/or credited to other sources.

Generally, funds from dedicated collections are financed by specifically identified revenues, often supplemented by other financing sources, provided to the Government by non-Federal sources, which remain available over time. These specifically identified revenues and other financing sources are required by statute to be used for designated activities, benefits, or purposes and must be accounted for separately from the Government's general revenues. Funds from dedicated collections generally include trust funds, public enterprise revolving funds (not including credit reform financing funds), and special funds. As discussed in Note 1.B for new standards issued and implemented, in accordance with SFFAS No. 27, as amended by SFFAS No. 43, effective in fiscal year 2013, funds from dedicated collections specifically exclude any fund established to account for pensions, other retirement benefits, other postemployment or other benefits provided for federal employees (civilian and military). In addition, SFFAS No. 43 changed the terminology for these funds from "earmarked funds" to "funds from dedicated collections."

In the Federal budget, the term "trust fund" means only that the law requires a particular fund be accounted for separately, used only for a specified purpose, and designated as a trust fund. A change in law may change the future receipts and the terms under which the fund's resources are spent. In the private sector, trust fund refers to funds of one party held and managed by a second party (the trustee) in a fiduciary capacity. The activity of funds from dedicated collections differs from fiduciary activities primarily in that assets within funds from dedicated collections are Government-owned. For further information related to fiduciary activities, see Note 23—Fiduciary Activities.

Public enterprise revolving funds include expenditure accounts authorized by law to be credited with offsetting collections, mostly from the public, that are generated by and dedicated to finance a continuing cycle of business-type operations. Some of the financing for these funds may be from appropriations.

Special funds are Federal funds dedicated by law for a specific purpose. Special funds include the special fund receipt account and the special fund expenditure account.

The tables above depict major funds from dedicated collections chosen based on their significant financial activity and importance to taxpayers. All other Government funds from dedicated collections not shown separately are aggregated as "all other."

Total assets represent the unexpended balance from all sources of receipts and amounts due to the funds from dedicated collections, regardless of source, including related Governmental transactions. These are transactions between two different entities within the Government (for example, monies received by one entity of the Government from another entity of the Government).

The intragovernmental assets are comprised of fund balances with Treasury, investments in Treasury securities— including unamortized amounts, and other assets that include the related accrued interest receivable on Federal investments. These amounts were eliminated in preparing the principal financial statements.

The non-Federal assets represent only the activity with individuals and organizations outside of the Government.

Most of the assets within funds from dedicated collections are invested in intragovernmental debt holdings. The Government does not set aside assets to pay future benefits or other expenditures associated with funds from dedicated collections. The cash receipts collected from the public for funds from dedicated collections are deposited in the U.S. Treasury, which uses the cash for general Government purposes. Treasury securities are issued to Federal agencies as evidence of its receipts. Treasury securities are an asset to the Federal agencies and a liability to the U.S. Treasury and, therefore, they do not represent an asset or a liability in the *Financial Report*. These securities require redemption if a fund's disbursements exceeds its receipts. Redeeming these securities will increase the Government's financing needs and require more borrowing from the public (or less repayment of debt), or will result in higher taxes than otherwise would have been needed, or less spending on other programs than otherwise would have occurred, or some combination thereof. See Note 12—Federal Debt Securities Held by the Public and Accrued Interest for further information related to the investments in Federal debt securities.

Depicted below is a description of the major funds from dedicated collections shown in the above tables, which also includes the names of the Government agencies that administer each particular fund. In accordance with the requirements of SFFAS No. 43, four major funds: Military Retirement Fund, Civil Service Retirement and Disability Fund, Medicare-Eligible Retiree Health Care Fund (MERHCF), and the Civil Service Health Benefits Program Trust Funds, which were reported as earmarked funds in fiscal year 2012, were excluded from reporting as funds from dedicated collections. For detailed information regarding these funds from dedicated collections, please refer to the financial statements of the corresponding administering agencies. For information on the benefits due and payable liability associated with certain funds from dedicated collections, see Note 15—Benefits Due and Payable.

Federal Old-Age and Survivors Insurance Trust Fund

The Federal Old-Age and Survivors Insurance Trust Fund, administered by the SSA, provides a basic annuity to workers to protect them from loss of income at retirement and provide a guaranteed income to survivors in the event of the death of a family's primary wage earner.

Payroll and self-employment taxes primarily fund the Federal Old-Age and Survivors Insurance Trust Fund. Interest earnings on Treasury securities, Federal agencies' payments for the Social Security benefits earned by military and Federal civilian employees, and Treasury payments for a portion of income taxes collected on Social Security benefits provide the fund with additional income. The law establishing the Federal Old-Age and Survivors Insurance Trust Fund and authorizing the depositing of amounts to the credit of the fund is set forth in 42 U.S.C. § 401.

Federal Hospital Insurance Trust Fund (Medicare Part A)

The Federal Hospital Insurance Trust Fund, administered by HHS, finances the Hospital Insurance Program (Medicare Part A). This program funds the cost of inpatient hospital and related care for individuals age 65 or older who meet certain insured status requirements, and eligible disabled people.

The Federal Hospital Insurance Trust Fund is financed primarily by payroll taxes, including those paid by Federal agencies. It also receives income from interest earnings on Treasury securities and a portion of income taxes collected on Social Security benefits. The law establishing the Federal Hospital Insurance Trust Fund and authorizing the depositing of amounts to the credit of the fund is set forth in 42 U.S.C. § 1395i.

Federal Disability Insurance Trust Fund

The Federal Disability Insurance Trust Fund provides financial assistance and protection against the loss of earnings due to a wage earner's disability. The SSA administers this fund.

Like the Federal Old-Age and Survivors Insurance Trust Fund, payroll taxes primarily fund the Federal Disability Insurance Trust Fund. The fund also receives income from interest earnings on Treasury securities, Federal agencies' payments for the Social Security benefits earned by military and Federal civilian employees, and a portion of income taxes collected on Social Security benefits. The law establishing the Federal Disability Insurance Trust Fund and authorizing the depositing of amounts to the credit of the fund is set forth in 42 U.S.C. § 401.

Federal Supplementary Medical Insurance Trust Fund (Medicare Parts B and D)

The Federal Supplementary Medical Insurance Trust Fund, administered by HHS, finances the Supplementary Medical Insurance Program (Medicare Part B) and the Medicare Prescription Drug Benefit Program (Medicare Part D). These programs provide supplementary medical insurance for enrolled eligible participants to cover physician and outpatient services not covered by Medicare Part A and to obtain qualified prescription drug coverage, respectively. Medicare Part B financing is not based on payroll taxes; it is primarily based on monthly premiums, income from the General Fund of the Treasury, and interest earnings on Treasury securities. The law establishing the Federal Supplementary Medical Insurance Trust Fund and authorizing the depositing of amounts to the credit of the fund is set forth in 42 U.S.C. § 1395t.

Medicare Part D was created by the *Medicare Prescription Drug, Improvement, and Modernization Act of 2003* (Public Law No. 108-173). Medicare Part D financing is similar to Part B; it is primarily based on monthly premiums and income from the General Fund of the Treasury, not on payroll taxes. It also receives transfers from States. The law creating the Medicare prescription drug account within the Federal Supplementary Medical Insurance Trust Fund and authorizing the depositing of amounts to the credit of the fund is set forth in 42 U.S.C. § 1395w-116.

All Other Funds from Dedicated Collections

The Government is responsible for the management of numerous funds from dedicated collections that serve a wide variety of purposes. The funds from dedicated collections presented on an individual basis in the above tables represent the majority of the Government's net position attributable to funds from dedicated collections. All other activity attributable to funds from dedicated collections is aggregated in accordance with SFFAS No. 27, as amended by SFFAS No. 43. For the years ending September 30, 2013, and 2012, there were approximately 648 and 660 funds from dedicated collections, respectively. The funds from dedicated collections within the "all other" aggregate, along with the agencies that administer them, include the following:

- Exchange Stabilization Fund—administered by Treasury.
- Railroad Retirement Trust Fund—administered by RRB.
- National Flood Insurance Program—administered by DHS.
- Land and Water Conservation Fund, Reclamation Fund, and Water and Related Resources Fund—administered by DOI.
- Government National Mortgage Association—administered by HUD.
- Unemployment Trust Fund (UTF) and Black Lung Disability Trust Fund (BLDTF)—administered by DOL.
- Highway Trust Fund and Airport and Airway Trust Fund—administered by DOT.
- Decommissioning and Decontamination Fund—administered by DOE.
- Crime Victims Fund—administered by DOJ.
- National Telecommunications and Information Administration Digital Television Transition and Public Safety Fund and Broadband Technology Opportunities Program-Recovery Act Fund—administered by the Department of Commerce (DOC).
- Salaries and Expenses Fund and Investor Protection Fund—administered by the Securities and Exchange Commission (SEC).
- Universal Service Fund—administered by the Federal Communication Commission (FCC).
- Superfund (Hazardous Substance) and Leaking Underground Storage Tanks—administered by the Environmental Protection Agency (EPA).

In accordance with SFFAS No. 43, any funds established to account for pension, other retirement, or other post-employment benefits to civilian or military personnel are excluded from the reporting requirements related to funds from dedicated collections. This exclusion is applied retroactively to fiscal year 2012 reporting in this first year implementation. As a result, any such funds previously included in fiscal year 2012 within the "all other" aggregate have been excluded to reflect the implementation impact on the reporting for these funds.

Unemployment and Excise Taxes

Unemployment Taxes

The Unemployment Trust Fund (UTF), within the "all other" aggregate, represents all the unemployment tax revenues attributable to funds from dedicated collections shown on the consolidated Statement of Operations and Changes in Net Position.

The Unemployment Trust Fund provides temporary assistance to workers who lose their jobs. The program is administered through a unique system of Federal and State partnerships, established in Federal law, but executed through conforming State laws by State officials. DOL administers the Federal operations of the program.

Employer taxes provide the primary funding source for the UTF and constitute all the unemployment tax revenues attributable to funds from dedicated collections as shown on the consolidated Statement of Operations and Changes in Net Position. However, interest earnings on Treasury securities also provide income to the fund. For the years ending September 30, 2013, and 2012, UTF unemployment tax revenues were $54.0 billion and $66.5 billion, respectively. Appropriations have supplemented the fund's income during periods of high and extended unemployment. The law establishing the UTF and authorizing the depositing of amounts to the credit of the fund is set forth in 42 U.S.C. § 1104.

Excise Taxes

There are 10 funds from dedicated collections within the "all other" aggregate that represent all of the dedicated excise tax revenue attributable to funds from dedicated collections shown on the consolidated Statement of Operations and Changes in Net Position. The Highway Trust Fund and the Airport and Airway Trust Fund, combined, represent more than 90 percent of all dedicated excise tax revenues. Both of these funds are administered by the DOT. For more detailed information regarding them, please refer to DOT's financial statements.

The Highway Trust Fund was established to promote domestic interstate transportation and to move people and goods. The fund provides Federal grants to States for highway construction, certain transit programs, and related transportation purposes. The law establishing the Highway Trust Fund and authorizing the depositing of amounts to the credit of the fund is set forth in 26 U.S.C. § 9503. Funding sources include designated excise taxes on gasoline and other fuels, certain tires, the initial sale of heavy trucks, and highway use by commercial motor vehicles. For the years ending September 30, 2013, and 2012, Highway Trust Fund excise tax revenues were $36.5 billion and $40.2 billion, respectively. As funds are needed for payments, the Highway Trust Fund corpus investments are liquidated and funds are transferred to the Federal Highway Administration, the Federal Transit Administration, or other DOT entities, for payment of obligations.

The Airport and Airway Trust Fund provides for airport improvement and airport facilities maintenance. It also funds airport equipment, research, and a portion of the Federal Aviation Administration's administrative operational support. The law establishing the Airport and Airway Trust Fund and authorizing the depositing of amounts to the credit of the fund is set forth in 26 U.S.C. § 9502. Funding sources include:

- Taxes received from transportation of persons and property in the air and fuel used in commercial and general aviation.
- International departure taxes.
- Interest earnings on Treasury securities.

For the years ending September 30, 2013, and 2012, Airport and Airway Trust Fund excise tax revenues were $12.9 billion and $12.5 billion, respectively.

Miscellaneous Earned Revenues

Miscellaneous earned revenues due to activity attributable to funds from dedicated collections primarily relate to royalties retained by various funds within DOI.

Restatement

As was stated above, in accordance with the requirements of SFFAS No. 43, various funds, primarily the Military Retirement Fund, the Civil Service Retirement and Disability Fund, the Medicare-Eligible Retiree Health Care Fund, and the Civil Service Health Benefits Program Trust Fund, reported as earmarked funds in fiscal year 2012, were excluded from the reporting requirements related to funds from dedicated collections. This resulted in a restatement of balances and activity attributable to funds from dedicated collections as presented in this note and on the consolidated Statement of Operations and Changes in Net Position. In addition, the fiscal year 2012 ending net position attributable to funds from dedicated collections was restated on the consolidated Balance Sheet. As a result of the implementation of SFFAS No. 43, the Government recorded a prior-period adjustment to increase fiscal year 2012 beginning net position for funds from dedicated collections by $2,335.0 billion and to decrease beginning net position for funds other than those from dedicated collections by the same amount. In addition, and unrelated to the implementation of SFFAS No. 43, the Government also recorded a fiscal year 2012 prior-period adjustment to decrease fiscal year 2012 beginning net position for funds from dedicated collections by $0.6 billion and to increase beginning net position for funds other than those from dedicated collections by the same amount. Therefore, these net prior-period adjustments increase fiscal year 2012 beginning net position for funds from dedicated collections by $2,334.4 billion and decrease beginning net position for funds other than those from dedicated collections by the same amounts, as reflected in the consolidated Statement of Operations and Changes in Net Position. Therefore, there was no effect on total ending net position for fiscal year 2012. Most of this prior-period adjustment was primarily due to the exclusion of the above four funds, which collectively contributed $2,327.4 billion toward the prior-period adjustment amount.

In addition, the Exchange Stabilization Fund is no longer reported separately and is instead included in the "all other funds" aggregate in the above tables. The reporting for this fund was not restated with the implementation of SFFAS No. 43.

Lastly, and as allowed by SFFAS No. 43, the presentation for funds from dedicated collections are now on a combined basis and is depicted as such in the Note 22 tables. This change in presentation is applied retroactively to fiscal year 2012, which were formerly presented on a consolidated basis. Therefore, no intra-fund elimination column is shown in the Note 22 tables as was reflected in prior years' reporting for these funds.

Note 23. Fiduciary Activities

Fiduciary activities are the collection or receipt, and the management, protection, accounting, investment and disposition by the Government of cash or other assets in which non-Federal individuals or entities have an ownership interest that the Government must uphold. Fiduciary cash and other assets are not assets of the Government and accordingly are not recognized on the consolidated Governmentwide Balance Sheet. Examples of the Government's fiduciary activities include the Thrift Savings Plan (the Plan), which is administered by the Federal Retirement Thrift Investment Board, and the Indian Tribal and individual Indian Trust Funds, which are administered by the DOI.

Schedule of Fiduciary Net Assets as of September 30, 2013, and 2012

(In billions of dollars)	2013	2012
FRTIB-Thrift Savings Plan	374.3	329.2
Department of the Interior	4.7	4.5
All other	(0.4)	5.7
Total fiduciary net assets	378.6	339.4

In accordance with the requirements of SFFAS No. 31, *Accounting for Fiduciary Activities,* fiduciary investments in Treasury securities and fund balance with Treasury held by fiduciary funds are to be recognized on the Governmentwide Balance Sheet as debt held by the public and a liability for fiduciary fund balance with Treasury, respectively. Refer to Note 12—Federal Debt Securities Held by the Public and Accrued Interest for more information on Treasury securities.

As of September 30, 2013, total fiduciary investments in Treasury securities and in non-Treasury securities are $176.8 billion and $206 billion, respectively. As of September 30, 2012, total fiduciary investments in Treasury securities and in non-Treasury securities were $158.2 billion and $175.2 billion, respectively. As of September 30, 2013, and 2012, the total fiduciary fund balance with Treasury is $1.1 billion and $1.2 billion, respectively. A liability for this fiduciary fund balance with Treasury is reflected as other miscellaneous liabilities in Note 17—Other Liabilities.

As of September 30, 2013, and 2012, collectively, the fiduciary investments in Treasury securities and fiduciary fund balance with Treasury held by all Government entities represent $4.0 billion and $4.3 billion, respectively, of unrestricted cash included within cash held by Treasury for Governmentwide Operations shown in Note 2—Cash and Other Monetary Assets.

Federal Retirement Thrift Investment Board (FRTIB)-Thrift Savings Plan

The TSP is administered by an independent Government agency, the FRTIB, which is charged with operating the TSP prudently and solely in the interest of the participants and their beneficiaries. Assets of the TSP are maintained in the Thrift Savings Fund.

The TSP is a retirement savings and investment plan for Federal employees and members of the uniformed services. It was authorized by the United States Congress in the *Federal Employees' Retirement System Act of 1986.* The Plan provides Federal employees and members of the uniformed services with a savings and tax benefit similar to what many private sector employers offer their employees. The Plan was primarily designed to be a key part of the retirement package (along with a basic annuity benefit and Social Security) for employees who are covered by the FERS.

Federal employees, who are participants of FERS, the CSRS, or equivalent retirement systems, as provided by statute, and members of the uniformed services, are eligible to join the Plan immediately upon being hired. Generally, FERS employees are those employees hired on or after January 1, 1984, while CSRS employees are employees hired before January 1, 1984, who have not elected to convert to FERS. Each group has different rules that govern contribution rates. As of December 31, 2012, and 2011, there were approximately 4.6 million and 4.5 million participants in the TSP, respectively, with approximately 2.9 million contributing their own money. For further information about FRTIB and the TSP, please refer to the FRTIB website at http://www.frtib.gov.

As of September 30, 2013, and 2012, the TSP held $374.3 billion and $329.2 billion, respectively, in net assets, which included $52.5 billion and $153.9 billion, respectively, of U.S. Government Securities (amounts are unaudited). A delay in raising the statutory debt limit existed as of September 30, 2013. When delays in raising the statutory debt limit occur, the Department of the Treasury often must deviate from its normal debt management operations and take a number of extraordinary measures to meet the government's obligations as they come due without exceeding the debt limit. Many extraordinary measures taken by Treasury during the period of May 20, 2013 through September 30, 2013, resulted in federal debt securities not being issued to certain federal government accounts. As reported in Note 17, as a result of Treasury securities not being issued to the Federal Retirement Thrift Investment Board (FRTIB) for the G Fund, Treasury reported miscellaneous liabilities in the amount of $120.4 billion that represent uninvested principal and related interest for TSP's G Fund that would have been reported as federal debt securities had there not been a delay in raising the statutory debt limit as of September 30, 2013, and had the securities been issued. The most recent audited financial statements for the TSP are as of December 31, 2012, and 2011. As of December 31, 2012, and 2011, the TSP held $334.9 billion and $298.1 billion, respectively, in net assets, which included $158.5 billion and $147.7 billion, respectively, of U.S. Government Securities. These unaudited amounts above are included to enhance comparability of the TSP net assets with the remainder of the Government's fiduciary net assets as of September 30, 2013, and 2012.

DOI–Indian Trust Funds

As stated above, DOI has responsibility for the assets held in trust on behalf of American Indian Tribes and individuals, and these account for all of DOI's fiduciary net assets. DOI maintains accounts for Tribal and Other Trust Funds (including the Alaska Native Escrow Fund and Individual Indian Money Trust Funds) in accordance with the American Indian Trust Fund Management Reform Act of 1994. The fiduciary balances that have accumulated in these funds have resulted from land use agreements, royalties on natural resource depletion, other proceeds derived directly from trust resources, judgment awards, settlements of claims, and investment income. These funds are maintained for the benefit of individual Native Americans as well as for designated Indian tribes. DOI maintains separate financial statements for these trust funds which were prepared using the cash or modified cash basis of accounting, a comprehensive basis of accounting other than GAAP. The independent auditors' reports were qualified as it was not practical to extend audit procedures sufficiently to satisfy themselves as to the fairness of the trust fund balances. For further information related to these assets, see the financial statements of the DOI.

All Other Entities with Fiduciary Activities

The Government is responsible for the management of other fiduciary net assets on behalf of various non-Federal entities. The component entities presented individually in the table on the previous page represent the vast majority of the Government's fiduciary net assets. All other component entities with fiduciary net assets are aggregated in accordance with SFFAS No. 31. As of September 30, 2013, and 2012, including FRTIB and DOI, there are a total of 20 and 16 Federal entities, respectively, with fiduciary activities at a grand total of 66 and 59 fiduciary funds, respectively. SBA, LOC, and Treasury are the significant agencies relating to the fiduciary activities of the remaining component entities within the "all other" aggregate balance. As of September 30, 2013, "all other" fiduciary net assets were ($0.4) billion, compared to $5.7 billion as of September 30, 2012; this decrease is due to NCUA reporting ($6.1) billion of net assets.

Note 24. Social Insurance

The Statement of Social Insurance presents the projected actuarial present value of the estimated future revenue and estimated future expenditures of the Social Security, Medicare, Railroad Retirement, and Black Lung social insurance programs which are administered by the SSA, HHS, RRB, and DOL, respectively. These estimates are based on the economic and demographic assumptions presented later in this note as set forth in the relevant Social Security and Medicare trustees' reports and in the agency financial reports of HHS, SSA, and DOL and in the relevant agency performance and accountability report for RRB. The projections are based on the continuation of program provisions contained in current law. The estimates in the consolidated SOSI of the open group measures are for persons who are participants or eventually will participate in the programs as contributors (workers) or beneficiaries (retired workers, survivors, and disabled) during the 75-year projection period (Black Lung is projected only through September 30, 2040, because the program will terminate on that date).

Contributions and dedicated taxes consist of: payroll taxes from employers, employees, and self-employed persons; revenue from Federal income taxation of Old-Age Survivors and Disability Insurance (OASDI) and railroad retirement benefits; excise tax on coal (Black Lung); premiums from, and State transfers on behalf of, participants in Medicare; and reimbursements from the General Fund of the Treasury to the OASDI trust funds to make up for reductions in payroll tax revenue due to temporary payroll tax rate reductions. Income for all programs is presented from a consolidated perspective. Future interest payments and other future intragovernmental transfers have been excluded upon consolidation. Expenditures include scheduled benefit payments and administrative expenses. Scheduled benefits are projected based on the benefit formulas under current law. However, current Social Security and Medicare law provides for full benefit payments only to the extent that there are sufficient balances in the trust funds.

Actuarial present values of estimated future revenue (excluding interest) and estimated future expenditures for the Social Security, Medicare, and Railroad Retirement social insurance programs are presented for three different groups of participants: (1) current participants who have attained eligibility age, (2) current participants who have not attained eligibility age, and (3) future participants who are new entrants expected to become participants in the future. Current participants in the Social Security and Medicare programs form the "closed group" of taxpayers and/or beneficiaries who are at least 15 years of age at the start of the projection period. Since the projection period for the Social Security, Medicare, and Railroad Retirement social insurance programs consists of 75 years, the period covers virtually all of the current participants' working and retirement years, a period that could be greater than 75 years in a relatively small number of instances. Future participants for Social Security and Medicare include births during the projection period and individuals below age 15 as of January 1 of the valuation year. Railroad Retirement's future participants are the projected new entrants as of January 1 of the valuation year.

The present values of future expenditures in excess of future revenue are calculated by subtracting the actuarial present values of future scheduled contributions and dedicated tax income by and on behalf of current and future participants from the actuarial present value of the future scheduled benefit payments to them or on their behalf. To determine a program's funding shortfall over any given period of time, the starting trust fund balance is subtracted from the present value of expenditures in excess of revenues over the period.

The trust fund balances as of the valuation date for the respective programs, including interest earned, are shown in the table below. Substantially all of the Social Security (OASDI) and Medicare Hospital Insurance (HI), and Supplementary Medical Insurance (SMI) trust fund balances consist of investments in special nonmarketable U.S. Treasury securities that are backed by the full faith and credit of the U.S. Government.

Social Insurance Programs Trust Fund Balances [1]

(In billions of dollars)	2013	2012	2011	2010	2009
Social Security	2,732	2,678	2,609	2,540	2,419
Medicare					
HI	220	244	272	304	321
SMI Part B	66	80	71	76	59
SMI Part D	1	1	1	1	1
Railroad Retirement	26	24	26	25	22
Black Lung	(6)	(6)	(6)	(6)	(6)

[1] As of the valuation date of the respective programs.

Social Security

The Old-Age and Survivors Insurance (OASI) program, created in 1935, and the Disability Insurance (DI) program, created in 1956, collectively referred to as OASDI or "Social Security," provides cash benefits for eligible U.S. citizens and residents. Eligibility and benefit amounts are determined under the laws applicable for the period. Current law provides that the amount of the monthly benefit payments for workers, or their eligible dependents or survivors, is based on the workers' lifetime earnings histories.

The primary financing of the OASDI Trust Funds are taxes paid by workers, their employers, and individuals with self-employment income, based on work covered by the OASDI Program. Refer to the Unaudited Required Supplementary Information—Social Insurance section for additional information on Social Security program financing.

That portion of each trust fund not required to pay benefits and administrative costs is invested, on a daily basis, in interest-bearing obligations of the U.S. Government. The Social Security Act authorizes the issuance by the Treasury of special nonmarketable, intragovernmental debt obligations for purchase exclusively by the trust funds. Although the special issues cannot be bought or sold in the open market, they are redeemable at any time at face value and thus bear no risk of fluctuation in principal value due to changes in market yield rates. Interest on the bonds is credited to the trust funds and becomes an asset to the funds and a liability to the General Fund of the Treasury. These Treasury securities and related interest are eliminated in consolidation at the Governmentwide level.

Medicare

The Medicare Program, created in 1965, has two separate trust funds: the HI (Medicare Part A) and SMI (Medicare Parts B and D) Trust Funds. HI pays for inpatient acute hospital services and major alternatives to hospitals (skilled nursing services, for example) and SMI pays for hospital outpatient services, physician services, and assorted other services and products through the Part B account and pays for prescription drugs through the Part D account. Though the events that trigger benefit payments are similar, HI and SMI have different dedicated financing structures. Similar to OASDI, HI is financed primarily by payroll contributions. Other income to the HI Trust Fund includes a small amount of premium income from voluntary enrollees, a portion of the Federal income taxes that beneficiaries pay on Social Security benefits and interest credited on Treasury securities held in the HI Trust Fund. These Treasury securities and related interest are eliminated in the consolidation at the Governmentwide level.

For SMI, transfers from the General Fund of the Treasury represent the largest source of income for both Parts B and D. Generally, beneficiaries finance the remainder of Parts B and D costs via monthly premiums to these programs. With the introduction of Part D drug coverage, Medicaid is no longer the primary payer for beneficiaries dually eligible for Medicare and Medicaid. For those beneficiaries, States must pay a portion of their estimated foregone drug costs into the Part D account (referred to as State transfers). As with HI, interest received on Treasury securities held in the SMI Trust Fund is credited to the fund and these Treasury securities and related interest are eliminated in consolidation at the Governmentwide level. By accounting convention, the transfers of general revenues are eliminated in the consolidation of the SOSI at the government-wide level and as such, the general revenues that are used to finance Medicare Parts B and D are not included in these calculations even though the expenditures on these programs are included. For the fiscal year 2013 and 2012 SOSI, the amounts eliminated totaled $22.5 trillion and $21.6 trillion, respectively. Refer to Unaudited Required Supplementary Information—Social Insurance section for additional information on Medicare program financing.

The Medicare Prescription Drug, Improvement, and Modernization Act (MMA), enacted on December 8, 2003, created the Part D account in the SMI Trust Fund to account for the prescription drug benefit that began in 2006. The MMA established within SMI two Part D accounts related to prescription drug benefits: the Medicare Prescription Drug Account and the Transitional Assistance Account. The Medicare Prescription Drug Account was used in conjunction with the broad, voluntary prescription drug benefits that commenced in 2006. The Transitional Assistance Account was used to provide transitional assistance benefits, beginning in 2004 and extending through 2005, for certain low-income beneficiaries prior to the start of the new prescription drug benefit.

Affordable Care Act (ACA)

The financial projections for the Medicare program reflect substantial, but very uncertain, cost savings deriving from provisions of the Affordable Care Act. However, it is important to note that the improved results for HI and SMI Part B since 2010 depend in part on the long-range feasibility of the various cost-saving measures in the Affordable Care Act–in particular, the lower increases in Medicare payment rates to most categories of health care providers. Under the ACA, the rate of increase of Medicare payment rates is equal to the prior law rate of increase (equal to the rate of increase in the prices of inputs used to produce Medicare services) less the rate of increase of total economy multifactor productivity. Without fundamental change in the current delivery system, these productivity-related adjustments to Medicare payment rates would probably not be viable indefinitely. It is possible that health care providers could improve their productivity, reduce wasteful expenditures, and take other steps to keep their cost growth within the bounds imposed by the Medicare price limitations. For such efforts to be successful in the long range, providers would have to generate and sustain unprecedented levels of productivity gains–a very challenging and uncertain prospect.

A transformation of health care in the United States, affecting both the means of delivery and the method of paying for care, is also a possibility. The Affordable Care Act takes important steps in this direction by initiating programs of research into innovative payment and service delivery models, such as accountable care organizations, patient-centered "medical homes," improvement in care coordination for individuals with multiple chronic health conditions, improvement in coordination of post-acute care, payment bundling, "pay for performance," and assistance for individuals in making informed health choices. If researchers and policy makers can demonstrate that the new approaches developed through these initiatives will improve the quality of health care and/or reduce costs, then the Secretary of Health and Human Services can adopt them for Medicare without further legislation. Such changes have the potential to reduce health care costs and cost growth rates and could, as a result, help lower Medicare cost growth rates to levels compatible with the lower price updates payable under current law.

The ability of new delivery and payment methods to significantly lower cost growth rates is uncertain at this time, since specific changes have not yet been designed, tested, or evaluated. Hopes for success are high, but at this time there is insufficient evidence to support an assumption that improvements in efficiency can occur of the magnitude needed to align with the statutory Medicare price updates.

The reduction in provider payment updates, if implemented for all future years as required under current law, could have secondary impacts on provider participation, beneficiary access to care; quality of services; and other factors. These possible impacts are very speculative and at present there is no consensus among experts as to their potential scope. Further research and analysis will help to better inform this issue and may enable the development of specific projections of secondary effects under current law in the future. In addition, the Medicare Part B projections reflect a reduction of almost 25 percent in payment rates for physician services in 2014, as estimated in the 2013 Trustee Report, which is assumed to be implemented as required by the Sustainable Growth Rate (SGR) provisions of current law. If lawmakers act to prevent this decrease, as they did all SGR payment rate reductions scheduled between 2003 through 2013, and do not offset this action with reductions in other provisions of the program, then actual Part B and total SMI costs will significantly exceed the projections shown in this report.

The SOSI projections are based on current law. Therefore, the productivity adjustments are assumed to occur in all future years, as required by the Affordable Care Act. In addition, an approximate 25 percent reduction in Medicare payment rates for physician services in January 2014, as estimated in the 2013 Trustees Report, is assumed to be implemented as required under current law, despite the virtual certainty that Congress will continue to override this reduction[1]. Therefore, it is important to note that the actual future costs for Medicare are likely to exceed those shown by these current-law projections.

The extent to which actual future Part A and Part B costs exceed the projected current-law amounts due to changes to the productivity adjustments and physician payments depends on both the specific changes that might be legislated and on whether Congress would pass further provisions to help offset such costs. As noted, these examples only reflect hypothetical changes to provider payment rates. It is likely that in the coming years, Congress will consider, and pass a number of other legislative proposals affecting Medicare. Many of these will likely be designed to reduce costs in an effort to make the program more affordable. In practice, it is not possible to anticipate what actions Congress might take, either in the near term or over longer periods.

The Medicare Board of Trustees, in their annual report to Congress, references an alternative scenario to illustrate when possible, the potential understatement of Medicare costs and projection results. This alternative scenario assumes that the productivity adjustments are gradually phased down during 2020 to 2034 and that the physician fee reductions are overridden. These examples were developed for illustrative purposes only; the calculations have not been audited; no endorsement of the illustrative alternative to current law by the Trustees, CMS, or the CMS Office of the Actuary, should be inferred; and the examples do not attempt to portray likely or recommended future outcomes. Thus the illustrations are useful only as general indicators of the substantial impacts that could result from future legislation affecting the productivity adjustments and physician payments under Medicare and of the broad range of uncertainty associated with such impacts. The table below contains a comparison of the Medicare 75-year present values of income and expenditures under current law with those under the alternative scenario illustration.

---

[1] The Pathway for SGR Reform Act of 2013, enacted December 26, 2013, replaced the almost 25 percent reduction in Medicare payment rates with an increase of 0.5 percent for the period January 1, 2014, through March 31, 2014.

Medicare Present Values (in billions) (Unaudited)

	2013 Consolidated SOSI	Illustrative Alternative Scenario [1,2]
Income		
Part A	$16,192	$16,214
Part B [3]	5,718	7,364
Part D [4]	2,340	2,343
Total Income	$24,250	$25,921
Expenditures		
Part A	$20,964	$25,396
Part B	21,377	27,510
Part D	9,211	9,224
Total Expenditures	$51,552	$62,130
Part A	$4,772	$9,182
Part B	15,659	20,146
Part D	6,871	6,881
Excess of Expenditures over Income	$27,302	$36,209

[1] These amounts are not presented in the 2013 Trustees Report.

[2] At the request of the Trustees, the Office of the Actuary at CMS has prepared an illustrative set of Medicare Trust Fund projections that differ from current law. No endorsement of the illustrative alternative to current law by the Trustees, CMS, or the Office of the Actuary should be inferred.

[3] Excludes $15,659 billion and $20,146 billion of General Revenue Contributions from the 2013 Consolidated SOSI projection and the Illustrative Alternative Scenario's projection, respectively; i.e., to reflect Part B income on a consolidated Governmentwide basis.

[4] Excludes $6,871 billion and $6,881 billion of General Revenue Contributions from both the 2013 Consolidated SOSI projection and the Illustrative Alternative Scenario's projection, respectively; i.e., to reflect Part D income on a consolidated Governmentwide basis.

Note: Amounts may not add due to rounding.

As expected, the differences between the current-law projections and the illustrative alternative are substantial for Part A and Part B, although both represent a sizeable improvement in the financial outlook for Medicare compared to the laws in effect prior to the ACA. This difference in outlook serves as a compelling reminder of the importance of developing and implementing further means of reducing health care cost growth in the coming years. All Part A fee-for-service providers are affected by the productivity adjustments, so the current law projections reflect an estimated annual Part A cost growth averaging 0.8 percent through 2029 and 1.1 percent in each year thereafter. If the productivity adjustments were gradually phased out, as illustrated under the alternative scenario, the present value of Part A expenditures is estimated to be roughly 20 percent higher than the current-law projection. As indicated above, the present value of Part A income is basically unaffected under the alternative scenario.

The Part B expenditure projections are significantly higher under the alternative scenario than under current law, both because of the assumed gradual phase-out of the productivity adjustments and the assumption that the scheduled physician fee reductions would be overridden and based on 0.7 percent annual increases through 2022, as is consistent with the recent historical experience and the recommendation of the 2010-2011 Medicare Technical Review Panel. The productivity adjustments are assumed to affect more than half of Part B expenditures at the time their phase-out is assumed to begin. Similarly, physician fee schedule services are assumed to be roughly 25 percent higher under the alternative scenario than under current law at that time. The combined effect of these two factors results in a present value of Part B expenditures under the alternative scenario that is approximately 29 percent higher than the current-law projection.

The Part D projections are the same in the alternative projection as they are in the current law projection because the services are not impacted by the productivity adjustments or the physician fee schedule reductions. The very minor impact is the result of a slight change in the discount rates that are used to calculate present values.

Social Security and Medicare–Demographic and Economic Assumptions

The Boards of Trustees[2] of the OASDI and Medicare Trust Funds provide in their annual reports to Congress short-range (10-year) and long-range (75-year) actuarial estimates of each trust fund. Because of the inherent uncertainty in estimates for 75 years into the future, the Boards use three alternative sets of economic and demographic assumptions to show a range of possibilities. Assumptions are made about many economic and demographic factors, including Gross Domestic Product (GDP)[3], earnings, the Consumer Price Index (CPI), the unemployment rate, the fertility rate, immigration, mortality, disability incidence and terminations and, for the Medicare projections, health care cost growth. The assumptions used for the most recent set of projections shown in Table 1A (Social Security) and Table 1B (Medicare) are generally referred to as the "intermediate assumptions," and reflect the trustees' reasonable estimate of expected future experience. For further information on Social Security and Medicare demographic and economic assumptions, refer to SSA's and HHS' Agency Financial Reports.

---

[2] There are six trustees: the Secretaries of the Treasury (managing trustee), Health and Human Services, and Labor; the Commissioner of the Social Security Administration; and two public trustees who are generally appointed by the President and confirmed by the Senate for a 4-year term. By law, the public trustees are members of two different political parties.

[3] In July 2013, the Bureau of Economic Analysis (BEA) revised upward the historical values for GDP beginning with estimates for 1929. The Social Security and Medicare projections do not reflect this change as they are based on 2013 Trustees Reports issued in May 2013. If this change had been available in time to include in the 2013 Trustees Reports, it would not have had any significant effect on earnings projections.

Table 1A
Social Security – Demographic and Economic Assumptions

Demographic Assumptions

Year	Total Fertility Rate[1]	Age-Sex Adjusted Death Rate (per 100,000)[2]	Net Annual Immigration (persons per year)[3]	Period Life Expectancy at Birth[4]	
				Male	Female
2013	1.91	722.2	1,155,000	76.4	81.2
2020	2.06	670.2	1,250,000	77.4	82.0
2030	2.03	613.0	1,110,000	78.6	83.0
2040	2.00	564.1	1,080,000	79.7	83.9
2050	2.00	521.1	1,060,000	80.8	84.7
2060	2.00	483.3	1,055,000	81.7	85.5
2070	2.00	449.7	1,055,000	82.6	86.2
2080	2.00	419.8	1,055,000	83.4	86.9

Economic Assumptions

Year	Real Wage Differential (percent)[5]	Average Annual Wage In Covered Employment (percent change)[6]	CPI (percent change)[7]	Real GDP (percent change)[8]	Total Employment (percent change)[9]	Average Annual Interest Rate (percent)[10]
2013	0.87	2.67	1.80	2.2	1.2	1.6
2020	1.35	4.15	2.80	2.3	0.7	5.6
2030	1.20	4.00	2.80	2.0	0.4	5.7
2040	1.15	3.95	2.80	2.2	0.6	5.7
2050	1.11	3.91	2.80	2.1	0.5	5.7
2060	1.10	3.90	2.80	2.0	0.4	5.7
2070	1.10	3.90	2.80	2.1	0.5	5.7
2080	1.13	3.93	2.80	2.1	0.4	5.7

[1] The total fertility rate for any year is the average number of children that would be born to a woman in her lifetime if she were to experience, at each age of her life, the birth rate observed in, or assumed for, the selected year, and if she were to survive the entire childbearing period.

[2] The age-sex-adjusted death rate is based on the enumerated total population as of April 1, 2000, if that population were to experience the death rates by age and sex observed in, or assumed for, the selected year. It is a summary measure and not a basic assumption; it summarizes the basic assumptions from which it is derived.

[3] Net annual immigration is the number of persons who enter during the year (both legally and otherwise) minus the number of persons who leave during the year. It is a summary measure and not a basic assumption; it summarizes the effects of the basic assumptions from which it is derived.

[4] The period life expectancy, at a given age for a given year, is the average remaining number of years expected prior to death for a person at that exact age, born on January 1, using the mortality rates for that year over the course of his or her remaining life. It is a summary measure and not a basic assumption; it summarizes the effects of the basic assumptions from which it is derived.

[5] The real-wage differential is the annual percentage change in the average annual wage in covered employment, less the annual percentage change in the CPI. Values are rounded after computations.

[6] The average annual wage in covered employment is the total amount of wages and salaries for all employment covered by the OASDI program in a year divided by the number of employees with any such earnings during the year. It is a summary measure and not a basic assumption; it summarizes the basic assumptions from which it is derived.

[7] The CPI is the Consumer Price Index for Urban Wage Earners and Clerical Workers (CPI-W).

[8] The real GDP is the value of total output of goods and services produced in the U.S., in 2005 dollars. It is a summary measure and not a basic assumption; it summarizes the effects of the basic assumptions from which it is derived.

[9] Total employment is total U.S. military and civilian employment. It is a summary measure and not a basic assumption; it summarizes the basic assumptions from which it is derived.

[10] The average annual interest rate is the average of the nominal interest rates, which compound semiannually, for special public-debt obligations issuable to the OASI and DI Funds in each of the 12 months of the year. It is a summary measure and not a basic assumption; it summarizes the basic assumptions from which it is derived.

Table 1B
Medicare – Demographic and Economic Assumptions

Demographic Assumptions

Year	Total Fertility Rate[1]	Age-Sex Adjusted Death Rate (per 100,000)[2]	Net Annual Immigration (persons per year)[3]
2013	1.91	722.2	1,155,000
2020	2.06	670.2	1,255,000
2030	2.03	613.0	1,115,000
2040	2.00	564.1	1,080,000
2050	2.00	521.1	1,065,000
2060	2.00	483.3	1,060,000
2070	2.00	449.7	1,055,000
2080	2.00	419.8	1,055,000

Economic Assumptions

Year	Real Wage Differential (percent)[4]	Average Annual Wage In Covered Employment (percent change)[5]	CPI (percent change)[6]	Real GDP (percent change)[7]	Per Beneficiary Cost[8] (percent change) HI	SMI Part B	SMI Part D	Real Interest Rate (percent)[9]
2013	0.87	2.67	1.80	2.2	(0.9)	0.4	0.3	(0.3)
2020	1.35	4.15	2.80	2.3	3.9	5.3	6.6	2.8
2030	1.20	4.00	2.80	2.0	4.7	4.9	5.5	2.9
2040	1.15	3.95	2.80	2.2	5.3	4.5	5.3	2.9
2050	1.11	3.91	2.80	2.1	4.2	4.1	5.0	2.9
2060	1.10	3.90	2.80	2.0	3.9	4.0	4.8	2.9
2070	1.10	3.90	2.80	2.1	4.1	4.0	4.7	2.9
2080	1.13	3.93	2.80	2.1	3.8	3.8	4.5	2.9

[1] The total fertility rate for any year is the average number of children that would be born to a woman in her lifetime if she were to experience, at each age of her life, the birth rate observed in, or assumed for, the selected year, and if she were to survive the entire childbearing period.

[2] The age-sex-adjusted death rate is based on the enumerated total population as of April 1, 2000, if that population were to experience the death rates by age and sex observed in, or assumed for, the selected year. It is a summary measure and not a basic assumption; it summarizes the basic assumptions from which it is derived.

[3] Net annual immigration is the number of persons who enter during the year (both legally and otherwise) minus the number of persons who leave during the year. It is a summary measure and not a basic assumption; it summarizes the effects of the basic assumptions from which it is derived.

[4] The real-wage differential is the annual percentage change in the average annual wage in covered employment less the annual percentage change in CPI. Values are rounded after computations.

[5] The average annual wage in covered employment is the total amount of wages and salaries for all employment covered by the OASDI program in a year, divided by the number of employees with any such earnings during the year. It is a summary measure and not a basic assumption; it summarizes the basic assumptions from which it is derived.

[6] The CPI is the Consumer Price Index for Urban Wage Earners and Clerical Workers (CPI-W).

[7] The real GDP is the value of total output of goods and services produced in the U.S., in 2005 dollars. It is a summary measure and not a basic assumption; it summarizes the effects of the basic assumptions from which it is derived.

[8] These increases reflect the overall impact of more detailed assumptions that are made for each of the different types of service provided by the Medicare program (for example, hospital care, physician services, and pharmaceutical costs). These assumptions include changes in the payment rates, utilization, and intensity of each type of service.

[9] The real interest rate is the average rate of interest earned on new trust fund securities, above and beyond the rate of inflation.

Railroad Retirement

The Railroad Retirement and Survivor Benefit program pays full retirement annuities at age 60 to railroad workers with 30 years of service. The program pays disability annuities based on total or occupational disability. It also pays annuities to spouses and divorced spouses of retired workers and to widow(er)s, remarried widow(er)s, surviving divorced spouses, children, and parents of deceased railroad workers. Medicare covers qualified railroad retirement beneficiaries in the same way as it does Social Security beneficiaries. The Railroad Retirement and Survivors' Improvement Act of 2001 (RRSIA) liberalized benefits for 30-year service employees and their spouses, eliminated a cap on monthly benefits for retirement and disability benefits, lowered minimum service requirements from 10 to 5 years, and provided for increased benefits for widow(er)s.

The RRB and the SSA share jurisdiction over the payment of retirement and survivor benefits. RRB has jurisdiction if the employee has at least 10 years (5 if performed after 1995) of railroad service. For survivor benefits, RRB requires that the employee's last regular employment before retirement or death be in the railroad industry. If a railroad employee or his or her survivors do not qualify for railroad retirement benefits, the RRB transfers the employee's railroad retirement credits to SSA.

Payroll taxes paid by railroad employers and their employees are a primary source of income for the Railroad Retirement and Survivor Benefit Program. By law, railroad retirement taxes are coordinated with Social Security taxes. Employees and employers pay tier I taxes at the same rate as Social Security taxes and tier II taxes to finance railroad retirement benefit payments that are higher than Social Security levels.

Other sources of program income include: financial transactions with the Social Security and Medicare Trust Funds, earnings on investments, Federal income taxes on railroad retirement benefits, and appropriations (provided after 1974 as part of a phase out of certain vested dual benefits). The financial interchange between RRB's Social Security Equivalent Benefit (SSEB) Account, the Federal Old-Age and Survivors Insurance Trust Fund, the Disability Insurance Trust Fund, and the Federal Hospital Insurance Trust Fund is intended to put the latter three trust funds in the same position they would have been had railroad employment been covered under the Social Security Act. From a Governmentwide perspective, these future financial interchanges and transactions are intragovernmental transfers and are eliminated in consolidation.

Railroad Retirement–Employment, Demographic and Economic Assumptions

The most recent set of projections are prepared using employment, demographic and economic assumptions and reflect the Board Members' reasonable estimate of expected future experience.

Three employment assumptions were used in preparing the projections and reflect optimistic, moderate and pessimistic future passenger rail and freight employment. The average railroad employment is assumed to be 230,000 in 2013 under the moderate employment assumption. This employment assumption, based on a model developed by the Association of American Railroads, assumes that (1) passenger service employment will remain at the level of 45,000 and (2) the employment base, excluding passenger service employment, will decline at a constant 2.0 percent annual rate for 25 years, at a falling rate over the next 25 years, and remain level thereafter. All the projections are based on an open-group (i.e., future entrants) population.

The moderate (middle) economic assumptions include a long-term cost of living increase of 2.8 percent, an interest rate of 7.0 percent, and a wage increase of 3.8 percent. The cost of living assumption reflects the expected level of price inflation. The interest (or investment) rate assumption reflects the expected rate of return on NRRIT investments. The wage increase reflects the expected increase in railroad employee earnings.

Sources of the demographic assumptions including mortality rates and total termination rates, remarriage rates for widow(er)s, retirement rates and withdrawal rates, are listed in Table 2. For further details on the employment, demographic, economic and all other assumptions, refer to the *U.S. Railroad Retirement Board Annual Report*, and the 25th *Actuarial Valuation of the Assets and Liabilities under the Railroad Retirement Acts* (Valuation Report) as of December 31, 2010, with Technical Supplement.

Table 2
Railroad Retirement Demographic Actuarial Assumptions (Sources)

Mortality Rates [1]	Mortality after age retirement	2010 RRB Annuitants Mortality Table
	Mortality after disability retirement	2010 RRB Disabled Mortality Table for Annuitants with Disability Freeze
		2010 RRB Disabled Mortality Table for Annuitants without Disability Freeze
	Mortality during active service	2006 RRB Active Service Mortality Table
	Mortality of widow annuitants	1995 RRB Mortality Table for Widows
Total Termination Rates [2]	Termination for spouses	2010 RRB Spouse Total Termination Table
	Termination for disabled children	2004 RRB Total Termination Table for Disabled Children
Widow Remarriage Rates [3]	1997 RRB Remarriage Table	
Retirement Rates [4]	Age retirement	See the Valuation Report.
	Disability retirement	See the Valuation Report.
Withdrawal Rates [5]	See the Valuation Report.	

[1] These mortality tables are used to project the termination of eligible employee benefit payments within the population.

[2] Total termination rates are used to project the termination of dependent benefits to spouses and disabled children.

[3] This rate is used to project the termination of spousal survivor benefits.

[4] The retirement rates are used to determine the expected annuity to be paid based on age and years of service for both age and disability retirees.

[5] The withdrawal rates are used to project all withdrawals from the railroad industry and resultant effect on the population and accumulated benefits to be paid.

Black Lung–Disability Benefit Program

The Black Lung Disability Benefit Program provides for compensation and medical benefits for eligible coal miners who are totally disabled due to pneumoconiosis (black lung disease) as a result of their coal mine employment. The same program also provides for survivor benefits for eligible survivors of coal miners who died due to pneumoconiosis. DOL operates the Black Lung Disability Benefit Program.

Black lung disability benefit payments are funded by excise taxes from coal mine operators based on the sale of coal, as are the fund's administrative costs. These taxes are collected by the Internal Revenue Service (IRS) and transferred to the BLDTF, which was established under the authority of the Black Lung Benefits Revenue Act, and administered by the Treasury.

P.L. 110-343, Division B-Energy Improvement and Extension Act of 2008, enacted on October 3, 2008, among other things, restructured the BLDTF debt by refinancing the outstanding high interest rate repayable advances with low interest rate discounted debt instruments similar in form to zero-coupon bonds, plus a one-time appropriation. This Act also allowed that any subsequent debt issued by the BLDTF may be used to make benefit payments, other authorized expenditures, or to repay debt and interest from the initial refinancing.

Black Lung–Demographic and Economic Assumptions

The demographic assumptions used for the most recent set of projections are the number of beneficiaries and their life expectancy. The beneficiary population data is updated from information supplied by the program. The beneficiary population is a nearly closed universe in which attrition by death exceeds new entrants by a ratio of more than ten to one. SSA Life Tables are used to project the life expectancies of the beneficiary population.

The economic assumptions used for the most recent set of projections are coal excise tax revenue estimates, the tax rate structure, Federal civilian pay raises, and medical cost inflation.

Estimates of future receipts of the black lung excise tax are based on projections of future coal production and sale prices prepared by the Energy Information Agency of DOE. Treasury's Office of Tax Analysis provides the first 11 years of tax receipt estimates. The remaining years are estimated using a growth rate based on both historical tax receipts and Treasury's estimated tax receipts. The coal excise tax rate structure is $1.10 per ton of underground-mined coal and $0.55 per ton of surface-mined coal sold, with a cap of 4.4 percent of sales price until the earlier of December 31, 2018, or the first December 31, in which there exist no (1) balance of repayable debt described in section 9501 of the Internal Revenue Code and (2) unpaid interest on the debt. At that time, the tax rates revert to $0.50 per ton of underground-mined coal and $0.25 per ton of surface-mine coal sold, and a limit of 2.0 percent of sales price.

OMB supplies assumptions for future monthly benefit rate increases based on increases in the Federal pay scale and future medical cost inflation based on increases in the CPIM, which are used to calculate future benefit costs. During the current projection period, future benefit rate increases 2.78 percent in 2014, 3.47 percent in 2015, and 3.4 percent in each year thereafter, and medical cost increases 3.7 percent in 2014, and 3.8 percent in each year thereafter. Estimates for administrative costs for the first 11 years of the projection are supplied by DOL's Budget Office, based on current year enacted amounts, while later years are based on the number of projected beneficiaries.

Statement of Changes in Social Insurance Amounts

The Statement of Changes in Social Insurance Amounts reconciles the change (between the current valuation and the prior valuation) in the present value of future revenue less future expenditures for current and future participants (the open group measure) over the next 75 years (except Black Lung is projected only through September 30, 2040). The reconciliation identifies several components of the changes that are significant and provides reasons for the changes. The following disclosures relate to the Statement of Changes in Social Insurance Amounts including the reasons for the components of the changes in the open group measure during the reporting period from the end of the previous reporting period for the Government's social insurance programs. The Statement of Changes in Social Insurance Amounts shows two reconciliations: (1) changing from the period beginning on January 1, 2012, to the period beginning on January 1, 2013, and (2) changing from the period beginning on January 1, 2011, to the period beginning on January 1, 2012.

Social Security

All estimates relating to the Social Security Program in the Statement of Changes in Social Insurance Amounts represent values that are incremental to the prior change. As an example, the present values shown for economic data, assumptions, and methods, represent the additional effect of these new data, assumptions, and methods after considering the effects from demography and the change in the valuation period.

Assumptions Used for the Components of the Changes for the Social Security Program

The present values included in the Statement of Changes in Social Insurance Amounts are for the current and prior years and are based on various economic and demographic assumptions used for the intermediate assumptions in the Social Security Trustees Reports for these years. Table 1A summarizes these assumptions for the current year.

Period Beginning on January 1, 2012, and Ending January 1, 2013

Present values as of January 1, 2012, are calculated using interest rates from the intermediate assumptions of the 2012 Social Security Trustees Report. All other present values in this part of the Statement of Changes in Social Insurance Amounts are calculated as a present value as of January 1, 2013. Estimates of the present value of changes in social insurance amounts due to changing the valuation period and changing demographic data, assumptions, and methods are presented using the interest rates under the intermediate assumptions of the 2012 Social Security Trustees Report. Since interest rates are an economic estimate and all estimates in the table are incremental to the prior change, all other present values in this part of the Statement of Changes in Social Insurance Amounts are calculated using the interest rates under the intermediate assumptions of the 2013 Social Security Trustees Report.

Period Beginning on January 1, 2011, and Ending January 1, 2012

Present values as of January 1, 2011, are calculated using interest rates from the intermediate assumptions of the 2011 Social Security Trustees Report. All other present values in this part of the Statement of Changes in Social Insurance Amounts are calculated as a present value as of January 1, 2012. Estimates of the present value of changes in social insurance amounts due to changing the valuation period and changing demographic data, assumptions, and methods are presented using the interest rates under the intermediate assumptions of the 2011 Social Security Trustees Report. Since interest rates are an economic estimate and all estimates in the table are incremental to the prior change, all other present values in this part of the Statement of Changes in Social Insurance Amounts are calculated using the interest rates under the intermediate assumptions of the 2012 Social Security Trustees Report.

Changes in Valuation Period

Period Beginning on January 1, 2012, and Ending January 1, 2013

The effect on the 75-year present values of changing the valuation period from the prior valuation period (2012-2086) to the current valuation period (2013-2087) is measured by using the assumptions for the prior valuation and extending them to cover the current valuation. Changing the valuation period removes a small negative net cashflow for 2012, replaces it with a much larger negative net cashflow for 2087, and measures the present values as of January 1, 2013, one year later. Thus, the present value of future net cashflows (excluding the combined OASI and DI Trust Fund asset reserves at the start of the period) decreased (became more negative) when the 75-year valuation period changed from 2012-2086 to 2013-2087.

Period Beginning on January 1, 2011, and Ending January 1, 2012

The effect on the 75-year present values of changing the valuation period from the prior valuation period (2011-2085) to the current valuation period (2012-2086) is measured by using the assumptions for the prior valuation and extending them to cover the current valuation. Changing the valuation period removes a small negative net cashflow for 2011, replaces it with a much larger negative net cashflow for 2086, and measures the present values as of January 1, 2012, one year later. Thus, the present value of future net cashflows (excluding the combined OASI and DI Trust Fund assets at the start of the period) decreased (became more negative) when the 75-year valuation period changed from 2011-2085 to 2012-2086.

Changes in Demographic Data, Assumptions, and Methods

Period Beginning on January 1, 2012, and Ending January 1, 2013

For the current valuation (beginning on January 1, 2013), changes in ultimate assumptions and recent data for immigration have significant but largely offsetting effects.

- The assumed ultimate annual immigration of "other immigrants", that is, those entering the country without legal permanent resident (LPR) status, is 1.4 million in the current valuation, compared with 1.5 million assumed for the prior valuation.
- The assumed ultimate annual number of persons attaining LPR status is 1.05 million for the current valuation, compared with 1.03 million assumed for the prior valuation. The distribution of the ultimate number between those entering the country with LPR status and those adjusting status after having already entered the country was also revised.

Reasons for these changes include: (1) the expectation of continued tighter border control in the future; (2) the assumed continuation of a recent increase in the number attaining LPR status as immediate relatives; and (3) the assumed continuation of a recent increase in the proportion of persons attaining LPR status upon entering the country (rather than adjusting status after entry).

These changes to immigration assumptions increased the present value of future cashflows.

Otherwise, the ultimate demographic assumptions for the current valuation are the same as those for the prior valuation. However, the starting demographic values, and the way these values transition to the ultimate assumptions, were changed.

- Final mortality data for 2008 and 2009 show substantially larger reductions in death rates for the current valuation than were expected in the prior valuation. The new data show a lower starting level of death rates and a faster rate of decline in death rates over the next 25 years.
- Final fertility (birth) data for 2009 and 2010, and preliminary data for 2011, indicate lower birth rates for these years than were assumed in the prior valuation.
- New historical data for marital status, for the number of new marriages, for "other immigration", and for the size of the population (based on the 2010 Census) were used in the current valuation.

Inclusion of the new mortality and fertility data decreased the present value of future net cashflows, while the inclusion of the remaining data increased the present value of future net cashflows.

Period Beginning on January 1, 2011, and Ending January 1, 2012

The ultimate demographic assumptions for the current valuation (beginning on January 1, 2012) are the same as those for the prior valuation. However, the starting demographic values, and the way these values transition to the ultimate assumptions, were changed.

- Preliminary birth rate data for 2009 and 2010 are lower than were expected in the prior valuation. During the period of transition to their ultimate values, the birth rates in the current valuation are generally lower than they were in the prior valuation.
- The current valuation incorporates final data on legal immigration levels for 2010. The levels are slightly lower than the estimates used in the prior valuation.
- Updated starting population levels and the interaction of these levels with the changes in the fertility and immigration assumptions result in higher ratios of retirement age population to working age population than in the prior valuation.

Inclusion of each of these demographic data sets decreased the present value of future net cashflows.

Changes in Economic Data, Assumptions, and Methods

Period Beginning on January 1, 2012, and Ending January 1, 2013

The ultimate economic assumptions for the current valuation (beginning on January 1, 2013) are the same as those for the prior valuation. Other changes include:

- The real interest rate is projected to be lower over the first ten years of the current valuation.
- The starting economic values and near-term economic growth rate assumptions were updated.

The projection of lower real interest rates decreased the present value of future net cashflows, while the changes to starting economic values and near-term economic growth rates increased the present value of future net cashflows.

Period Beginning on January 1, 2011, and Ending January 1, 2012

The ultimate economic assumptions for the current valuation (beginning January 1, 2012) are the same as those for the prior valuation except for the assumed annual rate of change in average hours worked. The current valuation assumes a decline in average hours worked of 0.05 percent per year rather than no change, as was assumed in the prior valuation. This change lowers the ultimate annual real-wage differential by 0.05 percentage point from the prior valuation, and decreases the present value of future cashflows. In addition, the starting economic values and near-term economic growth rate assumptions were updated to reflect recent developments.

- For the current valuation, OASDI taxable earnings are lower in the starting year, 2011, than were projected for the prior valuation.
- Price inflation in 2011 was higher than expected, with the cost-of-living adjustment to benefits in December 2011 being 2.9 percentage points higher than was assumed in the prior valuation.
- The real interest rate is projected to be lower over the first ten years of the current valuation.

Inclusion of each of these economic revisions decreased the present value of future net cashflows.

Changes in Law or Policy

Period Beginning on January 1, 2012, and Ending January 1, 2013

The current valuation (beginning on January 1, 2013) reflects the enactment of one law and the implementation of one policy change.

- The American Taxpayer Relief Act of 2012 was enacted on January 2, 2013. The Act reduces Federal marginal income tax rates for most beneficiaries and thus lowers projected revenue from taxation of benefits.
- The Deferred Action for Childhood Arrivals (DACA) policy was implemented on June 15, 2012. DACA provides protection from deportation and an opportunity to work legally for many unauthorized immigrants who entered the country before age 16 and were under age 31 on June 15, 2012.

Inclusion of the American Taxpayer Relief Act of 2012 decreased the present value of future net cashflows, while inclusion of DACA increased the present value of future net cashflows.

Period Beginning on January 1, 2011, and Ending January 1, 2012

There were no legislative changes, included in the current valuation (beginning on January 1, 2012) and not in the prior valuation, that are projected to have a significant effect on the present value of the 75-year net cashflows.

Changes in Methodology and Programmatic Data

Period Beginning on January 1, 2012, and Ending January 1, 2013

Several methodological improvements and updates of program-specific data are included in the current valuation (beginning on January 1, 2013). The most significant are identified below.

- The alignment of projected labor force participation rates with future trends in disability, longevity, and population levels was altered. Future changes in disability prevalence now affect labor force participation, and the starting year for longevity changes used in the participation rate projections is now consistent with the starting year for those projections.
- Ultimate age-sex specific unemployment rates based on the relative levels of long-term historical patterns were developed through the most recent historical year. This improvement is expected to substantially reduce the volatility in projected levels of these rates between valuations.
- The modeling of the number of workers insured under the programs was separated into two groups by residency status: (1) citizens and immigrants with legal permanent resident status; and (2) other immigrants. Separate modeling for these groups is important because their relative sizes in the total population have been changing and will continue to do so.
- The historical sample of earnings histories for new beneficiaries was updated to reflect new benefit entitlements in 2008 for the current valuation. The prior valuation used a sample, which reflected new benefit entitlements in 2007.
- The projections of revenue from taxation of benefits were better aligned between the first 10 years and the remaining years of the projection period.
- There were also minor updates to programmatic data, method changes for projecting beneficiaries and benefit levels over the first 10 years of the projection period, other small methodological improvements, and interactions.

Inclusion of each of these methodological improvements and updates of program-specific data increased the present value of future net cashflows.

Period Beginning on January 1, 2011, and Ending January 1, 2012

Several methodological improvements and updates of program-specific data are included in the current valuation (beginning on January 1, 2012). The most significant are identified below.

- Compared to the prior valuation, the ultimate age-adjusted disability incidence rates increased by 2 percent for males and 5 percent for females. Inclusion of these changes to disability incidence rates projections increased the number of disability beneficiaries.
- Projected earnings of new beneficiaries were made more consistent with projected economy-wide covered worker rates. This change led to increases in projected benefit levels for workers who become eligible for benefits in the future.
- Average benefit levels for retired-worker and disabled-worker beneficiaries were slightly increased for their first two years of benefit entitlement. The method for estimating these average benefit levels was changed to exclude beneficiaries who first start receiving benefits two or more years after their initial entitlement date, who tend to have lower benefits.

Inclusion of each of these methodological improvements and updates of program-specific data revisions decreased the present value of future net cashflows.

Medicare

All estimates relating to the Medicare program in the Statement of Changes in Social Insurance Amounts represent values that are incremental to the prior change. As an example, the present values shown for demographic assumptions, represent the additional effect that these assumptions have, once the effects from the change in the valuation period and projection base have been considered.

Assumptions Used for the Components of the Changes for the Medicare Program

The present values included in the Statement of Changes in Social Insurance Amounts are for the current and prior years and are based on various economic and demographic assumptions used for the intermediate assumptions in the Medicare Trustees Reports for these years. Table 1B summarizes these assumptions for the current year.

Period Beginning on January 1, 2012, and Ending January 1, 2013

Present values as of January 1, 2012, are calculated using interest rates from the intermediate assumptions of the 2012 Medicare Trustees Report. All other present values in this part of the Statement of Changes in Social Insurance Amounts are calculated as a present value as of January 1, 2013. Estimates of the present value of changes in social insurance amounts due to changing the valuation period, projection base, demographic assumptions, and law are determined using the interest rates under the intermediate assumptions of the 2012 Medicare Trustees Report. Since interest rates are economic assumptions, the estimates of the present values of changes in economic assumptions are presented using the interest rates under the intermediate assumptions of the 2013 Medicare Trustees Report.

Period Beginning on January 1, 2011, and Ending January 1, 2012

Present values as of January 1, 2011, are calculated using interest rates from the intermediate assumptions of the 2011 Medicare Trustees Report. All other present values in this part of the Statement of Changes in Social Insurance Amounts are calculated as a present value as of January 1, 2012. Estimates of the present value of changes in social insurance amounts due to changing the valuation period, projection base, demographic assumptions, and law are determined using the interest rates under the intermediate assumptions of the 2011 Medicare Trustees Report. Since interest rates are economic assumptions, the estimates of the present values of changes in economic assumptions are presented using the interest rates under the intermediate assumptions of the 2012 Medicare Trustees Report.

Changes in Valuation Period

Period Beginning on January 1, 2012, and Ending January 1, 2013

The effect on the 75-year present values of changing the valuation period from the prior valuation period (2012-2086) to the current valuation period (2013-2087) is measured by using the assumptions for the prior valuation period and applying them, in the absence of any other changes, to the current valuation period. Changing the valuation period removes a small negative net cashflow for 2012 and replaces it with a much larger negative net cashflow for 2087. The present value of future net cashflow (including or excluding the combined Medicare Trust Fund assets at the start of the period) was therefore decreased (made more negative) when the 75-year valuation period changed from 2012-2086 to 2013-2087.

Period Beginning on January 1, 2011, and Ending January 1, 2012

The effect on the 75-year present values of changing the valuation period from the prior valuation period (2011-2085) to the current valuation period (2012-2086) is measured by using the assumptions for the prior valuation period and applying them, in the absence of any other changes, to the current valuation period. Changing the valuation period removes a small negative net cashflow for 2011 and replaces it with a much larger negative net cashflow for 2086. The present value of future net cashflow (including or excluding the combined Medicare Trust Fund assets at the start of the period) was therefore decreased (made more negative) when the 75-year valuation period changed from 2011-2085 to 2012-2086.

Changes in Demographic Data, Assumptions, and Methods

Period Beginning January 1, 2012, and Ending January 1, 2013

The demographic assumptions used in the Medicare projections are the same as those used for the OASDI and are prepared by the Office of the Chief Actuary at the SSA.

For the current valuation (beginning on January 1, 2013), changes in ultimate assumptions and recent data for immigration have significant effects.

- The assumed ultimate annual immigration of "other immigrants", that is, those entering the country without legal permanent resident (LPR) status, is 1.4 million in the current valuation, compared with 1.5 million assumed for the prior valuation.
- The assumed ultimate annual number of persons attaining LPR status is 1.05 million for the current valuation, compared with 1.03 million assumed for the prior valuation. The distribution of the ultimate number between those entering the country with LPR status and those adjusting status after having already entered the country was also revised.

Otherwise, the ultimate demographic assumptions for the current valuation period are the same as those for the prior valuation period. However, the starting demographic values, and the way these values transition to the ultimate assumptions, were changed.

- Final mortality data for 2008 and 2009 show substantially larger reductions in death rates for the current valuation than were expected in the prior valuation. The new data show a lower starting level of death rates and a faster rate of decline in death rates over the next 25 years.
- Final fertility (birth) data for 2009 and 2010, and preliminary data for 2011, indicate lower birth rates for these years than were assumed in the prior valuation.
- New historical data for marital status, for the number of new marriages, for "other immigration", and for the size of the population (based on the 2010 Census) were used in the current valuation.

These changes increased the Part A present values of future expenditures and income. Since overall population projections are higher compared to the prior valuation, these changes increase the Part B and Part D present values of expenditures.

Period Beginning January 1, 2011, and Ending January 1, 2012

The demographic assumptions used in the Medicare projections are the same as those used for the OASDI and are prepared by the Office of the Chief Actuary at the SSA.

The ultimate demographic assumptions for the current valuation period are the same as those for the prior valuation period. However, the starting demographic values were changed.

- Preliminary birth rate data for 2009 and 2010 are lower than were expected in the prior valuation. During the period of transition to their ultimate values, the birth rates in the current valuation are generally lower than they were in the prior valuation.
- The current valuation incorporates final data on legal immigration levels for 2010. The levels are slightly lower than the estimates used in the prior valuation.
- Updated starting population levels and the interaction of these levels with the changes in the fertility and immigration assumptions result in higher ratios of retirement age population to working age population than in the prior valuation.

These changes have little impact on the Part A present values of future expenditures and revenue. However, since overall population projections are lower compared to the prior valuation, these changes decrease the Part B and Part D present values of expenditures.

Changes in Economic and Other Health Care Assumptions

Period Beginning January 1, 2012, and Ending January 1, 2013

The economic assumptions used in the Medicare projections are the same as those used for OASDI and are prepared by the Office of the Chief Actuary at SSA.

The ultimate economic assumptions for the current valuation (beginning on January 1, 2013) are the same as those for the prior valuation. Other changes include:

- The real interest rate is projected to be lower over the first ten years of the current valuation.
- The starting economic values and near-term economic growth rate assumptions were updated.

The health care assumptions are specific to the Medicare projections. The following health care assumptions were changed in the current valuation.

- Utilization rate and case mix increase assumptions for skilled nursing facilities were decreased.
- Lower projected Medicare Advantage program costs that reflect recent data suggesting that certain provisions of the Affordable Care Act will reduce growth in these costs by more than was previously projected.

- Administrative action that increased Medicare Advantage payment rates beginning in 2014 to reflect assumed future legislative overrides of the physician payment reductions.
- Larger than previously projected impact from patent expiration of several major prescription drugs in 2012.
- Lower projected prescription drug trend for 2013.

The net impact of these changes resulted in a slight increase in the future net cashflow for total Medicare. For Part A, these changes resulted in a decrease to the present value of expenditures and income, with an overall slight increase in the future net cashflow. For Part B, these changes increased the present value of expenditures. On the other hand, the above-mentioned changes lowered the present value of expenditures for Part D.

Period Beginning January 1, 2011, and Ending January 1, 2012

The economic assumptions used in the Medicare projections are the same as those used for the OASDI and are prepared by the Office of the Chief Actuary at the SSA.

The ultimate economic assumptions for the current valuation period are the same as those for the prior valuation period. However, the starting economic values and near-term economic growth rate assumptions were changed. The economic recovery has been slower than was assumed for the prior valuation period.

- For the current valuation period, HI taxable earnings are considerably lower for the starting year, 2011, than were projected for the prior valuation period. The projected level of taxable earnings grows more slowly through 2017 for the current valuation period.
- Price inflation in 2011 was higher than expected, with the cost-of-living adjustment in December 2011 being 2.9 percentage points higher than was assumed in the prior valuation.
- The real interest rate is projected to be lower over the first 10 years of the current valuation period.

Inclusion of each of these economic revisions decrease the present value of future net cashflow.

The health care assumptions are specific to the Medicare projections. The following health care assumptions were changed in the current valuation.

- Case mix growth assumptions for inpatient hospitals were lowered.
- Utilization rate and case mix increase assumptions for skilled nursing facilities and home health agencies were increased.
- Growth in hospice services were increased.
- Increase in average pre-ACA "baseline" growth rate from GDP+1 percent to GDP+1.4 percent to better account for the level of payment rate updates for Medicare (prior to the ACA) compared to private health insurance and other payers of health insurance in the U.S.
- Use of the "factors contributing to growth" model, developed by the Office of the Actuary at CMS, for year-by-year growth rate assumptions in long range.
- Lower assumed growth rate for prescription drug expenditures in the U.S. overall.
- Explicit projection of Part B services indexed by the CPI (e.g., Ambulatory Surgical Center, lab and DME services).

The net impact of these changes resulted in a decrease in the future net cashflow for total Medicare. For Part A, these changes resulted in an increase to the present value of expenditures and a very slight decrease to the present value of revenue, with an overall decrease on the future net cashflow. For Part B, these changes increased the present value of expenditures. On the other hand, the above-mentioned changes lowered the present value of expenditures for Part D.

Changes in Law or Policy

Period Beginning January 1, 2012, and Ending January 1, 2013

Although Medicare legislation was enacted since the prior valuation date, many of the provisions have a negligible impact on the present value of the 75-year revenue, expenditures, and net cashflow. The American Taxpayer Relief Act of 2012 included several provisions that had an impact on the Medicare program. These include the extension of the 0 percent physician payment update through 2013, which slightly increases the present value of Part B expenditures; payments for inpatient hospital services in 2014-2017 are reduced in order to recoup $11 billion in overpayments associated with documentation and coding adjustments during 2008-2010 that were not previously recovered, which lowers the present value of Part A expenditures; reductions to the end-stage renal disease (ESRD) bundled payment rate to reflect changes in the utilization of certain drugs and biological and a delay in the inclusion of oral-only ESRD drugs in the rate, which reduces the present value of Part B expenditures and increases the present value of Part D expenditures; and the coding intensity adjustment used in determining payments to Medicare Advantage plans was revised, which decreases the present value of Part A and Part B expenditures.

Period Beginning January 1, 2011, and Ending January 1, 2012

Although Medicare legislation was enacted since the prior valuation date, many of the provisions have a negligible impact on the present value of the 75-year revenue, expenditures, and net cashflow. However, there were three specific provisions enacted that had a fairly substantial impact on the Medicare program. These include the sequestration of up to two percent of Medicare provider expenditures from February 2013 through January 2022 as required by the Budget Control Act of 2011, which reduces the present value of expenditures for Medicare; the extension of the 0 percent physician payment update through calendar year 2012 required by the Temporary Payroll Tax Cut Continuation Act of 2011 and the Middle Class Tax Relief and Job Creation Act of 2012, which slightly increases the present value of Part B expenditures; and the reduction in bad debt payments required by the Middle Class Tax Relief and Job Creation Act of 2012, which decreases the present value of Part A and Part B expenditures.

Change in Projection Base

Period Beginning January 1, 2012, and Ending January 1, 2013

Actual revenue and expenditures in 2012 were different than what was anticipated when the 2012 Medicare Trustees Report projections were prepared. Part A revenue and expenditures were lower than anticipated, based on actual experience. Part B total revenue and expenditures were also lower than estimated based on actual experience. For Part D, actual revenue and expenditures were both slightly lower than prior estimates. The net impact of the Part A, B, and D projection-base changes is an increase in the future net cashflow. Actual experience of the Medicare Trust Funds between January 1, 2012 and January 1, 2013 is incorporated in the current valuation and is slightly more than projected in the prior valuation.

Period Beginning on January 1, 2011, and Ending January 1, 2012

Actual revenue and expenditures in 2011 were different than what was anticipated when the 2011 Medicare Trustees Report projections were prepared. Part A revenue was slightly higher than estimated and Part A expenditures were lower than anticipated, based on actual experience. Part B total revenue and expenditures were higher than estimated based on actual experience. For Part D, actual revenue and expenditures were both slightly lower than prior estimates. The net impact of the Part A, B, and D projection-base changes is an increase in the future net cashflow. Actual experience of the Medicare Trust Funds between January 1, 2011, and January 1, 2012 is incorporated in the current valuation and is slightly more than projected in the prior valuation.

Railroad Retirement

The present values included in the Statement of Changes in Social Insurance Amounts are for the current and prior years and are based on various employment, demographic and economic assumptions that reflect the RRB's reasonable estimate of expected future financial and actuarial status of the trust funds. Selected economic assumptions were updated in 2013 along with the following other components of changes in the open group measure.

Changes in Valuation Period

Period Beginning January 1, 2012, and Ending January 1, 2013

The effect on the 75-year present values of changing the valuation period from the prior valuation period (2012-2086) to the current valuation period (2013-2087) was a $1.5 billion decrease (became more negative) on the open group measure between January 1, 2012, and January 1, 2013.

Period Beginning January 1, 2011, and Ending January 1, 2012

The effect on the 75-year present values of changing the valuation period from the prior valuation period (2011-2085) to the current valuation period (2012-2086) was a $1.9 billion decrease on the open group measure between January 1, 2011, and January 1, 2012.

Changes in Demographic Data and Assumptions

Period Beginning January 1, 2012, and Ending January 1, 2013

Demographic assumptions were not changed between the Statement of Social Insurance as of January 1, 2012 and the Statement of Social Insurance as of January 1, 2013. Changes in demographic data resulted in an increase of $1.5 billion in the open group measure between January 1, 2012, and January 1, 2013.

Period Beginning January 1, 2011, and Ending January 1, 2012

Some demographic assumptions, such as the Annuitants Mortality Table, the Disabled Mortality Table for Annuitants with Disability Freeze, the Disabled Mortality Table for Annuitants without Disability Freeze, the Active Service Mortality Table, the Spouse Total Termination Table, the probability of a spouse, the rates of immediate age retirement, the rates of immediate disability retirement, the rates of eligibility for disability freeze, the rates of final withdrawal, service months, salary scales, and family characteristics, were changed between the Statement of Social Insurance as of January 1, 2011 and the Statement of Social Insurance as of January 1, 2012. These changes and the changes in demographic data resulted in an increase of $2.8 billion on the open group measure between January 1, 2011 and January 1, 2012.

Changes in Economic Data and Assumptions

Period Beginning January 1, 2012, and Ending January 1, 2013

Ultimate economic assumptions were not changed between the Statement of Social Insurance as of January 1, 2012 and the Statement of Social Insurance as of January 1, 2013, but selected economic assumptions were. The actual COLA of 1.7 percent was used for 2013 in place of the 2.0 percent COLA assumed for 2013 in the prior year's report. A 1.8 percent COLA was assumed for 2014 instead of a 2.4 percent COLA, and a 2.3 percent COLA was assumed for 2015 instead of a 2.8 percent COLA. Also, the actual 2012 interest rate (investment return) of 13.9 percent was higher than the assumed 7.0 percent interest rate used for 2012 in the prior year's report. Changes in economic data and assumptions had a relatively small effect of a $0.5 billion decrease in the open group measure between January 1, 2012, and January 1, 2013.

Period Beginning January 1, 2011, and Ending January 1, 2012

Both select and ultimate economic assumptions were changed between January 1, 2011, and January 1, 2012. The actual COLA of 3.6 percent was used for 2012 in place of the 3.0 percent COLA assumed for 2012 in the prior year's report. Assumed COLAs of 2.0 percent in 2013, 2.4 percent in 2014, and 2.8 percent in 2015 and thereafter were used rather than the 3.0 percent COLA assumed in the prior year's report. A wage increase rate of 3.5 percent was used for 2011 rather than the assumed 4 percent wage increase rate used for 2011 in the prior year's report. A wage increase rate of 3.8 percent was used for 2012 and thereafter rather than the 4 percent wage increase rate used in the prior year's report. Also, the actual 2011 interest rate (investment return) of 1.6 percent was lower than the assumed 7.5 percent interest rate used for 2011 in the prior year's report. An assumed interest rate of 7 percent was used for 2012 and all subsequent years rather than the 7.5 percent rate used in the prior year's report. Changes in economic data and assumptions resulted in a decrease of about $1.8 billion on the open group measure from January 1, 2011 to January 1, 2012.

Changes in Methodology and Programmatic Data

Period Beginning January 1, 2012, and Ending January 1, 2013

There were no changes in methodology and programmatic data.

Period Beginning January 1, 2011, and Ending January 1, 2012

There were no changes in methodology and programmatic data.

Changes in Law or Policy

Period Beginning January 1, 2012, and Ending January 1, 2013

There were no changes in law or policy.

Period Beginning January 1, 2011, and Ending January 1, 2012

There were no changes in law or policy.

Black Lung

The significant assumptions used in the projections of the Black Lung social insurance program presented in the Statement of Social Insurance are the number of beneficiaries, life expectancy, coal excise tax revenue estimates, the tax rate structure, Federal civilian pay raises and medical cost inflation. These assumptions also affect the amounts reported on the Statement of Changes in Social Insurance Amounts.

During fiscal year 2013, the decrease in the open group measure was primarily due to projected lower coal excise tax revenues and changes in the interest rates used to discount cashflows from 2.75 percent in fiscal year 2012 to between 2.79 and 2.95 percent in fiscal year 2013 offset in part due to lower beneficiary costs. In fiscal year 2013, the matching between the timing of cashflows and interest rates was enhanced and the approach for selecting the interest rate assumptions was refined by selecting discount rates based on OMB's interest rate assumptions which were interpolated to reflect the average duration of payments between 21.3 and 25.4 years for income payments, medical payments, administrative expenses and coal excise tax collections. For fiscal years 2009 to 2012, the projections were discounted using an interest rate published by Treasury as of the start of the projection period for Treasury loans to government agencies for loans with a duration that approximated the projection period.

During fiscal year 2012, the decrease in the open group measure was primarily due to changes in the assumptions about coal excise tax revenues and changes in the assumptions about beneficiaries, including cost (not associated with medical inflation or Federal civilian pay raises), number, type, age, and life expectancy, which were offset in part due to the change in the assumption about the interest rate that was used to discount the cashflows from 3.375 percent to 2.75 percent. For fiscal year 2012, the coal excise tax revenue projections were revised to reflect current year experience and a decrease in future collections. The assumptions about the beneficiaries were revised to reflect current year experience and an increase in future costs. The interest rate was revised to reflect the Treasury rate for loans to government agencies with a duration that approximated the projection period as of the start of the projection period.

Note 25. Stewardship Land and Heritage Assets

Stewardship land is federally-owned land that is set aside for the use and enjoyment of present and future generations, and land on which military bases are located. Except for military bases, this land is not used or held for use in general Government operations. Stewardship land is land that the Government does not expect to use to meet its obligations, unlike the assets listed in the Balance Sheets. Stewardship land is measured in non-financial units such as acres of land and lakes, and a number of National Parks and National Marine Sanctuaries. Examples of stewardship land include national parks, national forests, wilderness areas, and land used to enhance ecosystems to encourage animal and plant species, and to conserve nature. This category excludes lands administered by the Bureau of Indian Affairs and held in trust.

The majority of public lands that are under the management of DOI were acquired by the Government during the first century of the Nation's existence between 1781 and 1867.

Stewardship lands are used and managed in accordance with the statutes authorizing their acquisition or directing their use and management. Additional detailed information concerning stewardship land, such as agency stewardship policies, physical units by major categories, and the condition of stewardship land, can be obtained from the financial statements of DOI, DOC, DOD, and USDA.

Heritage assets are Government-owned assets that have one or more of the following characteristics:
- Historical or natural significance.
- Cultural, educational, or artistic importance.
- Significant architectural characteristics.

The cost of heritage assets often is not determinable or relevant to their significance. Like stewardship land, the Government does not expect to use these assets to meet its obligations. The most relevant information about heritage assets is non-financial. The public entrusts the Government with these assets and holds it accountable for their preservation. Examples of heritage assets include the Mount Rushmore National Memorial and Yosemite National Park. Other examples of heritage assets include the Declaration of Independence, the U.S. Constitution, and the Bill of Rights preserved by the National Archives. Also included are national monuments/structures such as the Vietnam Veterans Memorial, the Jefferson Memorial, and the Washington Monument, as well as the Library of Congress. Many other sites such as battlefields, historic structures, and national historic landmarks are placed in this category, as well.

Many laws and regulations govern the preservation and management of heritage assets. Established policies by individual Federal agencies for heritage assets ensure the proper care and handling of the assets under their control and preserve these assets for the benefit of the American public.

Some heritage assets are used both to remind us of our heritage and for day-to-day operations. These assets are referred to as multi-use heritage assets. One typical example is the White House. The cost of acquisition, betterment or reconstruction of all multi-use heritage assets is capitalized as general PP&E and is depreciated.

The Government classifies heritage assets into two broad categories: collection type and non-collection type. Collection type heritage assets include objects gathered and maintained for museum and library collections. Non-collection type heritage assets include national wilderness areas, wild and scenic rivers, natural landmarks, forests, grasslands, historic places and structures, memorials and monuments, buildings, national cemeteries, and archeological sites.

The discussion of the Government's heritage assets is not all-inclusive. Rather, it highlights significant heritage assets reported by Federal agencies. Please refer to the individual financial statements of the DOC, VA, State, DOD, National Archives and Records Administration, and Web sites for the Library of Congress (http://www.loc.gov/index.html), the Smithsonian Institution (http://www.si.edu), and the Architect of the Capitol (http://aoc.gov) for additional information on multi-use heritage assets, agency stewardship policies, and physical units by major categories and conditions.

Note 26. Subsequent Events

Statutory Debt Limit

A delay in raising the statutory debt limit existed on September 30, 2013. When delays in raising the statutory debt limit occur, Treasury often must deviate from its normal debt management operations and take extraordinary measures to meet the government's obligations as they come due without exceeding the debt limit. Extraordinary measures taken by Treasury during the period of May 20, 2013, through September 30, 2013, resulted in federal debt securities not being issued to certain federal government funds. As a result of Treasury securities not being issued to the Government Securities Investment Fund (G-Fund) of the Federal Retirement Thrift Investment Board, Treasury reported in Note 17—Other Liabilities miscellaneous liabilities in the amount of $120.4 billion, representing uninvested principal of and related interest for G-Fund that would have been reported in Note 12–Federal Debt Securities Held by the Public and Accrued Interest had there not been a delay in raising the statutory debt limit on September 30, 2013, and had the securities been issued. The uninvested principal amount of the G-Fund was $119.9 billion. Additionally, the related interest that would have been accrued and/or paid during the period of May 20, 2013, through September 30, 2013, would have been $476 million.

On October 1, 2013, the Secretary of the Treasury notified Congress that Treasury had begun using the final extraordinary measures and that these measures would be exhausted no later than October 17, 2013. In accordance with the Continuing Appropriations Act, 2014 (Public Law No. 113-46), which was enacted on October 17, 2013, the President submitted a written certification to Congress that, absent a suspension of the statutory debt limit under 31 U.S.C. § 3101(b), the Secretary of the Treasury would be unable to issue debt to meet existing commitments. As a result, the debt limit was suspended for the period of October 17, 2013 through February 7, 2014. On October 17, 2013, Treasury discontinued its use of the extraordinary measures and resumed normal debt management operations. On this date, in accordance with relevant laws, Treasury restored uninvested principal amount to the G-Fund of $173.9 billion. On October 18, 2013, in accordance with relevant laws, Treasury restored the interest related to the uninvested principal in the amount of $653 million. Treasury has also restored uninvested principal and interest to the Civil Service Retirement and Disability Fund and Postal Service Retiree Health Benefits Fund and uninvested principal to the Exchange Stabilization Fund, in accordance with relevant laws.

On February 7, 2014, Treasury again began using extraordinary measures to temporarily avoid exceeding the statutory debt limit of $17,211.6 billion. Legislation suspending the debt limit through March 15, 2015 was signed by the President on February 15, 2014, making further use of these measures unnecessary. In accordance with relevant laws, restoration of principal and interest to funds affected by the measures began on February 18, 2014, and will be completed on June 30, 2014.

Updates to Troubled Asset Relief Program (TARP) Investments

Ally Financial, Inc.

In January 2014, the Office of Financial Stability (OFS) sold approximately 410,000 shares of Ally Financial, Inc. common stock in a private placement for $3.0 billion. OFS' remaining Ally Financial Inc. holdings consist of approximately 572,000 shares of common stock.

General Motors

Between October 1, 2013 and December 20, 2013, OFS sold its remaining 101 million shares of General Motors common stock for approximately $3.8 billion.

See Note 5 – Troubled Asset Relief Program (TARP) – Direct Loans and Equity Investments, Net for further information on TARP investments related to Ally Financial, Inc. and General Motors.

This page is intentionally blank.

United States Government Required Supplementary Information (Unaudited) For the Years Ended September 30, 2013, and 2012

Fiscal Projections for the U.S. Government – Fiscal Year 2013

This section of the Financial Report of the U.S. Government (FR) is prepared pursuant to Statement of Federal Financial Accounting Standard (SFFAS) 36, *Reporting Comprehensive Long-Term Fiscal Projections for the U.S. Government*. It assesses whether current policies for spending and taxation can be sustained and the extent to which the cost of federal benefits received by current taxpayers will be shifted to future taxpayers under sustainable policies. This assessment requires prospective information about receipts and spending, the resulting debt, and how these amounts relate to the economy. A sustainable policy is defined here as one where the ratio of federal debt held by the public to GDP (the debt-to-GDP ratio) is ultimately stable or declining. This section of the FR does not assess the sustainability of State and local government fiscal policy.

The projections and analysis presented here are extrapolations based on an array of assumptions described in detail below. Among these is the assumption that current Federal policy will not change. This assumption is made so as to inform the question of whether current fiscal policy is sustainable and, if it is not sustainable, the magnitude of needed reforms to make fiscal policy sustainable. The projections are therefore neither forecasts nor predictions. If policy changes are implemented, perhaps in response to projections like those presented here, then actual financial outcomes will of course be different than those projected.

The methods and assumptions underlying the projections are still evolving.

Statement of Long Term Fiscal Projections

Table 1 on the following page reports the present value of 75-year projections for various categories of Federal Government's receipts and non-interest spending[1] . Estimates from last year's Financial Report are included in Table 1 for comparison. The Table 1 estimates are expressed in present value dollars and as a percentage of the present value of Gross Domestic Product (GDP)[2] as of September 30, 2013 and, in the case of last year's Financial Report, September 30, 2012. The present value of a future amount, for example $1 billion in October 2088, is the amount of money that if invested on September 30, 2013 in an account earning the government borrowing rate would have a value of $1 billion in October 2088.[3]

The present value of a receipt or expenditure category over 75 years is the sum of the annual present value amounts. When expressing a receipt or expenditure category over 75 years as a percent of GDP, the present value dollar amount is divided by the present value of GDP over 75 years. Measuring receipts and expenditures as a percentage of GDP is a useful indicator of the economy's capacity to sustain federal government programs. As is true for prior Financial Reports, the assumptions for GDP, interest rates, and other economic factors underlying this year's projections are the same assumptions

---

[1] For the purposes of this analysis, spending is defined in terms of outlays. In the context of Federal budgeting, spending can either refer to budget authority – the authority to commit the government to make a payment; to obligations – binding agreements that will result in payments, either immediately or in the future; or to outlays – actual payments made.

[2] GDP is a standard measure of the overall size of the economy and represents the total market value of all final goods and services produced domestically during a given period of time. The components of GDP are: private sector consumption and investment, government consumption and investment, and net exports (exports less imports). Equivalently, GDP is a measure of the gross income generated from domestic production over the same time period.

[3] Present values recognize that a dollar paid or collected in the future is worth less than a dollar today because a dollar today could be invested and earn interest. To calculate a present value, future amounts are thus reduced using an assumed interest rate, and those reduced amounts are summed.

that underlie the most recent Social Security and Medicare trustees' report projections. The use of discount factors consistent with the Social Security trustees' rate allows for consistent present value budget calculations over 75 years between this report and the trustees' reports. Present value calculations under higher and lower interest rate scenarios are presented in the "Alternative Scenarios" section.

Table 1: Long-Term Fiscal Projections of Federal Receipts and Spending						
	75-Year Present Values[1]					
	Dollars in Trillions			% GDP[2]		
Receipts:	2013	2012	Change	2013	2012	Change
Social Security Payroll Taxes...............	46.1	42.1	3.9	4.2	4.3	-0.1
Medicare Payroll Taxes......................	15.4	14.1	1.3	1.4	1.5	0.0
Individual Income Taxes....................	113.2	97.5	15.7	10.4	10.0	0.3
Other Receipts..................................	41.5	37.9	3.6	3.8	3.9	-0.1
Total Receipts...................................	216.2	191.6	24.6	19.8	19.7	0.1
Non-interest Spending:						
Social Security..................................	62.4	57.5	5.0	5.7	5.9	-0.2
Medicare Part A[3]............................	23.5	22.7	0.8	2.2	2.2	-0.1
Medicare Parts B&D[4]......................	24.4	22.2	2.2	2.2	2.4	-0.2
Medicaid..	25.2	26.1	-0.9	2.3	2.7	-0.4
Defense Discretionary.......................	23.1	30.4	-7.3	2.1	3.1	-1.0
Non-defense Discretionary.................	27.4	16.1	11.4	2.5	1.7	0.9
Other Mandatory..............................	34.0	33.2	0.8	3.1	3.4	-0.3
Total Non-interest Spending..............	220.2	208.2	12.0	20.2	21.4	-1.3
Non-interest Spending less Receipts.......	4.0	16.5	-12.6	0.4	1.7	-1.3

[1] 75-year present value projections for 2013 are as of 9/30/2013 for the period FY 2014-2088; projections for 2012 are as of 9/30/2012 for the period FY 2013-2087.

[2] The 75-year present value of nominal GDP, which drives the calculations above is $1091.8 trillion starting in FY 2014, and was $971.3 trillion starting in FY 2013.

[3] Represents portions of Medicare supported by payroll taxes.

Represents portions of Medicare supported by general revenues. Consistent with the President's Budget, outlays for Parts B & D are presented net of premiums.

NOTE Totals may not equal the sum of components due to rounding.

Receipt categories in Table 1 include individual income taxes, Social Security and Medicare payroll taxes, and the residual "other receipts." On the spending side, the projections are broken down into: (1) discretionary spending that is funded through annual appropriations, such as spending for national security, and (2) mandatory (entitlement) spending that is generally financed with permanent or multi-year appropriations, such as spending for Social Security and Medicare. This year's projections for Social Security and Medicare are based on the same economic and demographic assumptions that underlie the 2013 Social Security and Medicare trustees' reports and the Statement of Social Insurance, while comparative information presented from last year's report is based on the 2012 Social Security and Medicare trustees' reports. Projections for the other categories of receipts and spending are consistent with the economic and demographic assumptions used from the respective trustees' reports. The projections assume the continuance of current policy which, as is explained below, can be different than current law in cases where lawmakers have in the past periodically changed the law in a consistent way.

The projections shown in Table 1 are made over a 75-year time frame, consistent with the time frame featured in the Social Security and Medicare trustees' reports. However, these projections are for fiscal years starting on October 1, whereas the trustees' reports feature calendar-year projections. This difference allows the projections to start from the actual budget results from fiscal years 2013 and 2012.

This year's estimate of the overall 75-year present value net excess of non-interest spending over receipts expressed in Table 1 is 0.4 percent of the 75-year present value of GDP ($4.0 trillion). This imbalance can be broken down by funding source. There is a surplus of receipts over spending of 1.3 percent of GDP ($14.5 trillion) among programs funded by the government's general revenues, but an imbalance of 1.7 percent of GDP ($18.5 trillion[4]) for the combination of Social Security (OASDI) and Medicare Part A, which under current law are funded with payroll taxes and not in any material

---

[4] The 75-year present value earmarked imbalance of $18.5 trillion is comprised of several line items from Table 1 – Social Security outlays net of Social Security Payroll Taxes ($16.3 trillion) and Medicare Part A outlays net of Medicare Payroll Taxes ($8.1 trillion) – as well as subcomponents of these programs not presented separately in the table. These subcomponents include Social Security and Medicare Part A administrative costs that are classified as non-defense discretionary spending ($0.6 trillion) and Social Security and Medicare Part A revenue other than payroll taxes: taxation of benefits (-$2.9 trillion), Federal employer share (-$1.1 trillion), and other income (-$2.5 trillion).

respect with general revenues.[5] [6] By comparison, last year's projections showed that programs funded by the government's general revenues had an excess of receipts over spending of 0.1 percent of GDP ($1.3 trillion) while the payroll tax-funded programs had an imbalance of spending over receipts of 1.8 percent of GDP ($17.9 trillion).

This year's estimate of the 75-year present value imbalance of spending over receipts expressed as a share of the 75-year present value of GDP is 1.3 percentage points lower than was estimated in last year's Report. Table 2 reports the sources of the change. The largest source of change, 0.5 percent of GDP ($4.9 trillion), was due to changes in the projections for Medicare and Medicaid as reflected in their respective actuarial reports. The 2013 Medicare trustees' report projected lower spending in most service categories and lower Medicare Advantage program costs, reflecting recent data that suggest certain provisions of the Affordable Care Act will reduce growth in these costs by more than was projected in the 2012 report. The 2012 Medicaid actuarial report reflected fewer beneficiaries and lower cost per beneficiary than the 2011 report, due to lower than projected base year expenditures, the Supreme Court decision on the Medicaid eligibility expansion, and slower projected per enrollee cost growth.

Table 2: Components of Change		
75-Year Present Values:	Trillions of $	% of 75-Year Present Value of GDP
Non-Interest Spending Less Receipts: FY 2012...................	16.5	1.7
Components of Change:		
Change due to Program-Specific Actuarial Assumptions.....	-4.9	-0.5
Change due to Enacted Legislation...................................	-3.2	-0.3
Change in Economic and Demographic Assumptions..........	-2.0	-0.3
Change due to Updated Budget Data..............................	-1.2	-0.1
Change in Reporting Period...	-0.9	-0.1
Change in Model Technical Assumptions.........................	-0.4	-0.0
Total...	-12.6	-1.3
Non-Interest Spending Less Receipts: FY 2013..................	4.0	0.4
NOTE: Totals may not equal the sum of components due to rounding.		

The next largest change noted in Table 2 – further lowering the imbalance by 0.3 percent of GDP ($3.2 trillion), is attributable to enactment of the American Taxpayer Relief Act (ATRA) in January 2013. ATRA permanently extended the 2001/2003 tax cuts (providing for lower marginal income tax rates and other tax cuts) for incomes up to $400,000 for individuals and $450,000 for couples while allowing them to expire for incomes above those thresholds.[7] The law also permanently indexed the Alternative Minimum Tax (AMT) to inflation. (In addition, it delayed the implementation of automatic spending cuts called for in the Budget Control Act of 2011 (BCA) for two months and extended a number of smaller tax and spending measures while allowing several other smaller tax provisions to expire.) Since the 2012 projections

---

[5] General fund transfers received by the OASDI trust fund, primarily in 2011 and 2012, to account for lost payroll taxes resulting from enactment of the temporary 2 percent reduction of the employee payroll taxes are not included in the 75-year present value of OASDI payroll taxes. Social Security and Medicare Part A expenditures can exceed payroll tax revenues in any given year to the extent that there are sufficient balances in the respective trust funds, balances that derive from past excesses of payroll tax revenues over expenditures and interest earned on those balances and represent the amount the general fund owes the respective trust fund programs. When spending does exceed payroll tax revenues, as has occurred each year since 2008 for Medicare Part A and 2010 for Social Security, the excess spending is financed first with interest due from the general fund and secondly with a drawdown of the general fund's loan balance; in either case, the spending is ultimately supported by general revenues or borrowing. Under current law, benefits for Social Security and Medicare Part A can be paid only to the extent that there are sufficient balances in the respective trust funds. In order for the projections here to reflect the full size of these program's commitments to pay future benefits, the projections assume that all scheduled benefits will be financed with borrowing to the extent necessary after the trust funds are exhausted.

[6] The fiscal imbalances reported in Table 1 are limited to future outlays and receipts. They do not include the initial level of publicly-held debt, which was $12.0 trillion in 2013 and $11.3 trillion in 2012, and therefore they do not by themselves answer the question of how large fiscal reforms must be to make fiscal policy sustainable, or how those reforms divide between reforms to Social Security and Medicare Part A and to other programs. Other things equal, past cashflows (primarily surpluses) for Social Security and Medicare Part A reduced federal debt at the end of 2013 by $3.0 trillion (the trust fund balances at that time); the contribution of other programs to federal debt at the end of 2013 was therefore $14.3 trillion. Because the $18.5 trillion imbalance between outlays and receipts over the next 75 years for Social Security and Medicare Part A does not take account of the Social Security and Medicare Part A trust fund balances, it overstates the magnitude of reforms necessary to make Social Security and Medicare Part A solvent over 75 years by $3.0 trillion. The $3.0 trillion combined Social Security and Medicare Part A trust fund balance represents a claim on future general revenues.

[7] The 2001/2003 tax rate cuts were extended for incomes up to $400,000 for individuals and $450,000 for couples; certain other provisions expired for individuals with incomes over $250,000 and couples with incomes over $300,000.

assumed extension of all the 2001/2003 tax cuts, including for those with incomes above $400,000/$450,000, the effect of ATRA was to raise revenue in the 2013 projections relative to the 2012 projections.

Revised economic and demographic assumptions—including the July 2013 comprehensive National Income and Product Accounts revisions to GDP—lowered the 75-year present value imbalance by 0.3 percent of GDP ($2.0 trillion), as higher nominal GDP and wages had a larger upward effect on the receipts projection than the spending projection. Finally, the projected 75-year present value imbalance was also lowered by a combined 0.3 percent of GDP ($2.8 trillion) due to: (1) updated actual budget results for fiscal year 2013 and other budget data used in formulating the projection ($1.2 trillion or 0.1 percent of GDP reduction), (2) the change in the reporting period from 2013-2087 to 2014-2088 ($0.9 trillion or 0.1 percent of GDP reduction), and (3) changes in model technical assumptions ($0.4 trillion or 0.0 percent of GDP reduction).

The Sustainability of Fiscal Policy

One of the important purposes of the Financial Report is to help citizens and policymakers assess whether current fiscal policy is sustainable and, if it is not, the urgency and magnitude of policy reforms necessary to make fiscal policy sustainable. A sustainable policy is one where the ratio of debt held by the public to GDP (the debt-to-GDP ratio) is ultimately stable or declining.

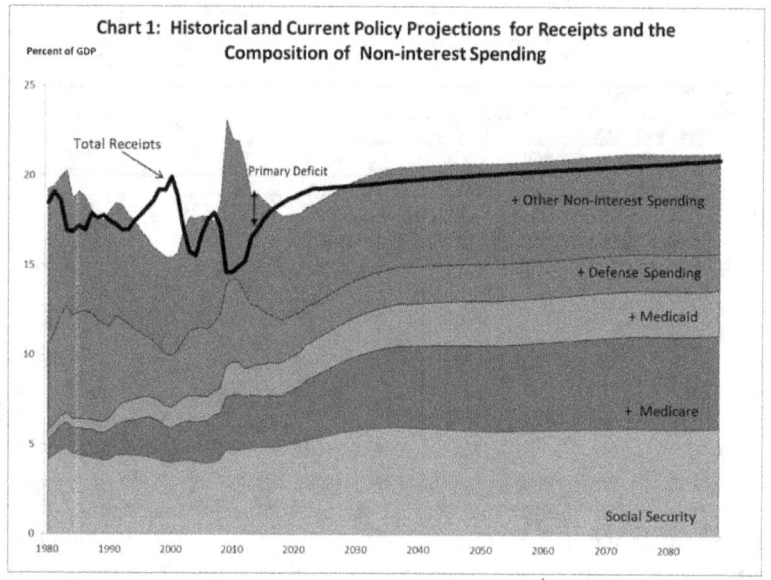

As discussed below, the projections in this report indicate that current policy is not sustainable. If current policy is left unchanged, the projections show the debt-to-GDP ratio falling by nearly 5 percentage points between 2014 to 2024, returning to its 2012 level of 70.1 percent of GDP by 2025, reaching 100 percent of GDP in 2039, and then steadily rising and eventually reaching 277 percent in 2088. Moreover, if the trends that underlie the 75-year projections were to continue, the debt-to-GDP ratio would continue to rise beyond the 75-year window. These conclusions are rooted in the projected trends in receipts, spending, and surpluses/deficits in the context of current law and policy, although, as described in the following pages, there is considerable uncertainty surrounding these estimates. For comparison, under the 2012 projections, the debt-to-GDP ratio increased by a little less than 2 percentage points from 2013 to 2015, fell slightly each year to reach its low point in 2019 (76.4 percent of GDP, roughly the same as its 2013 level), and was projected to equal 100 percent by 2030 and 395 percent in 2087.

Current Policy Projections for Primary Deficits

A key determinant of growth in the debt-to-GDP ratio and hence fiscal sustainability is the primary deficit-to-GDP ratio. The primary deficit is the difference between non-interest spending and receipts, and the primary deficit-to-GDP ratio is the primary deficit expressed as a percent of GDP. As shown in Chart 1, the primary deficit-to-GDP ratio grew rapidly in 2009 due to the financial crisis and the recession and the policies pursued to combat both. The ratio stayed large from 2010 to 2012 despite shrinking in each successive year, and fell significantly in 2013. The primary deficit is projected to shrink in the next few years as spending reductions called for in the BCA take effect and the economy recovers, becoming a primary surplus starting in 2017 that peaks at 1.1 percent of GDP in 2021. Between 2022 and 2037, however, increased spending for Social Security and health programs due to continued aging of the population is expected to cause the primary balance to steadily deteriorate and become a primary deficit in 2029 that grows to 0.8 percent of GDP in 2036. After 2037, the projected primary deficit-to-GDP ratio slowly declines to 0.4 percent of GDP in 2088 as the impact of the baby boom generation retiring dissipates.

The revenue share of GDP fell substantially in 2009 and 2010 and remained low in 2011 and 2012 because of the recession and tax reductions enacted as part of the 2009 American Recovery and Reinvestment Act (ARRA) and the Tax Relief, Unemployment Insurance Reauthorization, and Job Creation Act of 2010. The share rose to 17 percent in 2013 and is projected to return to near its long-run average as the economy recovers and higher tax rates called for by ATRA take effect. After the economy has fully recovered around 2020, receipts are projected to grow slightly more rapidly than GDP as increases in real incomes cause more taxpayers and a larger share of income to fall into the higher individual income tax brackets. Other possible paths for the receipts-to-GDP ratio and the implications for projected debt are analyzed in the "Alternative Scenarios" section.

On the spending side, the non-interest spending share of GDP is projected to stay at or below its current level of about 19 percent until 2029, and to then rise gradually to 20.6 percent of GDP in 2042 and 21.3 percent of GDP in 2088. The reductions in the non-interest spending share of GDP over the next two years are mostly due to the expected reductions in spending for overseas contingency operations (OCO), caps on discretionary spending and the automatic spending cuts mandated by the BCA, and the subsequent increases are principally due to faster growth in Medicare, Medicaid, and Social Security spending (see Chart 1). The retirement of the baby boom generation over the next 25 years is projected to increase the Social Security, Medicare, and Medicaid spending shares of GDP by about 1.2 percentage points, 1.6 percentage points, and 0.8 percentage points, respectively. After 2038, the Social Security spending share of GDP gradually declines and then returns to 2038 levels, while the Medicare and Medicaid spending share of GDP continues to increase, albeit at a slower rate, due to projected increases in health care costs.

The Patient Protection and Affordable Care Act, as amended by the Health Care and Education Reconciliation Act of 2010 (ACA) significantly affects projected spending for both Medicare and Medicaid. That legislation expands health insurance coverage, includes many measures designed to reduce health care cost growth, and significantly reduces Medicare payment rates. On net, the ACA is projected to substantially reduce federal expenditures over the next 75 years. The Medicare spending projections in Table 1 are based on the 2013 Medicare trustees' report's current law projections, and those projections show a substantial slowdown in Medicare cost growth. The projections assume that Medicaid cost per beneficiary grows at the same rate as Medicare cost growth per beneficiary, so the ACA is also estimated to substantially slow Medicaid cost growth. These projections are subject to much uncertainty about the ultimate effects of the ACA's provisions to reduce health care cost growth. Even if those provisions work as intended and as assumed in this projection, Chart 1 shows that there is still a long-term gap between projected receipts and projected total non-interest spending.

Current Policy Projections for Debt and Interest Payments

The primary deficit projections in Chart 1, along with projections for interest rates and GDP, determine the projections for the debt-to-GDP ratio that are shown in Chart 2 (right axis). That ratio was 72 percent at the end of fiscal year 2013, and under current policy is projected to be 69 percent in 2023, 112 percent in 2043, and 277 percent in 2088. The continuous rise of the debt-to-GDP ratio after 2024 indicates that current policy is unsustainable.

The change in debt held by the public from one year to the next is approximately equal to the unified budget deficit, the difference between total spending and total receipts.[8] Total spending is non-interest spending plus interest spending. Chart 2 (left axis) shows that the rapid rise in total spending and the unified deficit is almost entirely due to projected interest payments on the debt. As a percent of GDP, interest spending was 1.3 percent in 2013, and under current policy is projected to reach 4.6 percent in 2033 and 15 percent in 2088.

Another way of viewing the improvement in the financial outlook in this year's report relative to last year's report documented in Table 2 is in terms of the projected debt-to-GDP ratio in 2087. This ratio is projected to reach 272 percent in this year's report, which compares with 395 percent projected in last year's report.

---

[8] Debt held by the public is also affected by certain transactions not included in the unified budget deficit, such as changes in Treasury's cash balances and the nonbudgetary activity of Federal credit financing accounts. These transactions are assumed to hold constant at about 0.8 percent of GDP.

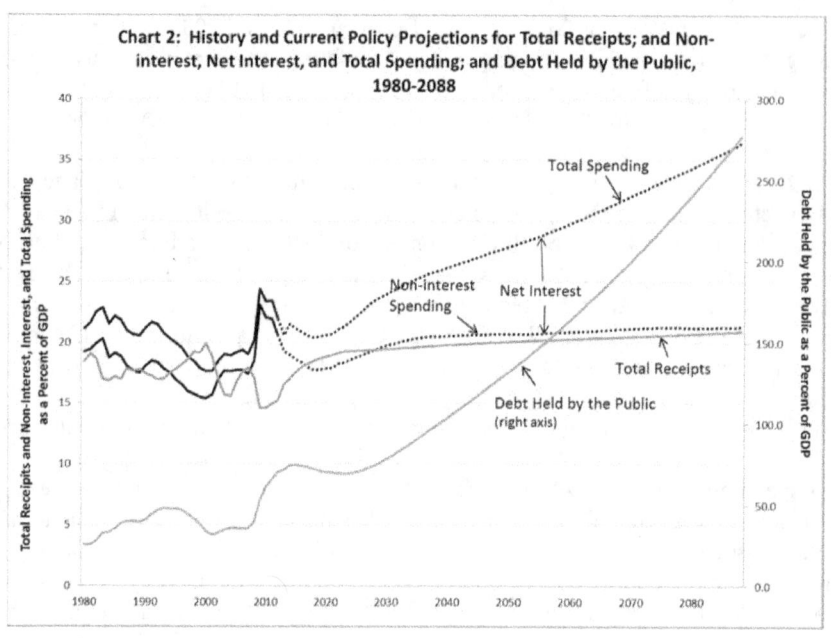

Chart 2: History and Current Policy Projections for Total Receipts; and Non-interest, Net Interest, and Total Spending; and Debt Held by the Public, 1980-2088

The Fiscal Gap

The fiscal gap measures how much the primary surplus (receipts less non-interest spending) must increase in order for fiscal policy to achieve a target debt-to-GDP ratio in a particular future year. In these projections, the fiscal gap is estimated over a 75-year period, from 2014 to 2088, and the target debt-to-GDP ratio is equal to the ratio at the beginning of the projection period, in this case the debt-to-GDP ratio at the end of fiscal year 2013 (72 percent of GDP).

Table 3 reports that the 75-year fiscal gap under current policy is estimated at 1.7 percent of GDP, which is 8.6 percent of the 75-year present value of projected receipts and 8.4 percent of the 75-year present value of non-interest spending. This is less than the 75-year fiscal gap projected in 2012 (2.7 percent of GDP).

Eliminating the primary deficit of 0.4 percent of GDP is not sufficient to close the fiscal gap. Because interest rates are assumed to exceed the growth rate of GDP, maintaining primary balance in each year would still leave debt rising relative to GDP. As noted in Table 1, the present value of the primary deficit, or the excess of projected programmatic (non-interest) spending over receipts, is 0.4 percent of GDP, which in nominal terms is equivalent to an average primary deficit over 75 years of 0.4 percent of GDP. In order to fully close the fiscal gap of 1.7 percent of GDP, annual primary surpluses over the next 75 years must average 1.3 percent of GDP (compared to the current projection of primary deficits of 0.4 percent of GDP).

The Cost of Delay in Closing the 75-Year Fiscal Gap

The longer policy action to close the fiscal gap is delayed, the larger the post-reform primary surpluses must be to stabilize the debt-to-GDP ratio by the end of the 75 year period. Varying the years in which reforms are initiated while holding constant the ultimate target ratio of debt to GDP helps to illustrate the cost of delaying policy changes that close the fiscal gap. The reforms considered here increase the primary surplus relative to current policy by a fixed percent of GDP starting in the reform year. Three such policies are considered, each one beginning in a different year. The analysis shows that the longer policy action is delayed, the larger the post-reform primary surplus must be to bring the debt-to-GDP ratio to 72 percent of GDP in 2088. Future generations are harmed by policy delay because delay necessitates higher primary surpluses during their lifetimes, and those higher primary surpluses must be achieved through some combination of lower government benefits and higher taxes.

As previously shown in Chart 1, under current policy, primary deficits occur in much of the projection period. Table 3 shows primary surplus changes necessary to make the debt-to-GDP ratio in 2088 equal to its level in 2013 under each of the three policies. If reform begins in 2014, then it is sufficient to raise the primary surplus share of GDP by 1.7 percentage points in every year between 2014 and 2088 in order to have a debt-to-GDP ratio in 2088 equal to the level in 2013. This raises the average 2014-2088 primary surplus-to-GDP ratio from -0.4 percent to +1.3 percent.

Table 3	
Costs of Delaying Fiscal Reform	
Period of Delay	**Change in Average Primary Surplus**
No Delay: Reform in 2014.........	1.7 percent of GDP between 2014 and 2088
Ten Years: Reform in 2024........	2.1 percent of GDP between 2024 and 2088
Twenty Years: Reform in 2034..	2.6 percent of GDP between 2034 and 2088

Note: Reforms taking place in 2013, 2023, and 2033 from the 2012 Report were 2.7, 3.2, and 4.1 percent of GDP.

In contrast to a reform that begins immediately, if reform is begun in 2024 or 2034, the primary surplus must be raised by 2.1 percent and 2.6 percent of GDP, respectively, in order to reach a debt-to-GDP ratio in 2088 equal to the level of 72 percent in 2013. The difference between the primary surplus increase necessary if reform begins in 2024 and 2034 (2.1 and 2.6 percent of GDP, respectively) and the increase necessary if reform begins in 2014 (1.7 percent of GDP) is a measure of the additional burden policy delay would impose on future generations. The costs of delay are due to increases in the debt-to-GDP ratio between 2013 and the year reform is initiated, which increases the amount of interest that must be covered with primary surpluses after reform begins.

These estimates likely understate the cost of lengthy policy delays because they assume interest rates will not rise as the debt-to-GDP ratio grows. Under the current projections, the debt-to-GDP ratio rises until 2015 and then falls for the next decade, but rises to exceed its 2012 level in 2026 and then grows steadily. If a higher debt-to-GDP ratio causes the government borrowing rate to rise, thus making it more costly for the government to service its debt and simultaneously slowing private investment, then the primary surplus required to return the debt-to-GDP ratio to its 2013 level would also increase. This dynamic may accelerate with higher ratios of debt to GDP, potentially resulting in there being no feasible level of taxes and spending that would reduce the debt-to-GDP ratio to its 2013 level. The potential impact on the projections of interest rates rising as the debt-to-GDP ratio rises is explored in the "Alternative Scenarios" section.

Assumptions Used and Relationship to Other Financial Statements

A fundamental assumption underlying the projections is that current Federal policy (defined below) does not change. The projections are therefore neither forecasts nor predictions. If policy changes are enacted, perhaps in response to projections like those presented here, then actual fiscal outcomes will of course be different than those projected.

Even if policy does not change, actual expenditures and receipts could differ materially from those projected here. Long-range projections are inherently uncertain and are necessarily based on simplifying assumptions. For example, one key simplifying assumption is that interest rates paid on public debt remain unchanged, regardless of the amount of debt outstanding. To the contrary, it is likely that future interest rates would increase if the debt-to-GDP ratio rises as in these projections. To help illustrate this uncertainty, present value calculations under higher and lower interest rate scenarios are presented in the "Alternative Scenarios" section.

The projections in this section focus on future cashflows, and do not reflect either the accrual basis or the modified-cash basis of accounting. These cash-based projections reflect receipts or spending at the time cash is received or when a payment is made by the Government. In contrast, accrual-based projections would reflect amounts in the time period in which income is earned or when an expense or obligation is incurred. The cash basis accounting underlying this section is consistent with methods used to prepare the Statement of Social Insurance (SOSI) and the generally cash-based Federal budget.

The following bullets summarize the assumptions used for the key categories of receipts and spending presented in Table 1 and in the related analysis:

- **Social Security:** Projected Social Security (OASDI) spending is net of administrative expenses, which are classified as discretionary spending, and is based on the projected expenditures in the 2013 Social Security trustees' report for benefits and the Railroad Retirement interchange. The projections of Social Security payroll taxes and future Social Security spending begin with actual budget data for FY 2013. The projected growth rates for future spending and payroll taxes are equal to the spending and tax growth rate projections underlying the 2013 Social Security trustees' report. More information about the assumptions for Social Security cost growth can be found in the Required Supplementary Information for Social Insurance.
- **Medicare:** Projected Medicare spending is also net of administrative expenses and is based on projected incurred expenditures from the 2013 Medicare trustees' report. However, some adjustments to the trustees' report projections are made. Medicare Part B and D premiums, as well as State contributions to Part D, are subtracted from gross spending in measuring Part B and Part D outlays, just as they are subtracted from gross cost to yield net cost in the

financial statements.[9] Here, as in the Federal budget, premiums are treated as "negative spending" rather than receipts since they represent payment for a service rather than payments obtained through the Government's sovereign power to tax. This is similar to the financial statement treatment of premiums as "earned" revenue as distinct from all other sources of revenue, such as taxes. The projections start with actual FY 2013 Medicare spending and assume spending growth accords with the growth rates projected in the Medicare trustees' report. Medicare Part A payroll taxes are projected similarly. More information about the assumptions for Medicare cost growth can be found in the Required Supplementary Information for Social Insurance. As discussed in Note 24, there is uncertainty about whether the reductions in health care cost growth projected in the Medicare trustees' report will be fully achieved. Note 24 illustrates this uncertainty by considering Medicare cost growth assumptions under varying policy assumptions.

- **Medicaid:** The Medicaid spending projections start with the projections from the *2012 Actuarial Report on the Financial Outlook for Medicaid* prepared by the Office of the Actuary, Centers for Medicare & Medicaid Services (CMS),[10] adjusted to accord with the latest budget data. Those projections end in 2021 and incorporate CMS's projected effect of the ACA (as modified by the June 2012 Supreme Court ruling) on Medicaid enrollment. After 2021, the number of Medicaid beneficiaries is expected to grow at the same rate as total population, and Medicaid costs per beneficiary are assumed to grow at the same rate as Medicare benefits per beneficiary, as is consistent with the experience since 1987. Between 1987 and 2012, the average annual growth rate of outlays per beneficiary for Medicaid and Medicare were within 0.2 percentage points of each other.

- **Other Mandatory Spending:** Other mandatory spending is projected in two steps. First, spending prior to the automatic spending cuts called for by the BCA is projected and, second, the effect of the BCA is projected. With regard to pre-BCA spending: (a) Current mandatory spending components that are judged permanent under current policy are assumed to increase by the rate of growth in nominal GDP starting in 2014, implying that such spending will remain constant as a percentage of GDP[11]; (b) Special assumptions are made for temporary mandatory spending authorized by ARRA and other stabilization measures, including temporary expansions in unemployment insurance benefits, and the Troubled Asset Relief Program (TARP) – the 75-year present value of projected spending for this category totals $0.1 trillion; and (c) Projected new spending for insurance exchange subsidies starting in 2014 follows the most recent Budget projections until 2023, and then grows in accordance with growth in the projected non-elderly population and growth in health care costs as projected for the Medicare program.

- **Discretionary Spending:** Through 2021, discretionary spending other than for Overseas Contingency Operations (OCO) is dictated by the spending caps and automatic spending cuts called for by the BCA. After 2021, this spending is assumed to grow at the same rate as nominal GDP, and thus plateaus in 2021 at a long-term level of 4.5 percent of GDP. The BCA is projected to reduce the present value of spending by $0.6 trillion through 2021, and by an additional $3.3 trillion between 2022 and 2088 because of the lower base spending in 2022. Projected OCO spending steadily declines and is fully phased out by 2023, and amounts to $0.3 trillion in present value. To illustrate uncertainty, present value calculations under alternative discretionary growth scenarios are presented in the "Alternative Scenarios" section.

- **Receipts (Other than Social Security and Medicare):** It is assumed that individual income taxes will equal the same share of wages and salaries as in the Administration's latest Budget current law baseline projection. That baseline accords with current policy as defined above, and incorporates the effects of the economic recovery and bracket creep. After reaching about 22 percent of wages and salaries in 2023, individual income taxes increase gradually to 28 percent of wages and salaries in 2088 as real taxable incomes rise over time and an increasing share of total income is taxed in the higher tax brackets. The ratio of all other receipts combined to GDP is projected to rise over the next several years as the economy recovers, and to then level off at 3.8 percent of GDP, the historical average between 1979 and 2012. To illustrate uncertainty, present value calculations under higher and lower receipts growth scenarios are presented in the "Alternative Scenarios" section.

- **Interest Spending:** Interest spending is determined by projected interest rates and the level of outstanding debt held by the public. The long-run interest rate assumptions for fiscal years accord with those for calendar years in the 2013

---

[9] Medicare Part B and D premiums and State contributions to Part D are subtracted from the Part B and D spending displayed in Table 1. The total 75-year present value of these subtractions is $9.0 trillion, or 0.8 percent of GDP.

[10] Christopher J. Truffer, John D. Klemm, Christian J. Wolfe, Kathryn E. Rennie, and Jessica F. Shuff, *2012 Actuarial Report on the Financial Condition for Medicaid*, Office of the Actuary, Centers for Medicare and Medicaid Services, United States Department of Health and Human Services, December 2012.

[11] This assumed growth rate for other mandatory programs exceeds the growth rate in the most recent OMB and CBO baselines.

Social Security trustees' report[12]. The average interest rate over the projection period is 5.5 percent. These rates are also used to convert future cashflows to present values as of the start of fiscal year 2014.

Departures of Current Policy from Current Law

The long-term fiscal projections are made on the basis of current Federal policy, which in some cases is different from current law. The notable differences between current policy that underlies the projections and current law are: (1) projected spending and receipts imply violation of the current statutory limit on Federal debt, (2) continued discretionary appropriations are assumed throughout the projection period, (3) scheduled Social Security and Medicare benefit payments are assumed to occur beyond the projected point of trust fund exhaustion, and (4) many mandatory programs with expiration dates prior to the end of the 75-year projection period are assumed to be reauthorized. As is true in the Medicare trustees' report and in the Statement of Social Insurance,[13] the projections incorporate programmatic changes already scheduled in law, such as the implementation of ACA exchange subsidies and the ACA productivity adjustment for non-physician Medicare services.

Alternative Scenarios

The long-run outlook for the budget is extremely uncertain. This section illustrates this inherent uncertainty by presenting alternative scenarios for the growth rate of health care costs, revenues, discretionary spending, and interest rates.

Not considered here are the effects of alternative assumptions for long-run trends in birth rates, mortality, and immigration.

The population is aging rapidly and will continue to do so over the next several decades, which puts pressure on programs such as Social Security, Medicare, and Medicaid nursing care. A shift in projected fertility, mortality, or immigration rates could have important long-run effects on the projections. Higher than projected immigration, fertility, or mortality rates would improve the long-term fiscal outlook. Conversely, lower than projected immigration, fertility, or mortality rates would result in deterioration in the long-term fiscal outlook.

Effect of Changes in Health Care Cost Growth

One of the most important assumptions underlying the projections is the projected growth of health care costs. Enactment of the ACA in 2010 reduced the projected long-run growth rates of health care costs, but these growth rates are still highly uncertain. As an illustration of the dramatic effect of variations in health care cost growth rates, Table 4 shows the effect on the size of reforms necessary to close the fiscal gap as well as the effect of delaying closure of the fiscal gap of per capita health care cost growth rates that are one percentage point higher or two percentage points higher than the growth rates in the base projection. As indicated earlier, if reform is initiated in 2014, eliminating the fiscal gap requires that the 2014-2088 primary surplus increase by an average of 1.7 percent of GDP in the base case. However, that figure increases to 4.7 percent of GDP if per capita health cost growth is assumed to be 1 percentage point higher, and 7.6 percent of GDP if per capita health cost growth is 2 percentage points higher. The cost of delaying reform is also increased if health care cost growth is higher, due to the fact that debt accumulates more rapidly during the period of inaction. For example, the lower part of Table 4 shows that delaying reform initiation from 2014 to 2024 requires that 2024-2088 primary surpluses be higher by an average of 0.3 percent of GDP in the base case, 1.0 percent of GDP if per capita health cost growth is 1 percentage point higher, and 1.6 percent of GDP if per capita health cost growth is 2 percentage points higher. The dramatic deterioration of the long-run fiscal outlook caused by higher health care cost growth shows the critical importance of managing health care cost growth, including through effective implementation of the ACA.

---

[12] As indicated in the more detailed discussion of Social Insurance in Note 24 to the financial statements.

[13] To prevent the reductions in Medicare physician fees that would have otherwise taken place, since 2003 Congress has repeatedly enacted statutes with temporary "physician fee relief" provisions, which increase health care expenditures. Since 2003, the majority of these statutes have also included other provisions that would reduce expenditures associated with Medicare or other types of health care ("health care cost savings provisions"). The assumption here that future reductions in Medicare payments for physicians' services will occur as scheduled under current law is comparable to an assumption that the reductions will be overridden by enactment of new temporary physician fee relief provisions but the resulting costs will be paid for through enactment of new health care cost savings provisions.

Table 4			
Impact of Alternative Health Cost Scenarios on Cost of Delaying Fiscal Reform			
	Primary Surplus Increase (% of GDP) Starting in:		
Scenario	**2014**	**2024**	**2034**
Base Case..	1.7	2.1	2.6
1% pt. higher per person health cost growth..........................	4.7	5.6	7.1
2% pt. higher per person health cost growth..........................	7.6	9.2	11.6
	Change in Primary Surplus Increase if Reform is Delayed From 2014 to:		
		2024	**2034**
Base Case..		0.4	0.9
1% pt. higher per person health cost growth..........................		1.0	2.4
2% pt. higher per person health cost growth..........................		1.6	4.0

NOTE: Increments may not equal the subtracted difference of the components due to rounding.

Effects of Changes in Interest Rates

A higher debt-to-GDP ratio is likely to increase the interest rate on Government debt, making it more costly for the Government to service its debt. Table 5 displays the effect of several alternative scenarios using different nominal interest rates than assumed in the base case on the size of reforms to close the fiscal gap as well as the effect of delaying closure of the fiscal gap. If reform is initiated in 2014, eliminating the fiscal gap requires that the 2014-2088 primary surplus increase by an average of 1.7 percent of GDP in the base case, 2.0 percent of GDP if the interest rate is 0.5 percentage point higher in every year, and 2.2 percent of GDP if the interest rate is 1.0 percentage point higher in every year. The cost of delaying reform is also increased if interest rates are higher, due to the fact that interest paid on debt accumulates more rapidly during the period of inaction. For example, the lower part of Table 5 shows that delaying reform initiation from 2014 to 2024 requires that 2024-2088 primary surpluses be higher by an average of 0.3 percent of GDP in the base case, 0.5 percent of GDP if the interest rate is 0.5 percentage point higher in every year, and 0.6 percent of GDP if the interest rate is 1.0 percentage point higher in every year. To show the effects of achieving primary balance and lowering long-term debt-to-GDP and interest rates, lowering nominal interest rates by one-half percentage point from the base projection starting in 2014 lowers the cost of reform over the three periods to 1.4 percent of GDP per year starting in 2014, 1.7 percent per year starting in 2024, and 2.1 percent per year starting in 2034.

Table 5			
Impact of Alternative Interest Rate Scenarios on Cost of Delaying Fiscal Reform			
	Primary Surplus Increase (% of GDP) Starting in:		
Scenario	**2014**	**2024**	**2034**
Base Case: Average of 5.5 percent over 75 years.................	1.7	2.1	2.6
0.5 percent higher interest rate in each year.......................	2.0	2.4	3.2
1.0 percent higher interest rate in each year.......................	2.2	2.8	3.8
0.5 percent lower interest rate in each year........................	1.4	1.7	2.1
	Change in Primary Surplus Increase if Reform is Delayed From 2014 to:		
		2024	**2034**
Base Case: Average of 5.5 percent over 75 years.................		0.4	0.9
0.5 percent higher interest rate in each year.......................		0.5	1.2
1.0 percent higher interest rate in each year.......................		0.6	1.6
0.5 percent lower interest rate in each year........................		0.3	0.6

NOTE: Increments may not equal the subtracted difference of the components due to rounding.

Effects of Changes in Discretionary Spending Growth

The growth of discretionary spending has a large impact on long term fiscal sustainability. The current base projection for discretionary spending assumes that after 2021, discretionary spending keeps pace with the economy and grows with GDP. An alternative assumption would be to allow discretionary spending to grow with inflation and population to effectively hold discretionary spending constant on a real per capita basis. (This assumption is still faster than the standard 10-year budget baseline, which assumes that discretionary spending grows with inflation.) Another possible long-range assumption is to allow discretionary spending to return in 2022 to levels established prior to the sequestration required by the failure of the Joint Select Committee on Deficit Reduction, and grow with GDP from that point forward. As shown in Table 6, the fiscal gap decreases significantly if discretionary spending grows with inflation and population from 1.7 percent of GDP to 0.3 percent of GDP. Conversely, if discretionary spending rises to the pre-Joint Committee sequestration levels and grows with GDP, the fiscal gap increases from 1.7 percent of GDP to 2.0 percent of GDP. The cost of delaying reform is greater when discretionary spending levels are higher. Initiating reforms in 2024 requires that the primary surplus increase by an average of 2.1 percent of GDP per year in the base case, and 2.4 percent of GDP if discretionary levels return to pre-Joint Committee sequestration levels. If delayed until 2034, the primary surplus must increase by an average of 2.6 percent of GDP in the base case, and 3.0 percent of GDP at pre-sequestration levels.

Table 6			
Impact of Alternative Discretionary Spending Growth Scenarios on Cost of Delaying Fiscal Reform			
	Primary Surplus Increase (% of GDP) Starting in:		
Scenario	2014	2024	2034
Base Case: Discretionary spending growth with GDP...	1.7	2.1	2.6
Growth with inflation and population..	0.3	0.3	0.4
Reversion in 2022 to pre-Joint Committee sequester levels and growth with GDP...	2.0	2.4	3.0
	Change in Primary Surplus Increase if Reform is Delayed From 2014 to:		
		2024	2034
Base Case: Discretionary spending growth with GDP...		0.4	0.9
Growth with inflation and population..		0.1	0.1
Reversion in 2022 to pre-Joint Committee sequester levels and growth with GDP...		0.4	1.0

NOTE: Increments may not equal the subtracted difference of the components due to rounding.

Effects of Changes in Individual Income Revenue Growth

The growth rate of revenues, specifically individual income taxes, is another key determinant of long term sustainability. The base projections assume growth in individual income taxes over time to account for the slow shift of individuals into higher tax brackets due to real wage growth ("real bracket creep"). This assumption approximates the long-term historical growth in individual income taxes relative to wages and salaries and is consistent with current tax code policy without change, as future legislation would be required to prevent real bracket creep from allowing individual income taxes to rise. As an illustration of the effect of variations in individual income tax growth, Table 7 shows the effect on the size of reforms necessary to close the fiscal gap and the effect of delaying closure of the fiscal gap if long-term revenue growth as a share of wages and salaries is allowed to be even more rapid than the base case as well as if no bracket creep is assumed. If reform is initiated in 2014, eliminating the fiscal gap requires that the 2014-2088 primary surplus increase by an average of 1.7 percent of GDP in the base case, only 0.7 percent of GDP if real bracket creep is higher, but 2.7 percent of GDP if no real bracket creep is assumed. The cost of delaying reform is also affected if revenue growth assumptions change, much as was the case in the previous alternative scenarios.

Table 7			
Impact of Alternative Revenue Growth Scenarios on Cost of Delaying Fiscal Reform			
	Primary Surplus Increase (% of GDP) Starting in:		
Scenario	2014	2024	2034
Base Case: Individual income tax bracket creep of 0.1% of wages and salaries per year.....	1.7	2.1	2.6
0 2% of wages and salaries per year..	0.7	0.8	1.0
0 0% of wages and salaries per year (no bracket creep)...	2.7	3.3	4.1
	Change in Primary Surplus Increase if Reform is Delayed From 2014 to:		
		2024	2034
Base Case: Individual income tax bracket creep of 0.1% of wages and salaries per year.....		0.4	0.9
0 2% of wages and salaries per year..		0.1	0.4
0 0% of wages and salaries per year (no bracket creep)...		0.6	1.4

NOTE: Increments may not equal the subtracted difference of the components due to rounding.

Fiscal Projections in Context

In this report, a sustainable policy has been defined as one where the federal debt-to-GDP ratio is stable or declining. However, this definition does not indicate what a sustainable debt-to-GDP ratio might be. Any particular debt ratio is not the ultimate goal of fiscal policy. Rather, the goal of fiscal policy is to finance government services in a way that is consistent with a strong and growing economy.

Economic theory suggests that high levels of national debt may contribute to higher interest rates, leading to lower investment and a smaller capital stock with which the economy can use to grow. Whether this has been the actual experience of countries remains an open research question. It is not possible to perform randomized experiments on economies, and historical experience, while valuable, is filled with confounding events and circumstances. Some countries with high debt-to-GDP ratios have been observed to experience lower than average growth, while other countries with similarly high debt ratios continue to enjoy robust growth. Analogously, low debt-to-GDP ratios are no guarantee of strong economic growth. Moreover, the direction of causality is unclear. High debt may undermine growth; low growth may contribute to high debt.

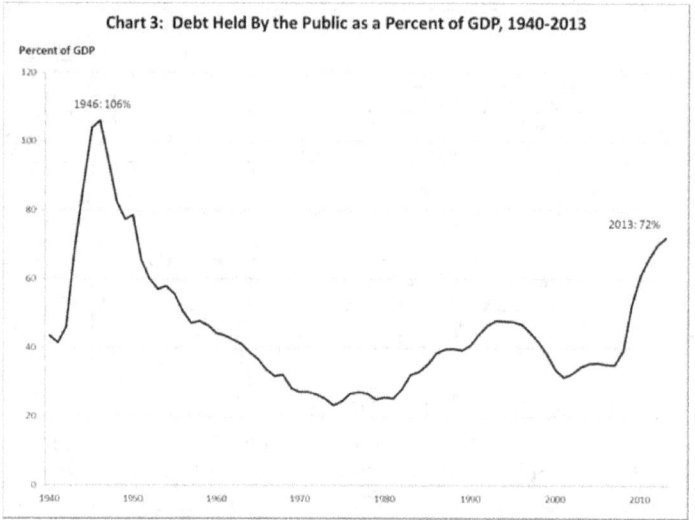

Nevertheless, to put the current and projected debt-to-GDP ratios in context, it is instructive to examine the experiences of other countries as well as that of the United States. The United States Government's debt as a percentage of GDP is relatively large compared with central government debt of other countries, but far from the largest among the countries in the Organization for Economic Co-operation and Development (OECD). Based on historical data as reported by the OECD for all of its 34 member countries, the debt-to-GDP ratio in 2010 ranged from 3 percent of GDP to 148 percent of GDP[14], with the United States the higher echelon.[15] However each country is different in how it finances its sovereign debt, how robustly its economy grows, how government responsibilities are shared between central and local governments, and how current policies compare with the past policies that determine the current level of debt.

The historical experience of the U.S. may also provide some perspective. As Chart 3 shows, the debt-to-GDP ratio was highest in the 1940s, following the debt buildup during World War II. In the projections in this report, the U.S. would reach the previous peak debt ratio in 2041. However, the origins of current and future Federal debt are quite different from the wartime debt of the 1940s, limiting the pertinence of past experience.

As the cross-country and historical comparisons suggest, there is a very imperfect relationship between the current level of central government debt and the sustainability of overall government policy. Past accrual of debt is certainly important, but current policies and their implications for future debt accumulation are as well.

---

[14] Central government debt was not yet reported to the OECD for the country of Japan for the year 2010, but based on its 2009 level of 184 percent of GDP, its 2010 number will exceed 148 percent reported for Greece, which is the highest level of the countries that have reported thus far.

[15] Central government debt, OECD National Accounts Statistics available at http://stats.oecd.org/Index.aspx?DatasetCode=GOV_DEBT

Conclusion

The United States took a potentially significant step towards fiscal sustainability in 2010 by reforming its system of health insurance through enactment of the ACA. The legislated changes for Medicare, Medicaid, and other health coverage hold the prospect of lowering the long-term growth trend for health care costs and significantly reducing the long-term fiscal gap. Furthermore, enactment of the BCA in August 2011 placed limits on future discretionary spending and established a process to ensure further deficit reduction of $1.2 trillion through fiscal year 2021, while enactment of ATRA in January 2013 increased revenues under current policy. But even with the new laws, the projections in this Financial Report indicate that if policy remains unchanged the debt-to-GDP ratio will continually increase over the next 75 years and beyond, which implies current policies are not sustainable and must ultimately change. Subject to the important caveat that policy changes are not so abrupt that they slow the economic recovery, the sooner policies are put in place to avert these trends, the smaller are the revenue increases and/or spending decreases necessary to return the Nation to a sustainable fiscal path.

Social Insurance

The social insurance programs consisting of Social Security, Medicare, Railroad Retirement, and Black Lung were developed to provide income security and health care coverage to citizens under specific circumstances as a responsibility of the Government. Because taxpayers rely on these programs in their long-term planning, social insurance program information should indicate whether the current statutory provisions of the programs can be sustained, and more generally what effect these provisions likely have on the Government's financial condition. The resources needed to run these programs are raised through taxes and fees. Eligibility for benefits depends in part on earnings and time worked by the individuals. Social Security benefits are generally redistributed intentionally toward lower-wage workers (i.e., benefits are progressive). In addition, each social insurance program has a uniform set of eligibility events and schedules that apply to all participants.

Social Security and Medicare

Social Security

The OASI Trust Fund was established on January 1, 1940, as a separate account in the Treasury. The DI Trust Fund, another separate account in the Treasury, was established on August 1, 1956. OASI pays cash retirement benefits to eligible retirees and their eligible dependents and survivors, and the much smaller DI fund pays cash benefits to eligible individuals who are unable to work because of medical conditions and certain family members of such eligible individuals. Though the events that trigger benefit payments are quite different, both trust funds have the same dedicated financing structure: primarily payroll taxes and income taxes on benefits. All financial operations of the OASI and DI Programs are handled through these respective funds. The two funds are often referred to as the combined OASDI Trust Funds. At the end of calendar year 2012, OASDI benefits were paid to approximately 57 million beneficiaries.

The primary financing source for these two funds are taxes paid by workers, their employers, and individuals with self-employment income, based on work covered by the OASDI Program. Since 1990, with the exception of calendar years 2011 and 2012, employers and employees have each paid 6.2 percent of taxable earnings and the self-employed paid 12.4 percent of taxable earnings. In 2011 and 2012, payroll tax rates paid by employees and the self-employed were each reduced by 2 percentage points and the General Fund of the Treasury reimbursed the OASDI trust fund for the resulting reduction in payroll tax revenues. Payroll taxes are levied on wages and net earnings from self-employment up to a specified maximum annual amount, referred to as maximum taxable earnings ($113,700 in 2013), that increases each year with economy-wide average wages.

Legislation passed in 1984 subjected up to half of OASDI benefits to income tax and allocated the revenue to the OASDI Trust Funds. In 1993 legislation increased the potentially taxed portion of benefits to 85 percent and allocated the additional revenue to the Medicare's Hospital Insurance Trust Fund.

Medicare

The Medicare Program, created in 1965, has two separate trust funds: the Hospital Insurance (HI) Trust Fund (otherwise known as Medicare Part A) and the Supplementary Medical Insurance (SMI) Trust Funds (which consists of the Medicare Part B and Part D[1] accounts). HI pays for inpatient acute hospital services and major alternatives to hospitals (skilled nursing services, for example). SMI pays for hospital outpatient services, physician services, and assorted other services and products through the Part B account and for prescription drugs through the Part D account.

Though the events that trigger benefit payments are similar, HI and SMI have different dedicated financing structures. Similar to OASDI, HI is financed primarily by payroll contributions. Currently, employers and employees each pay 1.45 percent of earnings, while self-employed workers pay 2.9 percent of their net earnings. Beginning in 2013, employees and self-employed individuals with earnings above certain thresholds pay an additional HI tax of 0.9 percent on earnings above those thresholds. Other income to the HI Trust Fund includes a small amount of premium income from voluntary enrollees, a portion of the Federal income taxes that beneficiaries pay on Social Security benefits (as explained above), and interest credited on Treasury securities held in the HI Trust Fund. As is explained in the next section, these Treasury securities and related interest have no effect on the consolidated statement of Governmentwide finances.

---

[1] Medicare legislation in 2003 created the new Part D account in the SMI Trust Fund to track the finances of a new prescription drug benefit that began in 2006. As in the case of Medicare Part B, approximately three-quarters of revenues to the Part D account will come from future transfers from the General Fund of the Treasury. Consequently, the nature of the relationship between the SMI Trust Fund and the Federal Budget described below is largely unaffected by the presence of the Part D account though the magnitude will be greater.

For SMI, transfers from the General Fund of the Treasury financed 75 percent and 74 percent of 2013 program costs for Parts B and D, respectively. Premiums paid by beneficiaries and, for Part D State transfers, financed the remainder of expenditures. With the introduction of Part D drug coverage, Medicaid is no longer the primary payer of drug benefits for beneficiaries dually eligible for Medicare and Medicaid. For those beneficiaries, States must pay the Part D account a portion of their estimated foregone drug costs for this population (referred to as State transfers). As with HI, interest received on Treasury securities held in the SMI Trust Fund is credited to the fund. These Treasury securities and related interest have no effect on the consolidated statement of Governmentwide finances. See Note 24—Social Insurance, for additional information on Medicare program financing.

Figure 1
Social Security, Medicare, and Governmentwide Finances

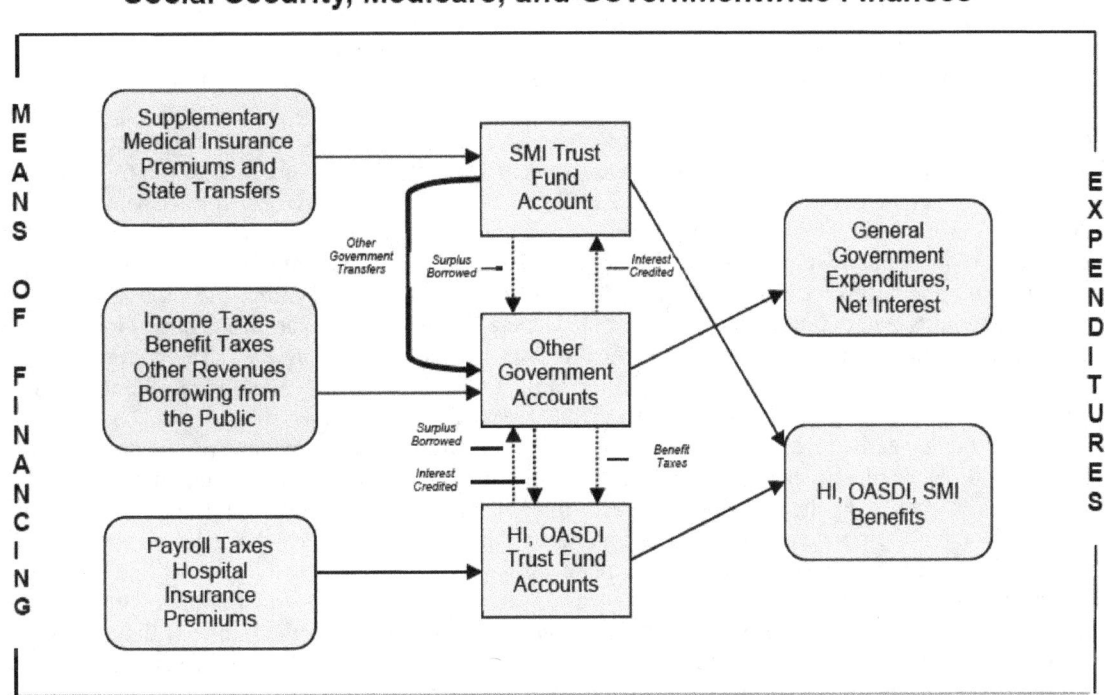

Social Security, Medicare, and Governmentwide Finances

The current and future financial status of the separate OASDI, HI and SMI Trust Funds is the focus of the Social Security and Medicare Trustees' Reports, a focus that may appropriately be referred to as the "trust fund perspective." In contrast, the Government primarily uses the *unified budget* concept as the framework for budgetary analysis and presentation. It represents a comprehensive display of all Federal activities, regardless of fund type or on- and off-budget status, and has a broader focus than the trust fund perspective that may appropriately be referred to as the "budget perspective" or the "Governmentwide perspective." Social Security and Medicare are among the largest expenditure categories of the U.S. Federal budget. Together, they now account for more than a third of all Federal spending and the percentage is projected to rise dramatically for the reasons discussed below. This section describes in detail the important relationship between the trust fund perspective and the Governmentwide perspective.

Figure 1 is a simplified depiction of the interaction of the Social Security and Medicare Trust Funds with the rest of the Federal budget.[2] The boxes on the left show sources of funding, those in the middle represent the trust funds and other Government accounts, which includes the General Fund into which that funding flows, and the boxes on the right show simplified expenditure categories. The figure is intended to illustrate how the various sources of program revenue flow through the budget to beneficiaries. The general approach is to group revenues and expenditures that are linked specifically to Social Security and/or Medicare separately from those for other government programs.

---

[2] The Federal unified budget encompasses all Government financing and is synonymous with a Governmentwide perspective.

Each of the trust funds has its own sources and types of revenue. With the exception of General Fund transfers to SMI, each of these revenue sources represents revenue from the public that are dedicated specifically for the respective trust fund and cannot be used for other purposes. In contrast, personal and corporate income taxes and other revenue go into the General Fund of the Treasury and are drawn down for any Government program for which Congress has approved spending.[3] The arrows from the boxes on the left represent the flow of the revenues into the trust funds and other Government accounts.

The heavy line between the top two boxes in the middle of Figure 1 represents intragovernmental transfers to the SMI Trust Fund from other Government accounts. The Medicare SMI Trust Fund is shown separately from the two Social Security trust funds (OASI and DI) and the Medicare HI Trust Fund to highlight the unique financing of SMI. SMI is currently only one of the programs that is funded through transfers from the General Fund of the Treasury, which is part of the other Government accounts (the SMI Part D account also receives transfers from the States). The transfers finance roughly three-fourths of SMI Program expenses. The transfers are automatic; their size depends on how much the program requires, not on how much revenue comes into the Treasury. If General Fund revenues become insufficient to cover both the mandated transfer to SMI and expenditures on other general Government programs, Treasury has to borrow to make up the difference. In the longer run, if transfers to SMI increase beyond growth in general revenues as shown below, they are projected to increase significantly in coming years—then Congress must either raise taxes, cut other Government spending, reduce SMI benefits, or borrow even more.

The dotted lines between the middle boxes of Figure 1 also represent intragovernmental transfers but those transfers arise in the form of "borrowing/lending" between the Government accounts. Interest credited to the trust funds arises when the excess of program income over expenses is loaned to the General Fund. The vertical lines labeled *Surplus Borrowed* represent these flows from the trust funds to the other Government accounts. These loans reduce the amount the General Fund has to borrow from the public to finance a deficit (or likewise increase the amount of debt paid off if there is a surplus). However, the General Fund has to credit interest on the loans from the trust fund programs, just as if it borrowed the money from the public. The credits lead to future obligations for the General Fund (which is part of the other Government accounts). These transactions are indicated in Figure 1 by the vertical arrows labeled *Interest Credited*. The credits increase trust fund income exactly as much as they increase credits (future obligations) in the General Fund. From the Governmentwide standpoint, at least in an accounting sense, these interest credits are a wash.

When the trust funds get the receipts that they loan to the General Fund, these receipts provide additional authority to spend on benefits and other program expenses. The General Fund, in turn, has taken on the obligation of paying interest on these loans every year and repaying the principal when trust fund income from other sources falls below expenditures.

How loans from the trust funds to the General Fund and later repayments of those loans affect tax income and expenditures of the General Fund is uncertain. Two extreme cases encompass the possibilities. At one extreme, each dollar the trust funds loan to the General Fund might reduce borrowing from the public by a dollar at the time the loan is extended, in which case the General Fund could repay all trust fund loans by borrowing from the public without raising the level of public debt above the level that would have occurred in the absence of the loans. At the other extreme, each dollar the trust funds loan to the General Fund might result in some combination of higher General Fund spending and lower General Fund revenues amounting to one dollar at the time the loans are extended, in which case General Fund loan repayments to the trust funds might initially be financed with borrowing from the public but must at some point be financed with a combination of higher general fund taxes and lower General Fund spending than would have occurred in the absence of the loans. In this latter extreme, trust fund loans result in additional largess (i.e., higher spending and/or lower taxes) in General Fund programs at the time the loans are extended, but ultimately that additional largess is financed with additional austerity (i.e., lower spending and/or higher taxes) in General Fund programs at later dates. The actual impact of trust fund loans to the General Fund and their repayment on General Fund programs is at one of these two extremes or somewhere in between.

Actual dollar amounts roughly corresponding to the flows presented in Figure 1 are shown in Table 1 for fiscal year 2013. In Table 1, revenues from the public (left side of Figure 1) and expenditures to the public (right side of Figure 1) are shown separately from transfers between Government accounts (middle of Figure 1). Note that the transfers ($258.2 billion) and interest credits ($118.1 billion) received by the trust funds appear as negative entries under "All Other" and are thus offsetting when summed for the total budget column. These two intragovernmental transfers are the key to the differences between the trust fund and budget perspectives.

From the Governmentwide perspective, only revenues received from the public (and States in the case of Medicare Part D) and expenditures made to the public are important for the final balance. Trust fund revenue from the public consists of

---

[3] Other programs also have dedicated revenues in the form of taxes and fees (and other forms of receipt) and there are a large number of dedicated trust funds in the Federal budget. Total trust fund receipts account for about 40 percent of total Government receipts with the Social Security and Medicare Trust Funds accounting for about two-thirds of trust fund receipts. For further discussion, see the report issued by the Government Accountability Office, *Federal Trust and Other Earmarked Funds*, GAO-01-199SP, January 2001. In the figure and the discussion that follows, all other programs, including these other dedicated trust fund programs, are grouped under "Other Government Accounts" to simplify the description and maintain the focus on Social Security and Medicare.

payroll taxes, benefit taxes, and premiums. For HI, the difference between total expenditures made to the public ($266.6 billion) and revenues ($233.6 billion) was $33.0 billion in 2013, indicating that HI had a relatively small negative effect on the overall budget outcome *in that year*. For the SMI account, revenues from the public (premiums) were relatively small, representing about a quarter of total expenditures made to the public in 2013. The difference ($234.3 billion) resulted in a net draw on the overall budget balance in that year. For OASDI, the difference between total expenditures made to the public ($813.3 billion) and revenues from the public ($714.3 billion) was $99.0 billion in 2013, indicating that OASDI had a negative effect on the overall budget outcome in that year. Combined OASDI payroll and benefit tax revenues were increased by $101.0 billion in fiscal year 2013.

The trust fund perspective is captured in the bottom section of each of the three trust fund columns. For HI, total expenditures exceeded total revenues by $23.0 billion in 2013, as shown at the bottom of the first column. This cash deficit was made up by calling in past loans made to the General Fund (i.e., by redeeming Trust Fund assets). For SMI, total expenditures exceeded total revenues by $4.6 billion. The total revenue for SMI is $310.2 billion ($80.5 + $229.7), which includes $229.7 billion transferred from other Government accounts (the General Fund). Transfers to the SMI Program from other Government accounts (the General Fund), amounting to about 72 percent of program costs, are obligated under current law and, therefore, appropriately viewed as revenue from the trust fund perspective. For OASDI, total revenues of $850.9 billion exceeded total expenditures of $813.3 billion by $37.6 billion. Total revenues for OASDI included $136.6 billion of transfers from the General Fund, principally interest credits and $30.9 billion in credits called for by Public Laws 111-312, 112-78 and 112-96 to make up for the reduction in payroll tax revenues attributable to the temporary payroll tax rate reductions.

Table 1

Revenues and Expenditures for Medicare and Social Security Trust Funds and the Total Federal Budget for the Fiscal Year ended September 30, 2013

	Trust Funds					
(In billions of dollars)	HI	SMI	OASDI	Total	All Other	Total [1]
Payroll taxes and other public revenues:						
Payroll and benefit taxes....................	227.2	-	714.3	941.5	-	941.5
Premiums................................	6.4	71.2	-	77.6	-	77.6
Other taxes and fees......................	-	9.3	-	9.3	1,745.6	1,754.9
Total..................................	233.6	80.5	714.3	1,028.4	1,745.6	2,774.0
Total expenditures to the public [2]...........	266.6	314.8	813.3	1,394.7	2,059.6	3,454.3
Net results—budget perspective [3]	(33.0)	(234.3)	(99.0)	(366.3)	(314.0)	(680.3)
Revenues from other Government accounts:						
Transfers..............................	0.1	227.2	30.9	258.2	(258.2)	
Interest credits........................	9.9	2.5	105.7	118.1	(118.1)	
Total..............................	10.0	229.7	136.6	376.3	(376.3)	
Net results—trust fund perspective perspective:[3]........................	(23.0)	(4.6)	37.6	10.0	N/A	N/A

[1] This column is the sum of the preceding two columns and shows data for the total Federal budget. The figure $680.3 was the total Federal deficit in fiscal year 2013.

[2] The OASDI figure includes $4.5 billion transferred to the Railroad Retirement Board for benefit payments and is therefore an expenditure to the public.

[3] Net results are computed as revenues less expenditures.

Notes: Amounts may not add due to rounding.
    "N/A" indicates not applicable.

Cashflow Projections

Background

Economic and Demographic Assumptions. The Boards of Trustees [4] of the OASDI and Medicare Trust Funds provide in their annual reports to Congress short-range (10-year) and long-range (75-year) actuarial estimates of each trust fund. Because of the inherent uncertainty in estimates for 75 years into the future, the Boards use three alternative sets of economic and demographic assumptions to show a range of possibilities. The economic and demographic assumptions used for the most recent set of intermediate projections for Social Security and Medicare are shown in the "Social Security" and "Medicare" sections of Note 24—Social Insurance.

---

[4] There are six trustees: the Secretaries of the Treasury (managing trustee), Health and Human Services, and Labor; the Commissioner of the Social Security Administration; and two public trustees who are appointed by the President and confirmed by the Senate for a 4-year term. By law, the public trustees cannot both be members of the same political party.

Beneficiary-to-Worker Ratio. The expenditure projections for both the OASDI and Medicare Programs reflect the aging of the large baby-boom generation, born in the years 1946 to 1964, and its ultimate passing. Chart 1 shows that the number of OASDI beneficiaries per 100 covered workers is projected to grow rapidly from 35 in 2013 to 48 in 2035 as the baby boom generation enter their retirement years and receives benefits. After 2035 the baby boom's influence will have dissipated, and it is projected that the beneficiary-worker ratio will continue to rise but at a slower pace due to increasing longevity, reaching 51 beneficiaries per 100 workers in 2087. (In rough terms, the beneficiary-to-worker ratio at any point in time reflects the birth rates experienced by the generations who are retired; the birth rates of the baby boom generations' parents were much higher than those of the baby boomer generations and the generations to follow them.) A similar demographic pattern confronts the Medicare Program.

**Chart 1—OASDI Beneficiaries per 100 Covered Workers
1970-2087**

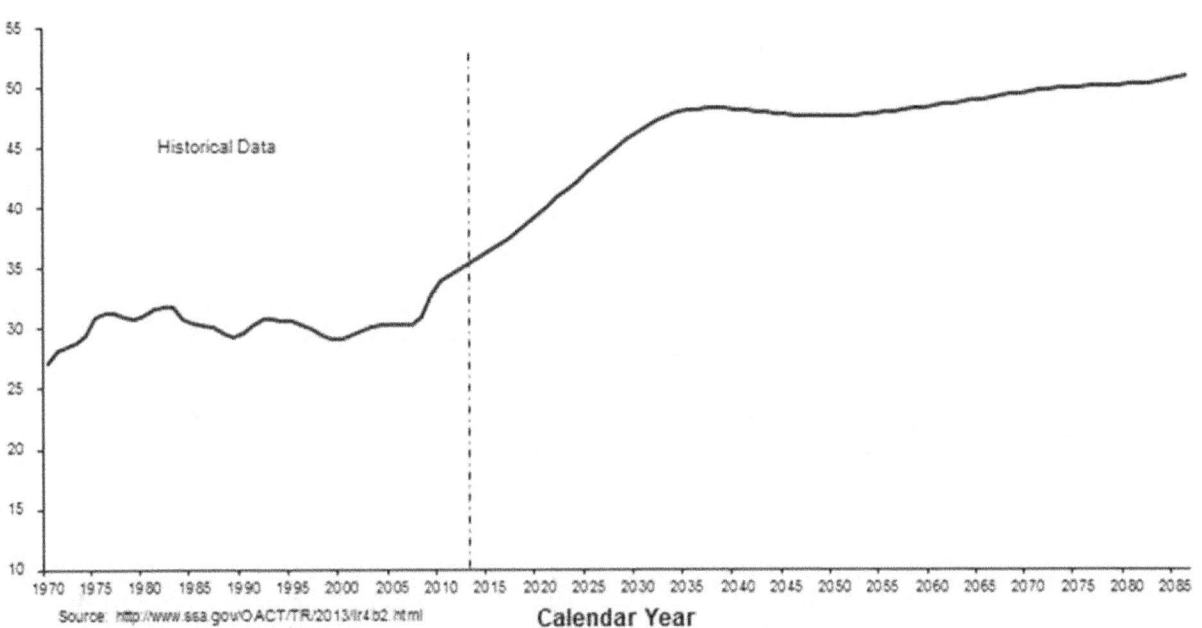

Social Security Projections

Income and Expenditures. Chart 2 shows historical values and actuarial estimates of combined OASDI annual noninterest income and expenditures for 1970-2087. The estimates are for the open-group population of all workers and beneficiaries projected to be alive in each year. The expenditure projections in Chart 2 and all subsequent charts assume all scheduled benefits are paid regardless of whether the income and assets are available to finance them.

Chart 2—OASDI Income (Excluding Interest) and Expenditures 1970-2087

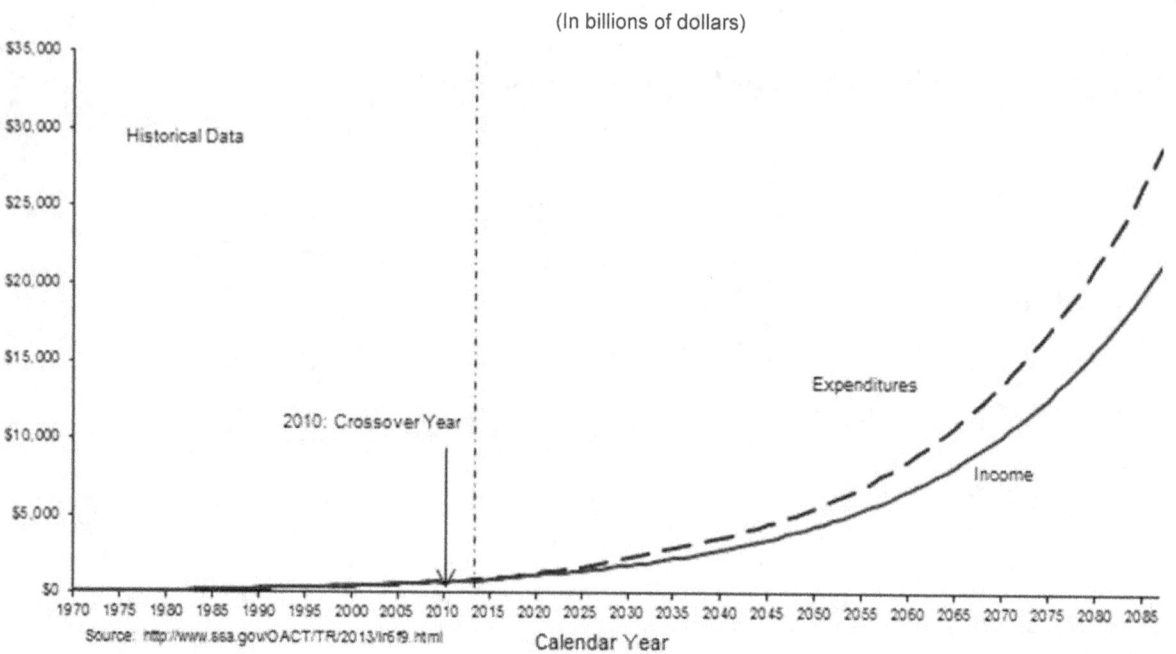

(In billions of dollars)

Source: http://www.ssa.gov/OACT/TR/2013/lr6f9.html

Calendar Year

Social Security's surplus of noninterest income over expenditures was positive every year between 1984 and 2009, negative in 2010 through 2012, and is projected to grow ever more negative over the next 75 years. This pattern reflects the aging of the population documented in Chart 1, as well as growth of the economy and growth in the price level. As described above, surpluses that occurred prior to 2010 were "loaned" to the General Fund and accumulated, with interest, increasing reserve spending authority for the trust fund. The reserve spending authority represents an obligation for the General Fund.

Income and Expenditures as a Percent of Taxable Payroll. Chart 3 shows annual noninterest income and expenditures expressed as percentages of taxable payroll, commonly referred to as the income rate and cost rate, respectively. Dividing noninterest income and expenditures by taxable payroll serves to isolate the effect of demographics on Social Security finances, and usefully gauges Social Security's financial imbalances against the size of the Social Security tax base. The time path of the cost rate in Chart 3 closely parallels that of the beneficiary-to-worker ratio in Chart 1. Social Security began using interest credits to meet full benefit obligations in 2010, and is projected to begin drawing down trust fund asset reserves starting in 2021 and to deplete those reserves in 2033. After trust fund asset reserves are depleted, noninterest income will continue to flow into the fund and will be sufficient to finance 77 percent of scheduled benefits in 2033 and 72 percent of scheduled benefits in 2087.

Chart 3—OASDI Income (Excluding Interest) and Expenditures as a Percent of Taxable Payroll 1970-2087

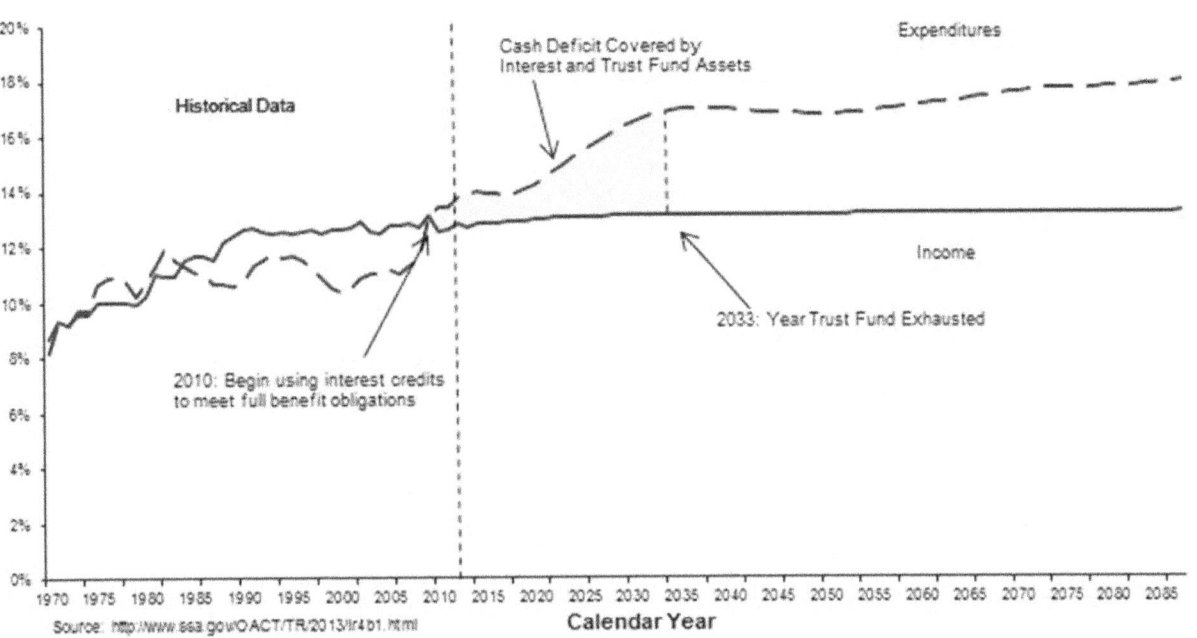

Source: http://www.ssa.gov/OACT/TR/2013/lr4b1.html

Income and Expenditures as a Percent of GDP. Chart 4 shows estimated annual noninterest income and expenditures, expressed as percentages of GDP, the total value of goods and services produced in the United States. This alternative perspective shows the size of the OASDI Program in relation to the capacity of the national economy to sustain it. The gap between expenditures and income generally widens with expenditures generally growing as a share of GDP and income declining slightly relative to GDP. Social Security's expenditures are projected to grow from 5.06 percent of GDP in 2013 to 6.20 percent in 2087. In 2087, expenditures are projected to exceed income by 1.64 percent of GDP.

Chart 4—OASDI Income (Excluding Interest) and Expenditures as a Percent of GDP
1970-2087

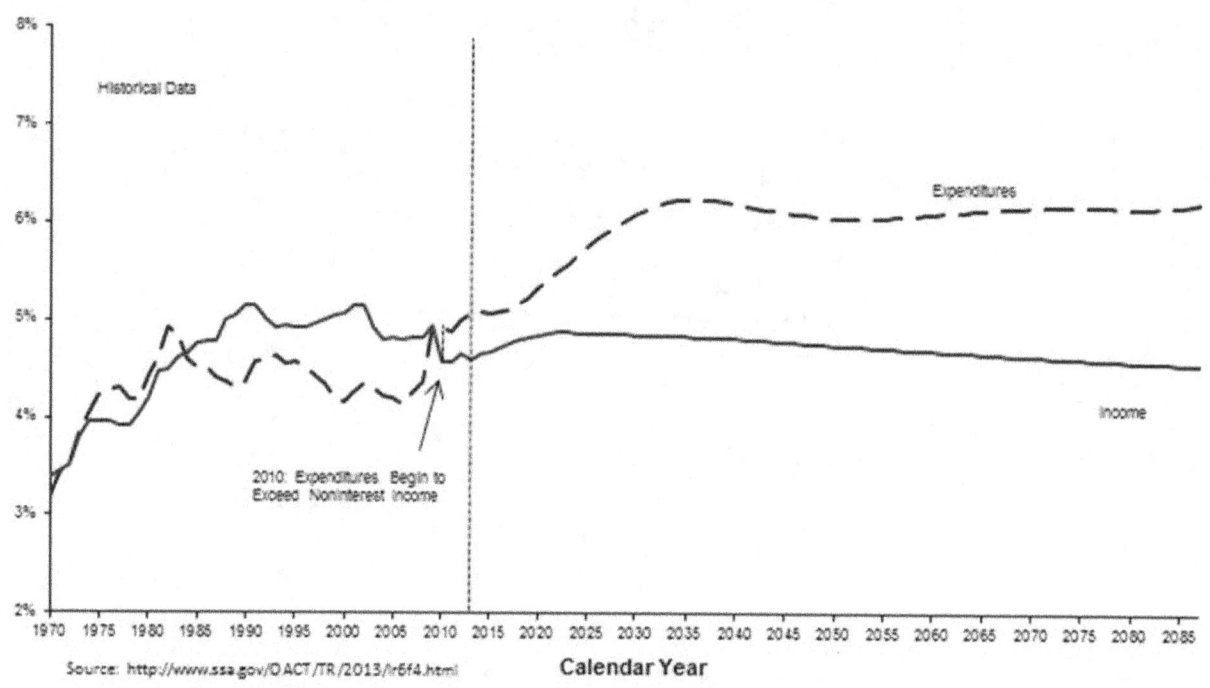

Source: http://www.ssa.gov/OACT/TR/2013/lr6f4.html

Sensitivity Analysis. Actual future income from OASDI payroll taxes and other sources and actual future expenditures for scheduled benefits and administrative expenses will depend upon a large number of factors: the size and composition of the population that is receiving benefits, the level of monthly benefit amounts, the size and characteristics of the work force covered under OASDI, and the level of workers' earnings. These factors will depend, in turn, upon future marriage and divorce rates, birth rates, death rates, migration rates, labor force participation and unemployment rates, disability incidence and termination rates, retirement age patterns, productivity gains, wage increases, cost-of-living increases, and many other economic and demographic factors.

This section presents estimates that illustrate the sensitivity of long-range expenditures and income for the OASDI Program to changes in *selected individual assumptions*. In this analysis, the intermediate assumption is used as the reference point, and one assumption at a time is varied. The variation used for each individual assumption reflects the levels used for that assumption in the low-cost (Alternative I) and high-cost (Alternative III) projections. For example, when analyzing sensitivity with respect to variation in real wages, income and expenditure projections using the intermediate assumptions are compared to the outcome when projections are done by changing only the real wage assumption to either low-cost or high-cost alternatives.

The low-cost alternative is characterized by assumptions that generally improve the financial status of the program (relative to the intermediate assumption) such as slower improvement in mortality (beneficiaries die younger). In contrast, assumptions under the high-cost alternative generally worsen the financial outlook. One exception occurs with the CPI assumption (see below).

Table 2 shows the effects of changing individual assumptions on the present value of estimated OASDI expenditures in excess of income (the *shortfall* of income relative to expenditures in present value terms). The assumptions are shown in parentheses. For example, the intermediate assumption for the annual rate of *reduction in age-sex-adjusted death rates* is 0.80 percent. For the low-cost alternative, a slower reduction rate (0.42 percent) is assumed as it means that beneficiaries die at a younger age relative to the intermediate assumption, resulting in lower expenditures. Under the low-cost assumption, the shortfall drops from $12,294 billion to $10,541 billion, a 14 percent smaller shortfall. The high-cost death rate assumption (1.21 percent) results in an increase in the shortfall, from $12,294 billion to $14,147 billion, a 15 percent increase in the shortfall. Clearly, alternative death rate assumptions have a substantial impact on estimated future cashflows in the OASDI Program.

A higher fertility rate means more workers relative to beneficiaries over the projection period, thereby lowering the shortfall relative to the intermediate assumption. An increase in the rate from 2.0 to 2.3 percent results in a 9 percent smaller shortfall (i.e., expenditures less income), from $12,294 billion to $11,161 billion.

Higher real wage growth results in faster income growth relative to expenditure growth. Table 2 shows that a real wage differential that is 0.60 percentage points greater than the intermediate assumption of 1.12 causes the shortfall to drop from $12,294 billion to $9,928 billion, a 19 percent decline. Decreasing the real wage differential by 0.60 percentage points results in a 13 percent increase in the shortfall from $12,294 billion to $13,921 billion.

The CPI change assumption operates in a somewhat counterintuitive manner, as seen in Table 2. A higher rate of change results in a lower shortfall. This arises as a consequence of holding the real wage assumption constant while varying the CPI so that wages (the income base) are affected sooner than benefits. If the rate is assumed to be 3.8 percent rather than 2.8 percent, the shortfall decreases about 5 percent, from $12,294 billion to $11,667 billion.

The effect of net immigration is similar to fertility in that, over the 75-year projection period, higher immigration results in proportionately more workers (taxpayers) than beneficiaries. The low-cost assumption for net immigration results in a 4 percent drop in the shortfall, from $12,294 billion to $11,816 billion, relative to the intermediate case; and the high-cost assumption results in a 5 percent higher shortfall.

Finally, Table 2 shows the sensitivity of the shortfall to variations in the real interest rate or, in present value terminology, the sensitivity to alternative discount rates assuming a higher discount rate results in a lower present value. The shortfall is 15 percent lower, decreasing from $12,294 billion to $10,487 billion, when the real interest rate is 3.4 percent rather than 2.9 percent. The shortfall is 18 percent higher, increasing to $14,556 billion, when the real interest rate is 2.4 percent rather than 2.9 percent.

Table 2
Present Values of Estimated OASDI Expenditures in Excess of Income Under Various Assumptions, 2013-2087

(Dollar values in billions; values of assumptions shown in parentheses)

Assumption	Financing Shortfall Range		
	Low	Intermediate	High
Average annual reduction in death rates..................	10,541 (0.42)	12,294 (0.80)	14,147 (1.21)
Total fertility rate	11,161 (2.3)	12,294 (2.0)	13,407 (1.7)
Real wage differential	9,928 (1.72)	12,294 (1.12)	13,921 (0.52)
CPI change	12,939 (1.8)	12,294 (2.8)	11,667 (3.8)
Net immigration..	11,816 (1,400,000)[1]	12,294 (1,095,000)[1]	12,861 (800,000)[1]
Real interest rate	10,487 (3.4)	12,294 (2.9)	14,556 (2.4)

[1] Amounts represent the average annual net immigration over the 75-year projection period.

Source: 2013 OASDI Trustees Report and SSA.

Medicare Projections

Medicare Legislation. The Affordable Care Act as amended by the Health Care and Education Reconciliation Act of 2010 (the "Affordable Care Act" or ACA) significantly improves projected Medicare finances. The most important cost saving provision in the ACA is a revision in payment rate updates for Parts A and B services other than for physicians' services. Relative to payment rates made under prior law that were generally based on the rate at which prices for inputs used to provide Medicare services increase, the ACA reduces those payment rate updates by the rate at which productive efficiency in the overall economy increases, which is projected to average 0.8 percent per year through 2029 and 1.1 percent per year thereafter. The ACA also achieves substantial cost savings by benchmarking payment rates for private health plans providing Parts A and B services (Part C or Medicare Advantage) to more closely match per beneficiary costs. Partly offsetting these changes was an increase in prescription drug coverage. In addition, the ACA increases Part A revenues by: (a) taxing high-cost employer-provided health care plans and thereby giving employers incentives to increase the share of compensation paid as taxable earnings, and (b) imposing a new 0.9 percent surtax on earnings in excess of $200,000 (individual tax return filers) or $250,000 (joint tax return filers) starting in 2013.

The ACA substantially reduces the Medicare cost projections. Growth in Medicare cost per beneficiary in excess of growth in per capita GDP is referred to as "excess cost growth." In the 2009 *Financial Report*, the last Report released prior to the passage of the ACA, excess cost growth was assumed to average 1 percentage point over the last 50 years of the 75-year projection period—that is, Medicare expenditures per beneficiary were assumed to grow, on average, about one percentage point faster than per capita GDP over the long range. That assumption for excess cost growth in Medicare was optimistic in the sense that it is smaller than in recent history; excess cost growth averaged 1.6 percentage points between 1990 and 2007.[1] In this year's *Financial Report*, as in the 2011 and 2012 Reports, long-term excess cost growth is essentially zero. As a result, the long term projected Medicare spending share of GDP in this *Financial Report* is driven primarily by the same demographic trends that drive the OASDI spending share of GDP.

The 2013 Medicare Trustees' Report warns that the "actual future costs for Medicare are likely to exceed those shown by the current-law projections" that underlie both the Trustees' Report and this Financial Report. This concern reflects the fact that statutory adjustments to payment rates for Medicare physicians' services mandated by a 1996 Medicare reform have been consistently overridden by new law, and also the possibility that the new productivity-based downward adjustments to Medicare payment rate updates may not be sustainable.

Changes in Projection Methods. For 2012, based on the recommendation of the 2010-2011 Medicare Technical Review Panel, the Medicare Board of Trustees adopted a pre-ACA baseline cost growth assumption of "GDP plus 1.4 percent" and used a "factors contributing to growth" model, to create specific, year-by-year declining growth rates during the last 50 years of the projection period. For 2013 the Trustees used the "factors contributing to growth" model as the basis for determining the long-range Medicare cost growth assumption and applied the "GDP plus" framework as a reasonableness check, which produced results consistent with a pre-ACA "GDP plus 1 percent" approach and a post-ACA weighted average growth rate for Medicare of 4.3 percent (which is equal to per capita GDP growth plus 0.2 percentage points).

---

[1] Congressional Budget Office, the Long-Term Budget Outlook, June 2011.

Total Medicare. Chart 5 shows expenditures and current-law noninterest revenue sources for HI and SMI combined as a percentage of GDP. The total expenditure line shows Medicare costs rising to 6.54 percent of GDP by 2087. Revenues from taxes and premiums (including State transfers under Part D) are expected to increase from 1.96 percent of GDP in 2013 to 3.0 percent of GDP in 2087. Payroll tax income increases gradually as a percent of GDP because the new tax on earnings in excess of $250,000 for joint tax return filers and $200,000 for individual tax return filers applies to an increasing share of earnings because the $250,000 and $200,000 thresholds are not indexed for price changes. Premiums combined for Parts B and D of SMI are approximately fixed as a share of Parts B and D costs, so they also increase as a percent of GDP. General revenue contributions for SMI, as determined by current law, are projected to rise as a percent of GDP from 1.49 percent to 2.97 percent over the same period. Thus, revenues from taxes and premiums (including State transfers) will fall substantially as a share of total noninterest Medicare income (from 57 percent in 2013 to 50 percent in 2087) while general revenues will rise (from 43 percent to 50 percent). The gap between total noninterest Medicare income (including general revenue contributions) and expenditures begins around 2009 and then steadily continues to widen after 2022, reaching 0.57 percent of GDP by 2087.

**Chart 5—Total Medicare (HI and SMI) Expenditures and Noninterest Income
as a Percent of GDP
1970-2087**

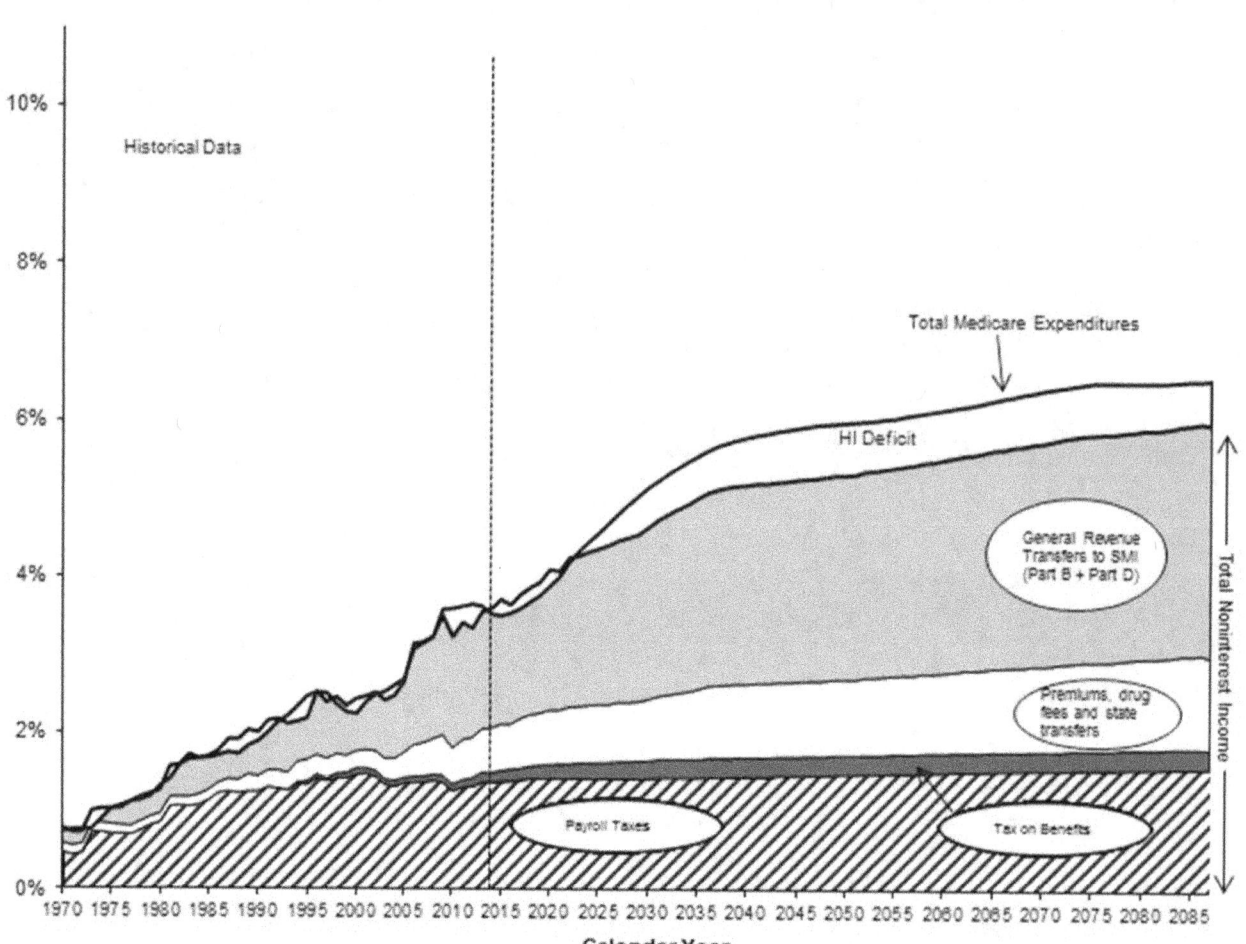

Medicare, Part A (Hospital Insurance)— Income and Expenditures. Chart 6 shows historical and actuarial estimates of HI annual income (excluding interest) and expenditures for 1970-2087 in nominal dollars. The estimates are for the open-group population.

Chart 6—Medicare Part A Income (Excluding Interest) and Expenditures
1970-2087

(In billions of dollars)

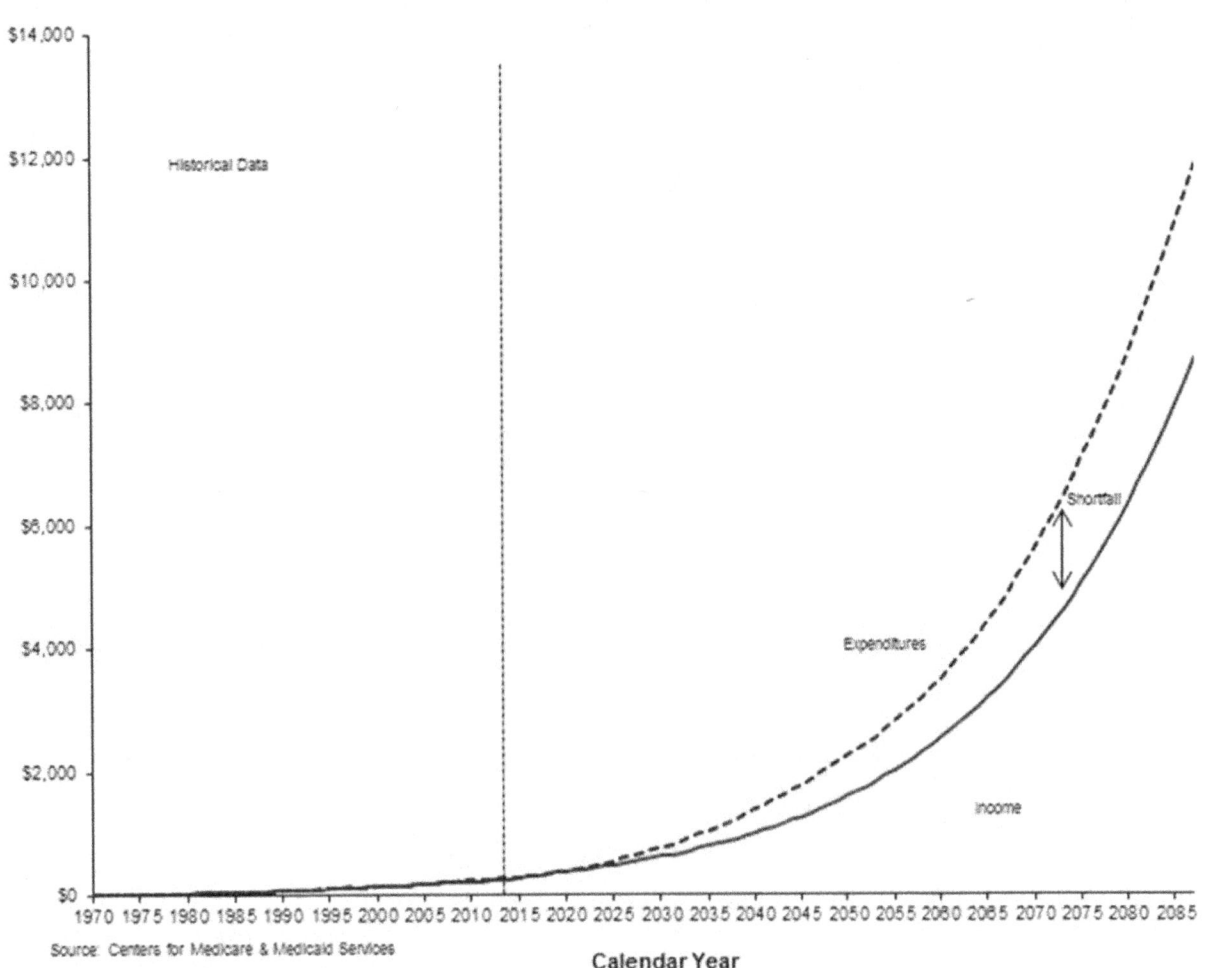

Source: Centers for Medicare & Medicaid Services

Calendar Year

Medicare, Part A Income and Expenditures as a Percent of Taxable Payroll. Chart 7 illustrates income (excluding interest) and expenditures as a percentage of taxable payroll over the next 75 years. The chart shows that beginning in 2005, the expenditure rate exceeds the income rate, and cash deficits continue thereafter. The projected initial decline in expenditures is due to the expected economic recovery, the savings provisions of the Affordable Care Act, and the 2-percent reduction in all Medicare expenditures for 2013-2022, as required by the Budget Control Act of 2011 and amended by the American Taxpayer Relief Act of 2012. Subsequent to 2022, the expenditure rate increases significantly due to retirements of those in the baby boom generation and continuing health services cost growth. The effect of these factors will be largely offset in 2045 and later under current law by the accumulating effect of the reduction in provider price updates, which will reduce the annual cost growth by an estimated 1.1 percent per year. Trust fund interest earnings and assets provide enough resources to pay full benefit payments until 2026 with general revenues used to finance interest and loan repayments to make up the difference between cash income and expenditures during that period. Pressures on the Federal budget will thus emerge well before 2026. Present tax rates would be sufficient to pay 87 percent of scheduled benefits after trust fund exhaustion in 2026 and 73 percent of scheduled benefits in 2087.

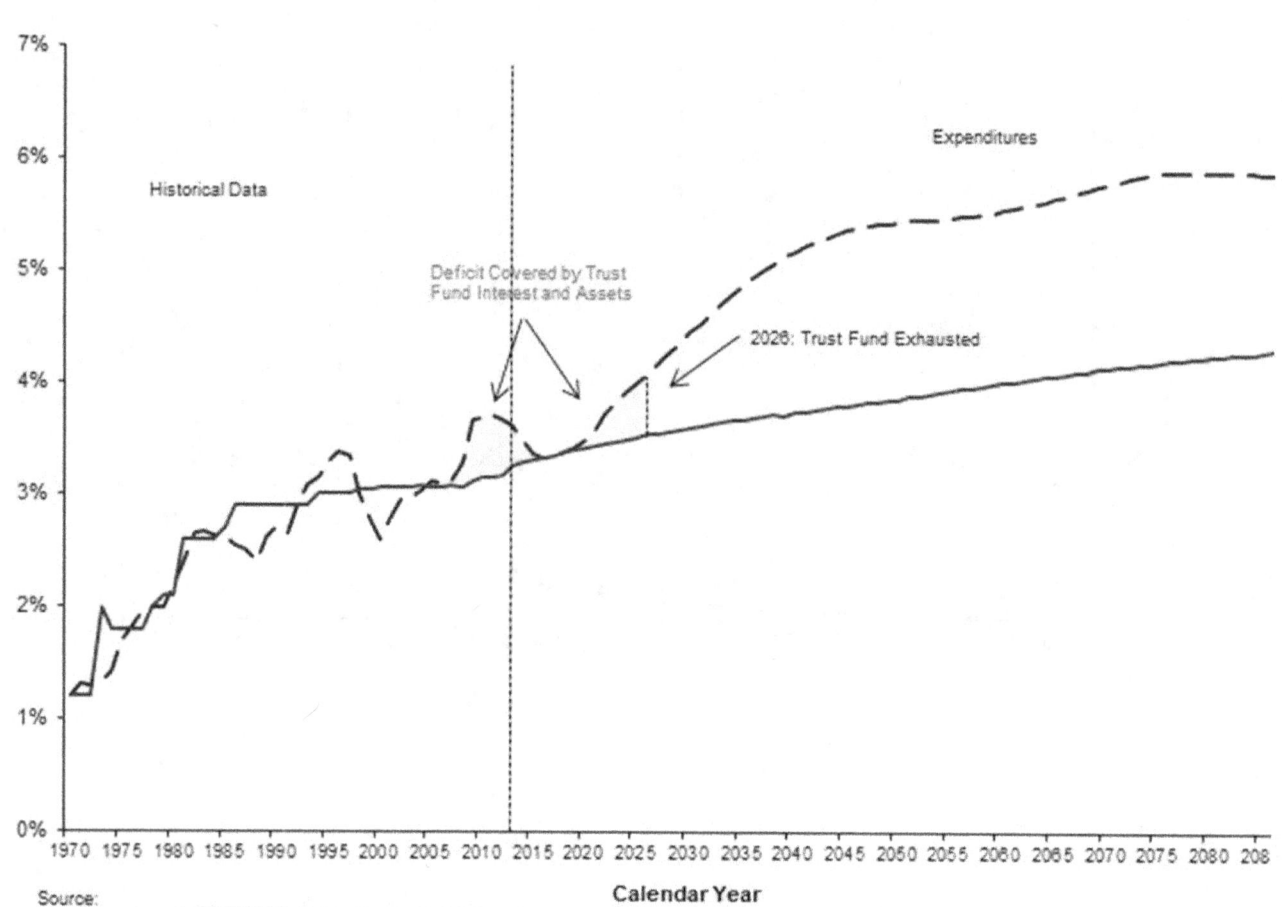

**Chart 7—Medicare Part A Income (Excluding Interest) and Expenditures
as a Percent of Taxable Payroll
1970-2087**

Source:
http://www.ssa.gov/OACT/TRSUM/images/LD_ChartB.html

Medicare, Part A Income and Expenditures as a Percent of GDP. Chart 8 shows estimated annual noninterest income and expenditures, expressed as percentages of GDP, the total value of goods and services produced in the United States. This alternative perspective shows the size of the HI Program in relation to the capacity of the national economy to sustain it. Medicare Part A's expenditures are projected to grow steadily from 1.63 percent of GDP in 2013, to 2.45 percent in 2046 and then remain fairly level throughout the rest of the 75-year period, as the accumulated effects of the price update reductions are realized. The gap between expenditure and income shares of GDP widens to 0.72 percent in 2046, remains fairly stable through 2080 and then commences a slight decline, reaching 0.68 percent of GDP in 2087.

**Chart 8—Medicare Part A Income (Excluding Interest) and Expenditures
as a Percent of GDP
1970-2087**

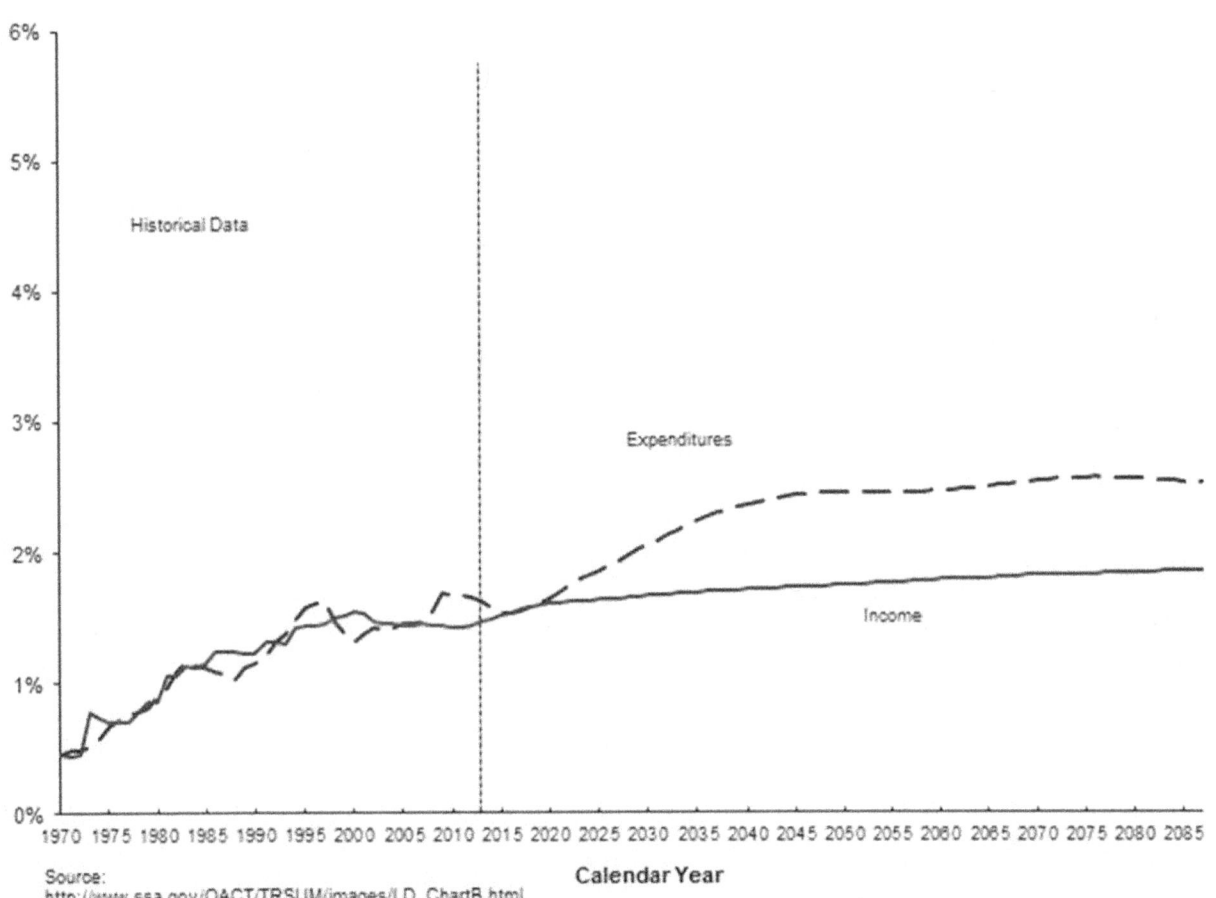

Source:
http://www.ssa.gov/OACT/TRSUM/images/LD_ChartB.html

Medicare, Parts B and D (Supplementary Medical Insurance). Chart 9 shows historical and actuarial estimates of Medicare Part B and Part D premiums (and Part D State transfers) and expenditures for each of the next 75 years, in dollars. The gap between premiums, drug fees and State transfer revenues and program expenditures, a gap that will need to be filled with transfers from general revenues, grows throughout the projection period.

Chart 9—Medicare Part B and Part D Premium and State Transfer Income and Expenditures 1970-2087

(In billions of dollars)

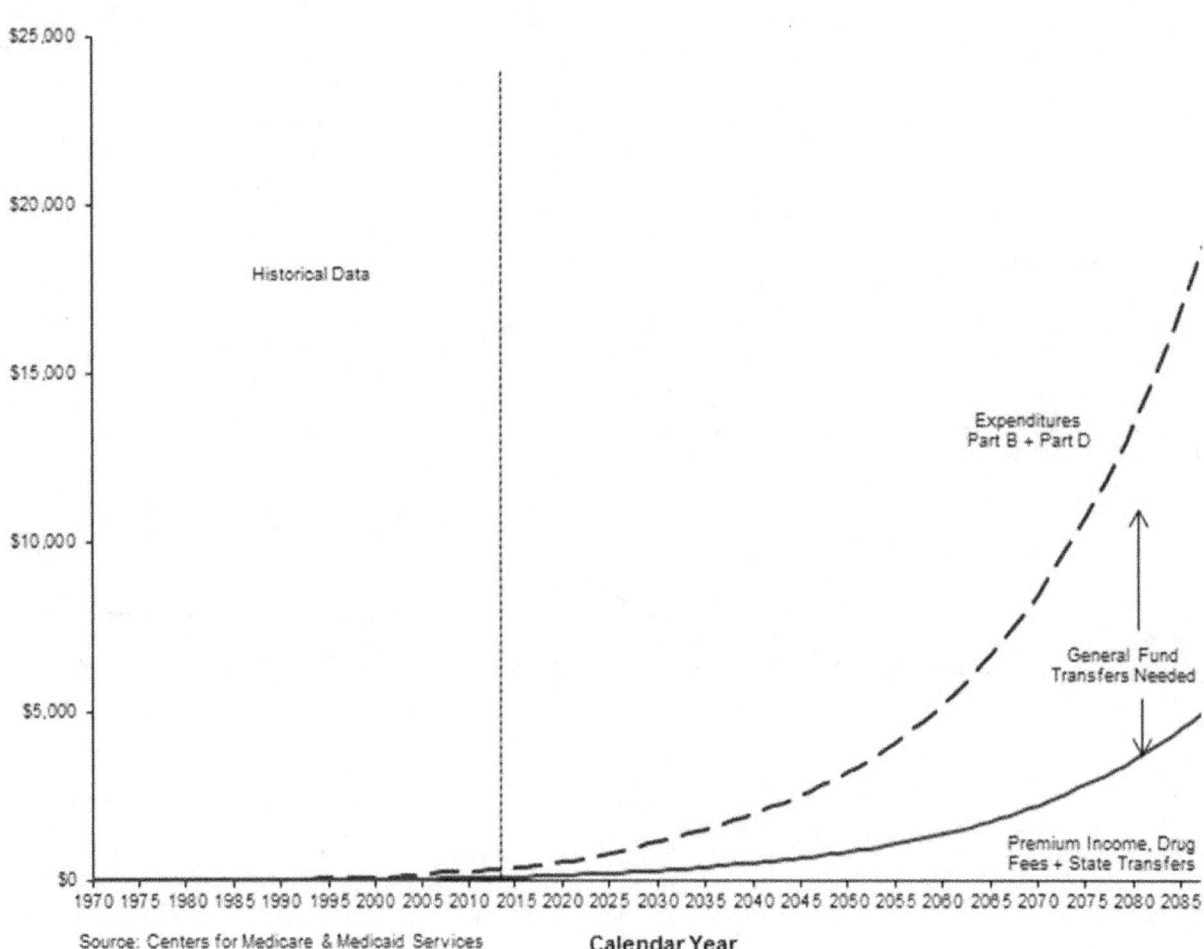

Source: Centers for Medicare & Medicaid Services

Medicare Part B and Part D Premium and State Transfer Income and Expenditures as a Percent of GDP. Chart 10 shows expenditures for the Supplementary Medical Insurance Program over the next 75 years expressed as a percentage of GDP, providing a perspective on the size of the SMI Program in relation to the capacity of the national economy to sustain it. SMI expenditures as a share of GDP are expected to grow rapidly from 1.99 percent in 2013 to 3.31 percent in 2035, and then grow more slowly reaching 4.01 in 2087. This growth pattern reflects growth in Medicare spending per beneficiary that is positive for the first half of the projection period (through 2035) as the baby boom generation move into their advanced years and then slows to a modest pace consistent with increasing longevity. As a share of GDP premium and State transfer income grows from about 0.52 percent in 2013 to 1.06 percent of GDP in 2087. The portion of SMI expenditures financed by General Fund transfers to SMI is projected to be about 74 percent throughout the projections period.

**Chart 10—Medicare Part B and Part D Premium and State Transfer
Income and Expenditures as a Percent of GDP
1970-2087**

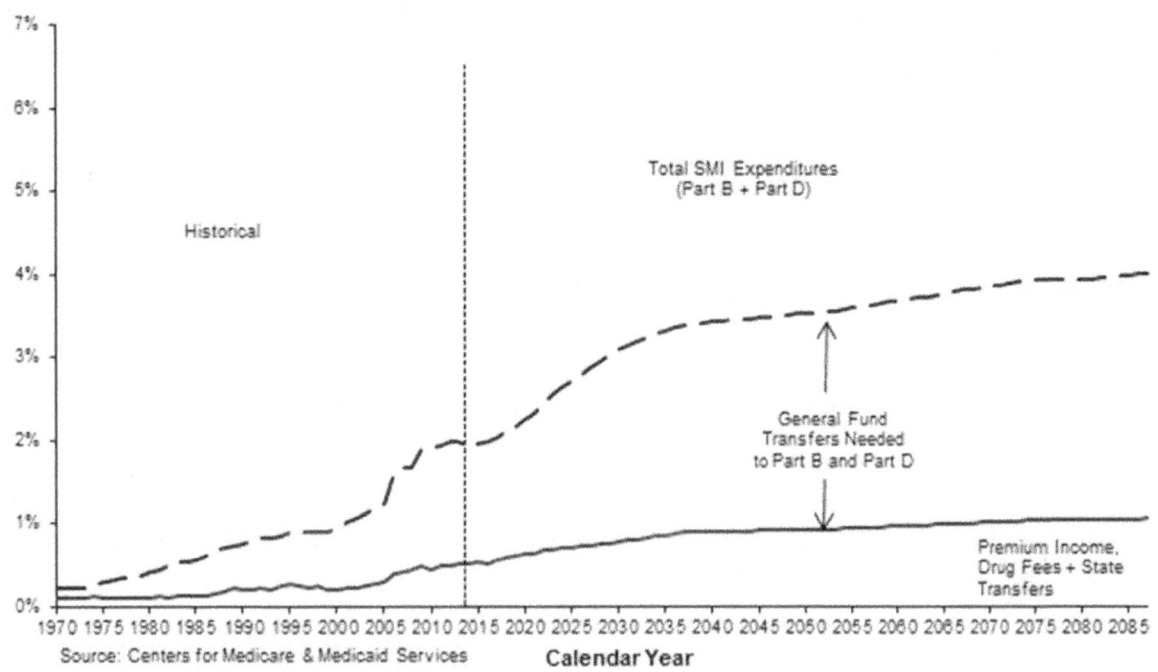

Medicare Sensitivity Analysis. This section illustrates the sensitivity of long-range cost and income estimates for the Medicare Program to changes in *selected individual assumptions*. As with the OASDI analysis, the intermediate assumption is used as the reference point, and one assumption at a time is varied. The variation used for each individual assumption reflects the levels used for that assumption in the low-cost and high-cost projections (see description of sensitivity analysis for OASDI).

Table 3 shows the effects of changing various assumptions on the present value of estimated HI expenditures in excess of income (the *shortfall* of income relative to expenditures in present value terms). The assumptions are shown in parentheses. Clearly, net HI expenditures are extremely sensitive to alternative assumptions about the growth in health care cost. For the low-cost alternative, the slower growth in health costs causes the shortfall to drop from $4,772 billion to a surplus of $1,242 billion, a 126 percent change. The high-cost assumption results in a tripling of the shortfall, from $4,772 billion to $14,352 billion.

The low and high real wage growth rate scenarios result in about a -21 and +11 percent, respectively, change in the shortfall relative to the intermediate case. Wages are a key cost factor in the provision of health care. Higher wages also result in greater payroll tax income. CPI inflation, fertility and net immigration changes have very little effect on net HI expenditures. (When CPI inflation is varied, the real interest rate is held constant, which implies that the nominal interest rate changes one for one with the assumed rate of CPI inflation.) Higher immigration decreases the net shortfall modestly as the 75-year projection period captures a higher share of additional immigrants tax payments than it does of their benefits.

Table 3 also shows that the present value of net HI expenditures is 17 percent lower if the real interest rate is 3.4 percent rather than 2.9 percent and 22 percent higher if the real interest rate is 2.4 percent rather than 2.9 percent.

Table 3
Present Values of Estimated Medicare Part A Expenditures in Excess of Income Under Various Assumptions, 2013-2087

(Dollar values in billions; values of assumptions shown in parentheses)

Assumption[1]	Financing Shortfall Range		
	Low	Intermediate	High
Average annual growth in health costs [2]	(1,242)	4,772	14,352
	(3.3)	(4.3)	(5.3)
Total fertility rate [3]	4,378	4,772	5,159
	(2.3)	(2.0)	(1.7)
Real wage differential	3,753	4,772	5,310
	(1.7)	(1.1)	(0.5)
CPI change	4,976	4,772	4,548
	(1.8)	(2.8)	(3.8)
Net immigration	4,731	4,772	4,848
	(1,400,000)[4]	(1,095,000)[4]	(800,000)[4]
Real interest rate	3,954	4,772	5,800
	(3.4)	(2.9)	(2.4)

[1] The sensitivity of the projected HI net cashflow to variations in future mortality rates also is of interest. At this time, however, relatively little is known about the relationship between improvements in life expectancy and the associated changes in health status and per beneficiary health expenditures. As a result, it is not possible at present to prepare meaningful estimates of the Part A, mortality sensitivity.

[2] Annual growth rate is the aggregate cost of providing covered health care services to beneficiaries. The low-cost and high-cost alternatives assume that costs increase 1 percent slower or faster, respectively, than the intermediate assumption, relative to growth in taxable payroll.

[3] The total fertility rate for any year is the average number of children who would be born to a woman in her lifetime if she were to experience the birth rates by age observed in, or assumed for, the selected year and if she were to survive the entire childbearing period.

[4] Amount represents the average annual net immigration over the 75-year projection period.

Source: Center for Medicare & Medicaid Services.

Table 4 shows the effects of various assumptions about the growth in health care costs on the present value of estimated SMI (Medicare Parts B and D) expenditures in excess of income. As with III, net SMI expenditures are very sensitive to changes in the health care cost growth assumption. For the low-cost alternative, the slower assumed growth in health costs reduces the Governmentwide resources needed for Part B from $15,659 billion to $11,359 billion and in Part D from $6,871 billion to $4,852 billion, about a 27 percent and 29 percent difference for Part B and Part D, respectively. The high-cost assumption increases Governmentwide resources needed to $22,348 billion for Part B and to $10,069 billion for Part D, about a 43 percent and a 47 percent difference for Part B and Part D, respectively.

Table 4
Present Values of Estimated Medicare Parts B and D Future Expenditures Less Premium Income and State Transfers Under Three Health Care Cost Growth Assumptions, 2013-2087

(In billions of dollars)

Medicare Program[1]	Governmentwide Resources Needed		
	Low (3.3)	Intermediate (4.3)	High (5.3)
Part B	11,359	15,659	22,348
Part D	4,852	6,871	10,069

[1] Annual growth rate is the aggregate cost of providing covered health care services to beneficiaries. The low and high scenarios assume that costs increase one percent slower or faster, respectively, than the intermediate assumption.

Source: Centers for Medicare & Medicaid Services.

Sustainability of Social Security and Medicare

75-Year Horizon

According to the 2013 Medicare Trustees Report, the HI Trust Fund is projected to remain solvent until 2026 and, according to the 2013 Social Security Trustees Report, the OASDI Trust Funds are projected to remain solvent until 2033. In each case, some general revenues must be used to satisfy the authorization of full benefit payments until the year of trust fund depletion. This occurs when the trust fund interest income and balances accumulated during prior years are needed to pay benefits, which leads to a transfer from general revenues to the trust funds. Moreover, under current law, General Fund transfers to the SMI Trust Fund will occur into the indefinite future and will continue to grow with the growth in health care expenditures.

The potential magnitude of future financial obligations under these three social insurance programs is, therefore, important from a unified budget perspective as well as for understanding generally the growing resource demands of the programs on the economy. A common way to present future cashflows is in terms of their *present value*. This approach recognizes that a dollar paid or collected next year is worth less than a dollar today because a dollar today could be saved and earn a year's worth of interest.

Table 5 shows the magnitudes of the primary expenditures and sources of financing for the three trust funds computed on an open-group basis for the next 75 years and expressed in present values. The data are consistent with the Statements of Social Insurance included in the principal financial statements. For HI, revenues from the public are projected to fall short of total expenditures by $4,772 billion in present value terms which is the additional amount needed in order to pay scheduled benefits over the next 75 years.[1] From the trust fund perspective, the amount needed is $4,552 billion in present value after subtracting the value of the existing trust fund balances (an asset to the trust fund account but an intragovernmental transfer to the overall budget). For SMI, revenues from the public for Part B and D combined are estimated to be $22,530 billion less

---

[1] Interest income is not a factor in this table as dollar amounts are in present value terms.

than total expenditures for the two accounts, an amount that, from a budget perspective, will be needed to keep the SMI program solvent for the next 75 years. From the trust fund perspective, however, the present values of total revenues and total expenditures for the SMI Program are roughly equal due to the annual adjustment of revenue from other Government accounts to meet program costs.[2] For OASDI, projected revenues from the public fall short of total expenditures by $12,294 billion in present value dollars, and, from the trust fund perspective, by $9,562 billion.

From the Governmentwide perspective, the present value of the total resources needed for the Social Security and Medicare Programs over and above current-law funding sources (payroll taxes, benefit taxes, and premium payments from the public) is $39,596 billion. From the trust fund perspective, which counts the trust funds ($3,019 billion in present value) and the general revenue transfers to the SMI Program ($22,530 billion in present value) as dedicated funding sources, additional resources needed to fund the programs are $14,047 billion in present value.

Table 5
Present Values of Costs Less Revenues of 75-Year Open Group Obligations HI, SMI, and OASDI

(In billions of dollars, as of January 1, 2013)

	HI	SMI Part B	SMI Part D	OASDI	Total
Revenues from the public:					
Taxes	16,192	-	-	48,918	65,110
Premiums, State transfers	-	5,718	2,340	-	8,058
Total	16,192	5,718	2,340	48,918	73,168
Total costs to the public	20,964	21,377	9,211	61,212	112,764
Net results - budget perspective*	4,772	15,659	6,871	12,294	39,596
Revenues from other Government accounts	-	15,659	6,871	-	22,530
Trust fund balances as of 1/1/2013	220	66	1	2,732	3,019
Net results - trust fund perspective*	4,552	(66)	(1)	9,562	14,047

*Net results are computed as costs less revenues and trust fund balances. Negative values are indicative of surpluses.

Note: Details may not add to totals due to rounding.

Source: 2013 OASDI and Medicare Trustees' Report

Infinite Horizon

The 75-year horizon represented in Table 5 is consistent with the primary focus of the Social Security and Medicare Trustees' Reports. For the OASDI Program, for example, an additional $12.3 trillion in present value will be needed above currently scheduled taxes to pay for scheduled benefits ($9.6 trillion from the trust fund perspective). Yet, a 75-year projection can be a misleading indicator of all future financial flows. For example, when calculating unfunded obligations, a 75-year horizon includes revenue from some future workers but only a fraction of their future benefits. In order to provide a more complete estimate of the long-run unfunded obligations of the programs, estimates can be extended to the infinite horizon. The open-group infinite horizon net obligation is the present value of all expected future program outlays less the present value of all expected future program tax and premium revenues. Such a measure is provided in Table 6 for the three trust funds represented in Table 5.

From the budget or Governmentwide perspective, the values in line 1 plus the values in line 4 of Table 6 represent the value of resources needed to finance each of the programs into the infinite future. The sums are shown in the last line of the table (also equivalent to adding the values in the second and fifth lines). The total resources needed for all the programs sums

---

[2] The SMI Trust Fund has $67 billion of existing assets.

to $69.0 trillion in present value terms. This need can be satisfied only through increased borrowing, higher taxes, reduced program spending, or some combination.

The second line shows the value of the trust fund at the beginning of 2013. For the HI and OASDI Programs this represents, from the trust fund perspective, the extent to which the programs are funded. From that perspective, when the trust fund is subtracted, an additional $23.1 trillion is needed to sustain the OASDI program into the infinite future, while an additional $3.5 trillion is needed to sustain the HI program. However, looking just at present values ignores timing differences in the underlying projected cashflows; the HI Trust Fund is projected to remain solvent only until 2026. As described above, from the trust fund perspective, the SMI Program is fully funded, from a Governmentwide basis, the substantial gap that exists between premiums and State transfer revenue and program expenditures in the SMI Program ($25.0 trillion and $14.4 trillion for Parts B and D, respectively) represents future general revenue obligations of the Federal budget.

In comparison to the analogous 75-year number in Table 5, extending the calculations beyond 2087, captures the full lifetime benefits, and taxes and premiums of all current and future participants. The shorter horizon understates the total financial needs by capturing relatively more of the revenues from current and future workers and not capturing all of the benefits that are scheduled to be paid to them.

Table 6
Present Values of Costs Less Tax, Premium and State Transfer Revenue through the Infinite Horizon, HI, SMI, OASDI

(In trillions of dollars, as of January 1, 2013)

	HI	SMI Part B	SMI Part D	OASDI	Total
Present value of future costs less future taxes, premiums, and State transfers for current participants	9.6	13.1	4.9	26.4	54.0
Less current trust fund balance........................	0.2	0.1	-	2.7	3.0
Equals net obligations for past and current participants...	9.4	13.0	4.9	23.7	51.0
Plus net obligations for future participants	(5.9)	12.0	9.5	(0.6)	15.0
Equals net obligations through the infinite future for all participants	3.5	25.0	14.4	23.1	66.0
Present values of future costs less the present values of future income over the infinite horizon	3.7	25.1	14.4	25.8	69.0

Details may not add to totals due to rounding.

Source: 2013 OASDI and Medicare Trustees' Reports.

Railroad Retirement, Black Lung, and Unemployment Insurance

Railroad Retirement

The Railroad Retirement Board (RRB) was created in the 1930s to establish a retirement benefit program for the Nation's railroad workers. As the Social Security Program legislated in 1935 would not give railroad workers credit for service performed prior to 1937, legislation was enacted in 1934, 1935, and 1937 (collectively the Railroad Retirement Acts of the 1930s) to establish a railroad retirement program separate from the Social Security Program.

Railroad retirement pays full retirement annuities at age 60 to railroad workers with 30 years of service. The program pays disability annuities based on total or occupational disability. It also pays annuities to spouses, divorced spouses, widow(er)s, remarried widow(er)s, surviving divorced spouses, children, and parents of deceased railroad workers. Medicare covers qualified railroad retirement beneficiaries in the same way as it does Social Security beneficiaries.

Payroll taxes paid by railroad employers and their employees provide a primary source of income for the Railroad Retirement and Survivors' Benefit Program. By law, railroad retirement taxes are coordinated with Social Security taxes. Employees and employers pay tier I taxes at the same rate as Social Security taxes. Tier II taxes finance railroad retirement benefit payments that are higher than Social Security levels.

Other sources of program income include: the RRB-SSA-CMS Financial Interchanges with the Social Security and Medicare trust funds, earnings on investments, Federal income taxes on railroad retirement benefits, and appropriations (provided after 1974 as part of a phase out of certain vested dual benefits). See Note 24—Social Insurance, for additional information on railroad retirement program financing.

The RRSIA liberalized benefits for 30-year service employees and their spouses, eliminated a cap on monthly benefits for retirement and disability benefits, lowered minimum service requirements from 10 to 5 years, and provided for increased benefits for widow(er)s. Per the RRSIA, amounts in the Railroad Retirement Account and the SSEB Account that are not needed to pay current benefits and administrative expenses may be transferred to the NRRIT or used to offset transfers from the NRRIT to the Railroad Retirement Account. The NRRIT's sole purpose is to manage and invest railroad retirement assets. NRRIT's Board of Trustees is empowered to invest trust assets in nongovernmental assets, such as equities and debt, as well as in Government securities. Prior to RRSIA, all investments were limited to Government securities.

Since its inception, NRRIT has received $21.3 billion from RRB (including $19.2 billion in fiscal year 2003, pursuant to RRSIA) and returned $15.2 billion. During fiscal year 2013, the NRRIT made net transfers of $1.6 billion to the RRB to pay retirement benefits. Administrative expenses of the trust are paid out of trust assets. The balance as of September 30, 2013, and 2012, of non-Federal securities and investments of the NRRIT are disclosed in Note 8—Debt and Equity Securities.

Cashflow Projections

Economic and Demographic Assumptions. The economic and demographic assumptions used for the most recent set of projections are shown in the "Railroad Retirement" section of Note 24—Social Insurance.

Income and Expenditures. Chart 11 shows, in dollars, estimated railroad retirement income (excluding interest and financial interchange income) and expenditures for the period 2013-2087 based on the intermediate set of assumptions used in the RRB's actuarial evaluation of the program. The estimates are for the open-group population, which includes all persons projected to participate in the Railroad Retirement Program as railroad workers or beneficiaries during the period. Thus, the estimates include payments from, and on behalf of, those who are projected to be employed by the railroads during the period as well as those already employed at the beginning of the period. They also include expenditures made to, and on behalf of, such workers during that period.

Chart 11—Estimated Railroad Retirement Income
(Excluding Interest and Financial Interchange Income) and Expenditures
2013-2087

(In billions of dollars)

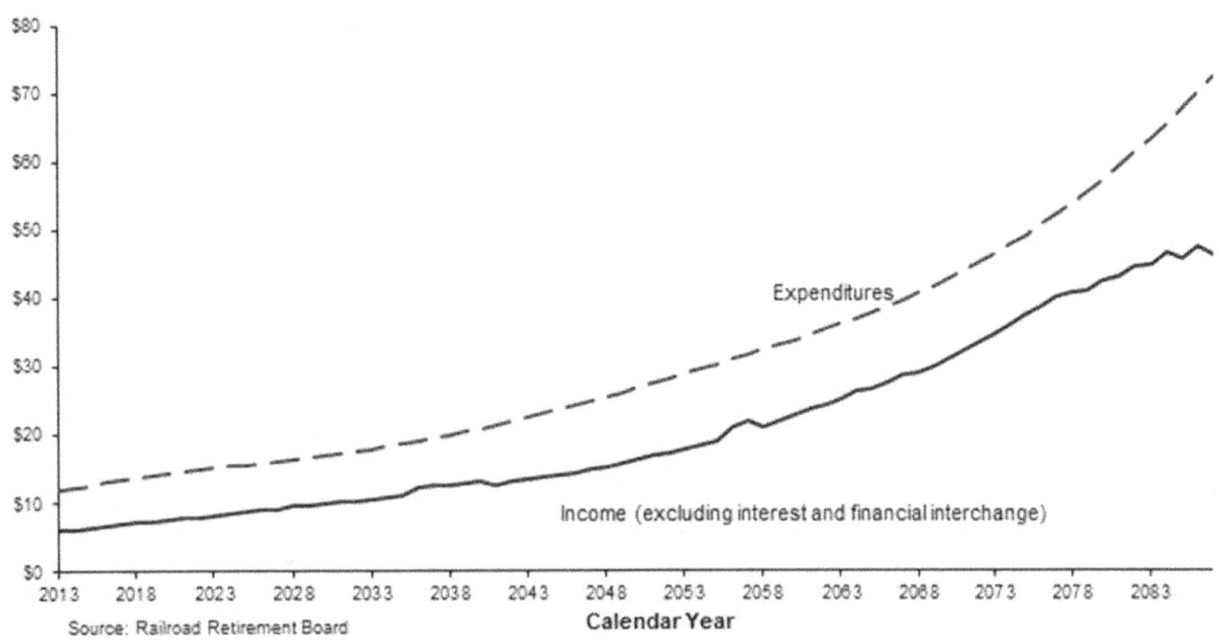

Source: Railroad Retirement Board

As Chart 11 shows, expenditures are expected to exceed tax income for the entire projection period. The imbalance generally grows at a moderate amount until about 2078 when it begins to grow more rapidly.

Income and Expenditures as a Percent of Taxable Payroll. Chart 12 shows estimated expenditures and income as a percent of tier II taxable payroll. Expenditures as a percentage of payroll increase from 2013 through 2016 primarily due to the anticipated retirement of a large percentage of the current workforce combined with the projected decline in railroad employment.

Chart 12—Estimated Railroad Retirement Income
(Excluding Interest and Financial Interchange Income) and Expenditures
as a Percent of Tier II Taxable Payroll
2013-2087

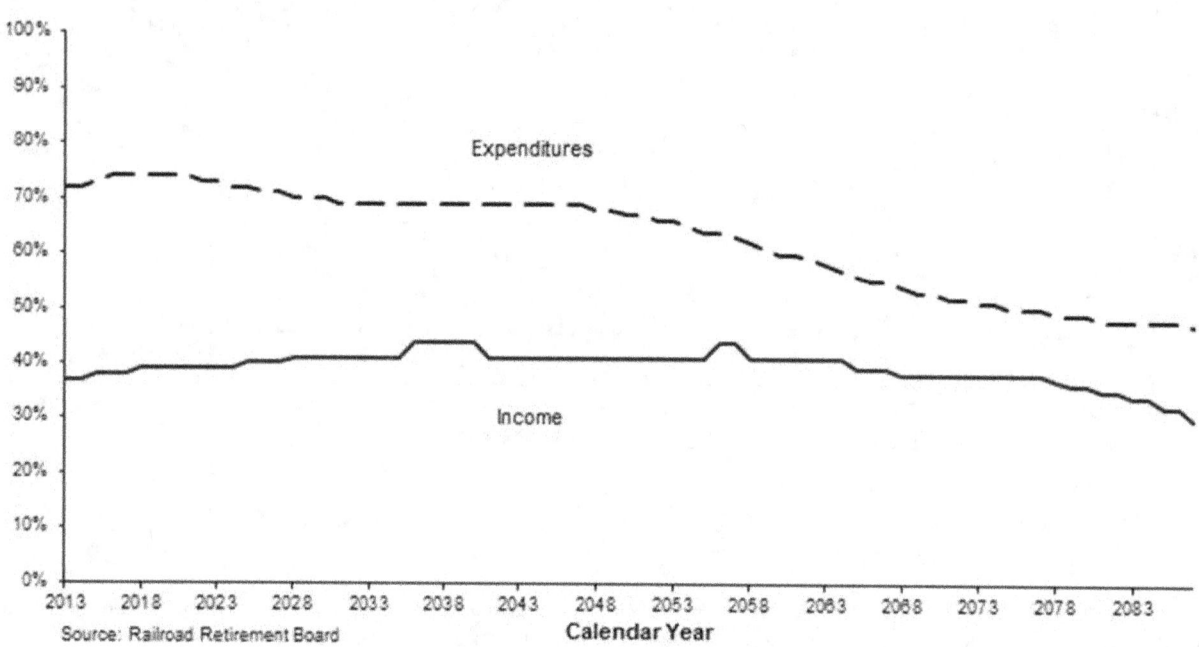

Sensitivity Analysis. Actual future income from railroad payroll taxes and other sources and actual future expenditures for scheduled benefits and administrative expenses will depend upon a large number of factors as mentioned above. Two crucial assumptions are employment growth and the interest rate. The interest rate assumption reflects the expected rate of return on NRRIT investments. Table 7 shows the sensitivity of the shortfall in the Railroad Retirement Program to variations in these two assumptions. The low-cost employment scenario has a 6.6 percent smaller shortfall of income to expenditures, and the high-cost scenario has a 6.1 percent higher shortfall. A higher discount rate reduces future values relative to a lower rate. As seen in the table, the shortfall is 26.7 percent lower if the interest rate is 10.0 percent rather than 7.0 percent and 65.0 percent higher when the interest rate is 4.0 percent rather than 7.0 percent.

Table 7
Present Values of Railroad Retirement Expenditures in Excess of Income Under Various Employment and Interest Rate Assumptions, 2013-2087

(Dollar values in billions; values of assumptions shown in parentheses)

Assumption	Low	Middle	High
Employment[1]	100.3	107.4	114.0
	(-0.5%)	(-2.0%)	(-3.5%)
Interest rate	78.7	107.4	177.2
	(10.0%)	(7.0%)	(4.0%)

[1] The low and middle employment scenarios have passenger service employment remaining at 45,000 workers per year and the remaining employment base declining at 0.5 percent and 2.0 percent, respectively, for 25 years, at a reducing rate over the next 25 years, and remaining level thereafter. The high-cost scenario has passenger service employment declining by 500 workers per year until a level of 35,000 is reached with the remaining employment base declining by 3.5 percent per year for 25 years, at a reducing rate over the next 25 years, and remaining level thereafter.

Source: Railroad Retirement Board

Sustainability of Railroad Retirement

Table 8 shows the magnitudes of the primary expenditures and sources of financing for the Railroad Retirement Program computed on an open-group basis for the next 75 years and expressed in present values as of January 1, 2013. The data are consistent with the Statements of Social Insurance.

From a Governmentwide perspective, revenues are expected to fall short of expenditures by approximately $107.4 billion, which represents the present value of resources needed to sustain the Railroad Retirement Program. From a trust fund perspective, when the trust fund balance and the financial interchange and transfers are included, the combined balance of the NRRIT, the Railroad Retirement Account, and the SSEB Account show a slight surplus.

Table 8
Present Values of 75-Year Projections of Revenues and Expenditures for the Railroad Retirement Program[1,2]

(In billions of present-value dollars as of January 1, 2013)

Estimated future income (excluding interest) received from or on behalf of:[3]

Current participants who have attained retirement age	6.9
Current participants not yet having attained retirement age	60.1
Those expected to become participants	78.8
All participants	145.8

Estimated future expenditures:[4]

Current participants who have attained retirement age	122.6
Current participants not yet having attained retirement age	96.2
Those expected to become participants	34.3
All participants	253.1

Net obligations from budget perspective (expenditures less income)	107.4
Railroad retirement program assets (mostly investments stated at market) [5]	25.5
Financial interchange from Social Security Trust	83.5
Net obligations from trust fund perspective	(1.6)

[1] Represents combined values for the Railroad Retirement Account, SSEB Account, and NRRIT, based on middle employment assumption.

[2] The data used reflect the provisions of RRSIA of 2001.

[3] Future income (excluding interest) includes tier I taxes, tier II taxes, and income taxes on benefits.

[4] Future expenditures include benefits and administrative expenditures.

[5] The value of the fund reflects the 7.0 percent interest rate assumption. The RRB uses the relatively high rate due to investments in private securities.

Note: Detail may not add to totals due to rounding. Employee and beneficiary status as are determined as of 1/1/2012, whereas present values are as of 1/1/2013.

Source: Railroad Retirement Board

Black Lung

The Federal Coal Mine Health and Safety Act of 1969 created the Black Lung Disability Benefit Program to provide compensation, medical, and survivor benefits for eligible coal miners who are totally disabled due to pneumoconiosis (black lung disease) arising out of their coal mine employment and to eligible survivors of coal miners who died due to pneumoconiosis. DOL operates the Black Lung Disability Benefit Program. The beneficiary population is a nearly closed universe in which attrition by death exceeds new entrants by a ratio of more than ten to one.

Excise taxes on coal mine operators, based on the sale of coal, are the primary source of financing black lung disability payments and related administrative costs. The *Black Lung Benefits Revenue Act* provided for repayable advances to the BLDTF from the General Fund of the Treasury, in the event that BLDTF resources were not adequate to meet program obligations. Prior to legislation enacted in 2008 that allowed for the restructuring of BLDTF debt, the trust fund had accumulated large liabilities from significant and growing shortfalls of excise taxes relative to benefit payments and interest expenses.

The *Energy Improvement and Extension Act of 2008* (Public Law 110-343), enacted on October 3, 2008, contained several provisions that significantly improved the BLDTF's financial position, including:

- Continuation of a previously-enacted increase in coal excise tax rates for an additional 5 years, through December 2018;
- Provision for the restructuring of BLDTF debt by refinancing the outstanding repayable advances with proceeds from issuing new debt instruments with lower interest rates; and
- Establishment of a one-time appropriation that significantly reduced the outstanding debt of the BLDTF.

This Act also allowed that any debt issued by the BLDTF subsequent to the refinancing may be used to make benefit payments, other authorized expenditures, or to repay debt and interest from the initial refinancing. All debt issued by the BLDTF was effected as borrowing from the Treasury's Bureau of the Fiscal Service.

On September 30, 2013, total liabilities of the BLDTF exceeded assets by $5.9 billion. Prior to the enactment of Public Law 110-343, this shortfall was funded by repayable advances to the BLDTF, which are repayable with interest. Pursuant to Public Law 110-343, any shortfall will be financed with debt instruments similar in form to zero-coupon bonds.

From the budget or consolidated financial perspective, Chart 13 shows projected black lung expenditures (excluding interest) and excise tax collections for the period 2014-2040 in constant dollars. The significant assumptions used in the most recent set of projections are coal excise tax revenue estimates, the tax rate structure, the number of beneficiaries, life expectancy, Federal civilian pay raises, medical cost inflation, the interest rate on new debt issued by the BLDTF, and the CPI-U for goods and services. The projected decrease in cash inflows in the year 2019 and, thereafter, is the result of a scheduled reduction in the tax rate on the sale of coal. This rate reduction is projected to result in a 37.6 percent decrease in the amount of excise taxes collected between the years 2018 and 2019.

Chart 13—Estimated Black Lung Income and Expenditures (Excluding Interest) In Constant (or Inflation-Adjusted) Dollars 2014-2040

(In millions of dollars)

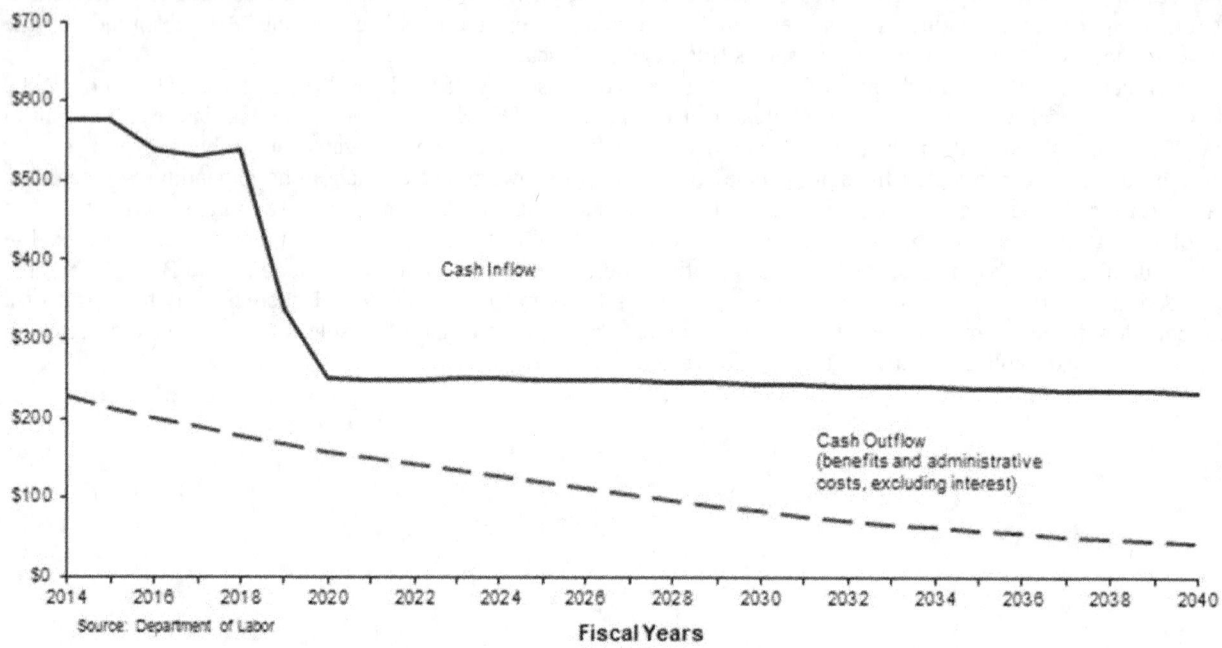

Source: Department of Labor

Fiscal Years

Table 9
Present Values of 27-Year Projections of Expenditures and Revenues
for the Black Lung Disability Benefit Program

(In billions of present value dollars as of September 30, 2013)

Projected future expenditures	2.9
Projected future tax income	7.5
Net obligations from budget perspective (expenditures less income)	(4.6)
Accumulated balance due General Fund	5.9
Net obligations from trust fund perspective	1.3

Note: Detail may not add to totals due to rounding.
Source: Department of Labor

Table 9 shows present values of 27-year projections of expenditures and revenues for the Black Lung Disability Benefit Program computed as of September 30, 2013. Cashflows were discounted using rates that ranged from 2.79 percent to 2.95 percent. From a Governmentwide (budget) perspective, the present value of expenditures is expected to be less than the present value of income by $4.6 billion (a surplus). From a trust fund perspective, a large balance ($5.9 billion) is owed to the General Fund. From that perspective, when that accumulated balance is combined with the cashflow surplus, the program has a shortfall of $1.3 billion in present value dollars. This compares to a shortfall of $1.7 billion reported in last year's *Financial Report*.

Unemployment Insurance

The Unemployment Insurance Program was created in 1935 to provide temporary partial wage replacement to workers who lost their jobs. The program is administered through a unique system of Federal and State partnerships established in Federal law but administered through conforming state laws by state agencies. The program includes the 50 states and Puerto Rico, U.S. Virgin Islands, and the District of Columbia. DOL interprets and enforces Federal law requirements and provides broad policy guidance and program direction, while program details such as benefit eligibility, duration, and amount of benefits are established through individual state unemployment insurance statutes and administered through State unemployment insurance agencies.

The program is financed through the collection of Federal and state unemployment taxes that are credited to the UTF and reported as Federal tax revenue. The fund was established to account for the receipt, investment, and disbursement of unemployment taxes. Federal unemployment taxes are used to pay for Federal and state administration of the Unemployment Insurance Program, veterans' employment services, state employment services, and the Federal share of extended unemployment insurance benefits. Federal unemployment taxes also are used to maintain a loan account within the UTF, from which insolvent state accounts may borrow funds to pay unemployment insurance benefits.

Chart 14 shows the projected cash contributions and expenditures over the next 10 years under expected economic conditions (described below) in constant dollars. The significant assumptions used in the projections include total unemployment rates, civilian labor force levels, percent of unemployed receiving benefits, total wages, distribution of benefit payments by State, State tax rate structures, State taxable wage bases, and interest rates on UTF investments. These projections, excluding interest earnings, indicate a positive net cashflow in fiscal year 2014 through fiscal year 2022.

The *Federal/State Extended Unemployment Compensation Act of 1970* provides for the extension of the duration of unemployment insurance benefits during periods of high unemployment to individuals who have exhausted their regular unemployment benefits. When the insured unemployment level within a state, or in some cases total unemployment, reaches certain specified levels, the state must extend benefit duration by 50 percent, up to a combined maximum of 39 weeks; certain states voluntarily extended the benefit duration up to a combined maximum of 46 weeks. These extended benefits are financed one-half by State unemployment taxes and one-half by Federal unemployment taxes. However, the ARRA of 2009 began temporary 100 percent Federal funding of extended benefits. Subsequent legislation, most recently P.L. 112-240, the *American Taxpayer Relief Act of 2012*, authorized continuing 100 percent Federal funding of extended unemployment benefits to December 31, 2013.

During prolonged periods of high unemployment, Congress may authorize the payment of emergency unemployment benefits to supplement extended Unemployment Insurance (UI) benefit payments. Emergency benefits began in July 2008, authorized under the *Supplemental Appropriations Act, 2008*. This emergency program was temporarily extended and additionally funded by the ARRA of 2009 and has been subsequently modified several times, most recently by P.L. 112-240, the *American Taxpayer Relief Act of 2012*, which extended the emergency unemployment insurance program to January 1, 2014.

**Chart 14—Estimated Unemployment Trust Fund Cashflow
Using Expected Economic Conditions
In Constant (or Inflation-Adjusted) Dollars
2014-2023**

(In billions of dollars)

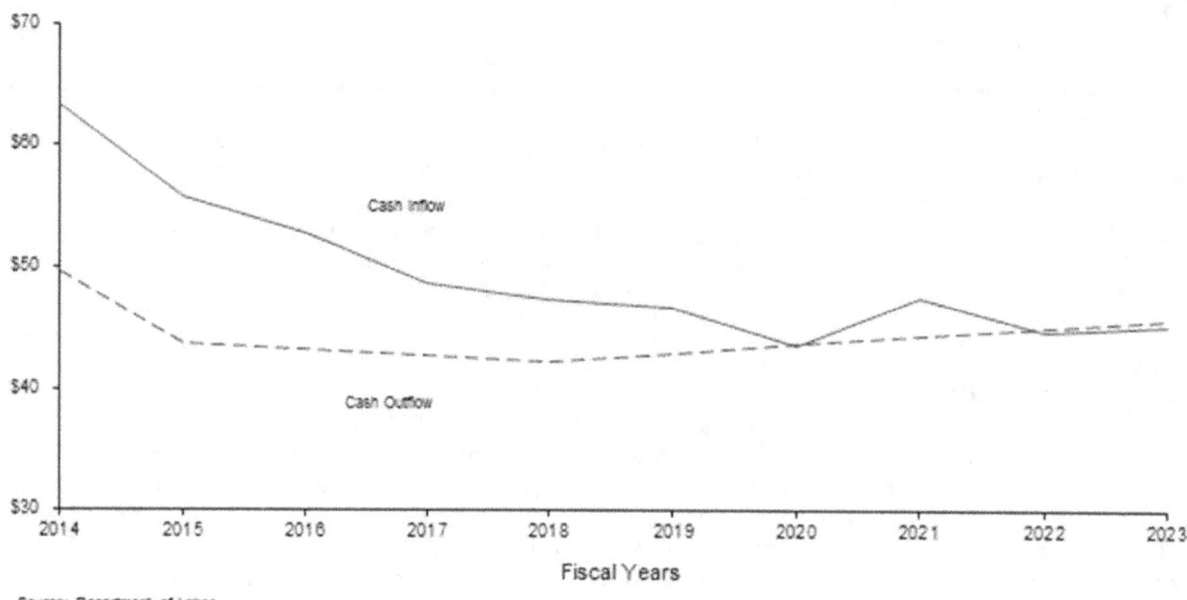

Source: Department of Labor

Table 10 shows 10-year projections of revenues and expenditures for the Unemployment Insurance Program in constant dollars. Three sets of numbers are presented in order to show the effects of varying economic conditions as reflected in different assumptions about the unemployment rate. For expected economic conditions, the estimates are based on an unemployment rate of 7.10 percent during fiscal year 2014, decreasing steadily to 5.40 percent in fiscal year 2018 and thereafter. Under Scenario One which utilizes a lower than expected unemployment rate of 6.91 in fiscal year 2014, net cash inflows peak in fiscal year 2014 and continue to be positive through 2023. Under Scenario Two, which utilizes a higher than expected unemployment rate of 9.11 in fiscal year 2014, net cash outflows, including interest earnings and expenses, are projected to be negative in fiscal years 2014 through 2015. Net cash inflows are reestablished in fiscal year 2016 and peak in fiscal year 2018 with a drop in the unemployment rate to 7.05 percent and then lower rates for fiscal years 2019 through 2023.

Each scenario uses an open group that includes current and future participants of the Unemployment Insurance Program. Table 10 shows the impact on the UTF projections of varying projected unemployment rates. For example, in Scenario Two, while tax income is projected to increase as higher layoffs result in higher employer taxes, benefit outlays increase even more. From the Governmentwide (budget) perspective, under expected conditions, the present value of income exceeds the present value of expenditures by $52.6 billion. From the same perspective, under Scenario Two, the present value of income exceeds the present value of expenditures by $26.0 billion. From a trust fund perspective, which takes into account the ($0.1) billion trust fund balance, the program has a surplus of $52.5 billion under expected conditions. As explained below, the negative trust fund balance reflects loans extended by the General Fund to the states.

Table 10
10-Year Projections of Expenditures and Revenues for
Unemployment Insurance in Constant (or Inflation-Adjusted) Dollars
Under Three Alternative Scenarios for Economic Conditions

(In billions of present value dollars as of September 30, 2013)

		Economic Conditions	
	Expected	**Scenario One**	**Scenario Two**
Projected future expenditures	443.3	436.9	550.9
Projected future cash income	495.9	489.4	576.9
Net obligations from budget perspective (expenditures less income)	(52.6)	(52.5)	(26.0)
Trust fund assets	(0.1)	(0.1)	(0.1)
Net obligations from trust fund perspective [1]	(52.5)	(52.4)	(25.9)

[1] Net obligations from the trust fund perspective equals net obligations from the budget perspective minus trust fund assets. The negative values in this line are indicative of surpluses.

Note: Data may not add to totals due to rounding.

Source: Department of Labor.

Unemployment Trust Fund Solvency

Each state's accumulated UTF net assets or reserve balance should provide a defined level of benefit payments over a defined period. To be minimally solvent, a state's reserve balance should provide for one year's projected benefit payment needs based on the highest levels of benefit payments experienced by the state over the last 20 years. A ratio of 1.0 or greater indicates a state is minimally solvent. States below this level are vulnerable to exhausting their funds in a recession. States exhausting their reserve balance borrow funds from the Federal Unemployment Account to make benefit payments.

Chart 15 presents the state by state results of this analysis as of September 30, 2013. As the chart illustrates, 37 state funds plus the funds of Puerto Rico and the U.S. Virgin Islands were below the minimal solvency ratio of 1.0 at September 30, 2013.

Chart 15—Unemployment Trust Fund Solvency as of September 30, 2013

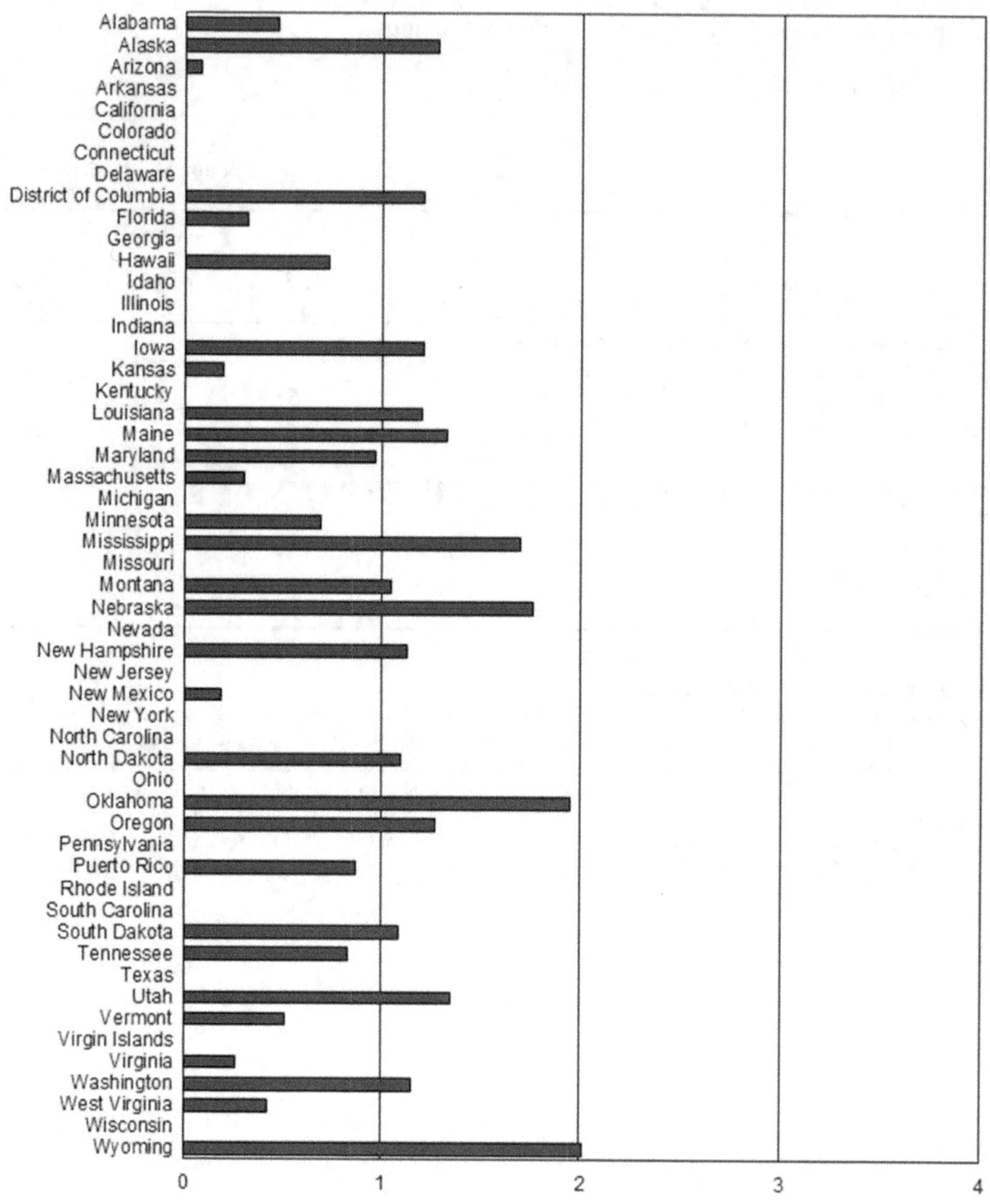

Years of benefit payments held in reserve

Deferred Maintenance and Repairs

Deferred maintenance and repairs are the estimated cost to bring Government-owned property, plant, and equipment to an acceptable condition, resulting from not performing maintenance on a timely basis. Deferred maintenance and repairs exclude the cost of expanding the capacity of assets or upgrading them to serve needs different from those originally intended. The consequences of not performing regular maintenance and repairs could include increased safety hazards, poor service to the public, higher costs in the future, and inefficient operations. Estimated deferred maintenance and repairs costs are not accrued in the Statements of Net Cost or recognized as a liability on the Balance Sheets.

The amounts disclosed for deferred maintenance and repairs are allowed to be measured using one of the following three methods:

- Condition assessment surveys are periodic inspections of the Government-owned property to determine the current condition and estimated cost to bring the property to an acceptable condition.
- Life-cycle cost forecast is an acquisition or procurement technique that considers operation, maintenance, and other costs in addition to the acquisition cost of assets.
- Management analysis method is founded on inflation-adjusted reductions in maintenance funding since the base year.

The amounts disclosed in the table below have all been measured using the condition assessment survey method. The standards for acceptable operating condition and the changes in these standards and changes in asset condition vary widely between the Federal entities.

Some deferred maintenance and repairs have been deemed critical. Such amounts and conditions are defined by the individual agencies with responsibility for the safekeeping of these assets. The critical maintenance amount is not included in the low or high estimates amounts and is reported separately. Low and high estimates are based on the materiality of the estimated cost of returning the asset to the acceptable condition versus the total value of the corresponding asset.

Deferred Maintenance and Repairs as of September 30, 2013, and 2012

(In billions of dollars)	Deferred Maintenance and Repairs Cost Range				Critical Maintenance	
	Low Estimate		High Estimate			
	2013	2012	2013	2012	2013	2012
Asset category:						
Buildings, structures and facilities.....	29.5	31.5	32.3	34.5	99.5	106.3
Furniture, fixtures, and equipment	0.1	0.1	0.1	0.1	2.3	1.3
Other general property, plant, and equipment.........................	5.9	5.3	6.0	5.3	0.9	0.7
Heritage assets	0.8	0.9	0.8	0.8	3.6	1.7
Stewardship land..............................	5.6	5.8	8.1	8.4	-	-
Total deferred maintenance	41.9	43.6	47.3	49.1	106.3	110.0

Please refer to the individual financial statements of DOI, DOD, USDA, DOE, HHS, and VA for detailed significant information on deferred maintenance and repairs, including the standards used for acceptable operating condition and changes in asset condition.

Other Claims for Refunds

Management has estimated amounts that may be paid out as other claims for tax refunds. This estimate represents an amount (principal and interest) that may be paid for claims pending judicial review by the Federal courts or, internally, by appeals. The total estimated payout (including principal and interest) for claims pending judicial review by the Federal courts is $0.8 billion and $6.1 billion for fiscal years 2013 and 2012, respectively. For those under appeal, the estimated payout is $3.5 billion and $5.3 billion for fiscal years 2013 and 2012, respectively. There are also unasserted claims for refunds of certain excise taxes. Although these refund claims have been deemed to be probable, they do not meet the criteria in SFFAS No. 5 for reporting the amounts in the balance sheets or for disclosure in the Notes to the Financial Statements. However, they meet the criteria in SFFAS No. 7 for inclusion as Required Supplementary Information. To the extent judgments against the Government for these claims prompt other similarly situated taxpayers to file similar refund claims, these amounts could become significantly greater.

Tax Assessments

The Government is authorized and required to make inquiries, determinations, and assessments of all taxes that have not been duly paid. Unpaid assessments result from taxpayers filing returns without sufficient payment, as well as enforcement programs such as examination, under-reporter, substitute for return and combined annual wage reporting. Assessments with little or no future collection potential are called write-offs. Although compliance assessments and write-offs are not considered receivables under Federal accounting standards, they represent legally enforceable claims of the Government. There is, however, a significant difference in the collection potential between compliance assessments and receivables.

Compliance assessments and pre-assessment work in process are $87.3 billion and $89.6 billion for fiscal years 2013 and 2012, respectively. The amount of allowance for uncollectible amounts pertaining to compliance assessments cannot be reasonably estimated, and thus the net realizable value of the value of the pre-assessment work-in-process cannot be determined. The amount of assessments that agencies have statutory authority to collect at the end of the period but that have been written off and excluded from accounts receivable are $130.3 billion and $125.1 billion for fiscal years 2013 and 2012, respectively.

Risk Assumed

Risk assumed information is important for all Federal insurance and guarantee programs, except social insurance, life insurance, and loan guarantee programs. Risk assumed is generally measured by the present value of unpaid losses net of associated premiums, based on the risk inherent in the insurance or guarantee coverage in force. In addition to the liability for unpaid insurance claims included in Note 16—Insurance and Guarantee Program Liabilities, for events that have already occurred, the Government also is required to report as supplementary information risk assumed amounts and the periodic changes in those amounts.

The assessments of losses based on the risk assumed are based on actuarial or financial methods that include information and assumptions applicable to the economic, legal, and policy environment in force at the time the assessments are made. Management has estimated the loss amounts based on the risk assumed as well as the periodic changes.

Please refer to the individual financial statements of the PBGC, USDA, and DHS for further detailed information, including information as to the indicators of the range of uncertainty around expected estimates and the indicators of the sensitivity of the estimates to changes in major assumptions. We note that this table does not include all federal insurance and guarantee programs.

Risk Assumed Information as of September 30, 2013, and 2012

(In billions of dollars)	2013	2012
Present value of unpaid losses, net of associated premiums:		
Pension Benefit Guaranty Corporation	328.8	321.7
Department of Agriculture	4.5	18.3
Department of Homeland Security	0.6	0.6
All other	0.5	3.7
Total	334.4	344.3
Period changes in risk assumed amounts:		
Pension Benefit Guaranty Corporation	7.1	71.5
National Credit Union Administration	(3.2)	(4.0)
Department of Agriculture	(13.8)	9.5
Total	(9.9)	77.0

This page is intentionally blank.

Federal Oil and Gas Resources

DOI plays an integral part in the implementation of the President's *Blueprint for a Clean and Secure Energy Future*, designed to build a safe, secure energy future by using cleaner, alternative fuels to power our homes and economies, producing more oil and gas at home, and improving energy efficiency. The DOI is responsible for managing the nation's oil and natural gas resources and the mineral revenues on federal lands, both onshore and on the Outer Continental Shelf. This management process can be broken down into six essential analysis components: pre-leasing, post-leasing and preproduction, production and post-production, revenue collection, fund disbursement, and compliance.

Schedule of Estimated Federal Oil and Gas Petroleum Royalties
Assets Present Values as of September 30, 2013

(In billions of dollars)	Offshore	Onshore	Total
Oil and Lease Condensate...........	36.4	15.0	51.4
Natural Gas, Wet After Lease Separation	4.6	25.8	30.4
Total..	41.0	40.8	81.8

The above table presents the estimated present value of future federal royalty receipts on estimated proved reserves[1] as of September 30, 2013. The federal government's estimated petroleum royalties have as their basis the DOE's Energy Information Administration (EIA) estimates of proved reserves. The EIA provides such estimates directly for federal offshore areas and are adjusted to extract the federal subset of onshore proved reserves. The federal proved reserves were then further adjusted to correspond with the effective date of the actual production for calendar year 2011, the most recently published EAI proved reserves report and then are projected, separately for oil and natural gas, over time to simulate a schedule of when the reserves would be produced. Future royalties are then calculated from these production streams by applying future price estimates by the OMB, and effective royalty rates, adjusted for transportation allowances and other allowable deductions. The valuation method used for gas captures royalties from three products – dry gas, wet gas and natural gas liquids which collectively are reported as natural gas, wet after lease separation. The present value of these royalties are then determined by discounting the revenue stream back to the effective date at a public discount rate assumed to be equal to the OMB's estimates of future 30-Year Treasury Bill rates. The 30-year rate was chosen because this maturity life most closely approximates the productive lives of the proved reserves estimates.

---

[1] Per the EIA, lease condensate is a mixture consisting primarily of pentanes and heavier hydrocarbons which is recovered as a liquid from natural gas in lease separation facilities. This category excludes natural gas plant liquids, such as butane and propane, which are recovered at downstream natural gas processing plants or facilities. Also per the EIA, natural gas, wet after lease separation, is the volume of natural gas remaining after removal of lease condensate in lease and/or field separation facilities, if any, and after exclusion of nonhydrocarbon gases where they occur in sufficient quantity to render the gas unmarketable. Natural gas liquids may be recovered from volume of natural gas, wet after lease separation, at natural gas processing plants (see http://www.eia.gov/dnav/ng/TblDefs/ng_deep_tbldef2.asp).

Estimated Federal Oil and Gas Petroleum Royalties (Proved Reserves)
As of September 30, 2013

Petroleum Category	Quantity (in Millions)	Average Purchase Price ($)	Average Royalty Rate (%)
Oil and Lease Condensate (Bbl):			
Offshore	4,412.1	105.89	13.82
Onshore	1,984.4	89.92	12.11
Total	6,396.5		
Natural Gas, Wet After Lease Separation (Mcf):			
Offshore	8,443.3	4.12	13.66
Onshore	57,563.5	3.94	10.40
Total	66,006.8		

Bbl = barrels
Mcf = 1,000 cubic feet

The table above provides the estimated quantity, and a weighted average purchase price, and a weighted average royalty rate by category of estimated federal petroleum royalties at the end of fiscal year 2013[2]. The estimated quantities, average purchase prices and royalty rates vary by region; the above table reflects an overall weighted average purchase price and royalty rate, and is not presented on a regional basis, but is instead calculated based on regional averages. The prices and royalty rates are based upon historical (or estimated) averages, excluding prior-period adjustments, if any, and are affected by such factors as accounting adjustments and transportation allowances, resulting in effective average prices and royalty rates. Prices are valued at the lease rather than at the market center, and differ from those used to compute the asset estimated present values, which are forecasted and discounted based upon OMB economic assumptions. For further details on federal oil and gas resources, refer to the financial statements of DOI.

---

[2] Gulf of Mexico proved reserves are royalty bearing volumes. In the Gulf of Mexico, an additional 964.8 million bbl of proved oil reserves and 1,798.2 million Mcf of proved gas reserves are not reflected in these totals as they are estimated to be producible royalty free under various royalty relief provisions. The net present value of the royalty value of the royalty free proved reserves volumes in the Gulf of Mexico is estimated to be $8.8 billion.

United States Government
Other Information (Unaudited) For the
Years Ended September 30, 2013, and 2012

Unexpended Budget Balances

The President's budget and Federal budget process largely use obligational accounting–a distinct administrative control through which Federal agencies control, monitor, and report on the status of funds at their disposal. Unexpended budget balances consist of the unobligated and obligated, but unliquidated, budget balances.

Unobligated budget balances, including amounts for trust funds, are the cumulative amount of budget balances that are not obligated and that remain available for obligation. In 1-year accounts, the unobligated balance is not available for new obligations after the end of the fiscal year. In multiyear accounts, the unobligated balance may be carried forward and remains available for obligation for the period specified. In no-year accounts, the unobligated balance is carried forward until specifically rescinded by law or the head of the agency concerned determines that the purposes for which it was provided have been accomplished and disbursements have not been made against the appropriation for two consecutive years. The total unobligated budget balances as of September 30, 2012, and 2011, are $745.2 billion and $829.4 billion, respectively.

Obligated budget balances are the cumulative budget balances that have been obligated but not liquidated. The obligated balance can be carried forward for a maximum of 5 years after the appropriation has expired. The total obligated budget balances as of September 30, 2012, and 2011, are $1442.3 billion and $1,428.5 billion, respectively.

The President's Budget is located at www.whitehouse.gov/omb; unexpended budget balances are shown in the supporting documentation section under "Balances of Budget Authority." The President's Fiscal Year 2014 Budget (issued on April 10, 2013) includes the actual unobligated and obligated amounts for fiscal year 2012. The President's Budget with fiscal year 2013 actual amounts is expected to be published in February 2014.

Tax Burden

The Internal Revenue Code provides for progressive tax rates, whereby higher incomes are generally subject to higher tax rates. The following tables present the latest available information on income tax and related income, deductions, and credit: for individuals by income level, and for corporations by size of assets.

Individual Income Tax Liability for Tax Year 2011

Adjusted Gross Income (AGI)	Number of Taxable Returns (In thousands)	AGI (in millions of dollars)	Total Income Tax (in millions of dollars)	Average AGI Per Return (in whole dollars)	Average Income Tax per Return (in whole dollars)	Income Tax as a Percentage of AGI
Under $15,000	38,456	87,540	2,304	2,276	60	2.6%
$15,000 under $30,000	31,078	682,619	19,113	21,965	615	2.8%
$30,000 under $50,000	25,504	996,783	55,287	39,083	2,168	5.5%
$50,000 under $100,000	30,876	2,197,423	189,342	71,169	6,132	8.6%
$100,000 under $200,000	14,756	1,977,406	248,968	134,007	16,872	12.6%
$200,000 under $500,000	3,802	1,080,932	212,403	284,306	55,866	19.6%
$500,000 or more	898	1,351,440	318,094	1,504,944	354,225	23.5%
Total	145,370	8,374,143	1,045,511			

Corporation Income Tax Liability for Tax Year 2010

Total Assets (In thousands of dollars)	Income Subject to Tax (in millions of dollars)	Total Income Tax After Credits (in millions of dollars)	Percentage of Income Tax After Credits to Taxable Income
Zero Assets	15,068	4,789	31.8%
$1 under $500	6,167	1,178	19.1%
$500 under $1,000	3,231	741	22.9%
$1,000 under $5,000	10,274	2,970	28.9%
$5,000 under $10,000	6,890	2,162	31.4%
$10,000 under $25,000	10,312	3,358	32.6%
$25,000 under $50,000	9,900	3,175	32.1%
$50,000 under $100,000	12,955	4,150	32.0%
$100,000 under $250,000	23,640	7,143	30.2%
$250,000 under $500,000	29,057	8,732	30.1%
$500,000 under $2,500,000	109,072	30,770	28.2%
$2,500,000 or more	785,609	153,801	19.6%
Total	1,022,175	222,969	

Tax Gap

The tax gap is the difference between what taxpayers should pay and what they actually pay due to not filing tax returns, not paying their reported tax liability on time, or failing to report their correct tax liability. The tax gap, about $450.0 billion based on updated fiscal year 2006 estimates, represents the amount of noncompliance with the tax laws. Underreporting of income tax, employment taxes, and other taxes represents 84 percent of the gross tax gap. The IRS remains committed to finding ways to increase compliance and reduce the tax gap, while minimizing the burden on the vast majority of taxpayers who pay their taxes accurately and on time.

The tax gap is the aggregate amount of tax (i.e., excluding interest and penalties) that is imposed by the tax laws for any given tax year but is not paid voluntarily and timely. The tax gap arises from three types of noncompliance: not filing required tax returns on time or at all (the nonfiling gap), underreporting the correct amount of tax on timely filed returns (the underreporting gap), and not paying on time the full amount reported on timely filed returns (the underpayment gap). Of these three components, only the underpayment gap is observed; the nonfiling gap and the underreporting gap must be estimated. Each instance of noncompliance by a taxpayer contributes to the tax gap, whether or not the IRS detects it, and whether or not the taxpayer is even aware of the noncompliance. Obviously, some of the tax gap arises from intentional (willful) noncompliance, and some of it arises from unintentional mistakes.

The collection gap is the cumulative amount of assessed tax, penalties, and interest that has been assessed over many years, but has not been paid by a certain point in time and which the IRS expects to remain uncollectible. In essence, it represents the difference between the total balance of unpaid assessments and the net taxes receivable reported on the IRS' balance sheet. The tax gap and the collection gap are related and overlapping concepts, but they have significant differences. The collection gap is a cumulative balance sheet concept for a particular point in time, while the tax gap is like an income statement item for a single year. Moreover, the tax gap estimates include all noncompliance, while the collection gap includes only amounts that have been assessed (a small portion of all noncompliance).

Unmatched Transactions and Balances

(in millions of dollars)	Fiscal Year 2013	Fiscal Year 2012
Change in intragovernmental unmatched balances:		
Debt/investment	5.5	(0.5)
Interest payable/receivable	4.9	(6.5)
Loans payable/receivable	(9.0)	17.6
Benefit program contributions payable/receivable	(207.3)	160.8
Accounts payable/receivable	831.2	(1,267.5)
Advances from/to others & deferred credits/prepayments	506.6	97.2
Transfers payable/receivable	(178.7)	134.6
	953.2	(864.3)
Unmatched intragovernmental transactions:		
Federal securities interest revenue/expense—investment exchange	8.8	6.5
Borrowings interest revenue/expense-exchange	9.4	71.3
Borrowings gains/losses	(19.7)	9.3
Nonexpenditure transfers-in/out	123.1	35.9
Expenditure transfers-in/out	110.3	122.8
Transfers-in/out without reimbursement	(537.2)	(1,013.2)
Imputed financing source/cost	(25.7)	(17.8)
Benefit program revenue/cost	(240.1)	(725.2)
	(571.1)	(1,510.4)
General fund transactions:		
Fund balance with Treasury	(2,935.2)	5,656.4
Appropriations of unavailable special or trust fund receipts—transfers-out/in	(48.0)	(50.9)
Appropriations received/warrants issued	19,010.9	2,361.2
Other taxes and receipts/trust fund warrants	(16,672.0)	3,588.0
Custodial and non-entity collections transferred out/in	19,767.2	(54,161.4)
Other General Fund transactions	(29,326.9)	65,725.2
	(10,204.0)	23,118.5
Net intra-agency reporting errors and restatements	801.6	(568.4)
Unmatched transactions and balances, net	(9,020.3)	20,175.4

( ) Parentheses indicate a decrease to Net Position.

The Statement of Operations and Changes in Net Position includes an amount for unmatched transactions and balances that result from the consolidation of Federal reporting entities. Transactions between Federal entities must be eliminated in consolidation to calculate the financial position of the Government. Many of the amounts included in the table represent intragovernmental activity and balances that differed between Federal agency trading partners and often totaled significantly more in the absolute than the net amounts shown. In addition, included in the "General Fund Transactions" section are certain intragovernmental accounts, primarily related to agency unreconciled transactions with the General Fund. The table also reflects other consolidating adjustments and other adjustments that contributed to the unmatched transactions and balances amount.

Unmatched transactions and balances between Federal entities impact not only in the period in which differences originate but also in the periods where differences are reconciled. As a result, it would not be proper to conclude that increases or decreases in the unmatched amounts shown in the "Unmatched Transactions and Balances" table reflect improvements or deteriorations in the Government's ability to reconcile intragovernmental transactions. The Federal community considers the identification and accurate reporting of intragovernmental activity a priority.

This page is intentionally blank.

United States Government Required Supplementary Stewardship Information (Unaudited) for the Years Ended September 30, 2013, and 2012

Stewardship Investments

Stewardship investments focus on Government programs aimed at providing long-term benefits by improving the Nation's productivity and enhancing economic growth. These investments can be provided through direct Federal spending or grants to State and local governments for certain education and training programs, research and development, and federally financed but not federally owned property, such as bridges and roads. When incurred, these investments are included as expenses in determining the net cost of operations. Stewardship investments for the current year and for the immediately preceding 4 years are shown below in Table 11.

Table 11
Stewardship Investments for the Years Ended
September 30, 2009, through 2013

(In billions of dollars)	Fiscal Year 2013	Fiscal Year 2012	Fiscal Year 2011	Fiscal Year 2010	Fiscal Year 2009
Investment in non-Federal Physical property	66.1	68.1	69.9	66.7	65.1
Investments in human capital	58.7	87.1	91.9	122.3	60.3
Research and development:					
Investments in basic research	35.2	34.2	35.7	31.5	27.4
Investments in applied research	28.0	29.1	28.8	26.2	19.1
Investments in development	64.1	67.0	71.7	77.3	101.0
Total investments	252.1	285.5	298.0	324.0	272.9

Non-Federal Physical Property

The Government makes grants and provides funds for the purchase, construction, and/or major renovation of State and local government physical properties. Costs for non-Federal physical property programs are included as expenses in the Statements of Net Cost and are reported as investments in Table 11. They are measured on the same accrual basis of accounting used in the *Financial Report* statements. DOT, HUD, and EPA had $56 billion (85 percent), $3.7 billion (6 percent), and $3.7 billion (6 percent), respectively, of the total non-Federal physical property investments in fiscal year 2013 as shown in Table 11. Within DOT, the Federal Highway Administration invested $42.1 billion during fiscal year 2013, primarily via reimbursement from the Highway Trust Fund, for States' construction costs of interstate and national highways. The States' contribution is 10 percent for the Interstate System and 20 percent for most other programs.

Human Capital

The Government runs several programs that invest in human capital. Those investments go toward increasing and maintaining a healthy economy by educating and training the general public. Costs do not include training expenses for Federal workers.

Education, VA, and DOL had $33.4 billion (57 percent), $13.2 billion (22 percent), and $6.4 billion (11 percent), respectively, of the total human capital investments in fiscal year 2013 as shown in Table 11. In comparison over the past five years, Education had a decrease in human capital investments in fiscal year 2013 due to a significant decrease in direct loan subsidies related to its Federal Student Aid Expense. Prior to that, Education had an increase in human capital investments in fiscal year 2010, due to an increase in the net cost for the Federal Family Education Loan, Direct Loan, Grant Programs, and Other Programs, including the *American Recovery and Reinvestment Act of 2009*; while VA increased in fiscal years 2009 through 2012 due to implementation of the Post 9/11 GI Bill. Education administers a wide variety of programs related to general public education and training programs that are intended to increase or maintain national economic productive capacity. The Office of Federal Student Aid administers need-based financial assistance programs for students pursuing postsecondary education and makes available Federal grants, direct loans, and work-study funding to eligible undergraduate and graduate students.

The significant human capital programs administered by DOL relate to grants for job training and employment programs. The significant human capital programs administered by VA also relate to grants for job training and rehabilitation programs for veterans.

Research and Development

Federal investments in Research and Development (R&D) comprise those expenses for basic research, applied research, and development that are intended to increase or maintain national economic productive capacity or yield other future benefits.

- Investments in basic research are for systematic studies to gain knowledge or understanding of the fundamental aspects of phenomena and of observable facts without specific applications toward processes or products in mind.
- Investments in applied research are for systematic studies to gain knowledge or understanding necessary for determining the means by which a recognized and specific need may be met.
- Investments in development are the systematic use of the knowledge and understanding gained from research for the production of useful materials, devices, systems, or methods, including the design and development of prototypes and processes.

With regard to basic and applied research, HHS had $18.1 billion (51 percent) and $12 billion (43 percent), of the total basic and applied research investments, respectively, in fiscal year 2013 as shown in Table 11. HHS also had similar R&D investment amounts (and percentage contributions) in each of the preceding four years.

Within HHS, the National Institutes of Health (NIH) conducts almost all (97 percent) of the Department's basic and applied research. The NIH Research Program includes all aspects of the medical research continuum, including basic and disease-oriented research, observational and population-based research, behavioral research, and clinical research, including research to understand both health and disease states, to move laboratory findings into medical applications, to assess new treatments or compare different treatment approaches; and health services research.

The NIH regards the expeditious transfer of the results of its medical research for further development and commercialization of products of immediate benefit to improved health as an important mandate.

With regard to development, the DOD and NASA had $56 billion (87 percent) and $5.2 billion (8 percent), respectively, of total development investments in fiscal year 2013, as shown in Table 11. Development is comprised of five stages: advanced technology development, advanced component development and prototypes, system development and demonstration, management support, and operational systems development. Major outputs of DOD development are:

- Hardware and software components, and complete weapon systems ready for operational and developmental testing and field use, and
- Weapon systems finalized for complete operational and developmental testing.

NASA development includes activities to extend the knowledge of Earth, its space environment, and the universe, and to invest in new aeronautics and advanced space transportation technologies that support the development and application of technologies critical to the economic, scientific, and technical competitiveness of the United States.

This page is intentionally blank.

Appendix A: Reporting Entity

This appendix lists the organizations and agencies encompassed in the reporting entity for this publication as well as some organizations excluded from the reporting entity. The reporting entity is a specifically defined group of agencies, principally Cabinet departments and other agencies of the executive branch, as stated in the law and accounting guidance.

The determination as to which organizations and agencies will be included in the reporting entity is governed by Federal laws and is also based on guidance issued by the Federal Accounting Standards Advisory Board (FASAB) in their Statement of Federal Financial Accounting Concept No. 2, *Entity and Display*, which provides criteria for determining what should be included in the reporting entity for a consolidated Governmentwide report. FASAB is now considering more specific guidance on the reporting entity for this report.

There are a total of 154 organizations and agencies included in the *Financial Report of the United States Government*. The lists below describe three groups of entity/fund types that comprise the reporting entity for the *Financial Report* and include entities from all three branches of Government.

Twenty-Four Chief Financial Officer Act Agencies

Department of Agriculture
www.usda.gov
Department of Commerce
www.doc.gov
Department of Defense
www.defense.gov
Department of Education
www.ed.gov
Department of Energy
www.doe.gov
Department of Health and Human Services
www hhs.gov
Department of Homeland Security
www.dhs.gov
Department of Housing and Urban Development
www hud.gov
Department of the Interior
www.doi.gov
Department of Justice
www.usdoj.gov
Department of Labor
www.dol.gov
Department of State
www.state.gov

Department of Transportation
www.dot.gov
Department of the Treasury
www.treasury.gov
Department of Veterans Affairs
www.va.gov
Environmental Protection Agency
www.epa.gov
General Services Administration
www.gsa.gov
National Aeronautics and Space Administration
www nasa.gov
National Science Foundation
www.nsf.gov
Office of Personnel Management
www.opm.gov
Small Business Administration
www.sba.gov
Social Security Administration
www.ssa.gov
U.S. Agency for International Development
www.usaid.gov
U.S. Nuclear Regulatory Commission
www.nrc.gov

Eleven Additional Significant Entities

Export-Import Bank of the United States
     www.exim.gov
Farm Credit System Insurance Corporation
     www fcsic.gov
Federal Communications Commission
     www fcc.gov
Federal Deposit Insurance Corporation
     www fdic.gov
National Credit Union Administration
     www.ncua.gov
Pension Benefit Guaranty Corporation
     www.pbgc.gov

Railroad Retirement Board
     www.rrb.gov
Securities and Exchange Commission
     www.sec.gov
Smithsonian Institution
     www.si.edu
Tennessee Valley Authority
     www.tva.gov
U.S. Postal Service
     www.usps.gov

One Hundred Nineteen Additional Entities/Funds

Abraham Lincoln Bicentennial Commission*
Administrative Conference of the United States
Advisory Council on Historic Preservation
African Development Foundation
American Battle Monuments Commission
Antitrust Modernization Commission*
Appalachian Regional Commission
Architect of the Capitol
Architectural and Transportation Barriers Compliance
  Board
Armed Forces Retirement Home
Barry Goldwater Scholarship and Excellence in
  Education Foundation
Broadcasting Board of Governors
Bureau of Consumer Financial Protection
Central Intelligence Agency
Chemical Safety Hazard Investigation Board
Christopher Columbus Fellowship Foundation
Commission for the Preservation of America's
  Heritage Abroad
Commission of Fine Arts
Commission on Civil Rights
Commission on International Religious Freedom
Commission on Security and Cooperation in Europe
Commission on Weapons of Mass Destruction*
Committee for Purchase from People Who Are Blind
  or Severely Disabled
Commodity Futures Trading Commission
Congressional Budget Office
Congressional-Executive Commission on the People's
  Republic of China
Consumer Product Safety Commission
Corporation for National and Community Service
Council of the Inspectors General on Integrity and
  Efficiency
Court of Appeals for Veterans Claims
Court Services and Offender Supervision Agency
  for DC

DC Courts
DC Courts–Defender Services
Defense Nuclear Facilities Safety Board
Delta Regional Authority
Denali Commission
Dwight D. Eisenhower Memorial Commission
Election Assistance Commission
Environmental Dispute Resolution Fund
Equal Employment Opportunity Commission
Executive Office of the President
Farm Credit Administration
Federal Election Commission
Federal Financial Institutions Examination Council
  Appraisal Subcommittee
Federal Housing Finance Agency
Federal Labor Relations Authority
Federal Maritime Commission
Federal Mediation and Conciliation Service
Federal Mine Safety and Health Review Commission
Federal Retirement Thrift Investment Board
Federal Trade Commission
Financial Crisis Inquiry Commission*
Foreign Military Financing Program
Foreign Military Sales Program
Government Accountability Office
Government Printing Office
Gulf Coast Ecosystem Restoration Council
Harry S. Truman Scholarship Trust Fund
Indian Law and Order Commission
Institute of Museum and Library Services
Interagency Council on the Homeless
Inter-American Foundation
International Trade Commission
James Madison Memorial Fellowship Foundation
Japan-United States Friendship Commission
John C. Stennis Center
John F. Kennedy Center for the Performing Arts
Library of Congress

Marine Mammal Commission
Medicaid and Children's Health Insurance Program
  Payment and Access Commission
Medicare Payment Advisory Commission
Merit Systems Protection Board
Military Compensation and Retirement Modernization
  Commission
Millennium Challenge Corporation
Morris K. Udall Scholarship Foundation
National Archives and Records Administration
National Capital Planning Commission
National Commission on Libraries and Information
  Science*
National Council on Disability
National Endowment for the Arts
National Endowment for the Humanities
National Gallery of Art
National Labor Relations Board
National Mediation Board
National Railroad Passenger Corporation, Office of the
  Inspector General
National Railroad Retirement Investment Trust
National Transportation Safety Board
Neighborhood Reinvestment Corporation
Northern Border Regional Commission
Nuclear Waste Technical Review Board
Occupational Safety and Health Review Commission
Office of Compliance

Office of Government Ethics
Office of Navajo and Hopi Indian Relocation
Office of Special Counsel
Office of the Director of National Intelligence
Office of the Federal Coordination for Alaska Natural
  Gas Transportation Projects
Office of the Nuclear Waste Negotiator*
Open World Leadership Center
Overseas Private Investment Corporation
Patient Centered Outcomes Research Trust Fund
Peace Corps
Presidio Trust
Privacy and Civil Liberties Oversight Board
Public Defender Service
Ronald Reagan Centennial Commission
Recovery Act Accountability and Transparency Board
Selective Service System
Senate Preservation Fund
St. Lawrence Seaway Development Corporation
State Justice Institute
U.S. Capital Preservation Commission
U.S. China Security Review Commission
U.S. Holocaust Memorial Museum
U.S. Institute of Peace
U.S. Trade and Development Agency
Vietnam Education Foundation
Woodrow Wilson International Center for Scholars
WWI Centennial Commission

*These entities are no longer active and have either returned all remaining fund balances to Treasury during fiscal year 2013 or have remaining fund balances pending final return to Treasury as of September 30, 2013.

Legislative and Judicial Branches

There are no legal or other requirements for the legislative or judicial branches to prepare consolidated audited financial statements or to provide accrual-based accounting data for inclusion in the Governmentwide financial statements. Therefore, these consolidated statements do not include accrual-based accounting data for such entities as the U.S. Courts or the Congress. Some legislative branch entities voluntarily prepare and submit such information (e.g., Government Accountability Office, Government Printing Office, and Library of Congress). In addition to the 154 entities, the FR includes cash-based outlay data for the remainder of the legislative and judicial branches.

Entities Excluded from These Statements

The following entities are not part of the Governmentwide reporting entity based on an assessment of these entities in accordance with the indicative criteria stated in SFFAC No. 2, Entity and Display. However, this list is not all inclusive of all entities excluded from these statements.

Board of Governors of the Federal Reserve System
  (Including the Federal Reserve Banks)
Federal Home Loan Banks
Federal Home Loan Mortgage Corporation
  (Freddie Mac)
Federal National Mortgage Association (Fannie Mae)
Thrift Savings Fund

The Financing Corporation
National Railroad Passenger Corporation
  (does business as Amtrak)
Public-Private Investment Funds
Resolution Funding Corporation
Student Loan Marketing Association

This page is intentionally blank.

Appendix B: Acronyms

This appendix lists the acronyms used in the Financial Statements and Notes to the Financial Statements section of this *Financial Report*.

ABS	Asset-Backed Securities
ACA	Affordable Care Act
ACH	Automated Clearinghouse
AIG	American International Group, Inc.
AMT	Alternative Minimum Tax
ARRA	American Recovery and Reinvestment Act of 2009
ASC	Accounting Standards Codification
ATRA	American Taxpayer Relief Act of 2012
BLDTF	Black Lung Disability Trust Fund
CCC	Commodity Credit Corporation
CDCI	Community Development Capital Initiative
CERCLA	Comprehensive Environmental Response, Compensation, and Liability Act
CMS	Centers for Medicare and Medicaid Services
COLA	Cost of Living Adjustments
CPI	Consumer Price Index
CPIM	Consumer Price Index–Medical
CPP	Capital Purchase Program
CSRDF	Civil Service Retirement and Disability Fund
CSRS	Civil Service Retirement System
DHS	Department of Homeland Security
DI	Disability Insurance
DIF	Deposit Insurance Fund
DIP	Debtor in Possession
DOC	Department of Commerce
DOD	Department of Defense
DOE	Department of Energy
DOI	Department of the Interior
DOJ	Department of Justice
DOL	Department of Labor
DOT	Department of Transportation
Education	Department of Education
EESA	Emergency Economic Stabilization Act of 2008
EPA	Environmental Protection Agency
EOP	Executive Office of the President
ESF	Exchange Stabilization Fund
EUC	Unemployment Account

EUCA	Emergency Unemployment Compensation Account
Ex-Im Bank	Export-Import Bank
FAA	Federal Aviation Administration
Fannie Mae	Federal National Mortgage Association
FASAB	Federal Accounting Standards Advisory Board
FCC	Federal Communications Commission
FCRA	Federal Credit Reform Act of 1991
FDIC	Federal Deposit Insurance Corporation
FECA	Federal Employees' Compensation Act
FEGLI	Federal Employees' Group Life Insurance
FEHB	Federal Employees Health Benefits Program
FERS	Federal Employees Retirement System
FERSA	Federal Employees' Retirement System Act of 1986
FFAS	Farm and Foreign Agricultural Services
FFEL	Federal Family Education Loan
FHA	Federal Housing Administration
FHFA	Federal Housing Financing Agency
FHWA	Federal Highway Administration
FICA	Federal Insurance Contribution Act
FOMC	Federal Open Market Committee
FR System	Federal Reserve System
FRBNY	Federal Reserve Bank of New York
FRBs	Federal Reserve Banks
Freddie Mac	Federal Home Loan Mortgage Corporation
FRTIB	Federal Retirement Thrift Investment Board
FSA	Farm Service Agency
FUA	Federal Unemployment Account
FUTA	Federal Unemployment Tax Act
GAAP	U.S. Generally Accepted Accounting Principles
GAO	U.S. Government Accountability Office
GDP	Gross Domestic Product
Ginnie Mae	Government National Mortgage Association
GM	General Motors
GSA	General Services Administration
GSE	Government-Sponsored Enterprises
HBP	Health Benefits Program
HEA	Higher Education Act of 1965
HERA	Housing and Economic Recovery Act of 2008
HFA	Housing Financing Agencies
HHS	Department of Health and Human Services
HI	Hospital Insurance
HUD	Department of Housing and Urban Development

IMF	International Monetary Fund
IRS	Internal Revenue Service
LAC	Latest Acquisition Cost
MAC	Moving Average Cost
MBS	Mortgage-Backed Securities
MDBs	Multilateral Development Banks
MERHCF	Medicare Eligible Retiree Health Care Fund
MMA	Medicare Prescription Drug, Improvement, and Modernization Act
MRF	Military Retirement Fund
NAB	New Arrangement to Borrow
NASA	National Aeronautics and Space Administration
NCUA	National Credit Union Administration
NIH	National Institutes of Health
NRRIT	National Railroad Retirement Investment Trust
NSLI	National Service Life Insurance
NTIA	National Telecommunications and Information Administration
NYSE	New York Stock Exchange
OASDI	Old-Age, Survivors, and Disability Insurance
OASI	Old-Age and Survivors Insurance
OMB	Office of Management and Budget
OPEB	Other Postemployment Benefits
OPM	Office of Personnel Management
ORB	Other Retirement Benefits
PBGC	Pension Benefit Guaranty Corporation
PCF	Periodic Commitment Fee
PEFCO	Private Export Funding Corporation
PMAs	Power Marketing Authorities
PP&E	Property, Plant, and Equipment
PPIF	Public Private Investment Funds
PPIP	Public Private Investment Program
PPO	Preferred Provider Organization
PSRHB	Postal Service Retiree Health Benefits
QFI	Qualified Financial Institution
R&D	Research and Development
RCRA	Resource Conservation and Recovery Act
RD	Rural Development
REDUX	Military Retirement Reform Act of 1986
RRB	Railroad Retirement Board
RRSIA	Railroad Retirement and Survivors Improvement Act
RSI	Required Supplementary Information
SAFETEA-LU	Safe, Accountable, Flexible, Efficient Transportation Equity Act: A Legacy for Users

SAFRA	Student Aid and Fiscal Responsibility Act
Sallie Mae	Student Loan Marketing Association
SBA	Small Business Administration
SCSIA	Statement of Changes in Social Insurance Amounts
SDRs	Special Drawing Rights
SDRCs	SDR Certificates
SEC	Securities and Exchange Commission
SECA	Self-Employment Contributions Act
SFFAC	Statement of Federal Financial Accounting Concept
SFFAS	Statement of Federal Financial Accounting Standards
SFP	Supplementary Financing Program
SLMA	Student Loan Marketing Association
SMI	Supplementary Medical Insurance
SOMA	System Open Market Account
SOSI	Statement of Social Insurance
SPSPA	Senior Preferred Stock Purchase Agreements
SSA	Social Security Administration
SSEB	Social Security Equivalent Benefit
TALF	Term Asset-Backed Loan Facility
TARP	Troubled Asset Relief Program
TFL	TRICARE for Life
TIP	Targeted Investment Program
TIPS	Treasury Inflation-Protected Securities
TPTCCA	Temporary Payroll Tax Cut Continuation Act of 2011
Treasury	Department of the Treasury
TRIA	Terrorism Risk Insurance Act
TSP	Thrift Savings Plan
TVA	Tennessee Valley Authority
TVARS	Tennessee Valley Authority Retirement System
U.S.C.	United States Code
USDA	United States Department of Agriculture
USPS	United States Postal Service
UTF	Unemployment Trust Fund
VA	Department of Veterans Affairs
VRI	Veterans Reopened Insurance
VSLI	Veterans Special Life Insurance

This page is intentionally blank.

 U.S. GOVERNMENT ACCOUNTABILITY OFFICE

441 G St. N.W.
Washington, DC 20548

Independent Auditor's Report

The President
The President of the Senate
The Speaker of the House of Representatives

In our audits of the U.S. government's consolidated financial statements as of and for the fiscal years ended September 30, 2013, and 2012, we found the following:

- Certain material weaknesses[1] in internal control over financial reporting and other limitations on the scope of our work resulted in conditions that continued to prevent us from expressing an opinion on the accompanying accrual-based consolidated financial statements[2] as of and for the fiscal years ended September 30, 2013, and 2012.[3]

- Significant uncertainties (discussed in Note 24 to the consolidated financial statements), primarily related to the achievement of projected reductions in Medicare cost growth reflected in the 2013, 2012, 2011, and 2010 Statements of Social Insurance, prevented us from expressing an opinion on those statements as well as on the 2013 and 2012 Statements of Changes in Social Insurance Amounts. The Statement of Social Insurance for 2009 is presented fairly, in all material respects, in accordance with U.S. generally accepted accounting principles.[4]

- Material weaknesses resulted in ineffective internal control over financial reporting for fiscal year 2013.

---

[1]A material weakness is a deficiency, or combination of deficiencies, in internal control over financial reporting, such that there is a reasonable possibility that a material misstatement of the entity's financial statements will not be prevented, or detected and corrected, on a timely basis. A deficiency in internal control exists when the design or operation of a control does not allow management or employees, in the normal course of performing their assigned functions, to prevent, or detect and correct, misstatements on a timely basis.

[2]The accrual-based consolidated financial statements as of and for the fiscal years ended September 30, 2013, and 2012, consist of the (1) Statements of Net Cost, (2) Statements of Operations and Changes in Net Position, (3) Reconciliations of Net Operating Cost and Unified Budget Deficit, (4) Statements of Changes in Cash Balance from Unified Budget and Other Activities, and (5) Balance Sheets, including the related notes to these financial statements. Most revenues are recorded on a modified cash basis. The 2013, 2012, 2011, 2010, and 2009 Statements of Social Insurance and the 2013 and 2012 Statements of Changes in Social Insurance Amounts, including the related notes, are also included in the consolidated financial statements.

[3]We previously reported that certain material weaknesses and, for some years, other limitations on the scope of our work prevented us from expressing an opinion on the accrual-based consolidated financial statements of the U.S. government for fiscal years 1997 through 2012.

[4]Statements of Social Insurance are presented for the current year and each of the 4 preceding years in accordance with U.S. generally accepted accounting principles. Also, both the Statements of Social Insurance and the Statements of Changes in Social Insurance Amounts do not interrelate with the accrual-based consolidated financial statements. In addition, the valuation date is January 1 for all social insurance programs except the Black Lung program, which has a valuation date of September 30.

- Our tests of compliance with selected provisions of applicable laws, regulations, contracts, and grant agreements for fiscal year 2013 were limited by the material weaknesses and other scope limitations discussed in this audit report.

The following sections discuss in more detail (1) our report on the accompanying consolidated financial statements, which includes (a) two emphasis of matters—equity investments related to the federal government's actions to stabilize financial markets and to promote economic recovery, and long-term fiscal challenges, (b) required supplementary information (RSI), required supplementary stewardship information (RSSI), and other information included with the consolidated financial statements in the *Fiscal Year 2013 Financial Report of the United States Government* (*2013 Financial Report*), and (c) information on Chief Financial Officers (CFO) Act agency financial management systems; (2) our report on internal control over financial reporting; (3) our report on compliance with laws, regulations, contracts, and grant agreements; and (4) the Department of the Treasury's (Treasury) and the Office of Management and Budget's (OMB) comments on a draft of this audit report. Appendix I discusses the objectives, scope, and methodology of our work.

Report on the Consolidated Financial Statements

The Secretary of the Treasury, in coordination with the Director of OMB, is required to annually submit audited financial statements for the U.S. government to the President and Congress. GAO is required to audit these statements.[5] As noted above, the consolidated financial statements are comprised of the accrual-based consolidated financial statements as of and for the fiscal years ended September 30, 2013, and 2012; the 2013, 2012, 2011, 2010, and 2009 Statements of Social Insurance; the 2013 and 2012 Statements of Changes in Social Insurance Amounts; and the related notes to the financial statements.

We performed sufficient audit work to provide this report on the consolidated financial statements. We considered the limitations on the scope of our work regarding the accrual-based consolidated financial statements; the 2013, 2012, 2011, and 2010 Statements of Social Insurance; and the 2013 and 2012 Statements of Changes in Social Insurance Amounts in forming our conclusions. We believe that the audit evidence we obtained is sufficient and appropriate to provide a basis for our audit opinion on the 2009 Statement of Social Insurance. Our work was performed in accordance with U.S. generally accepted government auditing standards.

Management's Responsibility

Management of the federal government is responsible for (1) the preparation and fair presentation of annual consolidated financial statements of the U.S. government in accordance with U.S. generally accepted accounting principles; (2) preparing, measuring, and presenting the RSI and RSSI in accordance with U.S. generally accepted accounting principles; and (3) preparing and presenting other information included in documents containing the consolidated financial statements and auditor's report, and ensuring the consistency of that information with the consolidated financial statements, RSI, and RSSI. This includes maintaining effective internal control over financial reporting, including the design, implementation, and maintenance of internal control relevant to the preparation and fair presentation of financial statements that are free from material misstatement, whether due to fraud or error.

---

[5]The Government Management Reform Act of 1994 has required such reporting, covering the executive branch of government, beginning with financial statements prepared for fiscal year 1997. 31 U.S.C. § 331(e). Treasury and OMB have elected to include certain financial information on the legislative and judicial branches in the consolidated financial statements as well.

Auditor's Responsibility

Our responsibility is to express opinions on these consolidated financial statements based on conducting the audit in accordance with U.S. generally accepted government auditing standards. We are also responsible for applying certain limited procedures to the RSI, RSSI, and other information included with the consolidated financial statements. Because of the matters discussed below, we were unable to obtain sufficient appropriate evidence to provide a basis for audit opinions on the consolidated financial statements, except for the 2009 Statement of Social Insurance.

For the 2009 Statement of Social Insurance, our responsibility is to express an opinion on this statement based on our audit. U.S. generally accepted government auditing standards require that we plan and perform the audit to obtain reasonable assurance about whether this financial statement is free from material misstatement.

Basis for Disclaimers of Opinion on the Consolidated Financial Statements, Except for the 2009 Statement of Social Insurance

Accrual-Based Consolidated Financial Statements as of and for the Fiscal Years Ended September 30, 2013, and 2012

The federal government is not able to demonstrate the reliability of significant portions of the accompanying accrual-based consolidated financial statements as of and for the fiscal years ended September 30, 2013, and 2012, principally resulting from limitations related to certain material weaknesses in internal control over financial reporting and other limitations affecting the reliability of these financial statements and the scope of our work as discussed below. As a result of these limitations, readers are cautioned that amounts reported in the accrual-based consolidated financial statements and related notes may not be reliable.

The federal government did not maintain adequate systems or have sufficient appropriate evidence to support certain material information reported in the accompanying accrual-based consolidated financial statements. The underlying material weaknesses in internal control, which have existed for years, contributed to our disclaimer of opinion on the accrual-based consolidated financial statements. Specifically, these weaknesses concerned the federal government's inability to

- satisfactorily determine that property, plant, and equipment and inventories and related property, primarily held by the Department of Defense (DOD), were properly reported in the accrual-based consolidated financial statements;

- reasonably estimate or adequately support amounts reported for certain liabilities, such as environmental and disposal liabilities, or determine whether commitments and contingencies were complete and properly reported;

- support significant portions of the reported total net cost of operations, most notably related to DOD, and adequately reconcile disbursement activity at certain federal entities;

- adequately account for and reconcile intragovernmental activity and balances between federal entities;

- ensure that the federal government's accrual-based consolidated financial statements were (1) consistent with the underlying audited entities' financial statements, (2) properly balanced, and (3) in accordance with U.S. generally accepted accounting principles; and

- ensure the consistency of (1) information used by Treasury to compute the budget deficit reported in the consolidated financial statements, (2) Treasury's records of cash transactions, and (3) information reported in federal entity financial statements and underlying financial information and records.

These material weaknesses continued to (1) hamper the federal government's ability to reliably report a significant portion of its assets, liabilities, costs, and other related information; (2) affect the federal government's ability to reliably measure the full cost as well as the financial and nonfinancial performance of certain programs and activities; (3) impair the federal government's ability to adequately safeguard significant assets and properly record various transactions; and (4) hinder the federal government from having reliable financial information to operate in an efficient and effective manner. Due to these material weaknesses and to other limitations on the scope of our work discussed below, additional issues may exist that could affect the accrual-based consolidated financial statements that were not identified. Appendix II describes these material weaknesses in more detail and highlights the primary effects of these material weaknesses on the accompanying accrual-based consolidated financial statements and on the management of federal government operations.

Statements of Social Insurance for 2013, 2012, 2011, and 2010 and the Statements of Changes in Social Insurance Amounts for 2013 and 2012

Significant uncertainties (discussed in Note 24 to the consolidated financial statements), that primarily relate to the achievement of projected reductions in Medicare cost growth, affect the 2013, 2012, 2011, and 2010 Statements of Social Insurance. As a result of these significant uncertainties, readers are cautioned that amounts reported in the 2013, 2012, 2011, and 2010 Statements of Social Insurance, the 2013 and 2012 Statements of Changes in Social Insurance Amounts, and the related notes to such financial statements may not fairly present, in all material respects, the financial condition and changes in the financial condition of the federal government's social insurance programs for those years, in accordance with U.S. generally accepted accounting principles.

These significant uncertainties include the following.

- Medicare projections in the 2013, 2012, 2011, and 2010 Statements of Social Insurance were based on benefit formulas in current law and included a significant decrease in projected Medicare costs from the 2009 Statement of Social Insurance related to (1) reductions in Medicare payment rates for physician services (totaling almost 25 percent in January 2014, as estimated in the 2013 Medicare Trustees Report) and (2) productivity improvements for most other categories of Medicare providers, based on full implementation of the provisions of the Patient Protection and Affordable Care Act, as amended (PPACA).[6] However, there are significant uncertainties concerning the achievement of these projected decreases in Medicare costs.

- Management has noted that actual future costs for Medicare are likely to exceed those shown by the current-law projections presented in the 2013, 2012, 2011, and 2010 Statements of Social Insurance due, for example, to the likelihood of modifications to the scheduled reductions in

---

[6]PPACA, Pub. L. No. 111-148, 124 Stat. 119 (Mar. 23, 2010), as amended by the Health Care and Education Reconciliation Act of 2010, Pub. L. No. 111-152, 124 Stat. 1029 (Mar. 30, 2010).

Medicare payment rates for physician services.[7] The extent to which actual future costs exceed the projected current-law amounts due to changes to the scheduled reductions in Medicare payment rates for physician services and productivity adjustments depends on both the specific changes that might be legislated and whether such legislation would include further provisions to help offset such costs.

- Management has developed an illustrative alternative projection intended to provide additional context regarding the long-term sustainability of the Medicare program and to illustrate the uncertainties in the Statement of Social Insurance projections. The present value of future estimated expenditures in excess of future estimated revenue for Medicare, included in the illustrative alternative projection, exceeds the $27.3 trillion estimate in the 2013 Statement of Social Insurance by $8.9 trillion.

Projections of Medicare costs are sensitive to assumptions about future decisions by policymakers and about the behavioral responses of consumers, employers, and health care providers as policy, incentives, and the health care sector change over time. Such secondary impacts are not fully reflected in the Statement of Social Insurance projections but could be expected to influence the excess cost growth rate used in the projections.[8] Key drivers of uncertainty about the excess cost growth rate include the future development and deployment of medical technology, the evolution of personal income, and the cost and availability of insurance, as well as federal policy changes, such as the implementation of PPACA.

Readers are cautioned that the uncertainties discussed previously also affect the projected Medicare and Medicaid costs reported in the Fiscal Projections for the U.S. Government and Social Insurance information included in the unaudited Required Supplementary Information section of the *2013 Financial Report* and summarized in Management's Discussion and Analysis. The Required Supplementary Information section of the *2013 Financial Report* includes unaudited information concerning how changes in various assumptions would change the present value of future estimated expenditures in excess of future estimated revenue. As discussed in that section, Medicare projections are very sensitive to changes in the health care cost growth assumption.

The Statement of Social Insurance presents the actuarial present value of the federal government's estimated future revenue to be received from or on behalf of participants and estimated future expenditures to be paid to or on behalf of participants, based on benefit formulas in current law and using a projection period sufficient to illustrate the long-term sustainability of the social insurance programs.[9] In preparing the Statements of Social Insurance, management considers and selects assumptions and data that it believes provide a reasonable basis for the assertions in the statement. However, because of the large number of factors that affect the Statement of Social Insurance and the fact that such assumptions are inherently subject to substantial uncertainty (arising from the likelihood

---

[7]Statutes have been enacted with provisions that prevented scheduled reductions in Medicare payment rates for physician services from taking effect from 2003 through March 2014, including the most recent provision enacted in the Pathway for SGR Reform Act of 2013, which replaced the almost 25 percent scheduled reductions in Medicare payment rates with an increase of 0.5 percent for the period of January 1, 2014, through March 31, 2014. Pub. L. No. 113-67, div. B, tit. I, § 1101, 127 Stat. 1165, 1196 (Dec. 26, 2013), which is classified at 42 U.S.C. § 1395w-4(d)(15). Some of these statutes also included provisions that reduced the federal government's spending on other categories of health care, which had the effect of helping to offset the increased costs related to the physician payment updates.

[8]The excess cost growth rate is the increase in health care spending per person relative to the growth of gross domestic product per person after removing the effects of demographic changes on health care spending.

[9]The projection period used for the Social Security, Medicare, and Railroad Retirement social insurance programs is 75 years. For the Black Lung program, the projections are through September 30, 2040.

of future events, significant uncertainties, and contingencies), there will be differences between the estimates in the Statement of Social Insurance and the actual results, and those differences may be material. In addition to the inherent uncertainty that underlies the expenditure projections prepared for all parts of Medicare, the Supplementary Medical Insurance Part D projections have an added uncertainty in that they were prepared using very little program experience upon which to base the estimates.

The scheduled future benefits presented in the Statement of Social Insurance are based on benefit formulas in current law. However, consistent with the respective annual Trustees Reports, the Social Security and Medicare programs are not projected to be sustainable under current financing arrangements. Also, the law concerning these programs can be changed at any time. Payment of Social Security and Medicare Hospital Insurance (Part A) benefits is limited by law to the balances in the respective trust funds. Consequently, future scheduled benefits are limited to future revenues plus existing trust fund assets.

As discussed in the unaudited Required Supplementary Information section of the *2013 Financial Report*, the Social Security and Medicare Hospital Insurance (Part A) trust funds are, based on achievement of the cost reductions discussed above, projected to be exhausted in 2033 and 2026, respectively, at which time they would be unable to pay the full amount of scheduled future benefits. For Social Security, as of January 1, 2013, future revenues were projected to be sufficient to pay 77 percent of scheduled benefits in 2033, the year of projected trust funds (combined) exhaustion, and decreasing to 72 percent of scheduled benefits in 2087.[10] For Medicare Hospital Insurance (Part A), as of January 1, 2013, future revenues were projected to be sufficient to pay 87 percent of scheduled benefits in 2026, the year of projected trust fund exhaustion, and then decreasing to 73 percent of scheduled benefits in 2087.

Other Limitations on the Scope of Our Work

For fiscal years 2013 and 2012, there were other limitations on the scope of our work, in addition to the material weaknesses and significant uncertainties noted above, that contributed to our disclaimers of opinion on the consolidated financial statements. Such limitations primarily relate to our ability to obtain adequate representations from management. Treasury and OMB depend on representations from certain federal entities to provide their representations to us regarding the U.S. government's consolidated financial statements. Treasury and OMB were unable to provide us with adequate representations regarding the U.S. government's accrual-based consolidated financial statements for fiscal years 2013 and 2012 primarily because of insufficient representations provided to them by certain federal entities, including DOD.

Disclaimers of Opinion on the Consolidated Financial Statements, Except for the 2009 Statement of Social Insurance

Accrual-Based Consolidated Financial Statements as of and for the Fiscal Years Ended September 30, 2013, and 2012

Because of the significance of the related matters described in the Basis for Disclaimer of Opinion paragraphs above, we were not able to obtain sufficient appropriate audit evidence to provide a basis for an audit opinion on the accrual-based consolidated financial statements. Accordingly, we do not

---

[10]The combined Social Security trust funds consist of the Federal Old-Age and Survivors Insurance (OASI) trust fund and the Federal Disability Insurance (DI) trust fund. The OASI and DI trust funds' assets are projected to be exhausted in 2035 and 2016, respectively.

express an opinion on the accrual-based consolidated financial statements as of and for the fiscal years ended September 30, 2013, and 2012.

Statements of Social Insurance for 2013, 2012, 2011, and 2010 and the Statements of Changes in Social Insurance Amounts for 2013 and 2012

Because of the significance of the related matters described in the Basis for Disclaimer of Opinion paragraphs above, we were not able to obtain sufficient appropriate audit evidence to provide a basis for an audit opinion on the Statements of Social Insurance for 2013, 2012, 2011, and 2010 as well as on the Statements of Changes in Social Insurance Amounts for 2013 and 2012. Accordingly, we do not express an opinion on the 2013, 2012, 2011, or 2010 Statements of Social Insurance or on the 2013 and 2012 Statements of Changes in Social Insurance Amounts.

Opinion on the Statement of Social Insurance for 2009

In our opinion, the Statement of Social Insurance for 2009 presents fairly, in all material respects, the financial condition of the federal government's social insurance programs for 2009, in accordance with U.S. generally accepted accounting principles.

Emphasis of Matters

The following key items deserve emphasis in order to put the information contained in the consolidated financial statements and the Management's Discussion and Analysis section of the *2013 Financial Report* into context. However, our disclaimers of opinion and our opinion noted above are not modified with respect to these matters.

Equity Investments Related to the Federal Government's Actions to Stabilize Financial Markets and to Promote Economic Recovery

The last economic recession and the federal government's actions to stabilize financial markets and promote economic recovery, among other factors, significantly affected the federal government's financial condition, including the addition of significant assets and liabilities. While the federal government has significantly reduced the assets and liabilities related to such actions, the accrual-based consolidated financial statements, as of September 30, 2013, and 2012, continue to include significant equity investments in certain entities. For example, as of September 30, 2013, reported investments in the Federal National Mortgage Association (Fannie Mae) and the Federal Home Loan Mortgage Corporation (Freddie Mac) totaled about $140 billion (reported net of about $54 billion in valuation reserves).

In valuing these equity investments, management considered and selected assumptions and data that it believed provided a reasonable basis for the estimated values reported in the accrual-based consolidated financial statements. However, as discussed in Note 1 to the consolidated financial statements, there are many factors affecting these assumptions and estimates that are inherently subject to substantial uncertainty arising from the uniqueness of the transactions and the likelihood of future changes in general economic, regulatory, and market conditions. As such, there will be differences between the estimated values as of September 30, 2013, and the actual results, and such differences may be material. Also, as discussed in Note 1 to the consolidated financial statements, the financial statements do not include the assets, liabilities, or results of operations of such entities in which Treasury holds either a direct, indirect, or beneficial equity interest. Treasury and OMB have determined that none of the entities meet the criteria for a federal entity.

Long-Term Fiscal Challenges

Increased attention to risks that could affect the federal government's financial condition is made more important because of the nation's longer-term fiscal challenges. The comprehensive long-term fiscal projections presented in the unaudited Required Supplementary Information section of the *2013 Financial Report* show that—absent policy changes—the federal government continues to face an unsustainable long-term fiscal path. The oldest members of the baby-boom generation are already eligible for Social Security retirement benefits and for Medicare benefits. Under these projections, spending for the major health and retirement programs will increase in coming decades as more members of the baby-boom generation become eligible for benefits and the health care cost for each enrollee increases. Over the long term, the imbalance between spending and revenue that is built into current law and policy will lead to continued growth of debt held by the public as a share of gross domestic product (GDP). This situation—in which debt grows faster than GDP—means the current federal fiscal path is unsustainable.

These projections, with regard to Social Security and Medicare, are based on the same assumptions underlying the information presented in the Statement of Social Insurance and assume that the provisions in law designed to slow the growth of Medicare costs are sustained and remain effective throughout the projection period. If, however, the Medicare cost containment measures are not sustained over the long term—a concern expressed by the Trustees of the Medicare trust funds, the Centers for Medicare & Medicaid Services' (CMS) Chief Actuary, the Congressional Budget Office, and others—spending on federal health care programs will grow much more rapidly.

GAO also prepares long-term federal fiscal simulations which continue to show debt rising as a share of GDP.[11] Under GAO's Alternative simulation,[12] which uses the CMS Office of the Actuary's alternative health care cost projections, future spending in excess of receipts would be greater and debt held by the public as a share of GDP would grow more quickly than the projections in the *2013 Financial Report*.

---

[11]GAO, *The Federal Government's Long-Term Fiscal Outlook: Spring 2013 Update*, GAO-13-481SP (Washington, D.C.: Apr. 11, 2013).

[12]GAO's Spring 2013 Alternative simulation incorporates the CMS Office of the Actuary's alternative projections for health care cost growth, which assume physician payments are not reduced as specified under current law and certain cost controls are not maintained over the long term. Also, in this simulation, expiring tax provisions, such as the research and experimentation tax credit, are extended to 2023. In the Alternative simulation, discretionary spending follows the original discretionary spending caps set by the Budget Control Act of 2011, but not the lower caps triggered by the automatic enforcement procedures. Over the long term, discretionary spending and revenue are held at their historical average share of GDP.

The Bipartisan Budget Act of 2013 (budget agreement),[13] which amended the Balanced Budget and Emergency Deficit Control Act (BBEDCA),[14] established new (higher) limits on defense and nondefense discretionary appropriations for fiscal years 2014 and 2015, extended sequestration for direct spending programs by 2 years through fiscal year 2023, and made other changes to direct spending and revenue.

Other Matters

Required Supplementary Information and Required Supplementary Stewardship Information

U.S. generally accepted accounting principles issued by the Federal Accounting Standards Advisory Board (FASAB) require that RSI[15] and RSSI[16] be presented in the *2013 Financial Report* to supplement the financial statements. Although not a part of the financial statements, FASAB considers this information to be an essential part of financial reporting for placing the financial statements in appropriate operational, economic, or historical context. We were unable to apply certain limited procedures to the RSI and RSSI in accordance with U.S. generally accepted government auditing standards because of the material weaknesses and other scope limitations discussed in this audit report. We did not audit and do not express an opinion or provide any assurance on the RSI or RSSI.

Other Information

Other information included in the *2013 Financial Report* contains a wide range of information, some of which is not directly related to the consolidated financial statements.[17] This information is presented for purposes of additional analysis and is not a required part of the consolidated financial statements, RSI, or RSSI. We read the other information included with the consolidated financial statements in order to identify material inconsistencies, if any, with the consolidated financial statements. We did not audit and do not express an opinion or provide any assurance on the other information in the *2013 Financial Report*.

Readers are cautioned that the material weaknesses, significant uncertainties, and other scope limitations discussed in this audit report may affect the reliability of certain information contained in the RSI, RSSI, and other information that is taken from the same data sources as the accrual-based

---

[13]Pub. L. No. 113-67, div. A, tit. I, § 101,127 Stat. 1165, 1166-69 (Dec. 26, 2013). The Continuing Appropriations Act, 2014, Pub. L. No. 113-76, 128 Stat. 5 (Jan. 17, 2014), enacted discretionary appropriations for fiscal year 2014 consistent with the limits established in the budget agreement and the Balanced Budget and Emergency Deficit Control Act (BBEDCA), as amended.

[14]The Budget Control Act of 2011, Pub. L. No. 112-25, 125 Stat. 240 (Aug. 2, 2011), which amended BBEDCA, imposed discretionary spending limits for fiscal years 2012 through 2021 to reduce projected spending by about $1 trillion. The Budget Control Act also established the Joint Select Committee on Deficit Reduction, which was tasked with proposing legislation to reduce the deficit by an additional $1.2 trillion through fiscal year 2021. The Joint Committee did not report a proposal, and Congress and the President did not enact legislation. This triggered the sequestration process in section 251A of BBEDCA, which is classified, as amended, at 2 U.S.C. § 901a. Section 251A required OMB to calculate, and the President to order, a sequestration of discretionary and direct spending on March 1, 2013. Section 251A also provides for an annual reduction of the discretionary spending limits and a sequestration of direct spending from fiscal years 2014 through 2021. The budget agreement enacted further changes amending section 251A of BBEDCA.

[15]RSI is comprised of Management's Discussion and Analysis and information in the Required Supplementary Information section of the *2013 Financial Report*.

[16]RSSI is comprised of information on stewardship investments in the Required Supplementary Stewardship Information section of the *2013 Financial Report*.

[17]Other information is comprised of information in the *2013 Financial Report* other than the consolidated financial statements, RSI, RSSI, the auditor's report, and the Statement of the Comptroller General of the United States.

consolidated financial statements; the 2013, 2012, 2011, and 2010 Statements of Social Insurance; and the 2013 and 2012 Statements of Changes in Social Insurance Amounts.

CFO Act Agency Financial Management Systems

The federal government's ability to efficiently and effectively manage and oversee its day-to-day operations and programs relies heavily on the ability of entity financial management systems to produce complete, reliable, timely, and consistent financial information for use by executive branch agencies and Congress.[18] The Federal Financial Management Improvement Act of 1996 (FFMIA) was designed to lead to system improvements that would result in CFO Act agency managers routinely having access to reliable, useful, and timely financial-related information with which to measure performance and increase accountability throughout the year.

The 24 CFO Act agencies are responsible for implementing and maintaining financial management systems that substantially comply with the requirements of FFMIA. FFMIA requires auditors, as part of the 24 CFO Act agencies' financial statement audits, to report whether those agencies' financial management systems substantially comply with (1) federal financial management systems requirements, (2) applicable federal accounting standards, and (3) the federal government's *U.S. Standard General Ledger* at the transaction level.

For both fiscal years 2013 and 2012, auditors for 11 of the 24 CFO Act agencies reported that the agencies' financial management systems did not substantially comply with one or more of the three FFMIA requirements. Agency management at the 24 CFO Act agencies also annually report on FFMIA compliance. For both fiscal years 2013 and 2012, agency management at 9 of the CFO Act agencies reported that their agencies' financial management systems were not in substantial compliance with one or more of the three FFMIA requirements. Based on agency financial reports, the differences in the assessments of substantial compliance between the auditors and agency management reflected differences in views between management and the auditors on the impact reported deficiencies had on agencies' financial management systems.

Long-standing financial management systems weaknesses at several large CFO Act agencies, along with the size and complexity of the federal government, continue to present a formidable management challenge in providing accountability to the nation's taxpayers and have contributed significantly to the material weaknesses and other limitations that have resulted in our disclaimers of opinion on the accrual-based consolidated financial statements.

Report on Internal Control over Financial Reporting

Management's Responsibility

Management of the federal government is responsible for (1) maintaining effective internal control over financial reporting, including the design, implementation, and maintenance of internal control relevant to the preparation and fair presentation of financial statements that are free from material misstatement,

---

[18]The Federal Financial Management Improvement Act of 1996, which is reprinted in 31 U.S.C. § 3512 note, defines "financial management systems" to include the financial systems and the financial portions of mixed systems necessary to support financial management, including automated and manual processes, procedures, controls, data, hardware, software, and support personnel dedicated to the operation and maintenance of system functions.

whether due to fraud or error, and (2) evaluating the effectiveness of internal control over financial reporting, based on criteria established under the Federal Managers' Financial Integrity Act (FMFIA).[19]

Auditor's Responsibility

The purpose of an audit of financial statements is to express an opinion on the financial statements. An audit of financial statements includes considering internal control over financial reporting to design audit procedures that are appropriate in the circumstances, but not for the purpose of expressing an opinion on the effectiveness of internal control over financial reporting. Accordingly, we do not express an opinion on the effectiveness of internal control over financial reporting. We did not consider all internal controls relevant to operating objectives as broadly established under FMFIA, such as those controls relevant to preparing performance information and ensuring efficient operations.

Our responsibility is to report any material weaknesses or significant deficiencies in internal control over financial reporting for fiscal year 2013 that come to our attention as a result of our audit. Based on the scope of our work and the effects of the other limitations on the scope of our audit noted throughout this audit report, our internal control work was not designed to, and would not necessarily, identify all deficiencies in internal control, including those that might be material weaknesses or significant deficiencies.[20] Therefore, additional material weaknesses or significant deficiencies may exist that were not identified. Our work was performed in accordance with U.S. generally accepted government auditing standards.

Definitions and Inherent Limitations of Internal Control over Financial Reporting

An entity's internal control over financial reporting is a process effected by those charged with governance, management, and other personnel, the objectives of which are to provide reasonable assurance that (1) transactions are properly recorded, processed, and summarized to permit the preparation of financial statements in accordance with U.S. generally accepted accounting principles, and assets are safeguarded against loss from unauthorized acquisition, use, or disposition, and (2) transactions are executed in accordance with laws governing the use of budget authority and with other applicable laws, regulations, contracts, and grant agreements that could have a direct and material effect on the financial statements.

Because of its inherent limitations, internal control over financial reporting may not prevent, or detect and correct, misstatements due to fraud or error.

Material Weaknesses Resulted in Ineffective Internal Control over Financial Reporting

The material weaknesses discussed in this audit report resulted in ineffective internal control over financial reporting. Consequently, the federal government's internal control did not provide reasonable assurance that a material misstatement of the consolidated financial statements would be prevented, or detected and corrected, on a timely basis.

In addition to the material weaknesses that contributed to our disclaimer of opinion on the accrual-based consolidated financial statements, which were discussed previously, we found the following three

---

[19]31 U.S.C. § 3512 (c), (d) (commonly referred to as FMFIA). This act requires executive agency heads to evaluate and report annually to the President and Congress on the adequacy of their internal control and accounting systems and on actions to correct significant problems.

[20]A significant deficiency is a deficiency, or a combination of deficiencies, in internal control that is less severe than a material weakness, yet important enough to merit attention by those charged with governance.

other material weaknesses in internal control. These other material weaknesses were the federal government's inability to

- determine the full extent to which improper payments occur and reasonably assure that appropriate actions are taken to reduce them,

- identify and resolve information security control deficiencies and manage information security risks on an ongoing basis, and

- effectively manage its tax collection activities.

These material weaknesses are discussed in more detail in appendix III, including the primary effects of the material weaknesses on the accompanying accrual-based consolidated financial statements and on the management of federal government operations.

We also found two significant deficiencies in the federal government's internal control related to implementing effective internal controls at certain federal entities for the following areas:

- loans receivable and loan guarantee liabilities and
- federal grants management.

Due to improvements during fiscal year 2013, we determined that control deficiencies related to loans receivable and loan guarantee liabilities, which were reported as a material weakness in fiscal year 2012, constitute a significant deficiency in fiscal year 2013. These significant deficiencies are discussed in more detail in appendix IV.

Further, individual federal entity financial statement audit reports identified additional control deficiencies that were reported by the entities' auditors as either material weaknesses or significant deficiencies at the individual entity level. We do not consider these additional deficiencies to represent material weaknesses or significant deficiencies with respect to the U.S. government's consolidated financial statements.

Intended Purpose of Report on Internal Control over Financial Reporting

The purpose of this report on internal control over financial reporting is solely to describe the scope of our consideration of internal control over financial reporting, and the results of our procedures, and not to provide an opinion on the effectiveness of internal control over financial reporting. This report on internal control over financial reporting is an integral part of an audit performed in accordance with U.S. generally accepted government auditing standards in considering internal control. Accordingly, this report on internal control over financial reporting is not suitable for any other purpose.

Report on Compliance with Laws, Regulations, Contracts, and Grant Agreements

Management's Responsibility

Management of the federal government is responsible for the federal government's compliance with laws, regulations, contracts, and grant agreements.

<u>Auditor's Responsibility</u>

An audit of federal financial statements includes testing compliance with selected provisions of applicable laws, regulations, contracts, and grant agreements that have a direct effect on the determination of material amounts and disclosures in the consolidated financial statements, and performing certain other limited procedures. Accordingly, we did not test the federal government's compliance with all laws, regulations, contracts, and grant agreements. Due to the limitations discussed below and the scope of our procedures, noncompliance may occur and not be detected by these tests.

Our objective was not to provide an opinion on the federal government's compliance with laws, regulations, contracts, and grant agreements. Accordingly, we do not express such an opinion. Our work was performed in accordance with U.S. generally accepted government auditing standards.

<u>Results of Our Tests for Compliance with Laws, Regulations, Contracts, and Grant Agreements</u>

Our work to test compliance with selected provisions of applicable laws, regulations, contracts, and grant agreements was limited by the material weaknesses and other scope limitations discussed in this audit report. U.S. generally accepted government auditing standards and OMB guidance require auditors to report on entities' compliance with selected provisions of applicable laws, regulations, contracts, and grant agreements. Certain component entity audit reports contain instances of noncompliance. None of these instances were deemed to be reportable noncompliance with regard to the accompanying U.S. government's consolidated financial statements.

<u>Intended Purpose of Report on Compliance with Laws, Regulations, Contracts, and Grant Agreements</u>

The purpose of this report on compliance with laws, regulations, contracts, and grant agreements is solely to describe the scope of our testing of compliance with selected provisions of applicable laws, regulations, contracts, and grant agreements, and the results of that testing, and not to provide an opinion on compliance. This report on compliance with laws, regulations, contracts, and grant agreements is an integral part of an audit performed in accordance with U.S. generally accepted government auditing standards in considering compliance. Accordingly, this report on compliance with laws, regulations, contracts, and grant agreements is not suitable for any other purpose.

Agency Comments

We provided a draft of this audit report to Treasury and OMB officials, who provided technical comments, which have been incorporated as appropriate. Treasury and OMB officials expressed their continuing commitment to address the problems this report outlines.

Robert F. Dacey
Chief Accountant
U.S. Government Accountability Office

February 19, 2014

Appendix I

Objectives, Scope, and Methodology

Our objectives were to audit the consolidated financial statements consisting of the (1) accrual-based consolidated financial statements as of and for the fiscal years ended September 30, 2013, and 2012; (2) 2013, 2012, 2011, 2010, and 2009 Statements of Social Insurance; and (3) 2013 and 2012 Statements of Changes in Social Insurance Amounts. Our objectives also included reporting on internal control over financial reporting and on compliance with selected provisions of applicable laws, regulations, contracts, and grant agreements.

The Chief Financial Officers Act of 1990 (CFO Act), as expanded by the Government Management Reform Act of 1994 (GMRA), requires the inspectors general of the 24 CFO Act agencies to be responsible for annual audits of agency-wide financial statements prepared by these agencies.[21] GMRA requires GAO to be responsible for the audit of the U.S. government's consolidated financial statements,[22] and the Accountability of Tax Dollars Act of 2002 (ATDA) requires most other executive branch entities to prepare and have audited annual financial statements.[23] The Office of Management and Budget and the Department of the Treasury (Treasury) have identified 35 federal entities that are significant to the U.S. government's consolidated financial statements, consisting of the 24 CFO Act agencies, several other federal executive branch agencies, and some government corporations (35 significant entities).[24] We consider these 35 entities to be significant component entities for purposes of our audit of the consolidated financial statements. Our work was performed in coordination and cooperation with the inspectors general and independent public accountants for these 35 significant component entities to achieve our respective audit objectives. Our audit approach regarding the accrual-based consolidated financial statements primarily focused on determining the current status of the material weaknesses that contributed to our disclaimer of opinion on the accrual-based consolidated financial statements and the other material weaknesses affecting internal control that we had reported in our report on the consolidated financial statements for fiscal year 2012.[25] We also separately audited the financial statements of certain component entities, and parts of a significant component entity, including the following.

- We audited and expressed an unmodified opinion on the Internal Revenue Service's (IRS) financial statements as of and for the fiscal years ended September 30, 2013, and 2012.[26] In fiscal years 2013 and 2012, IRS collected about $2.9 trillion and $2.5 trillion, respectively, in tax payments and paid about $364 billion and $373 billion, respectively, in refunds to taxpayers. For fiscal year 2013, we continued to report a material weakness in internal control over unpaid tax assessments that resulted in ineffective internal control over financial reporting. In addition, we continued to report a significant deficiency in IRS's internal control over financial reporting systems, which includes both recurring and newly identified issues that are collectively important enough to merit the attention of those charged with governance. We also reported that we found no reportable noncompliance for

---

[21] 31 U.S.C. § 3521(e). GMRA authorized the Office of Management and Budget to designate agency components that also would receive a financial statement audit. See 31 U.S.C. § 3515(c).

[22] GMRA, Pub. L. No. 103-356, § 405(c), 108 Stat. 3410, 3416-17 (Oct. 13, 1994), *codified at* 31 U.S.C. § 331(e)(2).

[23] ATDA, Pub. L. No. 107-289, 116 Stat. 2049 (Nov. 7, 2002), *codified at* 31 U.S.C. § 3515.

[24] See *Treasury Financial Manual*, volume I, part 2, chapter 4700, for a listing of the 35 entities.

[25] GAO, *Financial Audit: U.S. Government's Fiscal Years 2012 and 2011 Consolidated Financial Statements*, GAO-13-271R (Washington, D.C.: Jan. 17, 2013).

[26] GAO, *Financial Audit: IRS's Fiscal Years 2013 and 2012 Financial Statements*, GAO-14-169 (Washington, D.C.: Dec. 12, 2013).

fiscal year 2013 with provisions of applicable laws, regulations, contracts, and grant agreements we tested.

- We audited and expressed an unmodified opinion on the Schedules of Federal Debt Managed by Treasury's Bureau of the Fiscal Service (Fiscal Service) for the fiscal years ended September 30, 2013, and 2012.[27] For these 2 fiscal years, the schedules reported (1) approximately $12.0 trillion (2013) and $11.3 trillion (2012) of federal debt held by the public;[28] (2) about $4.8 trillion (2013) and $4.8 trillion (2012) of intragovernmental debt holdings;[29] and (3) about $247 billion (2013) and $245 billion (2012) of interest on federal debt held by the public. We also reported that although internal controls could be improved, Fiscal Service maintained, in all material respects, effective internal control over financial reporting relevant to the Schedule of Federal Debt as of September 30, 2013. In addition, we reported that we found no reportable noncompliance for fiscal year 2013 with provisions of applicable laws, regulations, contracts, and grant agreements we tested related to the Schedule of Federal Debt.

- We audited and expressed unmodified opinions on the U.S. Securities and Exchange Commission's (SEC) and its Investor Protection Fund's (IPF) financial statements as of and for the fiscal years ended September 30, 2013, and 2012.[30] We also reported that although internal controls could be improved, SEC maintained, in all material respects, effective internal control over financial reporting for both the entity as a whole and the IPF as of September 30, 2013. In addition, we reported that we found no reportable noncompliance for either SEC or IPF for fiscal year 2013 with provisions of applicable laws, regulations, contracts, and grant agreements we tested.

- We audited and expressed an unmodified opinion on the Federal Housing Finance Agency's (FHFA) financial statements as of and for the fiscal years ended September 30, 2013, and 2012.[31] We also reported that FHFA maintained, in all material respects, effective internal control over financial reporting as of September 30, 2013. In addition, we reported that we found no reportable noncompliance for fiscal year 2013 with provisions of applicable laws, regulations, contracts, and grant agreements we tested.

- We audited and expressed an unmodified opinion on the Office of Financial Stability's (OFS) financial statements for the Troubled Asset Relief Program (TARP) as of and for the fiscal years ended September 30, 2013, and 2012.[32] We also reported that OFS maintained, in all material respects, effective internal control over financial reporting as of September 30, 2013. In addition, we reported that we found no reportable noncompliance for fiscal year 2013 with provisions of applicable laws, regulations, contracts, and grant agreements we tested.

---

[27]GAO, *Financial Audit: Bureau of the Fiscal Service's Fiscal Years 2013 and 2012 Schedules of Federal Debt*, GAO-14-173 (Washington, D.C.: Dec. 12, 2013).

[28]Debt held by the public on the Schedules of Federal Debt represents federal debt issued by Treasury and held by investors outside of the federal government, including individuals, corporations, state or local governments, the Federal Reserve, and foreign governments.

[29]Intragovernmental debt holdings represent federal debt owed by Treasury to federal government accounts, primarily federal trust funds such as Social Security and Medicare.

[30]GAO, *Financial Audit: Securities and Exchange Commission's Fiscal Years 2013 and 2012 Financial Statements*, GAO-14-213R (Washington, D.C.: Dec. 16, 2013, reissued Dec. 23, 2013).

[31]GAO, *Financial Audit: Federal Housing Finance Agency's Fiscal Years 2013 and 2012 Financial Statements*, GAO-14-171R (Washington, D.C.: Dec. 16, 2013).

[32]GAO, *Financial Audit: Office of Financial Stability (Troubled Asset Relief Program) Fiscal Years 2013 and 2012 Financial Statements*, GAO-14-172R (Washington, D.C.: Dec. 11, 2013).

- We audited and expressed an unmodified opinion on the Bureau of Consumer Financial Protection's (CFPB) financial statements as of and for the fiscal years ended September 30, 2013, and 2012.[33] We also reported that although internal controls could be improved, CFPB maintained, in all material respects, effective internal control over financial reporting as of September 30, 2013. In addition, we reported that we found no reportable noncompliance for fiscal year 2013 with provisions of applicable laws, regulations, contracts, and grant agreements we tested.

In addition, we considered the CFO Act agencies' and certain other federal entities' fiscal years 2013 and 2012 financial statements and the related auditors' reports prepared by the inspectors general or contracted independent public accountants. Financial statements and audit reports for these entities provide information about the operations of each of the entities. The entity audit reports also contain details regarding any identified material weaknesses or significant deficiencies and related recommendations for the respective entity. We did not audit, and we do not express an opinion on, any of these individual federal entity financial statements.

We considered the Department of Defense's (DOD) assertion in the *DOD Agency Financial Report for Fiscal Year 2013* regarding its noncompliant financial management systems and lack of reasonable assurance that internal controls over financial reporting were effective. In addition, in the DOD Inspector General's fiscal year 2013 report on internal control over financial reporting, the Inspector General cited material weaknesses in several areas, including (1) property, plant, and equipment; (2) inventory and operating material and supplies; (3) environmental liabilities; (4) intragovernmental eliminations; and (5) material amounts of unsupported accounting entries needed to prepare DOD's annual consolidated financial statements.

Because of the significance of the amounts presented in the Statements of Social Insurance and Statements of Changes in Social Insurance Amounts related to the Social Security Administration (SSA) and the Department of Health and Human Services (HHS), our audit approach regarding these statements focused primarily on these two agencies. For each federal entity preparing a Statement of Social Insurance and Statement of Changes in Social Insurance Amounts,[34] we considered the entity's 2013, 2012, 2011, 2010, and 2009 Statements of Social Insurance and the 2013 and 2012 Statements of Changes in Social Insurance Amounts, as well as the related auditor's reports prepared by the inspectors general or contracted independent public accountants. We believe our audit, including internal control and substantive audit procedures, reperformance procedures, and review of the other auditors' Statement of Social Insurance-related audit work, provides a reasonable basis for our opinion on the 2009 Statement of Social Insurance.

We performed sufficient audit work to provide our reports on (1) the consolidated financial statements, (2) internal control over financial reporting, and (3) compliance with selected provisions of applicable laws, regulations, contracts, and grant agreements. We considered the limitations on the scope of our work regarding the accrual-based consolidated financial statements; the 2013, 2012, 2011, and 2010 Statements of Social Insurance; and the 2013 and 2012 Statements of Changes in Social Insurance Amounts in forming our conclusions. Our work was performed in accordance with U.S. generally accepted government auditing standards.

---

[33]GAO, *Financial Audit: Bureau of Consumer Financial Protection's Fiscal Years 2013 and 2012 Financial Statements*, GAO-14-170R (Washington, D.C.: Dec. 16, 2013).

[34]These entities are SSA, HHS, the Railroad Retirement Board, and the Department of Labor.

Appendix II

Material Weaknesses Contributing to Our Disclaimer of Opinion on the Accrual-Based Consolidated Financial Statements

The continuing material weaknesses discussed below contributed to our disclaimer of opinion on the federal government's accrual-based consolidated financial statements. The federal government did not maintain adequate systems or have sufficient appropriate evidence to support information reported in the accompanying accrual-based consolidated financial statements, as described below.

Property, Plant, and Equipment and Inventories and Related Property

The federal government could not satisfactorily determine that property, plant, and equipment (PP&E) and inventories and related property were properly reported in the accrual-based consolidated financial statements. Most of the PP&E and inventories and related property are the responsibility of the Department of Defense (DOD). As in past years, DOD did not maintain adequate systems or have sufficient records to provide reliable information on these assets. Certain other entities' auditors reported continued deficiencies in internal control procedures and processes related to PP&E.

Deficiencies in internal control over such assets could affect the federal government's ability to fully know the assets it owns, including their location and condition, and its ability to effectively (1) safeguard assets from physical deterioration, theft, or loss; (2) account for acquisitions and disposals of such assets and reliably report asset balances; (3) ensure that the assets are available for use when needed; (4) prevent unnecessary storage and maintenance costs or purchase of assets already on hand; and (5) determine the full costs of programs that use these assets.

Liabilities and Commitments and Contingencies

The federal government could not reasonably estimate or adequately support amounts reported for certain liabilities. For example, DOD was not able to estimate with assurance key components of its environmental and disposal liabilities. In addition, DOD could not support a significant amount of its estimated military postretirement health benefits liabilities included in federal employee and veteran benefits payable. These unsupported amounts related to the cost of direct health care provided by DOD-managed military treatment facilities. Further, the federal government could not determine whether commitments and contingencies, including any related to treaties and other international agreements entered into to further the federal government's interests, were complete and properly reported.

Problems in accounting for liabilities affect the determination of the full cost of the federal government's current operations and the extent of its liabilities. Also, deficiencies in internal control supporting the process for estimating environmental and disposal liabilities could result in improperly stated liabilities as well as adversely affect the federal government's ability to determine priorities for cleanup and disposal activities and to appropriately consider future budgetary resources needed to carry out these activities. In addition, to the extent disclosures of commitments and contingencies are incomplete or incorrect, reliable information is not available about the extent of the federal government's obligations.

Cost of Government Operations and Disbursement Activity

Reported net costs were affected by the previously discussed material weaknesses in reporting assets and liabilities; material weaknesses in financial statement preparation, as discussed below; and the lack of adequate reconciliations of disbursement activity at certain federal entities. As a result, the federal government was unable to support significant portions of the reported total net cost of operations, most notably those related to DOD.

With respect to disbursements, auditors of DOD and certain other federal entities reported continued material weaknesses and significant deficiencies in reconciling disbursement activity. For fiscal years 2013 and 2012, unreconciled disbursement activity, including unreconciled differences between federal entities' and the Department of the Treasury's (Treasury) records of disbursements and unsupported federal entity adjustments, totaled billions of dollars, which could also affect the balance sheet.

Unreliable cost information affects the federal government's ability to control and reduce costs, assess performance, evaluate programs, and set fees to recover costs where required or authorized. If disbursements are improperly recorded, this could result in misstatements in the financial statements and in certain data provided by federal entities for inclusion in *The Budget of the United States Government* (President's Budget) concerning obligations and outlays.

<u>Accounting for and Reconciliation of Intragovernmental Activity and Balances</u>

Significant progress was made in fiscal year 2013; however, the federal government continues to be unable to adequately account for and reconcile intragovernmental activity and balances between federal entities. Federal entities are responsible for properly accounting for and reporting their intragovernmental activity and balances in their entity financial statements. When preparing the consolidated financial statements, intragovernmental activity and balances between federal entities should be in agreement and must be subtracted out, or eliminated, from the financial statements. If the two federal entities engaged in an intragovernmental transaction do not both record the same intragovernmental transaction in the same year and for the same amount, the intragovernmental transactions will not be in agreement, resulting in errors in the consolidated financial statements. The Office of Management and Budget (OMB) and Treasury require the chief financial officers (CFO) of the 35 significant component entities to reconcile, on a quarterly basis, selected intragovernmental activity and balances with their trading partners. In addition, these entities are required to report to Treasury, their respective inspectors general, and GAO on the extent and results of intragovernmental activity and balance-reconciliation efforts as of the end of the fiscal year.

In fiscal year 2013, Treasury continued to actively work with federal entities to resolve intragovernmental differences. For example, Treasury expanded its quarterly scorecard process to include all 35 significant component entities,[35] highlighting differences requiring the entities' attention and encouraging the use of the dispute resolution process.[36] As a result of these and other actions, a significant number of intragovernmental differences were identified and resolved. While such progress was made, we continued to note that amounts reported by federal entity trading partners were not in agreement by significant amounts. Reasons for the differences cited by several CFOs included differing accounting methodologies, accounting errors, and timing differences. In addition, the auditor for DOD reported that DOD, which contributes significantly to the unreconciled amounts, could not accurately identify most of its intragovernmental transactions by customer and was unable to reconcile most intragovernmental transactions with trading partners, which resulted in adjustments that cannot be fully supported.

---

[35]For each quarter, Treasury produces a scorecard for each significant entity that reports various aspects of the entity's intragovernmental differences with its trading partners, including the composition of the differences by trading partner and category. Entities are expected to resolve, with the respective trading partners, the differences identified in their scorecards.
[36]When an entity and respective trading partner cannot resolve an intragovernmental difference, the entities must request Treasury to resolve the dispute. Treasury will review the dispute and issue a decision on how to resolve the difference, which the entities must follow.

Further, there are unreconciled transactions between the General Fund of the U.S. Government (General Fund)[37] and federal entity trading partners related to appropriations and other intragovernmental transactions, which amount to hundreds of billions of dollars. The ability to reconcile such transactions is hampered because only some of the General Fund is reported in Treasury's department-level financial statements. As a result of these circumstances, the federal government's ability to determine the impact of these differences on the amounts reported in the accrual-based consolidated financial statements is significantly impaired. In fiscal year 2013, Treasury continued to establish processes to account for and report General Fund activity and balances. As part of the quarterly scorecard process, Treasury provides entities information to assist them in complying with the proper use of the General Fund as a trading partner. In fiscal year 2014, Treasury plans to implement a process for federal entities to confirm and reconcile all of their activity and balances with the General Fund.

Resolving the intragovernmental transactions problem remains a difficult challenge and will require a strong and sustained commitment by federal entities to timely resolve differences with their trading partners, as well as continued strong leadership by Treasury and OMB.

Preparation of Consolidated Financial Statements

Treasury, in coordination with OMB, implemented corrective actions during fiscal year 2013 to address certain internal control deficiencies detailed in our previously issued report; however, the federal government continued to have inadequate systems, controls, and procedures to ensure that the consolidated financial statements are consistent with the underlying audited entity financial statements, properly balanced, and in accordance with U.S. generally accepted accounting principles (U.S. GAAP).[38] During our fiscal year 2013 audit, we found the following.

- Treasury's process for compiling the consolidated financial statements generally demonstrated that amounts in the Statement of Social Insurance and the Statement of Changes in Social Insurance Amounts were consistent with the underlying federal entities' financial statements and that the Balance Sheet, Statement of Net Cost, and Statement of Operations and Changes in Net Position were also consistent with the 35 significant component entities' financial statements prior to eliminating intragovernmental activity and balances. However, Treasury's process did not ensure that the information in the remaining two principal financial statements (Reconciliation of Net Operating Cost and Unified Budget Deficit, and Statement of Changes in Cash Balance from Unified Budget and Other Activities) was fully consistent with the underlying information in the 35 significant component entities' audited financial statements and other financial data.

- For fiscal year 2013, auditors reported internal control deficiencies at several entities regarding entities' financial reporting processes that could affect information included in the respective entities' closing packages.[39] Further, Treasury had to record significant adjustments to correct errors found in federal entities' audited closing package information. To ensure consistency of underlying entity information and financial data with the U.S. government's consolidated financial

---

[37]The General Fund is a central reporting entity that tracks core activities fundamental to funding the federal government (e.g., issued budget authority, operating cash, and debt financing activities).

[38]Most of the issues we identified in fiscal year 2013 existed in fiscal year 2012, and many have existed for a number of years. Most recently, in June 2013, we reported the issues we identified to Treasury and OMB and provided recommendations for corrective action. See GAO, *Management Report: Improvements Needed in Controls over the Preparation of the U.S. Consolidated Financial Statements*, GAO-13-540 (Washington, D.C.: June 28, 2013).

[39]The closing package methodology links federal entities' audited consolidated department-level financial statements to certain of the U.S. government's consolidated financial statements.

statements, entity auditors are required to separately audit and report on the financial information that the 35 significant component entities send to Treasury through closing packages.

- Treasury is unable to properly balance the accrual-based consolidated financial statements. To make the fiscal years 2013 and 2012 consolidated financial statements balance, Treasury recorded a net decrease of $9.0 billion and a net increase of $20.2 billion, respectively, to net operating cost on the Statements of Operations and Changes in Net Position, which were identified as "Unmatched transactions and balances."[40] Treasury recorded an additional net $5.9 billion and $1.8 billion of unmatched transactions in the Statement of Net Cost for fiscal years 2013 and 2012, respectively. The material weakness in the federal government's ability to account for and reconcile intragovernmental activity and balances, discussed above, significantly contributes to the unmatched transactions and balances and consequently impairs Treasury's ability to fully eliminate such intragovernmental activity and balances.

- The federal government has not established and implemented effective processes and procedures for identifying and reporting all items needed to (1) prepare the Statement of Changes in Cash Balance from Unified Budget and Other Activities and (2) reconcile the operating results to the budget results. Typical reconciling items would include both accrual-based costs that are not yet recognized in the unified budget deficit and budget costs that are not yet recognized in the net operating cost.

- Over the past several years, Treasury has taken significant actions to assist in ensuring that financial information is reported or disclosed in the consolidated financial statements in accordance with U.S. GAAP. However, Treasury's reporting of certain financial information required by U.S. GAAP continues to be impaired. Due to certain control deficiencies noted in this audit report—for example, commitments and contingencies related to treaties and other international agreements—Treasury is precluded from determining if additional disclosure is required by U.S. GAAP in the consolidated financial statements, and we are precluded from determining whether the omitted information is material. Further, Treasury's ability to report information in accordance with U.S. GAAP will also remain impaired until federal entities, such as DOD, can provide Treasury with complete and reliable information required to be reported in the consolidated financial statements.

- The consolidated financial statements include financial information for the executive, legislative, and judicial branches, to the extent that federal entities within those branches have provided Treasury such information. While progress was made in fiscal year 2013, undetermined amounts of assets, liabilities, costs, and revenues are not included, and the federal government did not provide evidence that the excluded financial information was immaterial.

- Other internal control deficiencies existed in the process for preparing the consolidated financial statements, involving (1) inadequate design and ineffective implementation of policies and procedures related to certain areas, such as analysis of federal entity-provided data and journal vouchers,[41] and (2) inadequate processes for monitoring and assessing internal controls over the preparation of the consolidated financial statements. As a result, we identified errors in draft consolidated financial statements that were subsequently corrected.

---

[40]Although Treasury was unable to determine how much of the unmatched transactions and balances, if any, relates to net operating cost, it reported this amount as a component of net operating cost in the accompanying consolidated financial statements.

[41]Treasury prepares journal vouchers to adjust the consolidated financial statements, for example, to correct errors in or omissions of federal entity-provided data.

- While progress was made in fiscal year 2013, Treasury did not have adequate systems and personnel to address the magnitude of the fiscal year 2013 financial reporting challenges it faced, such as control deficiencies in its process for preparing the consolidated financial statements noted above. Treasury has taken various steps to begin to address these issues, including (1) obtaining and utilizing certain interim financial information from federal entities in preparing initial financial statement drafts, (2) beginning to implement an automated tool to streamline the compilation process, (3) supplementing staff during the financial report preparation process, and (4) reassigning staff from other parts of Treasury and hiring new staff. However, there were not enough personnel in Treasury's Bureau of the Fiscal Service with specialized financial reporting experience that were involved in the preparation of the consolidated financial statements to help ensure reliable financial reporting. In addition, the federal government does not perform interim compilations at the government-wide level, which leads to almost all of the compilation effort being performed during a condensed time period at the end of the year.

- Treasury's and OMB's corrective action plans are not adequate to reasonably ensure that internal control deficiencies involving the process for preparing the consolidated financial statements are efficiently and effectively addressed. For example, these plans do not contain sufficiently detailed actions that must be performed to resolve each of the deficiencies, interim milestones so that interim actions and progress can be monitored and progress assessed, and outcome measures to assist in assessing the effectiveness of the corrective actions. Also, the corrective actions do not fully consider the interrelationships between deficiencies.

Until these internal control deficiencies have been fully addressed, the federal government's ability to ensure that the consolidated financial statements are consistent with the underlying audited federal entities' financial statements, properly balanced, and in accordance with U.S. GAAP will be impaired. Resolving these internal control deficiencies remains a difficult challenge and will require a strong and sustained commitment from Treasury and OMB as they continue to execute and implement corrective actions.

<u>Components of the Budget Deficit</u>

Both the Reconciliation of Net Operating Cost and Unified Budget Deficit and the Statement of Changes in Cash Balance from Unified Budget and Other Activities report a unified budget deficit for fiscal years 2013 and 2012 of about $0.7 trillion and $1.1 trillion, respectively.[42] The budget deficit is calculated by subtracting actual budget outlays (outlays) from actual budget receipts (receipts). Also, the Fiscal Projections for the U.S. Government included in the unaudited Required Supplementary Information section of the *Fiscal Year 2013 Financial Report of the United States Government* use such outlays and receipts.

Treasury and OMB continue to lack an effective process for ensuring the consistency of (1) information used by Treasury to compute the budget deficit reported in the consolidated financial statements, (2) Treasury's records of cash transactions, and (3) information reported in federal entity financial statements and underlying entity financial information and records. In fiscal year 2013, Treasury made progress through the development and implementation of procedures to reconcile certain outlays and receipts between Treasury's records used to compute the budget deficit reported in the consolidated financial statements and underlying federal entity financial information and records, which included obtaining from significant federal entities explanations of and support for certain differences. However, until Treasury develops and fully implements an effective process for ensuring

---

[42]The budget deficit, receipts, and outlays amounts are reported in Treasury's *Monthly Treasury Statement* and the President's Budget.

consistency as noted above and is able to fully reconcile this information, the effect on the U.S. government's consolidated financial statements will continue to be unknown.

In fiscal year 2013, we again noted that several entities' auditors reported internal control deficiencies related to monitoring, accounting, and reporting of budgetary transactions. These control deficiencies could affect the reporting and calculation of the net outlay amounts in the entities' Statements of Budgetary Resources. In addition, such deficiencies may also affect the entities' ability to report reliable budgetary information to Treasury and OMB and may affect the unified budget deficit reported in the accrual-based consolidated financial statements. The unified budget deficit is also reported by Treasury in its *Combined Statement of Receipts, Outlays, and Balances*,[43] and in other federal government publications.

---

[43]Treasury's *Combined Statement of Receipts, Outlays, and Balances* presents budget results and cash-related assets and liabilities of the federal government with supporting details. Treasury represents this report as the recognized official publication of receipts and outlays of the federal government based on entity reporting.

Appendix III

Other Material Weaknesses

Material weaknesses in internal control discussed in this audit report resulted in ineffective controls over financial reporting. In addition to the material weaknesses discussed in appendix II that contributed to our disclaimer of opinion on the accrual-based consolidated financial statements, we found the following three other material weaknesses in internal control.

Improper Payments

The federal government is unable to determine the full extent to which improper payments occur and reasonably assure that appropriate actions are taken to reduce them. Reducing improper payments is critical to safeguarding federal funds.[44] During fiscal year 2013, the federal government continued to make progress in identifying and reporting on improper payments. While the specific programs included in the government-wide improper payment estimate may change from year to year, a net of 10 additional programs were included when compared to fiscal year 2012. Most notably, the Department of Education's improper payment estimate for the Direct Loan program, approximately $1.1 billion, was included in the government-wide improper payment estimate for the first time in fiscal year 2013.

Nevertheless, the federal government continues to face challenges in determining the full extent of improper payments. For example, four federal entities did not report fiscal year 2013 estimated improper payment amounts for four risk-susceptible programs, including the Department of Health and Human Services' (HHS) Temporary Assistance for Needy Families. The Improper Payments Information Act of 2002 (IPIA), as amended by the Improper Payments Elimination and Recovery Act of 2010 (IPERA) and the Improper Payments Elimination and Recovery Improvement Act of 2012 (IPERIA),[45] requires federal executive branch entities to (1) review all programs and activities, (2) identify those that may be susceptible to significant improper payments, (3) estimate the annual amount of improper payments for those programs and activities, (4) implement actions to reduce improper payments and set reduction targets, and (5) report on the results of addressing the foregoing requirements. IPERA also established a requirement for entity inspectors general to report annually on entities' compliance with criteria listed in IPERA.[46]

The Office of Management and Budget (OMB) reported that the government-wide improper payment error rate decreased to 3.5 percent of program outlays in fiscal year 2013 from 3.7 percent in fiscal year 2012 when including the Department of Defense's (DOD) Defense Finance and Accounting Service (DFAS) Commercial Pay program. When excluding the DFAS Commercial Pay program, the reported government-wide error rate was 4.0 percent of program outlays in fiscal year 2013 compared to the

---

[44]Under the Improper Payments Information Act of 2002, as amended, improper payments are statutorily defined as any payment that should not have been made or that was made in an incorrect amount (including overpayments and underpayments) under statutory, contractual, administrative, or other legally applicable requirements. It includes any payment to an ineligible recipient, any payment for an ineligible good or service, any duplicate payment, any payment for a good or service not received (except for such payments where authorized by law), and any payment that does not account for credit for applicable discounts.

[45]IPIA, Pub. L. No. 107-300, 116 Stat. 2350 (Nov. 26, 2002), as amended by IPERA, Pub. L. No. 111-204, 124 Stat. 2224 (July 22, 2010), and IPERIA, Pub. L. No. 112-248, 126 Stat. 2390 (Jan. 10, 2013), and reprinted in 31 U.S.C. § 3321 note.

[46]The most recent inspectors general reports on compliance with the criteria listed in IPERA were issued in 2013 for fiscal year 2012. Pursuant to the Office of Management and Budget implementing guidance, inspectors general reports on fiscal year 2013 compliance with the criteria listed in IPERA are expected to be issued by April 2014.

revised 4.3 percent in fiscal year 2012.[47] In May 2013, we reported on major deficiencies in DOD's process for estimating fiscal year 2012 improper payments in the DFAS Commercial Pay program, including deficiencies in identifying a complete and accurate population of payments and developing a statistically valid sampling methodology.[48] According to its fiscal year 2013 Agency Financial Report, DOD is reevaluating its sampling methodology for fiscal year 2014 for the DFAS Commercial Pay program based on our recommendation. Consequently, the fiscal year 2013 improper payment estimate for the DFAS Commercial Pay program may not be reliable.

Without the DFAS Commercial Pay program, federal entity improper payment estimates totaled $105.8 billion in fiscal year 2013, a decrease from the prior year revised estimate of $107.1 billion. Decreases in reported estimates of improper payments were mostly attributable to three major programs: the decrease for the Department of Labor's Unemployment Insurance program was attributable to a decrease in reported outlays, and the decreases for HHS's Medicaid and Medicare Advantage (Part C) programs were attributable to decreases in reported error rates.[49] It is important to note that, pursuant to OMB implementing guidance, reported improper payment estimates include overpayments, underpayments, and payments for which adequate documentation was not found, and may also include amounts of payments for years prior to the current fiscal year.

In addition to the issues related to the DFAS Commercial Pay program discussed above, some federal entities face challenges in reporting on and reducing improper payments. Various inspectors general reported deficiencies related to compliance with the criteria listed in IPERA for fiscal year 2012 at their respective federal entities, including risk-susceptible programs that did not report improper payment estimates, estimation methodologies that were not statistically valid, and risk assessments that may not accurately assess the risk of improper payment.

While improper payment estimates have decreased, for fiscal year 2013, federal entities reported improper payment error rates for seven risk-susceptible programs, accounting for more than 50 percent of the government-wide improper payment estimate, that exceeded 10 percent.[50] Under IPERA, an entity reporting an improper payment rate of 10 percent or greater for any risk-susceptible program or activity must submit a plan to Congress describing the actions that the entity will take to reduce improper payment rates below 10 percent.[51]

Further, entity auditors continued to report internal control deficiencies over financial reporting in their fiscal year 2013 financial statement audit reports, such as financial system limitations and information

---

[47]In their fiscal year 2013 Performance and Accountability Reports (PAR) and Agency Financial Reports (AFR), three federal entities updated their fiscal year 2012 improper payment estimates to reflect changes since issuance of their fiscal year 2012 PARs and AFRs. These updates decreased the government-wide improper payment estimate for fiscal year 2012 from $107.7 billion to $107.1 billion and from 4.4 percent of program outlays to 4.3 percent.

[48]GAO, *DOD Financial Management: Significant Improvements Needed in Efforts to Address Improper Payment Requirements*, GAO-13-227 (Washington, D.C.: May 13, 2013).

[49]Reported error rates reflect the estimated improper payments as a percentage of total program outlays.

[50]The seven programs that reported improper payment estimates that exceeded 10 percent in fiscal year 2013 were (1) the U.S. Department of Agriculture's (USDA) School Breakfast program, (2) the Department of the Treasury's Earned Income Tax Credit program, (3) the Small Business Administration's (SBA) Disaster Assistance Loan program, (4) the Department of Veterans Affairs' State Home Per Diem Grants program, (5) USDA's National School Lunch program, (6) SBA's Contract Disbursements program, and (7) HHS's Medicare Fee-for-Service program.

[51]IPERA requires each inspector general to annually determine whether the entity is in compliance with the criteria listed in IPERA. Compliance includes an entity reporting an improper payment rate of less than 10 percent for each program and activity for which an estimate was published. Entities determined by the inspector general to not be in compliance with the criteria listed in IPERA must submit a plan to Congress describing the actions that the entity will take to come into compliance.

system control weaknesses. Such deficiencies could significantly increase the risk that improper payments may occur and not be detected promptly.

Finally, IPERIA was enacted in January 2013 to intensify efforts to identify, prevent, and recover payment error, waste, fraud, and abuse within federal spending. Among other things, IPERIA enacted into law elements of the President's "Do Not Pay List" initiative by requiring entities to review prepayment and pre-award procedures and ensure a thorough review of available databases to determine program or award eligibility before the release of any federal funds. IPERIA also directs OMB to annually identify a list of high-priority federal programs for greater levels of oversight and review and requires each entity responsible for administering one of these high-priority programs to annually submit a program report to its inspector general and make a report copy available to the public.

Until the federal government has implemented effective processes to determine the full extent to which improper payments occur and has taken appropriate actions across entities and programs to effectively reduce improper payments, it will not have reasonable assurance that the use of federal funds is adequately safeguarded.

Information Security

Although progress has been made, serious and widespread information security control deficiencies reported during fiscal year 2013 continue to place federal assets at risk of inadvertent or deliberate misuse, financial information at risk of unauthorized modification or destruction, sensitive information at risk of inappropriate disclosure, and critical operations at risk of disruption. Specifically, control deficiencies were identified related to (1) security management; (2) access to computer resources (data, equipment, and facilities); (3) changes to information system resources; (4) segregation of incompatible duties; and (5) contingency planning. We have reported information security as a high-risk area across government since February 1997.

Such information security control deficiencies unnecessarily increase the risk that data recorded in or transmitted by federal financial management systems are not reliable and available. A primary reason for these deficiencies is that federal entities generally have not yet fully institutionalized comprehensive security management programs, which are critical to identifying information security control deficiencies, resolving information security problems, and managing information security risks on an ongoing basis.

The federal government has taken important actions to improve information security, such as enhancing performance measures and reporting processes necessary for monitoring and assessing the effectiveness of entities' information security programs. In addition, the administration established goals to achieve, by the end of fiscal year 2014, 95 percent use of (1) trusted Internet connections to consolidate external telecommunication access points; (2) continuous monitoring of federal information systems; and (3) strong authentication through the increased use of federal smart card credentials, such as Personal Identity Verification and Common Access Cards. Until entities identify and resolve information security control deficiencies and manage information security risks on an ongoing basis, federal data and systems, including financial information, will remain at risk.

Tax Collection Activities

During fiscal year 2013, a material weakness continued to affect the federal government's ability to effectively manage its tax collection activities. Due to financial system limitations, as well as errors and delays in recording taxpayer information, the federal government's records did not always reflect the correct amount of taxes owed by the public to the federal government. Such errors and delays may cause undue burden and frustration to taxpayers who either have already paid taxes owed or who owe significantly lower amounts.

Collectively, these deficiencies indicate that internal controls were not effective in (1) ensuring that reported amounts of taxes receivable and other tax assessments were accurate on an ongoing basis and could be relied upon by management as a tool to aid in making and supporting resource allocation decisions and (2) supporting timely and reliable financial statements, accompanying notes, and required supplementary information and other information without extensive supplemental procedures and adjustments.

Appendix IV

Significant Deficiencies

In addition to the material weaknesses discussed in appendixes II and III, we found two significant deficiencies in the federal government's internal control related to implementing effective internal controls at certain federal entities, as described below.

Loans Receivable and Loan Guarantee Liabilities

Internal control deficiencies were identified at certain significant component entities accounting for the majority of the reported balances for loans receivable and loan guarantee liabilities. The deficiencies related to accounting and financial reporting issues involving loan servicing systems and a system used for managing certain guaranteed loans. During fiscal year 2013, the Department of Education, which accounted for the largest reported balance of loans receivable, implemented corrective actions to address certain of the systems deficiencies reported in fiscal year 2012. Due to these improvements, we determined that control deficiencies related to loans receivable and loan guarantee liabilities, which were reported as a material weakness in fiscal year 2012, constitute a significant deficiency in fiscal year 2013.

Control deficiencies related to accounting and financial reporting over loans receivable and loan guarantee liabilities increase the risk that misstatements in entity and government-wide financial statements could occur and go undetected.

Federal Grants Management

In fiscal year 2013, federal grants management internal control deficiencies were identified at several federal entities. Reported deficiencies primarily related to accounting for grant programs, monitoring procedures over grant activities, and the maintenance of related documentation. These internal control deficiencies could adversely affect the federal government's ability to ensure that grant funds are being properly reported and used in accordance with applicable program laws and regulations.